SPEECH & POWER

The African-American Essay and its Cultural Content From Polemics to Pulpit

VOLUME 1

Edited by

GERALD EARLY

D0950863

THE ECCO PRESS

To Ida, again.

Introduction and selection copyright © 1992 by Gerald Early
All rights reserved

The Ecco Press
100 West Broad Street
Hopewell, NJ 08525

Published simultaneously in Canada by
Penguin Books Canada Ltd., Ontario
Printed in the United States of America

Designed by Richard Oriolo

First Edition

Library of Congress Cataloging-in-Publication Data

Speech and power: the African-American essay and its cultural content
from polemics to pulpit / edited by Gerald Early—1st ed.
p.   cm.
Includes bibliographical references and index.
$16.95
1. American essays—Afro-American authors.
2. Afro-Americans—Civilization.   I. Early, Gerald Lyn.
PS683.A35S64   1990   814'.5080896073—dc20   90–49746   CIP
ISBN 0-88001-264-1

The text of this book is set in Electra.

Page 364 constitutes a continuation of this copyright page.

CONTENTS

PART IV: THE NUMBERS RUNNER

PART V: BOXING

PART VI: PORTRAITS, VOLUME 1

PART VII: PORTRAITS, VOLUME 2

PART VIII: PORTRAITS, VOLUME 3

PART IX: PORTRAITS, VOLUME 4

Donated By

The Lara-Cea Family

In Honor of
Ronald B. Takaki

GNOSTIC OR GNOMIC?

I dare; I also will essay to be.
—RALPH WALDO EMERSON

There are two remarkable and strikingly contrasting scenes from two of the classic black autobiographies of the twentieth century: Langston Hughes's *The Big Sea* was published in 1940, and Richard Wright's *Black Boy* was published five years later (an occurrence which caused Arna Bontemps to remark in a letter to Hughes that he—Hughes—must be starting an autobiography craze among black writers as Zora Neale Hurston had just published her *Dust Tracks on a Road* a few years before Wright). In the opening scene in Hughes's book, it is 1924: young Langston has just turned twenty-one and is about to leave Columbia University (where he had tried unsuccessfully for a year to follow his father's advice to become an engineer) and embark on a sea journey as a cabin boy, tossing his books into the sea:

> I looked down on deck and noticed that one of my books had fallen into the scupper. The last book. I picked it up and threw it far over the rail into the water below, that was too black to see. The wind caught the book and ruffled its pages quickly, then let it fall into the rolling darkness. I think it was a book by H. L. Mencken.[1]

Very near the end of his autobiography, Richard Wright tells the story of his arrival in Memphis in 1925, one year after Hughes's departure by ship, as, among other things, his literary awakening through his discovery of H. L. Mencken:

> One morning I arrived early at work and went into the bank lobby where the Negro porter was mopping. I stood at a counter and picked up the Memphis *Commercial Appeal* and began my free reading of the press. I came finally to the editorial page and saw an article dealing with one H. L. Mencken. I knew by hearsay that he was the editor of the *American Mercury*, but aside from that I knew nothing about him. The article was a furious denunciation of Mencken, concluding with one, hot, short sentence: Mencken is a fool.
>
> I wondered what on earth this Mencken had done to call down upon him the scorn of the South. . . .
>
> Now, how could I find out about this Mencken?[2]

In one of the most famous and compelling passages in modern American literature, Wright then explains how he convinced an Irish Catholic fellow worker at the optical company where both were employed to lend him his library card so he could borrow some books by Mencken from the "white" public library. With a forged note of his own making and a sufficiently "unbookish" facial expression, Wright succeeds in obtaining, among other Mencken works, A *Book of Prefaces:*

> That night in my rented room, while letting the hot water run over my can of pork and beans in the sink, I opened A *Book of Prefaces* and began to read. I was jarred and shocked by the style, the clear, clean, sweeping sentences. Why did he write like that? And how did one write like that? I pictured the man as a raging demon, slashing with his pen, consumed with hate, denouncing everything American, extolling everything European or German, laughing at the weaknesses of people, mocking God, authority. What was this? I stood up, trying to realize what reality lay behind the meaning of the words. . . . Yes, this man was fighting, fighting with words. . . . Then, maybe, perhaps, I could use them as a weapon?[3]

The differences between the two passages are both obvious and telling: Hughes wishes to escape the seductive entrapment of the life of the mind and the supremacy of intellect over experience, while Wright seeks his liberation from a provincial family and an oppressive political and social system through books. In one scene, the blackness of the sea stains and swallows the blackness of the print, while in the other "the clear, clean, sweeping sentences" of black print become a kind of illumination, a light in the literal darkness that consumes Wright's rented room. Here are two distinct rites concerning the politicization of literacy being performed. In the Hughes book we have an exorcism of whiteness (Hughes throws his books away as he is about to embark for Africa), an exorcism that is meant to be quite the ironic reversal of the common exorcisms of blackness that were taking place in the twenties in the form of lynchings. For Hughes, the world of white order and domination symbolized by literacy is ended not by fire (as lynchings were most memorably concluded; one has only to refer to the denouement, for instance, of James Weldon Johnson's 1912 novel, *The Autobiography of an Ex-Colored Man*), but by the blackness of water. Wright's rite is the reenactment of Prometheus; he steals the white fire and brings it to his own dark cave. He subverts the political system that denies him both light and life, creating disorder within a rigid, inhuman system of order. The epistemological question concerning politics and literacy has been engaged through these rites: Is black literacy a kind of gnostic subversion through dissimulation or is it the gnomic quest for consensus and belonging through individual, rebellious assertion? In some vital ways, the acts are truly fused and each can be defined as being the other. Is Wright really the dissimulator?[4] After all, everyone, all the white men at his job, knows that he reads. Is Hughes really the asserting rebel? After all, he comically undercuts his journey to Africa by saying that the sub-Saharan Africans thought him to be a white man. Thus, there may be more to be learned here from the similarities between the accounts than the differences. First, both Wright at 17 and Hughes at 21 are young black men who actively seek some sort of personal liberation while creating a kind of identity, through vaguely understood feelings, as expressive beings within the world of literature and art. Moreover, both scenes turn upon the presence of H. L Mencken: He wrote the last book that young Langston touches, the first serious book that Wright reads. Mencken becomes the alpha and omega of black male literary aspiration. Having mentioned Zora Neale Hurston earlier, I should make complete the extent of Mencken's influence here by mentioning that some of Hurston's most notable essays appeared in *American Mercury*, Mencken's magazine, in the 1940s. Of course, Mencken had ceased editing the *American Mercury* in 1933; nonetheless it was his editorial influence during the magazine's heyday in the twenties that made the publication of Hurston's essays possible.

Charles Scruggs in *The Sage in Harlem: H. L. Mencken and the Black Writers of the 1920s* (1984) makes an excellent case for Mencken's influence on many black writers of the Harlem Renaissance. What I think is central for our understanding of black American literature in the twentieth century is not so much the particular figure and personality of Mencken as a force but the particular figure and personality of the most vibrant and singular essayist in American letters (Mencken's influence can be seen in other noted American essayists from A. J. Leibling to Norman Mailer to Tom Wolfe) as a presence in black letters. Since black writing came of age in this country in the 1920s, the essay seems to be the informing genre behind it. Although there have been several outstanding black novels written in the twentieth century, black essays or essay collections have had generally as large, and in some cases an even larger impact on American life and letters than the most successful black novels: W. E. B. Du Bois's *The Souls of Black Folks* (1903), James Weldon Johnson's Preface to his *Book of American Negro Poetry* (1922), Alain Locke's essay "The New Negro" (1925), Langston Hughes's "The Black Artist and the Racial Mountain" (1926), Zora Neale Hurston's "Hoodoo in America" (1931), James Baldwin's *Notes of a Native Son* (1955), *Nobody Knows My Name* (1961), and *The Fire Next Time* (1963), Amiri Baraka's *Home: Social Essays* (1966), Eldridge Cleaver's *Soul on Ice* (1968), Martin Luther King's "Letter From a Birmingham Jail" (1964), Ralph Ellison's *Shadow and Act* (1964), Alice Walker's *In Search of Our Mother's Gardens* (1983), Albert Murray's *The Omni-Americans* (1970), George Jackson's *Soledad Brothers: The Prison Letters of George Jackson* (1970) are some of the collections or individual essays that have had an almost epochal effect in both popular and high cultures. There have been other black essays which, when placed in a certain context, have had a similarly dramatic and altering effect. Take, for instance, Richard Wright's "How Bigger Was Born," which was written in 1940, after the publication of *Native Son*, and which has been used subsequently as an introduction to the novel. The addition of the essay has altered the novel in such a way that it now resembles structurally Nathaniel Hawthorne's *The Scarlet Letter* (1850), where a similar lengthy autobiographical introductory essay becomes the tale (tail) that wags the dog. Other black essays have had a broad philosophical and ideological impact despite having limited distribution: Amiri Baraka's and Ron Karenga's essays on the Kawaida, the black value system they invented in the 1960s, have had a much longer and broader effect on black thinking than anyone could have imagined at the time of their publication for the tiny Third World Press. Those essays, which spawned among other concepts the idea of Kwanzaa or the black winter festival celebration, serve as a linchpin between earlier forms of Pan-Africanism and Negritude and the current idea of Afrocentricity. And there have been those black essays, ranging from the one printed in *The Voice of the Negro* at the turn of the century that refutes the popularly held belief that Eli Whitney invented the cotton gin—a black actually invented it, according to the article—to J. A. Rogers's pieces on the black ancestry of five American presidents, that have sought to uncover the obscured and hidden black (or African) subtext of human history and achievement. We cannot fully understand black American literature, the black writer, or the course of black culture as an intellectual construct during the 20th century without coming to grips with the meaning and function of the essay in the hands of the black American. It is on this simple yet vital premise that this collection is built.

It is not surprising that many black writers have been attracted to the essay as a literary form since the essay is the most exploitable mode of the confession and the polemic, the two variants of the essay that black writers have mostly used. (Few black writers have written what might be strictly called belles lettres–style essays.) The conditions under which many black writers felt they had to write (and live), and their coming to terms with these conditions, have constituted their most driving intellectual obsession. Thus, the black essay has been, in truth, a political provocation and a flawed example, if not a full representation, of a philosophical rumination even if the work itself was sometimes entangled in a thicket of sociological detail. Black writers could not help but see their writing as political, since they saw their *condition* in these terms and their writing and their *condition* have been largely inseparable. Both the discomfort and the disjuncture most apparent in the black essay (and black art generally) result from most of this writing having been produced by a bourgeois elite—which feels itself both insufferably proud and abysmally guilty that it is an elite, which is why this elite has so often tried to romanticize the poverty culture of lower- or under-class blacks. Some have argued, for instance, that the pathblazing filmmaker Spike Lee is the latest example of this self-conscious estrangement—those blacks who feel that they speak *for* blacks, or *for* something generically (if not cynically) referred to as a black or African-American experience, while in many instances not speaking *to* them. But this discomfort and disjuncture, whether fully and self-consciously exploited by the writers or not, has given most black essays a philosophical undertone or philosophical suggestiveness, representative not of the specific political experience of blacks but of the broader experience of a bourgeois, literary, and artistically self-conscious elite trying to reconcile its experience of otherness—which in most cases it insists is a whole replication of the group when, in fact, it is not. A significant portion of the artistic energy of this elite is generated by the uneasy and poorly synthesized realization that its replication does not wholly coincide, or only seemingly so, with its attempts in the art marketplace to act as a cultural broker and mediator and with its self-interests in that mediation and its relative powerlessness in that marketplace. This dilemma—massive in its magnitude as it involves ambition, status, and social justification, the very motives for the creation of any art—that any oppressed elite faces in the political negotiating between the individual rewards of a career and the necessity that the oppressed's art must serve the function of bringing about the provisions of the group's liberation, is the very unease and strain that makes virtually any elite capable of producing art in the first place. In this culture, we understand the function of blacks making art, in part, as the production of a cultured and mediated catharsis that changes both the oppressor and the oppressed. It is often this very limiting and entrapping creative and commercial dilemma for the black writer that has led some black intellectuals to argue for black publishing houses that would, in effect, give blacks a kind of vertical control over their own literary products and a horizontal control—through black bookstores, bookclubs and the like—over distribution to a sizable black bourgeois audience. To be sure, the existence of several or even one major black-controlled and black-aimed publishing house would change the way some black writers see their enterprise and might even bring to some a sense of psychic relief, but the essential nature of the dilemma of the black elite in a white-dominated society would not be changed.

This anthology has its antecedents in three important black essay collections that were published in the 1960s: Herbert Hill's *Anger, and Beyond: The Negro Writer in the United States* (1966)—a popular book with a red and black library dust jacket that I distinctly remember my sister carrying around during her undergraduate days along with the equally popular and tremendously influential *The Crisis of the Negro Intellectual* (1967) by Harold Cruse; as a junior high school student I was mightily impressed by the weightiness of it all—Addison Gayle's *Black Expression: Essays by and About Black Americans in the Creative Arts* (1969) and Darwin T. Turner's *Black American Literature Essays* (1969). It is interesting to note that although modern black literature anthologies are about seventy years old, black anthologies that are devoted exclusively to the essay are a phenomenon of the 1960s, an age fueled by contentiousness and ideology, when the essay would be a particularly useful form. (The 1960s gave us at one end Baldwin's *The Fire Next Time* (1963) and at the other end Cleaver's *Soul on Ice* (1968), easily the two most influential black books of the sixties and arguably the two most influential collections of essays produced in that decade.) As always with a new anthology, the editor would like to think, in some sense, that he or she is superseding the previous anthologies of its type. This is at least partly true in this instance; however, the Hill, Gayle, and Turner anthologies, as they capture well a certain cultural moment and a certain cultural excitement, cannot be superseded and ought to be read by the true student of the black anthology and the black essay. But it is capturing a particular cultural moment that limits the previous anthologies (and will undoubtedly limit this one eventually when someone decides it must be superseded).[5] For instance, both the Hill and the Turner anthologies have no black women writers represented, an unforgivable but not surprising oversight for a 1960s black anthology when the sexual tug of war between black men and black women was at least as charged, if not as explicit, as it is now. The Gayle anthology has five black women writers' essays represented out of a total of forty essays, a liberal number for 1969. This anthology tries to correct that imbalance by including a number of significant black women writers who have written nonfiction prose of quality and cultural significance, and whose work deserves to be more widely read. Also, this anthology is more open to diversity than the previous black essay anthologies. In sheer numbers, more essays are included here than in any collection of its type (or in any anthology of black writing at all) and a very broad group of writers is represented: most major black writers and many minor ones of the 20th century who have written a worthy essay for which it was possible to get permission to reprint. I have tried to include all political and social viewpoints and have tried to include essays from various sources, both black and white, both popular and highbrow. The 1990s is, at least ideally, the decade of inclusiveness and the celebration of diversity, and that is precisely what this anthology is trying to do: be inclusive and diverse. This will make it ultimately as time-bound as any other anthology. But what is hoped is that those values, those qualities—inclusiveness and diversity—will have a long shelf life, will prove more durable and more universal than some other qualities and criteria upon which other anthologies were built. All ages have their thematic values but some ages have better and more eternal values than others.

Some might take it as a sign of the sheer grandeur of this anthology (or its sheer pretension) that it is a two-volume work. Originally conceived as one large volume, serializing the collection was, in effect, an effort to make it more readable, more affordable, and more accessible as a reference and as a *work*. That the editor quakes a bit at the thought that the very act of making the work more *workable*, as it were, also makes it more diffuse and possibly more clumsy as a product is, naturally, understandable, but, it is to be hoped, finally, unwarranted.

A final word about this collection. The works included here are essays in the traditional accepted use of the term. That is to say, they are either magazine "articles," formal essays in the sense that they argue something in a fairly linear and logical way, or informal essays that are either autobiographical or meditative or both that may be a sort of free form enthymeme or purely intuitive and impressionistic. I spoke above of anthologies being captured by the very moment of their occasion which they hope, paradoxically, to supersede; the essay is a form that conversely tries to capture a moment; it is not simply a literary trial or attempt of some sort, but it is both a dispassionate and passionate effort to see something momentarily and of the moment clearly and precisely. A good essayist must be bound and blinded by his or her subject, by the unruly and unremitting moment of faith and inspiration that produces the essay. But the good essayist must also have what O. B. Hardison, Jr., referred to as ataraxia, the Greek term for detachment, calm, a certain bland and stylish coolness. The trick of the essay is: all write it hot, but all read it cool. The essay is a confession to the reader that the world is such a problem, such a jumble, and that writing is so inadequate and so fraught with possibilities of misunderstanding or falling prey to the overindulgences of sentimentality or minimalism, egotism or sheer emptiness that there can be only these attempts at capturing moments of passing. The essay announces its limitations, celebrates them in truth, even when it is its most omniscient, its most logical and reasonable, its most unflappable. These qualities for which the essay is often praised are merely conventions that the form uses to disguise its tendency to freedom, to fun, to indiscipline, to subverting the very business of logic, argument, style, and example upon which it is built. The essayist asks two questions: In seriousness, what do I know? In jest, who knows? Or, perhaps for many of us who practice the form, the serious and jesting adherents are reversed: we mock what we know and seriously consider what anyone can know about anything. As Carl H. Klaus[7] has perceptively said about the essay: it is indeed believed by essayists themselves to be "a rogue form of writing," "an antigenre." "Ultimately," Klaus writes, ". . . the essayists seem to conceive of the essay as a place of intellectual refuge, a domain sacred to the freedom of the mind itself."

I am also deeply gratified to edit a book that contains so much favorable work from black publications, most of which have received little attention from scholars and virtually none from the general reading public. To be able to showcase essays from *Opportunity* (the house organ of the National Urban League and one of the most important black publications of the Harlem Renaissance), *The Messenger* (edited by A. Philip Randolph and Chandler Owen and another important magazine of the black 1920s), *The Crisis* (the house organ of the National Association of the Advancement of Colored People and still another important literary presence of the 1920s), *Negro Digest* (a Johnson publication that was continued as *Black World* in the early 1970s), *Phylon, Obsidian, Black American Literature Forum, The Black Scholar, The Voice of the Negro, The Midwest Journal* (a scholarly publication of Lincoln University, an historically-black school in Jefferson City, Missouri), and the *Chicago Defender* (and these are only a portion of the many magazines and newspapers published by blacks that I read through during my research for this book) is a profound public duty, an honor, and a privilege. Much of our understanding of how black literary and cultural essays work and how they came to be, much of our understanding of the rich heritage of black expository writing, is largely the result of the existence of these magazines, newspapers, and journals. Without them, the black American essay as we understand it would not have existed.[8]

There are no speeches in this collection (although there are a few instances of writers who transformed speeches into essays for publication) or any excerpts from longer nonfiction works. The essays included here are complete, nonfiction prose expositions that develop or concentrate on a single theme and are meant, generally, to be read in a single sitting. None of the essays has been altered in any way from the way they appeared in their original sources unless it is a bracketed grammatical or syntactical correction. The essays are grouped by theme or subject matter but there is, obviously, a great deal of overlap and some essays could easily have been grouped in classifications other than the ones in which I placed them. This is largely done to make the collection more readable and not to "define" or "place" the essays in some tightly theoretical or critical structure. Most of the sections are meant to function almost as small books in themselves, each containing enough essays to make possible a fruitful consideration of both the historical development and the aesthetic and political dimensions of the black essay under that particular heading.

I would like to thank the Interlibrary Loan staff of Randolph-Macon Woman's College in Lynchburg, Virginia; the Interlibrary Loan staff of Washington University in St. Louis, particularly Ellen Raben who has been helpful beyond the call of duty and exceedingly forgiving about overdue loans; Marie Sanders and Lynnel Thomas, two delightful research assistants; and Jim McLeod, the former Director of the African and Afro-American Studies Program at Washington University, for his considerable support and very valued friendship. Finally, I would like to thank all the writers' agents, and editors who have generously permitted their work to be reprinted here. Although I cannot single out everyone here as I would like, I particularly appreciate the support and cooperation of Janet Dewart of the National Urban League, Fred Beaufort of the NAACP, Michael Brown of *The Chicago Defender*, Toni Tingle of *The Black Scholar* and the editors of *The Nation*, *American Scholar*, and *Esquire* who made available several very important works that make up this volume.

NOTES

1. Langston Hughes, *The Big Sea* (New York: Hill and Wang, 1978), pp. 3-4.

2. Richard Wright, *Black Boy* (New York: Harper and Row, 1966), p. 267.

3. Ibid., pp. 271-272.

4. Wright may be dissembling in other ways. In the chapter before the grand discovery of Mencken and serious literature, Wright states that he "began patronizing secondhand bookstores, buying magazines and books. In this way I became acquainted with periodicals like *Harper's Magazine*, *The Atlantic Monthly*, and the *American Mercury*." As Joseph Epstein tells us in his Foreword to H.L. Mencken's *A Carnival of Buncombe*: "During the years that [Mencken] edited the *American Mercury* it was sometimes alleged that entire issues of the monthly magazine read as if written by Mencken himself." This would indicate that Wright was far more familiar with the Mencken style than he lets on in his book and he certainly encountered it before he read *A Book of Prefaces*. The major point Wright wishes to make about his reading at this time in his life is that he had grown beyond the pulp literature that Harrison, the black boy who worked at a rival optical company and whom Wright was eventually manipulated into fighting, was reading. For our purposes, what is striking is that Wright had graduated from pulp fiction to magazines that were noted for publishing essays. (Incidentally, the Harrison character may not even have existed. Through his creation, Wright may have simply been dramatizing the battle of self-education and literacy that he felt was being waged in his own consciousness between the cheap mass entrapments of popular culture and the higher forms of American bourgeois literary productions.)

5. I suppose that this collection comes closest to emulating the Turner anthology. In his introduction, Turner states his purposes: "First, by furnishing samples of the styles of the best-known black essayists, it affords a comparison of their work with that of their more frequently anthologized white contemporaries. Second, it provides opportunity for examination of the changes in style from the nineteenth to the twentieth century. Third, the personal and cultural essays offer glimpses into the thoughts of individual men about subjects other than the social, economic, and political struggles of Negroes. In all of these, this collection reflects, in miniature, the history of essay writing by black Americans." This collection does not include work from the 19th century as I felt that a concentration on 20th century essays would make for a more unified and readable collection. Otherwise, I think that my aspirations for this collection generally coincide with Professor Turner's aspirations for his, although his third purpose in some ways begs the question—when is the Negro not thinking about social, economic, and political struggle which constitute the whole of his identity and his racial raison d'être, so to speak? When is he or she not consumed by the epistemology of his or her condition or status which often coincides with the epistemology of his or her being?

6. O. B. Hardison, Jr., "Binding Proteus: An Essay on the Essay" in *Essays on the Essay: Redefining the Genre*, Alexander J. Butrym (ed.), (Athens and London: the University of Georgia Press, 1989), p. 18.

7. Carl H. Klaus, "Essayists on the Essay," in Chris Anderson (ed.), *Literary Nonfiction: Theory, Criticism, Pedagogy* (Carbondale and Edwardsville: Southern Illinois University Press, 1989), pp. 160, 164.

8. Probably one of the finest essays on the black essay or more properly on black nonfiction prose is the introduction to the essay section of *The Negro Caravan*, edited by Arthur P. Davis, Ulysses Lee, and Sterling Brown and published in 1941. This piece explains the history of black nonfiction writing up to 1940 with a thoroughness that has not been matched since.

SPEECH AND POWER

VOLUME 1

I

ON BEING
BLACK

The essays in this section could have been classified in other sections of this book: some as autobiographical portraiture and others as political or cultural exposition. However, they all seem to work well together as a kind of composite of how blacks view, in a larger context, the meaning of their race in a society dominated, in most mundane and spiritual matters, by whites or at least by white sensibilities or what is convenient to the general comfort of whites. These essays range the entire span of the 20th century, from Du Bois's piece that thematically kicked off the Harlem Renaissance of the 1920s to Shelby Steele's late-1980s essay. The political views that inform the pieces differ markedly from each other—from the Marxist Marable to the assimilationist Steele—but each, in their contrast, seems to complement what the others say.

ON BEING BLACK

W. E. B. Du Bois was one of the most prominent
men of letters—sociologist, editor, novelist, poet, historian, essayist—in
American literary history. Born in Great Barrington, Massachusetts, in
1868, Du Bois earned a Ph.D. from Harvard, studied in Berlin, was one
of the young radicals who opposed the reign of Booker T. Washington as
national black leader (1895–1915), and eventually helped to found the
National Association for the Advancement of Colored People. He served
as editor of the NAACP's house organ, *The Crisis*, for nearly twenty
years. His *The Souls of Black Folk* (1903), a collection of essays, still
ranks as one of the most influential works written by a black American.
"On Being Black" was originally published on February 18, 1920 in the
New Republic and was reprinted in *Darkwater: Voices from Within the
Veil*, also published in 1920. Du Bois died in Ghana in 1963.

M y friend, who is pale and positive, said to me yesterday, as the tired
sun was nodding: "You are too sensitive."

I admit, I am—sensitive. I am artificial. I cringe or am bump-
tious or immobile. I am intellectually dishonest, art-blind, and I lack humor.

"Why don't you stop all this?" she retorts triumphantly.

You will not let us.

"There you go, again. You know that I—"

Wait! I answer. Wait!

I arise at seven. The milkman has neglected me. He pays little attention to
colored districts. My white neighbor glares elaborately. I walk softly, lest I disturb
him. The children jeer as I pass to work. The women in the streetcar withdraw
their skirts or prefer to stand. The policeman is truculent. The elevator man hates
to serve Negroes. My job is insecure because the white union wants it and does not

want me. I try to lunch, but no place near will serve me. I go forty blocks to Marshall's, but the Committee of Fourteen closes Marshall's; they say that white women frequent it.

"Do all eating places discriminate?"

No, but how shall I know which do not—except—

I hurry home through crowds. They mutter or get angry. I go to a mass-meeting. They stare. I go to a church. "We don't admit niggers!"

Or perhaps I leave the beaten track. I seek new work. "Our employees would not work with you; our customers would object."

I ask to help in social uplift.

"Why—er—we will write you."

I enter the free field of science. Every laboratory door is closed and no endowments are available.

I seek the universal mistress, Art; the studio door is locked.

I write literature. "We cannot publish stories of colored folks of that type." It's the only type I know.

This is my life. It makes me idiotic. It gives me artificial problems. I hesitate, I rush, I waver. In fine—I am sensitive!

My pale friend looks at me with disbelief and curling tongue.

"Do you mean to sit there and tell me that this is what happens to you each day?"

Certainly not, I answer low.

"Then you only fear it will happen?"

I fear!

"Well, haven't you the courage to rise above a—almost a craven fear?"

Quite—quite craven is my fear, I admit; but the terrible thing is—these things do happen!

"But you just said—"

They do happen. Not all each day—surely not. But now and then—now seldom; now, sudden; now after a week, now in a chain of awful minutes; not everywhere, but anywhere—in Boston, in Atlanta. That's the hell of it. Imagine spending your life looking for insults or for hiding places from them—shrinking (instinctively and despite desperate bolsterings of courage) from blows that are not always, but ever; not each day, but each week, each month, each year. Just, perhaps, as you have choked back the craven fear and cried, "I am and will be the master of my—"

"No more tickets downstairs; here's one to the smoking gallery."

You hesitate. You beat back your suspicions. After all, a cigarette with Charlie Chaplin—then a white man pushes by—

"Three in the orchestra."

"Yes, sir." And in he goes.

Suddenly your heart chills. You turn yourself away toward the golden twinkle of the purple night and hesitate again. What's the use? Why not always yield—always take what's offered—always bow to force, whether of cannon or dislike? Then the great fear surges in your soul, the real fear—the fear beside which other fears are vain imaginings; the fear lest right there and then you are losing your own soul; that you are losing your own soul and the soul of a people; that millions of unborn children, black and gold and mauve, are being there and then despoiled by you because you are a coward and dare not fight!

Suddenly that silly orchestra seat and the cavorting of a comedian with funny feet become matters of life, death, and immortality; you grasp the pillars of the universe and strain as you sway back to that befilled ticket girl. You grip your soul for riot and murder. You choke and sputter, and she, seeing that you are about to make a "fuss" obeys her orders and throws the tickets at you in contempt. Then you slink to your seat and crouch in the darkness before the film, with every tissue burning! The miserable wave of reaction engulfs you. To think of compelling puppies to take your hard-earned money; fattening hogs to hate you and yours; forcing your way among cheap and tawdry idiots—God! What a night of pleasure!

Why do not those who are scarred in the world's battle and hurt by its hardness travel to these places of beauty and drown themselves in the utter joy of life? I asked this one sitting in a Southern home. Outside the spring of a Georgia February was luring gold to the bushes and languor to the soft air. Around me sat color in human flesh—brown that crimsoned readily; dim soft-yellow that escaped description; creamlike duskiness that shadowed to rich tints of autumn leaves. And yet a suggested journey in the world brought no response.

"I should think you would like to travel," said the white one.

But no, the thought of a journey seemed to depress them.

Did you ever see a Jim Crow waiting room? There are always exceptions, as at Greensboro—but usually there is no heat in winter and no air in summer; with undisturbed loafers and train hands and broken, disreputable settees; to buy a ticket is torture; you stand and stand and wait and wait until every white person at the "other window" is waited on. Then the tired agent yells across, because all the tickets and money are over there—

"What d' ye want? What? Where?"

The agent browbeats and contradicts you, hurries and confuses the ignorant, gives many persons the wrong change, compels some to purchase their tickets on the train at a higher price, and sends you and me out on the platform burning with indignation and hatred!

The Jim Crow car is up next the baggage car and engine. It stops out beyond the covering in the rain or sun dust. Usually there is no step to help you climb on, and often the car is a smoker cut in two, and you must pass through the white smokers or else they pass through your part, with swagger and noise and stares. Your compartment is a half or a quarter or an eighth of the oldest car in service on the road. Unless it happens to be a through express, the plush is caked with dirt, the floor is grimy, and the windows dirty. An impertinent white newsboy occupies two seats at the end of the car and importunes you to the point of rage to buy cheap candy, Coca-Cola, and worthless, if not vulgar, books. He yells and swaggers, while a continued stream of white men saunters back and forth from the smoker, to buy and hear. The white train crew from the baggage car uses the Jim Crow to lounge in and perform their toilet. The conductor appropriates two seats for himself and his papers and yells gruffly for your tickets before the train has scarcely started. It is best not to ask him for information even in the gentlest tones. His information is for white persons chiefly. It is difficult to get lunch or clean water. Lunchrooms either don't serve niggers or serve them at some dirty and ill-attended hole in the wall. As for toilet rooms—don't! If you have to change cars, be wary of junctions which are usually without accommodation and filled with quarrelsome white persons who hate a "darky dressed up." You are apt to have the company of a sheriff and a couple of meek or sullen black prisoners on part of your way, and dirty colored section hands will pour in toward night and drive you to the smallest corner.

"No," said the little lady in the corner (she looked like an ivory cameo and her dress flowed on her like a caress), "we don't travel much."

Pessimism is cowardice. The man who cannot frankly acknowledge the Jim Crow car as a fact and yet live and hope is simply afraid either of himself or of the world. There is not in the world a more disgraceful denial of human brotherhood than the Jim Crow car of the Southern United States; but, too, just as true, there is nothing more beautiful in the universe than sunset and moonlight on Montego Bay in far Jamaica. And both things are true and both belong to this, our world, and neither can be denied.

High in the tower, where I sit above the loud complaining of the human sea, I know many souls that toss and whirl and pass, but none there are that intrigue me more than the Souls of White Folk.

Of them I am singularly clairvoyant. I see in and through them. I view them from unusual points of vantage. Not as a foreigner do I come, for I am native, not foreign, bone of their thought and flesh of their language. Mine is not the knowledge of the traveler or the colonial composite of dear memories, words, and wonder. Nor yet is my knowledge that which servants have of masters, or mass of class, or capitalist of artisan. Rather I see the working of their entrails. I know their thoughts and they know that I know. This knowledge makes them now embarrassed, now furious! They deny my right to live and be and call me misbirth! My word is to them mere bitterness and my soul, pessimism. And yet as they preach and strut and shout and threaten, crouching as they clutch at rags of facts and fancies to hide their nakedness, they go twisting, flying by my tired eyes and I see them ever stripped—ugly, human.

The discovery of personal whiteness among the world's peoples is a very modern thing—a nineteenth- and twentieth-century matter, indeed. The ancient world would have laughed at such a distinction. The Middle Ages regarded skin color with mild curiosity; and even up into the eighteenth century we were hammering our national manikins into one, great, Universal Man, with fine frenzy which ignored color and race even more than birth. Today we have changed all that, and the world in a sudden, emotional conversion has discovered that it is white and by that token, wonderful!

As we saw the dead dimly through rifts of battlesmoke and heard faintly the cursing and accusations of blood brothers, we darker men said: This is not Europe gone mad; this is not aberration nor insanity; this *is* Europe; this seeming Terrible is the real soul of white culture—back of all culture—stripped and visible today. This is where the world has arrived—these dark and awful depths, and not the shining and ineffable heights of which it boasted. Here is whither the might and energy of modern humanity has really gone.

But may not the world cry back at us and ask: "What better thing have you to show? What have you done or would do better than this if you had today the world rule? Paint with all riot of hateful colors the thin skin of European culture—is it not better than any culture that arose in Africa or Asia?"

It is. Of this there is no doubt and never has been; but why is it better? Is it better because Europeans are better, nobler, greater, and more gifted than other folk? It is not. Europe has never produced and never will in our day bring forth a single human soul who cannot be matched and overmatched in every line of human endeavor by Asia and Africa. Run the gamut, if you will, and let us have the Europeans who in sober truth overmatch Nefertari, Mohammed, Rameses, and Askia, Confucius, Buddha, and Jesus Christ. If we could scan the calendar of thousands of lesser men, in like comparison, the result would be the same; but we cannot do this because of the deliberately educated ignorance of white schools by which they remember Napoleon and forget Sonni Ali.

Why, then, is Europe great? Because of the foundations which the mighty past have furnished her to build upon: the iron trade of ancient black Africa, the religion and empire-building of yellow Asia, the art and science of the "dago" Mediterranean shore, east, south, and west, as well as north. And where she has builded securely upon this great past and learned from it, she has gone forward to greater and more splendid human triumph; but where she has ignored this past and forgotten and sneered at it, she has shown the cloven hoof of poor, crucified humanity—she has played, like other empires gone, the world fool!

ON BEING BLACK

ERIC D. WALROND was born in Guyana in 1898.
He wrote for a newspaper in Panama during World War I and came to
America at the age of twenty to attend City College of New York. He
worked intermittently both in the 1920s and in the 1930s as an associate
editor of Marcus Garvey's *Negro World* and *The Black Man*, respectively.
He also worked for *Opportunity* magazine, the house organ of the
National Urban League, as a business manager during the mid-twenties.
His major publication was a collection of ten short stories called *Tropic
Death* that was published in 1926. He also wrote a number of occasional
pieces for the *New Republic, Current History,* and the like. "On Being
Black" was originally published in the *New Republic* on November 1,
1922.

I

I go to an optician and ask for a pair of goggles. My eyes are getting bad and
my wife insists upon my getting them. For a long time I have hesitated to do
so. I hated to be literary—that is, to look literary. It is a fad, I believe. On an
afterthought I am convinced she is right; I need them. My eyes are paining me.
Moreover, the lights in the subway are blindingly dark, and head swirling. Again,
the glitter of spring sends needles through my skull. I need the things badly. I decide
to go to the optician's. I go. It is a Jewish place. Elderly is the salesman. I put my
cards on the table. . . . "Fine day, isn't it?" He rubs and twists his pigmy fingers
and ambles back to the rear. A moment later he returns. With him is a tray of
jewelry—lenses and gold rings, diamonds and silver frames. Fine, dainty, effemi-
nate things.

"Here is a nice one," chirps the old gentleman in a sing-song tone, as he tries to fit it on to my nose. "Just the right kind of goggles to keep the dust from going into your eyes. Only the other day I sold—"

At first I feel as if it is one of these confounded new fangled things. Overnight they come, these new styles. Ideas! Here, I whisper to myself, is a new one on me. But I look again. It has a perforated bit of tin on either side of it, like the black star-eyed guard on a horse's blinker.

"Oh, I can show you others, if you don't like that one. Want one with a bigger dust piece? I have others back here. Don't be afraid, I'll fix you up. All the colored chauffeurs on Cumberland Street buy their glasses here."

"But I am not a chauffeur," I reply softly. Were it a Negro store, I might have said it with a great deal of emphasis, of vehemence. But being what it is, and knowing that the moment I raise my voice I am accused of "uppishness," I take pains—oh such pains, to be discreet. I wanted to bellow into his ears, "Don't think every Negro you see is a chauffeur." But the man is overwhelmingly amused. His snow-white head is bent—bent over the tray of precious gold, and I can see his face wrinkle in an atrociously cynical smile. But I cannot stand it—that smile. I walk out.

II

I am a stenographer. I am in need of a job. I try the employment agencies. I battle with anaemic youngsters and giggling flappers. I am at the tail end of a long line—only to be told the job is already filled. I am ignorantly optimistic. America is a big place; I feel it is only a question of time and perseverance. Encouraged, I go into the tall office buildings on Lower Broadway. I try everyone of them. Not a firm is missed. I walk in and offer my services. I am black, foreign looking and a curio. My name is taken. I shall be sent for, certainly, in case of need. "Oh, don't mention it, sir. . . . Glad you came in. . . . Good morning." I am smiled out. I never hear from them again.

Eventually I am told that that is not the way it is done here. What typewriter do I use? Oh,——. Well, go to the firm that makes them. It maintains an employment bureau, for the benefit of users of its machine. There is no discrimination there; go and see them. Before I go I write stating my experience and so forth. Are there any vacancies? In reply I get a flattering letter asking me to call. I do so.

The place is crowded. A sea of feminine faces disarms me. But I am no longer sensitive. I've got over that—long since. I grind my teeth and confidently take my seat with the mob. At the desk the clerks are busy telephoning and making out cards. I am sure they do not see me. I am just one of the crowd. One by one the girls, and men, too, are sent out after jobs. It has been raining and my hair is frowsy. The Jewish girls are sweating in their war-paint. At last they get around to me. It is my turn.

I am sitting away down at the front. In order to get to me the lady is obliged to do a lot of detouring. At first I thought she was about to go out, to go past me. But I am mistaken. She takes a seat right in front of me, a smile on her wrinkled old-maidish face. I am sure she is the head of the department. It is a situation that requires a strong diplomatic hand. She does not send one of the girls. She comes herself. She is from Ohio, I can see that. She tries to make me feel at home by smiling broadly in my face.

"Are you Mr.——?"

"Yes."

"That's nice. Now how much experience you say you've had?"

She is about to write.

"I stated all that in the letter, I think. I've had five years. I worked for—"

"Oh yes, I have it right here. Used to be secretary to Dr.——. Then you worked for an export house, and a soap manufacturer. Also as a shorthand reporter on a South American paper. That is interesting; quite an experience for a young man, isn't it?"

I murmur unintelligibly.

"Well," continues the lady, "we haven't anything at present—"

"But I thought you said in your letter that there is a job vacant. I've got it here in my pocket. I hope I haven't left it at home—"

"That won't suit you. You see it—it—is a post that requires banking experience. One of the biggest banks in the city. Secretary to the vice-president. Ah, by the way; come to think of it, you're just the man for it. You know Mr.——of Lenox Avenue? You do! I think the number is—— Yes, here it is. Also one of his cards. Well, if I were you I would go and see him. Good day."

Dusk is on the horizon. I am once more on Broadway. I am not going to see the man on Lenox Avenue. It won't do any good. The man she is sending me to is a pupil of mine!

III

My wife's health is not very good and I think of sending her to the tropics. I write to the steamship company and in reply I receive a sheaf of booklets telling me all about the blueness of the Caribbean, the beauty of Montego Bay, and the fine à la carte service at the Myrtle Bank Hotel. I am intrigued—I think that is the word— by a three months' cruise at a special rate of $150. I telephone the company in an effort to get some information as to sailing dates, reservations, and so forth.

"I understand," I say to the young man who answers the telephone, "I understand that you have a ship sailing on the tenth. I would like to reserve a berth at the $150 you are at present offering."

"White or colored?"

"Colored."

Evidently the clerk is consulting someone. But his hand is over the mouthpiece and I cannot hear what he is saying. Presently—

"Better come in the office and make reservations."

"What time do you close?"

"Five o'clock."

"What time is it now, please?"

"Ten to."

"Good," I hurry, "I am at Park Place now. Do you think if I hop on a Broadway trolley I can make it before five?"

"I don't know," unconcernedly.

I am at the booking desk. It is three minutes to five. The clerks, tall, lean, light-haired youths, are ready to go home. As I enter a dozen pairs of eyes are fastened upon me. Murmuring. Only a nigger. Again the wheels of life grind on. Lots are cast—I am not speaking metaphorically. The joke is on the Latin. Down in Panama he is a government clerk. Over in Caracas, a tinterillo, and in Mexico, a scientifico. I know the type. Coming to New York, he shuns the society of Spanish Americans. On the subway at night he reads the *New York Journal* instead of *La Prensa*. And on wintry evenings, you can always find him around Seventy-second Street and Broadway. The lad before me is dark, has crystal brown eyes, and straight black hair.

"I would like," I begin, "to reserve a passage for my wife on one of your steamers to Kingston. I want to get it at the $150 rate."

"Well, it is this way." I am positive he is from Guayaquil. "It will cost you $178."

"Why $178?"

"You see, the passage alone is $170—"

"A hundred and seventy dollars! Why, this booklet here says $150 round trip. You must have made a mistake."

"You see, this $150 rate is for three in a room, and all the rooms on the ship sailing on the tenth are already taken up."

"All right," I decide, "the date is inconsequential. What I want is the $150 rate. Reserve a berth for me on any ship that is not already filled up. I don't care how late in the summer it is. I have brought a deposit along with me—"

I am not truculent. Everything I say I strive to say softly, unoffensively— especially when in the midst of a color-ordeal!

"Well, you'd have to get two persons to go with her." The Peruvian is independent. "There are only three berths in a stateroom, and if your wife wants to take advantage of the $150 rate, she will have to get two other colored persons to go with her."

"I s-e-e!" I mutter dreamily. And I did see!

"Come in tomorrow and pay a deposit on it, if you want to. It is five o'clock and—"

I am out on the street again. From across the Hudson a gurgling wind brings dust to my nostrils. I am limp, static, emotionless. There is only one line to Jamaica, and I am going to send her by it. It is the only thing to do. Tomorrow I am going back, with the $178. It pays to be black.

BLACK PRIDE

KIMBAL (STROUD) GOFFMAN apparently published only one piece in any major publication during her career. She died in October 1946 at the age of 41 in Colorado Springs, Colorado, where she had lived for 36 years, a member of the noted Stroud family of high-achieving blacks. Her husband was a chauffeur. "Black Pride" appeared in the *Atlantic Monthly* in February 1939.

I

"Yes, I beat 'im up. Nobody ain't gonna call me a nigger and get away with it. I got too much race pride for that."

These remarks were made by a small Negro lad who had just emerged victoriously from a fistic encounter with a white boy about the same size.

That was about twenty years ago on a school playground. The next day I had the opportunity of being a visitor at that school, where the same little boy sat in his classroom surrounded by his white classmates. The music supervisor was present, and every child was singing: "The Star-Spangled Banner," "Auld Lang Syne," "Home, Sweet Home," "Scotland's Burning," and many other old songs. Finally the teacher called for "Massa's in de Cold, Cold Ground." The Negro lad buried his face in his book and stopped singing. I know the teacher saw him. However, she at no time acted as if she were aware of his embarrassment. The children finished the song.

I must say that they did a splendid job, for which their supervisor complimented them. She went much further. She told them how the plantation songs which describe the days of slavery and work of the early Negroes are the only songs which America can call her own. She told of the number-one place those songs hold in our land. She even explained that Negroes sing these songs with more feeling, enthusiasm, and in better style than any other citizens of America. I know her intention was to relieve the Negro child of his embarrassment, and to encourage him to join his classmates in the singing.

The next song was the immortal "Old Folks at Home." The Negro boy again retreated into the covering of his book. I wondered to myself just what had become of all the race pride he had possessed the day before. The music which described the work and life of his ancestors he considered an insult and embarrassment. It was hard to account for such a sudden turn of character in our little champion of race pride. Perhaps the child had mistaken a case of personal anger for a serious insult to the entire race.

Are we Negroes of America champions of race pride or not? My personal answer is no. It is a shame that we people who are so conspicuous, who total such a large percentage of the population of these United States, who so often suffer from the rules of segregation and discrimination, who possess such a small amount of the wealth and political control of the nation, who have accomplished what we have accomplished through the most obscure and difficult of all channels, who are oftentimes despised and avoided by other men, should also be accused of a lack of race pride.

Negroes not only lack race pride and have an inferiority complex. They have a third handicap—white prejudice. Black people are more prejudiced in favor of the white race than white people are themselves. The black race is a distinctive creation; we possess characteristics which differ from those of any other people in the world. If there is one member of the black race present in an audience, one glance will find him. This is true of no other group. If the audience is large and everyone is dressed more or less alike, a definite search must be made to classify the different racial types with the exception of the Negro.

We have the honor of being exclusive, a distinction which every dealer in merchandise desires for his establishment; and the primary physical features which give us this distinction are black skin, kinky hair, thick lips, high cheekbones, large hands, feet, and nostrils. The whole world appreciates the exclusive community, home, food, dress, voice, book, and so on. There are, however, very few Negroes who are proud of their exclusive physical appearance.

If this statement is not true, why are so many manufacturers becoming rich through the manufacture of bleaching preparations? Why are hair-straightening combs found in nearly every Negro home? Why is the following remark made so often to a newborn baby, when grandma or auntie visits it for the first time? "Tell Mother she must pinch your nose every morning. If she doesn't, you're gonna have a sure 'nough darky nose."

The majority of us Negroes are not only ashamed of the physical features of our race, but also opposed to the habits and customs of the race that are ours through natural inheritance. I shall never forget the remark my mother made when my sister began to learn the Charleston dance. (I wish I were positive that she was the only person who made such a statement, but I doubt that seriously.) She said, "You act enough like a nigger now without adding that junk to it." Did that statement denote race pride? The Charleston is Negroid. Negroes originated it.

Why not be proud of it? Many individuals have commercialized dancing. Why shouldn't we Negroes commercialize our own ideas?

For generations other races have kept their individual customs. The white race takes pride in reviving, at regular intervals, some hand-me-down custom perhaps two hundred years old. Black Americans are not white Americans. Black Americans are only mimicking white Americans when they waltz, two-step, or fox-trot. When black Americans dance the Charleston, the Susie Q, or the Big Apple they become original. Originality is the backbone of all progress.

II

It was not until I married that I began to read periodicals published by Negroes. This seems a queer assertion for me to make; at present my boys are agents for every Negro periodical coming into our town, and we all read them. But my father was responsible for this situation.

When I was a small child about ten years of age, my father paid a year's subscription for two Negro periodicals, which came for three months. What they had in them I cannot say; I was too young to be interested in reading them. I do know, however, that my father was very angry when the agent visited our house. I cannot remember all the conversation, but I know he said, "Papers of that kind have no business in circulation. They do more to develop race hatred than anything else in the world. If I were alone, I might take a different attitude. I am not. I have seven children, and I don't intend to have them hate the white race before they are grown. Those papers do nothing but play up all the faults of white people. We can't live in the same country with white people and rear our children to hate them."

The agent asked him if it would be possible for him to read the publications and not let us youngsters see them. "I should say not," my father replied. "My youngsters are to read everything that comes into my house. The stuff in those papers is the most radical junk I have ever read. Whoever edits them has surely forgotten that the citizens of the United States have to live together." Then he laughed and said, "No, sir, there's nothing coming into my house that isn't fit for the children to read. If it comes in we're all going to read it. If it isn't fit for some of us to read, it isn't coming."

The agent then explained that he did not like to write that statement. The publishers would have to know why the papers were being stopped after three months when they had been paid for a year in advance. It was finally agreed that the subscription should be transferred to one of our neighbors, who wanted the periodicals and did not have the money to pay for them. That ended Negro publications in our home.

I have often wondered whether my father was right or wrong in his attitude. I have often wondered if those publications were written on a more radical basis in those days than now. That was more than twenty years ago. When I reached the age of adolescence and began to earn my own money I often wanted to subscribe for one of the Negro publications. I was curious; I wanted to know what was in them; I wanted to know why my father had become so angry. When I had reached that age, however, the family was in such poor circumstances that any surplus money had to be used to buy clothes. When I was twenty, my mother and father had a grand total of eleven children, and we older ones felt almost as much responsibility for the welfare of the little folk as my father and mother did.

When I married, nearly all the Negro periodicals came regularly to my new home, for my husband is greatly interested in current events of every nature. My father was a man of education; he had taught school and was a very deep thinker. My husband is uneducated, not from choice, but because an education was for him an impossibility. I believe he would have been a very successful student had he had the opportunity. My father enjoyed a book of economics, history, philosophy, or mathematics. My husband is more content with the daily newspaper or the *Reader's Digest*. One year during my married life I discovered we were receiving eight different weekly publications, the daily newspaper of our own home town, the daily paper from another town, and three monthly publications. I can't help feeling that this is some sort of record for a man who has never earned a salary of more than $100 a month.

It was during the first year of my married life that the case of the People of Detroit versus Ossian Sweet held the spotlight. That was the case of a Negro doctor who had a little more money than many of his associates, and who purchased a home within the boundaries of an all-white community. Racial trouble began. A man was killed. The trouble went into the courts, and the late Clarence Darrow represented Dr. Sweet. Mr. Darrow won the case so far as civil law is concerned. A few years later Mrs. Sweet's health broke and the family moved to Arizona, where she and the baby died.

I did not then, and I do not now, know Dr. Sweet. I know nothing about the circumstances which caused him to purchase that particular house. But I have often wondered why he could find no suitable place among his own people. I am not an advocate of racial segregation. I do not approve of having laws enacted which prohibit a person from living where he pleases in a democratic country. But on the other hand I do not approve of a statement of this kind: "Just as soon as I can get enough money I am going to get out of this trashy nigger neighborhood." I have heard that statement made by so many individuals of my own race that when I read about a case similar to the Sweet case I begin to wonder. I want to know why the Negro is moving away from his neighbors. Does he have a legitimate reason? Is the neighborhood overcrowded, and is there no room for the family? Is the property selling at too high a price within his neighborhood? I hope so. I hope the family are not moving because of a lack of race pride, or because a raise in salary has made them feel that the people and customs of the black race are too inferior for them to associate with.

As a home-town correspondent for some of the Negro newspapers, I have had a chance to talk to some of the leaders of the black race. In many instances, when I ask about a specific Negro enterprise in the city one of these leaders represents, I find he is so removed from the mass of his own people that he knows nothing about his next-door neighbors. It can't be true that a Negro who attains recognition and position through the help of his own race becomes too important to mingle socially with Negroes. He can't be ashamed of the customs and habits of his ancestors. Then why doesn't he develop the communities which other members of his race are forced to live in? This can be done by building new houses or remodeling old ones in his same neighborhood.

I hope Dr. Sweet, of that famous case, was forced to move because of the price of property or because of overcrowded conditions. If so, the case was won completely from the standpoint of both moral and civil law. If not, and he moved because he wanted to get out of that "trashy nigger neighborhood," the moral law was a total loss. Although on the surface we Negroes are challengers of race pride, we do very, very little to win the championship from the other races. Any person who will shun his own people is not, in my opinion, proving that he believes in race pride.

III

Another unfortunate attitude I find within my own race is regarding employment. We were given our freedom in 1865. Then came the problem of adjusting so many freed persons in the fields of industry. At that time, as a whole, Negroes were fitted only for agriculture and household service. From 1865 to 1910 we controlled the positions of servants in agriculture, hotels, restaurants, clubs, and private homes. Then what did we do? As we became educated, instead of systematically organizing this labor, we did not appreciate our opportunities. We wanted clerical or white-collar jobs. We began to feel that the work we were doing was made for no one but Negroes; and anything that is labeled "for Negroes only" is an insult in the heart of a black man.

We soon classed this employment as second-rate. What is the result? Since 1910 we have watched the Swedes, Germans, Irish, Chinese, Japanese, and so forth, replace our own workers. Why? Because Negroes have very little pride in their own achievements. We have sat idly by and let one of the largest industrial fields of the country, domestic labor, slip beyond our grasp. Domestic labor is an industry which, I dare say, would have produced many a wealthy person, had any other race of people had the chance to dominate it as we did. I have often thought of how the Jews would have made capital of such an opportunity. Household work, had it been monopolized by Jews, would have been one of the best-organized labor divisions in the United States by the time the New Deal inaugurated the now outlawed NRA.

When I speak of organization I do not mean merely organizing to start agitating and bickering for higher wages. That is only the cheap, small part of it. My idea of systematic organizing is first to classify the workers—rate them according to the service they give or the work they perform. If a worker gives expert service or does his work very well his labor is wanted. Employers will bid for a good and conscientious worker, and this condition will force a natural process of higher wages. Such a system would place the industry upon a high level that would command respect.

During the seventy-five years we have had our freedom, household work could have been placed upon such a high level that we should have been recognized everywhere as business managers. Workers would have had an urge to reach the highest in the classification scale. Wages would have been paid according to classification. An employer would know the minute he appeared at an employment agency just what to expect from each individual listed. He would know exactly what type of person he was employing before engaging that person. As it is, Negro labor varies in qualification, and the good have become so mingled with the worthless that employers have classified Negro servants as a whole on a lower level.

Because of our own lack of interest, an industry which provides the livelihood for numerous citizens of the United States is found completely unorganized, and under the new Social Security Unemployment Compensation law those employed in this field receive no protection. This is one result of the fact that Negroes have not been interested in things which were theirs through natural inheritance.

Nearly all my life I have lived in a community where domestic work furnishes the largest portion of employment. When we moved here Negroes held nine out of every ten of these jobs. Everywhere we heard: "All a darky can get to do in this town is housework. The place I came from employed Negroes everywhere." There was some sort of complaint registered in practically every Negro home. Whenever so many complaints are found, one may always be sure that those people are not doing their best work.

One by one Negroes lost their jobs and were replaced by other workers. In 1932 there were very few Negroes employed anywhere. Then the cry came in full blast: "The town would be all right, but a colored man can't get nothin' to do. Can't even get a job doing housework. I never in all my life saw such a place." They blamed the employment agencies. They accused the operators of being unfair. None of the complainers, however, seemed to have anything to offer as a remedy for the situation. I began to study the condition. From a complete survey I found that every Negro who still held his job was one I had never heard complaining, "All a darky can get to do in this town is housework."

I watched one man and his wife very closely. They were employed in a private family, where the woman was cook and her husband was yard man and butler. They had lived in the town since 1904, had worked in one family for over twenty years, and had been employed at their present place for ten years. I shall never forget what this man said to me one night. "I think a person should make a business out of any kind of work at which he might be employed. I am not an educated man, and I've got to make a living. This is the only thing I am fitted for, and believe me, I'm gonna do it. I'm gonna do everything I can to please the man I'm working for and make him like me, whether he wants to or not. Then, if I make a mistake sometime, maybe he'll overlook it, because he likes me, and I won't get fired. I look upon my job as a business, and I'm going to make my business a paying proposition."

That couple owns a downtown building now, the only one in this town owned by Negroes. They have built a home for the wife's mother (the husband's mother died when he was just a child). They own a 1938 Buick car and have more cash than any of the other Negroes. This was all due to the fact that they made a business out of a household job. If one Negro couple can do so much without an education, why has the whole of the black race, education and all, failed to organize such a profitable industry? Why are we allowing it gradually to slip from our grasp? I have only this answer: it was controlled by Negroes, and to the mass of black people anything which makes us exclusive has no value. It is but another example of false race pride in the hearts of black Americans.

IV

Here is another puzzle: why are we so ashamed of the historical background of our lives? Why do we object so forcefully to the stories, labors, art, and habits of the old slaves? It is true that slavery was all wrong, and that the civilized world should be 100 per cent against any suggestion of any type of slavery. To me, however, the relics of the old slave customs are antiques too valuable to be sold by the Negroes of to-day. There are very, very few of the old slaves left. Those who remain are too old to bring back the vivid and unusual past. How much of that life have we preserved? I dare say, had it not been for the fact that the white race took pride in preserving some of the quaint sayings and customs of those days, the beginning of the history of Negroes in America would be completely blotted out.

What is prettier than the quaint old-fashioned language of our ancestors? No race in the world spoke with the accent which the Negro slave used. I do not mean that we should make it universal to-day, but I do mean that every book, paper, magazine, and so forth, that contains any reference to that simple language should be clipped and kept as treasure. Had the white race not preserved the poems and works of Paul Laurence Dunbar in their original language, and had Joel Chandler Harris not portrayed the character of Uncle Remus in plantation style, the old-fashioned language of our own ancestors would be gone forever.

Slavery had many horrors—but what race has not had frightful experiences? Are we going to obliterate our past because we happen to have been slaves? Had the manners of the old Negro slave, the doorman, the butler, the maid, and the valet been preserved, we should have surpassed all other races in etiquette to this day. The man who possessed the best manners of all in my home town was a former slave. Many persons of wealth have singled him out as an example when trying to cultivate good manners among the men of their own families. There are very few of our modern youths who can be singled out as examples of courtesy. The younger generation has become so rude that at times we appear ridiculous.

We have become so afraid that we might be accused of acting like the old slaves that many of us are not wanted in good society. Had the good manners of the old slaves been retained, we should have been a pride to any nation. Any other race would have retained some of the better customs of the slave days. However we, who had the sole right to preserve the good parts, have thrown it all into the same heap and pushed it aside. Had it not been for slavery, such songs as "Steal Away," which bring so vividly to view a picture of the soul and heart found only in the body of a Negro slave, would have forever been unknown. Slavery is a black page in United States history, but that slavery produced the most unusual and exclusive history for a race of people that the world has ever known. But if we, the descendants of that unique race, do not preserve our history, our descendants will have nothing unusual, nothing supreme—just the common everyday background of every other race. The only possible chance for advancement for us as a race is to retain what is our own and add to it.

Not many years ago the senior class of our high school began to practice for their annual play, the setting of which was in the old South. There were a number of Negro slaves to be portrayed, and the instructors had decided to blacken the faces of a number of white students because they were afraid to ask the young Negroes to act those parts. They thought the Negro students would resent such assignments. My sister was a member of that class, and I suggested that she ask her Negro classmates to take the parts of the slaves. I hate imitation; I like real life. I wanted to see the part of the Negro slaves portrayed by Negroes. Out of a total of fifty-four students my sister was unable to find ten who would act those parts, but she did find six. The instructors were delighted, and managed to cut the number needed from ten to six, that they might use real life instead of imitation.

I had discovered what I had been trying to find out for a number of years previous to this experience: why it was that in mixed schools Negro students were seldom used in dramatics; why a white student blackened his face to portray a Negro. This experience answered those questions. We will not be ourselves. We like to imitate. Yet we seriously object to the statement, "Monkeys will imitate."

Since 1865 we have been recognized by other races as a free and independent group of American people. Have we recognized ourselves? Do we as a race recognize our own wealth when it is within reach? Do we exalt ourselves, or do we exalt other races? Many legal battles have been fought through the courts to force other people to respect us. Persons, whether they be white, yellow, brown, red, or black, who gain respect are those who command respect. As long as the following sentences are spoken by ourselves we cannot command respect:—

"I wouldn't marry a dark person."

"I don't want a lot of black, nappy-headed children running after me."

"I like her, but she's too dark."

"She'd get some place if she wasn't so dark."

"She's got brains, but there ain't no nigger going to hire anyone that dark, and I know the white folks ain't."

"That man's too black and ugly to be at the door; he'd drive the devil away."

If black Americans are prejudiced in favor of white Americans, why shouldn't white Americans be prejudiced in favor of white persons? If we are to accomplish and possess what is real and valuable in the world, we must search for the good within other races who are our neighbors, and we must also prove to the world that we are men and women capable of judging and finding the best that is within ourselves. If we exalt that best above all other factors, it is my hope that one day, not too far distant, my race will accept within itself the essential principle of race pride: pride for the things which, through the process of natural inheritance, belong to that particular and distinguished group—American Negroes.

ON BEING BLACK

The Burden of Race
and Class

MANNING MARABLE is one of the most prolific black
scholar-activists in the country. Aside from writing a weekly column that
appears in scores of black and white newspapers both here and abroad,
Marable has also published a number of scholarly articles and many
books. He has worked at a number of major universities. He models his
work and career after W. E. B. Du Bois. "On Being Black: The Burden
of Race and Class" is from his 1981 collection of essays, *Blackwater:
Historical Studies in Race, Class Consciousness and Revolution*.

I

At the dawn of the twentieth century, W. E. B. Du Bois predicted with
grim accuracy that the central crisis facing the world during the next 100
years would be "the problem of the color line—the relation of the darker
to the lighter races of men in Asia and Africa, in America and the islands of the
sea." A brilliant social scientist, researcher and political activist, Du Bois devoted
more than seven decades to patient investigation into what was once termed "The
Negro Problem." Nearing the end of his long and productive career in 1953, he
remarked that his initial research was deficient in two critical respects. The first was
the omission of "the influence of Freud" and the factors of "unconscious thought
and the cake of custom in the growth and influence of race prejudice." The second
and more important omission was "the tremendous impact on the modern world
of Karl Marx." Du Bois observed, "I still think today as yesterday that the color line
is a great problem of this country. But today I see more clearly than yesterday that
back of the problem of race and color, lies a greater problem which both obscures
and implements it: and that is the fact that so many civilized persons are willing to
live in comfort even if the price of this is poverty, ignorance and disease of the

majority of their fellowmen." The burden of racial prejudice or racism was more fundamentally the problem of class exploitation.

The question of whether it is race or class that lies at the heart of the inferior status of blacks broke out most recently in the October 5, 1980 issue of *The New York Times Magazine*. Carl Gershman, vice chairman of Social Democrats, USA, and a resident at the neoconservative Freedom House, was assigned the task of presenting the case for a class analysis of black social conditions. Black psychologist Kenneth Clark, author of *Dark Ghetto*, was asked to discuss black socioeconomic inequality as a function of race prejudice. Despite the widespread comment that the debate subsequently received on university campuses, neither Gershman nor Clark added anything that had not been said many times.

Gershman's approach to the crisis of black unemployment and discrimination was not very different from that of Daniel Patrick Moynihan; indeed, he begins his article with a defense of Moynihan's 1965 report, *The Negro Family: The Case for National Action*, which suggested that there was a "tangle of pathology" in the social fabric of the ghetto underclass. Black intellectual and activist protests against the Moynihan thesis "were frequently couched in radical-sounding terms," Gershman observed. "The sad irony in all of this," he went on, "is that what appeared to be a form of racial militancy was, in reality, a policy of racial accommodation. The new approach both rationalized and subsidized the underclass's continued existence." Gershman argues that Black Power was in effect an elitist movement which allowed the new black professional and managerial elite to become power brokers between the state and the permanent black underclass. He applauds the thesis of University of Chicago professor William Julius Wilson "that in the modern industrial period, unlike the earlier periods of slavery and industrialization, class plays a more significant role than race in determining a black's position in society." He concludes by observing paternally that "the crisis within the black movement" is related to the utter failure of a generation of black activists to comprehend what basic economic problems exist within their own ghetto.

Ironically, Kenneth Clark in his "rejoinder" found that he had much in common with Gershman on the race/class issue. First, Clark warned blacks not "to dismiss [Gershman's] article as another example of whites exercising their power to define contemporary civil rights problems primarily in terms of their own aspirations and interests." Clark agreed with Gershman that the Black Power movement and demands for black community–controlled schools were strategies of "racial accommodation" and neo–Booker T. Washingtonism. "While having some temporary cathartic value," he noted, Black Power "did not improve by one iota the educational and economic status of ghetto-entrapped underclass blacks." In short, both authors were confirmed integrationists on the question of black-white alliances. Both rejected categorically the idea that an autonomous black political and social movement could bring about meaningful change in the black urban enclaves. Both Clark and Gershman saw racism as a pattern of biased social attitudes and intolerant behavior by white people, rather than as a systemic or structural part of modern capitalist political economy. In their only significant area of disagreement, Clark maintained that the ghetto was a product of racial oppression. But even here, Clark views racism as "a dangerous social disease" and not the logical outcome of consistent and coherent social structure, world view and economic order. Both view "class" as a function of income or economic mobility, rather than as a group relationship to the means of production, distribution and ownership.

Black intellectuals had their own race/class debate during the years 1973 through 1975. Black Studies journals such as *Black World, The Black Scholar, Black Books Bulletin, The Journal of Black Studies* and others were filled with bitter polemics advancing either Marxist or black nationalist points of view. In the progressive wing of the modern Black Power movement, the debate began somewhat earlier in the late 1960s. Stokely Carmichael left the Black Panther Party in 1969, charging that Eldridge Cleaver, then the party's Minister of Information, and the Panthers were too preoccupied with class alliances with the New Left. Cleaver retorted that Carmichael was caught up in a "skin game," and that white members of the Students for a Democratic Society who had read Marcuse, Fanon and Malcolm were appropriate allies in the struggle against the system.

In the late 1970s, the debate took a new turn to the right. Stanford professor Thomas Sowell used the pages of *Commentary* magazine to debunk affirmative action. In Sowell's view, affirmative action was based on the rather vague notion that blacks as a group had been historically oppressed and that massive Federal intervention into the free market would halt racial discrimination. He ridiculed the idea that all blacks were equally oppressed and criticized the social democrat logic behind the legislation as harmful to both business interests and to unemployed blacks. William Julius Wilson went a step further in his controversial study *The Declining Significance of Race.* Wilson reviewed the political economy of black workers throughout US history, and argued that the civil rights movement and the progressive actions of corporate management had nearly created "the elimination of race in labor-management strife." Wilson's basic thesis was that racial discrimination is no longer a major bar to economic security or upward mobility by most blacks. Since the majority of blacks were now in the middle class, the time had come to shift legislative priorities from racial questions to the more specific problems of the economic underclass.

Recent events within the political economy seemingly validate many of Wilson's conclusions. The percentage of black families below the poverty level dropped from 55.1 percent in 1959 to 32.2 percent in 1969, but since then has remained about the same level. Black family heads with four years or more college education, however, earn about 90 percent of their white counterparts. Black married couples below the age of 35 in the Northern and Western states who both work earn median incomes at the same level of white couples. This new black strata of upper middle to upper income earners have articulated a clearly more conservative, class-conscious politics than the majority of blacks. The evidence for this is seen in the surprisingly high percentage (15 percent) of black votes for Reagan—the largest black total for any Republican Presidential candidate since the Nixon–Kennedy race in 1960. When the Reverend Ralph David Abernathy and other former associates of Martin Luther King, Jr. embraced Reagan, and after Leon Sullivan (the black director of the Opportunities Industrial Centers) endorsed the nomination of Alexander Haig as Secretary of State, a new political current was born—Black Reaganism. These "new accommodationists" exhibit the same electoral political behavior as white neoconservatives.

Actually, there have been two different debates on the race/class question over the last decade. White paternalists like Gershman and integrationist-oriented blacks like Clark and Wilson are asking a series of questions that are premised on the assumption that racial integration is a positive good and a worthy social ideal. Black nationalists and activists, both in the universities and in the streets, are raising a radically different series of theoretical and programmatic issues. From the white side, the concerns expressed include: Should public policy concentrate on racial problems and continue to use race as a central or critical variable? Should blacks concentrate their energies on matters of mutual racial interest, or should they begin to address the larger economic problems that transcend race entirely? From the black activist side, the questions include: What is white racism? Is it different from other "social diseases" like intolerance or bigotry? What is the relationship between racism as a system to the general economic order? What is the possibility of a political union or common program between black, Hispanic and progressive white groups, given the omni-presence of white racism and the disastrous history of multiracial alliance, from Populism to Black Power? Leaving aside the concerns of white social scientists for the moment, let us concentrate on the black side of the race/class dilemma.

II

There is a major difference between racial prejudice against blacks in the US and other forms of intolerance or persecution. Intolerance has existed as long as human beings have lived together in social units. The victims of intolerance are forced to give up their own group's belief systems, forms of cultural and social institutions, and so forth. The outsider must, for the good of the majority, renounce his differences and embrace those values defined as "normal" by those who control the social, cultural and economic hierarchies. Racial prejudice is radically different, developing gradually in the West as capitalism and nationalism emerged. Its purpose is to withdraw the dominant group's sympathy from an "inferior race," to facilitate its exploitation. Thus, some of the very goals of black liberation, which include the ability to control blacks' labor, the establishment of stable, independent communities and the opportunity to participate and to compete within the socioeconomic institutions of the dominant society according to our own self-interests, threaten white racist beliefs and social structures crucial to the continuation of white racial domination.

Black sociologist Oliver Cromwell Cox expressed the problem of racial prejudice succinctly by presenting the familiar analogies between blacks and Jews as victims in a new way. "The dominant group is intolerant of those whom it can define as antisocial, while it holds race prejudice against those whom it can define as subsocial. In other words, the dominant group or ruling class does not like the Jew at all, but it likes the Negro in his place." The function of white racist attacks against black children who are bused across town to attend a formerly all-white, suburban school is therefore fundamentally different from the bombing of a synagogue in Paris by neo-Nazis. Jews are objects of hatred for being different, e.g., non-Christian; blacks are hated for attempting to reverse the natural social order of things. Cox explains, "A Jewish pogrom is not exactly similar to a Negro lynching. In a pogrom, the fundamental motive is the extermination of the Jews; in a lynching, however, the motive is that of giving the Negro a lesson in good behavior."

A central theme in Frantz Fanon's *Peau Noire, Masques Blancs* is the examination of the similarities and differences between white anti-Semitism and white racism against the people of African descent. "No anti-Semite would ever conceive of the idea of castrating the Jew," Fanon observed. He is killed or sterilized. But the Negro is castrated. The penis, the symbol of manhood, is annihilated, which is to say that it is denied." The anti-Semite attacks the religious and cultural symbols that set Jews apart from other people within Western culture. This is a denial of history, as it were. But blacks *are assumed to have no history*, and are assaulted on radically different philosophical grounds. "All the same, the Jew can be unknown in his Jewishness." Fanon continued:

> One hopes, one waits. His actions, his behavior are the final determinant. He is a white man, and, apart from some rather debatable characteristics, he can sometimes go unnoticed. Granted, the Jews are harassed—what am I thinking of? They are hunted down, exterminated, cremated. But these are little family quarrels. The Jew is disliked from the moment he is tracked down. But in my case, everything takes on a *new* guise. I am given no chance. I am overdetermined from without. I am the slave not of the "idea" that others have of me but of my own appearance. I am *fixed*.

Thus, racism should be understood as an institutional process rather than a random pattern of intolerant collective behavior. Broadly defined, it is a process of persecution and violence in the service of white power; its purpose is the systemic exploitation of black life and labor. The key word here is *systemic*.

A social order can be characterized as distinctively racist if it exhibits the following characteristics. The most important of these is a political economy in which the surplus value produced by black workers is expropriated to a much greater degree than is that produced by white labor. In a precapitalist or primitive capitalist society, this exploitation usually takes the form of a system of compulsory black labor. W. Kloosterboer's *Involuntary Labour Since the Abolition of Slavery* defines compulsory labor "as that from which withdrawal from is generally considered a criminal offense, so that it engenders penal sanction, and/or for which [the laborer] has been accepted without his willing consent." Using this criterion, both chattel slavery (pre-1865) and sharecropping (post-1865) can be classified as kinds of involuntary labor exploitation in the black South. In advanced capitalist societies, black workers assume the role of a surplus labor pool which must be prepared to shift from one low-paying sector of the economy to another upon demand. Blacks are "the last hired, the first fired" under these unstable conditions. Moreover, since capitalism by its very nature cannot provide a full-employment economy, a permanent underclass of blacks is created, who are for all practical purposes outside the workplace. The managerial heights of the racist political economy are occupied almost totally by whites. Blacks as individuals may be appointed to managerial positions within the corporate hierarchy, but blacks as a group have absolutely no critical power other than as consumers.

Characteristics of any racist order is the historic and systemic pattern of physical isolation, exclusion and (in many cases) extermination of the oppressed race/class. This includes both *de facto* and *de jure* segregation, customary and legal forms of Jim Crow. To be sure, different cultural and social forms of racial isolation and exclusion have existed in the Americas. Brazilians have an obvious racial bias against people of African descent, but this has been muted and redirected in ways that a North American white could scarcely comprehend. The common saying in nineteenth-century Brazil, "Money lightens the skin," shows that blacks were almost always poor, but that wealth induced virtually color blindness. This was far from the case in countries settled by the English and Dutch, who practiced a radical form of collective exclusion and social isolation on their African laborers. The largest settler regimes which these two European nations founded, the United States of America and the Republic of South Africa, are still objectively the most racist countries to this day.

The third factor, to use Italian Marxist Antonio Gramsci's concept, is the ideological hegemony of white racism. The ideological apparatuses of the state— the universities, public schools, media, theater and all creative arts, religion, civic associations, political parties—provide the public rationale to justify, explain, legitimize or tolerate the previous two characteristics. Hegemony is the ideological or cultural glue through which collective consensus is achieved within any social order. Within the United States, racist hegemony is achieved in part through the media, which play down potentially disruptive information on the race question; inferior schooling for black children, which denies them necessary information and skills; a rewriting of cultural and social history so that racial conflict and class struggle are glossed over and the melting pot ideal stressed; religious dogma such as those espoused by fundamentalist Christians which divert and reaffirm the conservative values on which white middle class's traditional illusions of superiority are grounded.

The fourth variable involves the relationship between black people and the coercive apparatuses of the State—the police, armed forces, prisons, the criminal justice system, and white vigilante hate-groups such as the Ku Klux Klan. In all racist states, blacks make up a disproportionately large percentage of the prison population compared with their numbers in the society as a whole. In the United States, studies have shown that black, Hispanic and poor defendants on the whole receive harsher sentences and more meager legal services than middle class whites who commit identical crimes. The percentage of black policemen on metropolitan forces is almost always lower than the black urban population in the area. The percentage of blacks in managerial positions in any agency of coercion (the armed forces, police, penal systems) is always lower than the percentage of blacks who are employed in menial tasks. Generally, the coercive state apparatuses serve to disrupt, regulate and suppress the development of black social space—that is, the ability of blacks as a group to develop stable family units and neighborhoods, to construct social, cultural and alternative economic institutions, to strive for upward socioeconomic mobility within the predominantly white order of things.

The fifth category is philosophical—the redefinition of "blackness" in the light of the reality of "whiteness." As G.W.F. Hegel's *Lordship and Bondage* points out, human identity, that is, critical self-consciousness, is directly related to ideas of reciprocity and recognition. Human beings exist only as they are recognized by others. The dialectics of recognition, however, usually do not occur on the basis of equality. Furthermore, an important source of identity for human beings is the labor they perform.

In at least three respects, the racist order transforms both the master and the slave. First, the oppressed are unable to acquire meaning or purpose from the compulsory labor that is invariably their lot; in a contemporary capitalist economy, they are denied the opportunity to work at meaningful jobs. Work as a creative, productive endeavor ceases to exist for blacks as a group, and whites draw the erroneous conclusion that blacks do not like to work simply because they are black. Second, the ideological and coercive apparatuses of the State block the struggles of blacks to attain full equality, and in so doing, disrupt the development of a positive black identity. The African socialist theorist Amilcar Cabral suggested that when colonialism or compulsory labor began, African history was frozen or "stopped." Black revolutions represented an attempt "to return to the source"; rejecting the inequality of the white world, they sought a renaissance of the precolonial, preracist black culture and society.

In order for the racist order to function, any prior claim to an alternate set of human values, customs, and institutions that the oppressed might have had in the preracist state must be suppressed. Whites as a group have historically approached blacks not in the light of their "blackness"—perhaps a better term would be "African-ness"—but in light of what whites believed that blacks must become from the vantage point of their own "whiteness." Racist societies must invent "the Negro."

This transformation of African peoples into the status of "Negroes" took place even before black chattel slavery was established as the dominant means of production in the Southern United States. For example, many colonial historians have observed that white settlers always referred to the Native Americans or Indians as members of certain nations or tribes, or at worst, as "savages" or "heathens." Other than the term "redskin" (which is not pejorative), Indians were not described on the basis of skin color. Among white colonists, the principal perceived distinctions were obviously religious or ethnic. Blacks alone were set apart because of their skin color. And as early as 1660 in the Virginia colony, blackness itself was identical with the status of a chattel slave. Negroes ceased to be Africans; blackness was an ascribed status rising out of whites' demands for black labor, not a distinctive culture or even a condition of humanity.

The sixth factor is sexual. A major force behind all anti-black restrictions and regulations has always been the irrational yet very real anxiety white males have expressed concerning black sexuality. In *The White Man's Burden*, historian Winthrop Jordan argues that the threat of black slave revolts in the seventeenth and eighteenth centuries was usually perceived in sexual terms. "The notion existed that black men were particularly virile, promiscuous and lusted after white women. It is apparent that white men projected their own desires onto Negroes: their own passion for black women was not fully acceptable to society or the self and hence, not readily admissible." Black women, however, were naturally lascivious and passionate, and thus were fair game for sexual predation. The sexual pathology of whites became public policy through legal castration. Colony after colony, from Quaker Pennsylvania to the Carolinas, sanctioned castration as a form of lawful punishment for a whole set of black male offenses. At the root of this cruel punishment, Jordan contends, was the white man's "racking fear and jealousy" of what black men could do if their relative positions and powers were reversed. Their mastery in the world of economics and politics meant little if the very black man they belittled and abused "performed his nocturnal offices better than the white man. Perhaps, indeed, the white man's woman really wanted the Negro more than she wanted him."

Here again, Fanon's commentary is critical. "The civilized white man retains an irrational longing for unusual eras of sexual license, of orgiastic scenes, of unpunished rapes, of unrepressed incest. Projecting his own desires onto the Negro," Fanon noted, "the white man behaves 'as if' the Negro really had them." For the racist, the black male represents or symbolizes the fundamental biological fear:

> On the genital level, when a white man hates black men, is he not yielding to a feeling of impotence or of sexual inferiority? Since his ideal is an infinite virility, is there not a phenomenon of diminution in relation to the Negro, who is viewed as a penis symbol? Is the Negro's superiority real? Everyone *knows* that it is not. But that is not what matters. The prelogical thought of the phobic has decided that such is the case.

Racism, then, is not merely intolerance toward blacks, or the "superstructural justification" of the exploitation of black labor, or the collective projection of white psychosexual neuroses. All of these elements rise out of the social nexus of Western capitalist society and culture. Thus it seems unlikely that the simple transfer of state authority from one group of barbarous whites to another group of well-meaning whites (the Old Left, New Left, liberals or others) would change the basic dynamics of a system that is almost four centuries old.

III

Blacks, and blacks alone, must take the initial and decisive steps toward developing an adequate social theory to destroy white racism. This observation is not made out of black chauvinism, or disregard for the many sincere and dedicated white activists who gave their lives for the cause of black freedom—from John Brown and William Lloyd Garrison to Andrew Goodman and Michael Schwerner. It simply recognizes the fact that nothing in socialist or liberal political theory or practice to date indicates that white radicals and liberals have abandoned their respective infantile economic determinism and unrealistic belief in moral suasion. No long-range coalitions between white progressive organizations and black militant groups, such as the newly formed National Black Independent Political Party, can successfully mount a challenge to the New Right—a white social protest movement that is both intolerant and racist in character and intent—until this hard and painful theoretical work is done.

In *An American Dilemma*, Gunnar Myrdal observed that even during the Great Depression most blacks found it difficult to accept the Old Left's argument that socialism would quickly end the race problem. "When discussing communism in the Negro community," he wrote, "the most common black response was the comment, 'Even after a revolution, the country will be full of crackers.' " Only when American progressives, black and white, recognize the kernel of truth within this remark, and begin to construct a more realistic theoretical and programmatic response to white racism, can the promise of a truly nonracist society begin to be realized. The burden of race *and* class may be finally solved.

SOURCES

Kenneth Clark and Carl Gershman, "The Black Plight: Race and Class?" *The New York Times Magazine*, October 5, 1980.

Oliver Cromwell Cox, *Caste, Class, and Race: A Study in Social Dynamics*. New York and London: *Monthly Review*, 1970.

W. E. B. Du Bois, *The Souls of Black Folk, Essays and Sketches*. Greenwich, Connecticut: Fawcett Publications, 1961.

Frantz Fanon, *Black Skin, White Masks*, translated by Charles L. Markmann. New York: Grove Press, 1967.

H. Hoetink, *Slavery and Race Relations in the Americas: Comparative Notes on their Nature and Nexus*. New York: Harper & Row, 1973.

James Joll, *Antonio Gramsci*. New York: Penguin Books, 1978.

Winthrop D. Jordan, *The White Man's Burden: Historical Origins of Racism in the United States*. London and New York: Oxford University Press, 1974.

Manning Marable, *From the Grassroots: Social and Political Essays Towards Afro-American Liberation*. Boston: South End Press, 1980.

Edmund S. Morgan, *American Slavery, American Freedom: The Ordeal of Colonial Virginia*. New York: W. W. Norton, 1975.

Gunnar Myrdal, *An American Dilemma*. New York: Harper & Row, 1944.

Edward Peeks, *The Long Struggle for Black Power*. New York: Charles Scribner's Sons, 1971.

BEING BLACK
AND FEELING BLUE

Black Hesitation on the Brink

SHELBY STEELE is an associate professor of English at
San Jose University who has recently attracted quite a bit of attention
with his essays on race that have appear in *Harper's* magazine. These
essays and others were collected in the best-selling volume *The Content
of Our Character* (1990). He wrote and narrated a 1990 installment of
the PBS documentary series, "Frontline," that dealt with the Yusef
Hawkins murder in Bensonhurst. "Being Black and Feeling Blue: Black
Hesitation on the Brink" is from *The American Scholar*, Autumn 1989.

In the early seventies when I was in graduate school, I went out for a beer late
one afternoon with another black graduate student whom I'd only known
casually before. This student was older than I—a stint in the army had
interrupted his education—and he had the reputation of being bright and savvy, of
having applied street smarts to the business of getting through graduate school. I
suppose I was hoping for what would be called today a little mentoring. But it is
probably not wise to drink with someone when you are enamored of his reputation,
and it was not long before we stumbled into a moment that seemed to transform
him before my very eyes. I asked him what he planned to do when he finished his
Ph.D., fully expecting to hear of high aspirations matched with shrewd perceptions
on how to reach them. But, before he could think, he said with a kind of exhausted
sincerity, "Man, I just want to hold on, get a job that doesn't work me too hard,
and do a lot of fishing." Was he joking, I asked. "Hell no," he said with exaggerated
umbrage. "I'm not into it like the white boys. I don't need what they need."

I will call this man Henry and report that, until five or six years ago when I
lost track of him, he was doing exactly as he said he would do. With much guile
and little ambition he had moved through a succession of low-level administrative
and teaching jobs, mainly in black studies programs. Of course, it is no crime to
just "hold on," and it is hardly a practice limited to blacks. Still, in Henry's case

there was truly a troubling discrepancy between his ambition and a fine intelligence recognized by all who knew him. But in an odd way this intelligence was more lateral than vertical, and I would say that it was rechanneled by a certain unseen fear into the business of merely holding on. It would be easy to say that Henry had simply decided on life in a slower lane than he was capable of traveling in, or that he was that rare person who had achieved ambitionless contentment. But, if this was so, Henry would have had wisdom rather than savvy, and he would not have felt the need to carry himself with more self-importance than his station justified. I don't think Henry was uninterested in ambition; I think he was afraid of it.

It is certainly true that there is a little of Henry in most people. My own compulsion to understand him informs me that I must have seen many elements of myself in him. And though I'm sure he stands for a universal human blockage, I also believe that there is something in the condition of being black in America that makes the kind of hesitancy he represents one of black America's most serious and debilitating problems. As Henry reached the very brink of expanded opportunity, with Ph.D. in hand, he diminished his ambition almost as though his degree delivered him to a kind of semi-retirement. I don't think blacks in general have any illusions about semi-retirement, but I do think that, as a group, we have hesitated on the brink of new opportunities that we made enormous sacrifices to win for ourselves. The evidence of this lies in one of the most tragic social ironies of late twentieth-century American life—as black Americans have gained in equality and opportunity, we have also declined in relation to whites, so that by many socioeconomic and other measures we are further behind whites today than before the great victories of the civil rights movement. By one report, even the black middle class, which had made great gains in the seventies, began to lose ground to its white counterpart in the eighties. Most distressing of all, the black underclass continues to expand rather than shrink.

Of course, I don't suggest that Henry's peculiar inertia singularly explains social phenomena so complex and tragic. I do believe, however, that blacks in general are susceptible to the same web of attitudes and fears that kept Henry beneath his potential, and that our ineffectiveness in taking better advantage of our greater equality and opportunity has much to do with this. I think there is a specific form of racial anxiety that all blacks are vulnerable to that can, in situations where we must engage the mainstream society, increase our self-doubt and undermine our confidence so that we often back away from the challenges that, if taken, would advance us. I believe this hidden racial anxiety may well now be the strongest barrier to our full participation in the American mainstream—that it is as strong or stronger even than the discrimination we still face. To examine this racial anxiety, allow me first to look at how the Henry was born in me.

Until the sixth grade, I attended a segregated school in a small working-class black suburb of Chicago. The school was a dumping ground for teachers with too little competence or mental stability to teach in the white school in our district. In 1956 when I entered the sixth grade, I encountered a new addition to the menagerie of misfits that was our faculty—an ex-Marine whose cruelty was suggested during our first lunch hour when he bit the cap off his Coke bottle and spit it into the wastebasket. Looking back I can see that there was no interesting depth to the cruelty he began to show us almost immediately—no consumptive hatred, no intelligent malevolence. Although we were all black and he was white, I don't think he was even particularly racist. He had obviously needed us to like him though he had no faith that we would. He ran the class like a gang leader, picking favorites one day and banishing them the next. And then there was a permanent pool of outsiders, myself among them, who were made to carry the specific sins that he must have feared most in himself.

The sin I was made to carry was the sin of stupidity. I misread a sentence on the first day of school, and my fate was sealed. He made my stupidity a part of the classroom lore, and very quickly I in fact became stupid. I all but lost the ability to read and found the simplest math beyond me. His punishments for my errors rose in meanness until one day he ordered me to pick up all of the broken glass on the playground with my bare hands. Of course, this would have to be the age of the pop bottle, and there were sections of this playground that glared like a mirror in sunlight. After half an hour's labor I sat down on strike, more out of despair than rebellion.

Again, cruelty was no more than a vibration in this man, and so without even a show of anger he commandeered a bicycle, handed it to an eighth grader—one of his lieutenants—and told the boy to run me around the school grounds "until he passes out." The boy was also given a baseball bat to "use on him when he slows down." I ran two laps, about a mile, and then pretended to pass out. The eighth grader knew I was playing possum but could not bring himself to hit me and finally rode off. I exited the school yard through an adjoining cornfield and never returned.

I mention this experience as an example of how one's innate capacity for insecurity is expanded and deepened, of how a disbelieving part of the self is brought to life and forever joined to the believing self. As children we are all wounded in some way and to some degree by the wild world we encounter. From these wounds a disbelieving *anti-self* is born, an internal antagonist and saboteur that embraces the world's negative view of us, that believes our wounds are justified by our own unworthiness, and that entrenches itself as a lifelong voice of doubt. This anti-self is a hidden but aggressive force that scours the world for fresh evidence of our unworthiness. When the believing self announces its aspirations, the anti-self always argues against them, but never on their merits (this is a healthy function of the believing self). It argues instead against our worthiness to pursue these aspirations and, by its lights, we are never worthy of even our smallest dreams. The mission of the anti-self is to deflate the believing self and, thus, draw it down into inertia, passivity, and faithlessness.

The anti-self is the unseen agent of low self-esteem; it is a catalytic energy that tries to induce low self-esteem in the believing self as though it were the complete truth of the personality. The anti-self can only be contained by the strength of the believing self, and this is where one's early environment becomes crucial. If the childhood environment is stable and positive, if the family is whole and provides love, the schools good, the community safe, then the believing self will be reinforced and made strong. If the family is shattered, the schools indifferent, the neighborhood a mine field of dangers, the anti-self will find evidence everywhere with which to deflate the believing self.

This does not mean that a bad childhood cannot be overcome. But it does mean—as I have experienced and observed it—that one's *capacity* for self-doubt and self-belief are roughly the same from childhood on, so that years later when the believing self may have strengthened enough to control the anti-self, one will still have the same capacity for doubt whether or not one has the actual doubt. I think it is this struggle between our capacities for doubt and belief that gives our personalities one of their peculiar tensions and, in this way, marks our character.

My own anti-self was given new scope and power by this teacher's persecution of me, and it was so successful in deflating my believing self that I secretly vowed never to tell my parents what was happening to me. The anti-self had all but sold my believing self on the idea that I was stupid, and I did not want to feel that shame before my parents. It was my brother who finally told them, and his disclosure led to a boycott that closed the school and eventually won the dismissal of my teacher and several others. But my anti-self transformed even this act of rescue into a cause of shame—if there wasn't something wrong with me, why did I have to be rescued? The anti-self follows only the logic of self-condemnation.

But there was another dimension to this experience that my anti-self was only too happy to seize upon. It was my race that landed me in this segregated school and, as many adults made clear to me, my persecution followed a timeless pattern of racial persecution. The implications of this were rich food for the anti-self—my race was so despised that it had to be segregated; as a black my education was so unimportant that even unbalanced teachers without college degrees were adequate; and ignorance and cruelty that would be intolerable in a classroom of whites was perfectly all right in a classroom of blacks. The anti-self saw no injustice in any of this, but instead took it all as confirmation of a racial inferiority that it could now add to the well of personal doubt I already had. When the adults thought they were consoling me—"Don't worry. They treat all blacks this way"—they were also deepening the wound and expanding my capacity for doubt.

And this is the point. The condition of being black in America means that one will likely endure more wounds to one's self-esteem than others and that the capacity for self-doubt born of these wounds will be compounded and expanded by the black race's reputation of inferiority. The anti-self will most likely have more ammunition with which to deflate the believing self and its aspirations. And the universal human struggle to have belief win out over doubt will be more difficult.

And, more than difficult, it is also made inescapable by the fact of skin color, which, in America, works as a visual invocation of the problem. Black skin has more dehumanizing stereotypes associated with it than any other skin color in America, if not the world. When a black presents himself in an integrated situation, he knows that his skin alone may bring these stereotypes to life in the minds of those he meets and that he, as an individual, may be diminished by his race before he has a chance to reveal a single aspect of his personality. By the symbology of color that operates in our culture, black skin accuses him of inferiority. Under the weight of this accusation, a black will almost certainly doubt himself on some level and to some degree. The ever-vigilant anti-self will grab this racial doubt and mix it into the pool of personal doubt, so that when a black walks into an integrated situation—a largely white college campus, an employment office, a business lunch—he will be vulnerable to the entire realm of his self-doubt before a single word is spoken.

This constitutes an intense and lifelong racial vulnerability and anxiety for blacks. Even though a white American may have been wounded more than a given black, and therefore have a larger realm of inner doubt, his white skin with its connotations of privilege and superiority will actually help protect him from that doubt and from the undermining power of his anti-self, at least in relations with blacks. In fact, the larger the realm of doubt, the more he may be tempted to rely on his white skin for protection from it. Certainly in every self-avowed white racist, whether businessman or member of the Klan, there is a huge realm of self-contempt and doubt that hides behind the mythology of white skin. The mere need to pursue self-esteem through skin color suggests there is no faith that it can be pursued any other way. But if skin color offers whites a certain false esteem and impunity, it offers blacks vulnerability.

This vulnerability begins for blacks with the recognition that we belong quite simply to the most despised race in the human community of races. To be a member of such a group in a society where all others gain an impunity by merely standing in relation to us is to live with a relentless openness to diminishment and shame. By the devious logic of the anti-self, one cannot be open to such diminishment without in fact being inferior and therefore deserving of diminishment. For the anti-self, the charge verifies the crime, so that racial vulnerability itself is evidence of inferiority. In this sense, the anti-self is an internalized racist, our own subconscious bigot, that conspires with society to diminish us.

So when blacks enter the mainstream, they are not only vulnerable to society's racism but also to the racist within. This internal racist is not restricted by law, morality, or social decorum. It cares nothing about civil rights and equal opportunity. It is the self-doubt born of the original wound of racial oppression, and its mission is to establish the justice of that wound and shackle us with doubt.

Of course, the common response to racial vulnerability, as to most vulnerabilities, is denial—the mind's mechanism for ridding itself of intolerable possibilities. For blacks to acknowledge a vulnerability to inferiority anxiety, in the midst of a society that has endlessly accused us of being inferior, feels nothing less than intolerable— as if we were agreeing with the indictment against us. But denial is not the same as eradication, since it only gives unconscious life to what is intolerable to our consciousness. Denial reassigns rather than vanquishes the terror of racial vulnerability. This reassignment only makes the terror stronger by making it unknown. When we deny we always create a dangerous area of self-ignorance, an entire territory of the self that we cannot afford to know. Without realizing it, we begin to circumscribe our lives by avoiding those people and situations that might breach our denial and force us to see consciously what we fear. Though the denial of racial vulnerability is a human enough response, I think it also makes our public discourse on race circumspect and unproductive, since we cannot talk meaningfully about problems we are afraid to name.

Denial is a refusal of painful self-knowledge. When someone or something threatens to breach this refusal, we receive an unconscious shock of the very vulnerability we have denied—a shock that often makes us retreat and more often makes us intensify our denial. When blacks move into integrated situations or face challenges that are new for blacks, the myth of black inferiority is always present as a *condition* of the situation, and as such it always threatens to breach our denial of racial vulnerability. It threatens to make us realize consciously what is intolerable to us—that we have some anxiety about inferiority. We feel this threat unconsciously as a shock of racial doubt delivered by the racist anti-self (always the inner voice of the myth of black inferiority). Consciously, we will feel this shock as a sharp discomfort or a desire to retreat from the situation. Almost always we will want to intensify our denial.

I will call this shock "integration shock" since it occurs most powerfully when blacks leave their familiar world and enter into the mainstream. Integration shock and denial are mutual intensifiers. The stab of racial doubt that integration shock delivers is a pressure to intensify denial, and a more rigid denial means the next stab of doubt will be more threatening and therefore more intense. The symbiosis of these two forces is, I believe, one of the reasons black Americans have become preoccupied with racial pride, almost to the point of obsession over the past twenty-five or so years. With more exposure to the mainstream we have endured more integration shock, more jolts of inferiority anxiety. And I think we have often responded with rather hyperbolic claims of black pride by which we deny that anxiety. In this sense, our self-consciousness around pride, our need to make a point of it, is, to a degree, a form of denial. Pride becomes denial when it ceases to reflect self-esteem quietly and begins to compensate loudly for unacknowledged inner doubt. Here it also becomes dangerous since it prevents us from confronting and overcoming that doubt.

I think the most recent example of black pride-as-denial is the campaign (which seems to have been launched by a committee) to add yet another name to the litany of names that blacks have given themselves over the past century. Now we are to be African-Americans instead of, or in conjunction with, being black Americans. This self-conscious reaching for pride through nomenclature suggests nothing so much as a despair over the possibility of gaining the less conspicuous pride that follows real advancement. In its invocation of the glories of a remote African past and its wistful suggestion of homeland, this name denies the doubt black Americans have about their contemporary situation in America. There is no element of self-confrontation in it, no facing of real racial vulnerabilities, as there was with the name "black." I think "black" easily became the name of preference in the sixties precisely because it was not a denial but a confrontation of inferiority anxiety, with the shame associated with the color black. There was honest self-acceptance in this name, and I think it diffused much of our vulnerability to the shame of color. Even between blacks, "black" is hardly the drop-dead fighting word it was when I was a child. Possibly we are ready now for a new name, but I think "black" has been our most powerful name yet because it so frankly called out our shame and doubt and helped us (and others) to accept ourselves. In the name African-American there is too much false neutralization of doubt, too much looking away from the caldron of our own experience. It is a euphemistic name that hides us even from ourselves.

I think blacks have been more preoccupied with pride over the past twenty-five years because we have been more exposed to integration shock since the 1964 Civil Rights Bill made equal opportunity the law of the land (if not quite the full reality of the land). Ironically, it was the inequality of opportunity and all the other repressions of legal segregation that buffered us from our racial vulnerability. In a segregated society we did not have the same accountability to the charge of racial inferiority since we were given little opportunity to disprove the charge. It was the opening up of opportunity—anti-discrimination laws, the social programs of the Great Society, equal opportunity guidelines and mandates, fair housing laws, Affirmative Action, and so on—that made us individually and collectively more accountable to the myth of black inferiority and therefore more racially vulnerable.

This vulnerability has increased in the same proportion that our freedom and opportunity have increased. The exhilaration of new freedom is always followed by a shock of accountability. Whatever unresolved doubt follows the oppressed into greater freedom will be inflamed since freedom always carries a burden of proof, always throws us back on ourselves. And freedom, even imperfect freedom, makes blacks a brutal proposition: if you're not inferior, prove it. This is the proposition that shocks us and makes us vulnerable to our underworld of doubt. The whispers of the racist anti-self are far louder in the harsh accountability of freedom than in subjugation where the oppressor is so entirely to blame.

The bitter irony of all this is that our doubt and the hesitancy it breeds now help limit our progress in America almost as systematically as segregation once did. Integration shock gives the old boundaries of legal segregation a regenerative power. To avoid the shocks of doubt that come from entering the mainstream, or plunging more deeply into it, we often pull back at precisely those junctures where segregation once pushed us back. In this way we duplicate the conditions of our oppression and re-enact our role as victims even in the midst of far greater freedom and far less victimization. Certainly there is still racial discrimination in America, but I believe that the unconscious replaying of our oppression is now the greatest barrier to our full equality.

The way in which integration shock regenerates the old boundaries of segregation for blacks is most evident in three tendencies—the tendency to minimalize or avoid real opportunities, to withhold effort in areas where few blacks have achieved, and to self-segregate in integrated situations.

If anything, it is the presence of new opportunities in society that triggers integration shock. If opportunity is a chance to succeed, it is also a chance to fail. The vulnerability of blacks to hidden inferiority anxiety makes failure a much more forbidding prospect. If a black pursues an opportunity in the mainstream—opens a business, goes up for a challenging job or difficult promotion—and fails, that failure can be used by the anti-self to confirm both personal and racial inferiority. The diminishment and shame will tap an impersonal as well as personal source of doubt. When a white fails, he alone fails. His doubt is strictly personal, which gives him more control over the failure. He can discover *his* mistakes, learn the reasons *he* made them, and try again. But the black, laboring under the myth of inferiority, will have this impersonal, culturally determined doubt to contend with. This form of doubt robs him of a degree of control over his failure since he alone cannot eradicate the cultural myth that stings him. There will be a degree of impenetrability to his failure that will constitute an added weight of doubt.

The effect of this is to make mainstream opportunity more intimidating and risky for blacks. This is made worse in that blacks, owing to past and present deprivations, may come to the mainstream in the first place with a lower stock of self-esteem. High risk and low self-esteem are hardly the best combination with which to tackle the challenges of a highly advanced society in which others have been blessed by history with very clear advantages. Under these circumstances opportunity can seem more like a chance to fail than a chance to succeed. All this makes for a kind of opportunity aversion that I think was behind the hesitancy I saw in Henry, in myself, and in other blacks of all class backgrounds. It is also, I believe, one of the reasons for the sharp decline in the number of black students entering college, even as many colleges launch recruiting drives to attract more black students.

This aversion to opportunity generates a way of seeing that minimalizes opportunity to the point where it can be ignored. In black communities the most obvious entrepreneurial opportunities are routinely ignored. It is often outsiders or the latest wave of immigrants who own the shops, restaurants, cleaners, gas stations, and even the homes and apartments. Education is a troubled area in black communities for numerous reasons, but certainly one of them is that many black children are not truly imbued with the idea that learning is virtually the same as opportunity. Schools—even bad schools—were the opportunity that so many immigrant groups used to learn the workings and the spirit of American society. In the very worst inner city schools there are accredited teachers who teach the basics, but too often to students who shun those among them who do well, who see studying as a sucker's game and school itself as a waste of time. One sees in many of these children almost a determination not to learn, a suppression of the natural impulse to understand, that cannot be entirely explained by the determinism of poverty. Out of school, in the neighborhood, these same children learn everything. I think it is the meeting with the mainstream that school symbolizes that clicks them off. In the cultural ethos from which they come, it is always these meetings that trigger the aversion to opportunity behind which lies inferiority anxiety. Their parents and their culture send them a double message: go to school but don't really apply yourself. The risk is too high.

This same pattern of avoidance, this unconscious circumvention of possibility, is also evident in our commitment to effort—the catalyst of opportunity. Difficult, sustained effort—in school or career or family life—will be riddled with setbacks, losses, and frustrations. Racial vulnerability erodes effort for blacks by exaggerating the importance of these setbacks, by recasting them as confirmation of racial inferiority rather than the normal pitfalls of sustained effort. The racist anti-self greets these normal difficulties with an I-told-you-so attitude, and the believing self, unwilling to risk seeing that the anti-self is right, may grow timid and pull back from the effort. As with opportunity, racial vulnerability makes hard effort in the mainstream a high-risk activity for blacks.

But this is not the case in those areas where blacks have traditionally excelled.

In sports and music, for example, the threat of integration shock is effectively removed. Because so many blacks have succeeded in these areas, a black can enter them without being racially vulnerable. Failure carries no implication of racial inferiority, so the activity itself is far less risky than those in which blacks have no record of special achievement. Certainly in sports and music one sees blacks sustain the most creative and disciplined effort, and they seize opportunities where one would have thought there were none. But all of this changes the instant racial vulnerability becomes a factor. Across the country thousands of young black males take every opportunity and make every effort to reach the elite ranks of the NBA or the NFL. But in the classroom, where racial vulnerability is a hidden terror, they and many of their classmates put forth the meagerest effort and show a virtual indifference to the genuine opportunity that education is.

But the most visible circumvention that results from integration shock is the tendency toward self-segregation that, if anything, seems to have increased over the last twenty years. Along with opportunity and effort, it is also white people themselves who are often avoided. I hear young black professionals say they do not socialize with whites after work unless at some "command performance" that comes with the territory of their career. On largely white university campuses where integration shock is particularly intense, black students often try to enforce a kind of neo-separatism that includes black "theme" dorms, black student unions, Afro-houses, black cultural centers, black student lounges, and so on. There is a geo-politics involved in this activity, where race is tied to territory in a way that mimics the "whites only"/"coloreds only" designations of the past. Only now these race spaces are staked out in the name of pride.

I think this impulse to self-segregate, to avoid whites, has to do with the way white people are received by the black anti-self. Even if the believing self wants to see racial difference as essentially meaningless, the anti-self, that hidden perpetrator of racist doubt, sees white people as better than black people. Its mission is to confirm black inferiority, and so it looks closely at whites, watches the way they walk, talk, and negotiate the world, and then grants these styles of being and acting superiority. Somewhere inside every black is a certain awe at the power and achievement of the white race. In every barbershop gripe session where whites are put through the grinder of black anger, there will be a kind of backhanded respect—"Well, he might be evil, but that white boy is smart." True or not, the anti-self organizes its campaign against the believing self's faith in black equality around this supposition. And so, for blacks (as is true for whites in another way), white people in the generic sense have no neutrality. In themselves they are stimulants to the black anti-self, deliverers of doubt. Their color slips around the deepest need of blacks to believe in their immutable equality and communes directly with their self-suspicion.

So it is not surprising to hear black students on largely white campuses say that they are simply more comfortable with other blacks. Nor is it surprising to see them caught up in absurd contradictions—demanding separate facilities for themselves even as they protest apartheid in South Africa. Racial vulnerability is a species of fear, and, as such, it is the progenitor of countless ironies. More freedom makes us more vulnerable so that in the midst of freedom we feel the impulse to carve out segregated comfort zones that protect us more from our own doubt than from whites.

We balk before opportunity and pull back from effort just as these things would bear fruit. We reconstitute the boundaries of segregation just as they become illegal. By averting opportunity and curbing effort for fear of awakening a sense of inferiority, we make inevitable the very failure that shows us inferior.

One of the worst aspects of oppression is that it never ends when the oppressor begins to repent. There is a legacy of doubt in the oppressed that follows long after the cleanest repentance by the oppressor, just as guilt trails the oppressor and makes his redemption incomplete. These themes of doubt and guilt fill in like fresh replacements and work to duplicate the oppression. I think black Americans are today more oppressed by doubt than by racism and that the second phase of our struggle for freedom must be a confrontation with that doubt. Unexamined, this doubt leads us back into the tunnel of our oppression where we re-enact our victimization just as society struggles to end its victimization of us. We are not a people formed in freedom. Freedom is always a call to possibility that demands an overcoming of doubt. We are still new to freedom, new to its challenges, new even to the notion that self-doubt can be the slyest enemy of freedom. For us freedom has so long meant the absence of oppression that we have not yet realized that it also means the conquering of doubt.

Of course, this does not mean that doubt should become a lake we swim in, but it does mean that we should begin our campaign against doubt by acknowledging it, by outlining the contours of the black anti-self so that we can know and accept exactly what it is that we are afraid of. This is knowledge that can be worked with, knowledge that can point with great precision to the actions through which we can best mitigate doubt and advance ourselves. This is the sort of knowledge that gives the believing self a degree of immunity to the anti-self and that enables it to pile up little victories that, in sum, grant it even more immunity.

Certainly inferiority has long been the main theme of the black anti-self, its most lethal weapon against our capacity for self-belief. And so, in a general way, the acceptance of this piece of knowledge implies a mission: to show ourselves and (only indirectly) the larger society that we are not inferior on any dimension. That this should already be assumed goes without saying. But what "should be" falls within the province of the believing self where it has no solidity until the doubt of the anti-self is called out and shown false by demonstrable action in the real world. This is the proof that grants the "should" its rightful solidity, that transforms it from a well-intentioned claim into a certainty.

The temptation is to avoid so severe a challenge, to maintain a black identity, painted in the colors of pride and culture, that provides us with a way of seeing ourselves apart from this challenge. It is easier to be "African-American" than to organize oneself on one's own terms and around one's own aspiration and then, through sustained effort and difficult achievement, put one's insidious anti-self quietly to rest. No black identity, however beautifully conjured, will spare blacks this challenge that, despite its fairness or unfairness, is simply in the nature of things. But then I have faith that in time we will meet this challenge since this, too, is in the nature of things.

III

HARLEM, USA

Harlem, the uptown black ghetto of Manhattan, is probably the most famous, the most fabled black urban community in the world. Dark-skinned people all over the world have heard of the place and most are represented among its diverse population: American blacks, Caribbean Islanders, Latins, North and Sub-Saharan Africans. For a time it was the Mecca of the Non-white Imagination. Cab drivers in Dakar would ask black American visitors about Joe Louis, Ray Robinson, and Cab Calloway during Harlem's heyday as a nightclub and entertainment haven during the years of, say, 1920 to 1950. One could find blacks in the Bahamas who wore tee-shirts that said, "Resident of Harlem, USA." During the 1920s, Harlem was particularly a storied community, having just made the sociological shift from an upper-middle class white neighborhood to a burgeoning black community, largely made up of migrating southern blacks; it became the focal point of the artistic and intellectual movement called the New Negro Renaissance, now more commonly referred to as the Harlem Renaissance. Noted writers such as Countee Cullen, Langston Hughes, Wallace Thurman, W. E. B. Du Bois, Arna Bontemps, Claude McKay, Jessie Fauset, Nella Larsen were among those who became associated with both Harlem and its Renaissance. Political leaders such as Marcus Garvey, A. Philip Randolph, Adam Clayton Powell, Sr. and Jr., Father Divine were among the legendary voices in Harlem before the Second World War. Musicians such as Duke Ellington, Fletcher Henderson, James Reese Europe, Charlie Parker, Thelonious Monk and others helped to shape black culture and American culture at large while living and working there during the twenties, thirties, and forties. Famous nightclubs, dance halls, and theaters, from the Cotton Club to the Savoy Ballroom to Small's Paradise to the Apollo Theater were known throughout the entertainment world both here and abroad. Fidel Castro stayed at the Theresa Hotel in Harlem during his stay in America in the very early 1960s and Malcolm X made his reputation as both a hustler and a black political leader there. But if Harlem helped to produce, directly or indirectly, Josephine Baker and Zora Neale Hurston on the one hand, it was also a deeply impoverished community that produced more than its fair share of pimps, con men, hustlers, welfare mothers, abandoned children, substandard housing, inadequate schools, public policy neglect and mismanagement, violence, drug addiction, despair, blight, and frightening human waste. Harlem is among the worst urban ghettos in the United States. The following essays were written over a span of more than sixty years, from before the Renaissance to the post–Civil Rights era of the seventies, covering various aspects of life in Harlem. Some of the most notable essays written by black American writers have been about Harlem.

HUBERT H. HARRISON

Philosopher of Harlem

WILLIAM PICKENS According to Wilson J. Moses, among the earliest appearances of the phrase, "the New Negro," was in black novelist Sutton Griggs's *Imperium in Imperio* in 1899 and Booker T. Washington's *A New Negro for a New Century*, published in 1900. William Pickens (1881–1954) was an educator and writer who earned degrees from Yale, where he graduated Phi Beta Kappa in 1904, and Fisk Universities. He taught classics at various black colleges and became vice president of Morgan State College in Maryland. He became an official in the NAACP in 1920 and helped to established the Negro Officers Training Corps during World War I. "Hubert H. Harrison: Philosopher of Harlem" appeared in the *New York Amsterdam News* on February 7, 1923.

I t is not possible that Socrates could have outdone Hubert Harrison in making the most commonplace subject interesting. Here is a plain black man who can speak more easily, effectively and interestingly, on a greater variety of subjects than any other man we have ever met, even in any of the great universities. We do not like a platitude or a hackneyed phrase, but we know nothing better than to say that he is a "walking cyclopedia" of current human facts, and more especially of history and literature. And it makes no difference whether he is talking about "Alice in Wonderland" or the most extensive work of H.G. Wells; about the lightest shadows of Edgar Allan Poe or the heaviest depths of Kant; about music, or art, or science, or political history—he is equally interesting.

We know how hard it is to believe this, and we confess that we would never have believed it ourself, by report. But continual visits to the lectures which Harrison has been giving this winter in the New York Public Library, and elsewhere, under the auspices of the public school system, have convinced us. That is all. We had heard Harrison talk on the street corners before—and one is apt to be disgusted or disappointed with street-corner talks, because of the hearer's psychological state and discomforts, and because he seldom hears the tale out. But go and sit down comfortably, anywhere under the dome of heaven, and hear Hubert Harrison TALK, evenly, easily, readily, wittily, but not too wittily, about ANYTHING under the sun, and if you have brains you will concede him the palm as an educational lecturer.

When Mrs. Pickens, who is a persistent lecture and music fan, induced us to go the first time or two, we were interested, we acknowledged the excellence of the thing, but we had a sort of half-formed notion somewhere in our consciousness that he could not REPEAT; that he happened to be interesting and wonderful on those two subjects. We had no idea the man could keep up the same informing and interesting talk on a great variety of subjects, twice or more every week, for all winter!

And the unfortunate thing is, that a man like Hubert Harrison cannot yet find his proper place among us. He ought to be a lecturer in some great American university. No one out of a hundred of those lecturing in the universities have half his real information, and not one out of a thousand can convey it so interestingly. And we poor American people, white and black, have been so used to the white ideal, that it is next to impossible for us to believe that of any black man—until we have become convinced, for we will not even allow ourselves enough preliminary faith in the proposition to "Come and see!"

There is hardly a place for such a black man in America. If Mr. Harrison were white (and we say it boldly) he might be one of the most prominent lecturers and professors of Columbia University, under the shadow of which he is passing his days. Many white university people can be found sitting among the colored people at the Public Library on West 135th Street, or in some public school auditorium in Harlem, patiently listening to Harrison and writing rapidly in their note books—gathering material for their classes at the institution. And the strange human thing is, THAT THESE SAME WHITE DEVOTEES WOULD OBJECT AND PERHAPS WOULD EVEN REFUSE TO ATTEND COLUMBIA UNIVERSITY, IF HARRISON WAS TO BE THEIR LEC-TURER AND LEADER THERE. Of such poor stuff is human nature made. And yet these same students, if they bravely confessed, would acknowledge that they can listen interestedly to Harrison lecturing at ten o'clock at night on a subject in which their university professors could hardly interest them at ten o'clock in the morning.

Well, people used to go and sit on the hard rocks by the river to hear the Nazarene, or trudge through the woods to wilderness to listen to the Baptist, who would not have accepted either Jesus or John as heads or leaders in their synagogues. Fellows were charmed by Socrates on the corners of the small streets in the market places, who would have felt too "proud" to enroll in a school or university course headed up by that barefoot pot-gutted old gentleman.

Such is human nature—and when you add race prejudice and color mania to that!

Just as Charles Gilpin might have gone on in cheap vaudeville and back street shows for the rest of his life—but for an accident—so Hubert Harrison may go on for the rest of his life, with his full mind and most instructive deliverance, in the less prominent corners of public education—for accidents do not work so readily in his class of performance.

THE NEW POLITICS
FOR THE NEW NEGRO

HUBERT H. HARRISON (1883–1927) was one of
the leading black nationalists, a vehement Garveyite, and a compelling
Afrocentric thinker of the Renaissance period. He was a brilliant street
orator, knew several languages, and was an indefatigable propagandist for
the race. "The New Politics for the New Negro" and "A Negro for
President" are columns from his various publications that he published in
his collection, *When Africa Awakes* (1920).

The world of the future will look upon the world of today as an essentially
new turning point in the path of human progress. All over the world the
spirit of democratic striving is making itself felt. The new issues have
brought forth new ideas of freedom, politics, industry and society at large. The new
Negro living in this new world is just as responsive to these new impulses as other
people are.

In the "good old days" it was quite easy to tell the Negro to follow in the
footsteps of those who had gone before. The mere mention of the name Lincoln
or the Republican party was sufficient to secure his allegiance to that party which
had seen him stripped of all political power and of civil rights without protest—
effective or otherwise.

Things are different now. The new Negro is demanding elective representation
in Baltimore, Chicago and other places. He is demanding it in New York. The pith
of the present occasion is, that he is no longer begging or asking. He is demanding
as a right that which he is in position to enforce.

In the presence of this new demand the old political leaders are bewildered,
and afraid; for the old idea of Negro leadership by virtue of the white man's selection
has collapsed. The new Negro leader must be chosen by his fellows—by those
whose strivings he is supposed to represent.

Any man today who aspires to lead the Negro race must set squarely before his face the idea of "Race First." Just as the white men of these and other lands are white men before they are Christians, Anglo-Saxons or Republicans; so the Negroes of this and other lands are intent upon being Negroes before they are Christians, Englishmen, or Republicans.

Sauce for the goose is sauce for the gander. Charity begins at home, and our first duty is to ourselves. It is not what we wish but what we must, that we are concerned with. The world, as it ought to be, is still for us, as for others, the world that does not exist. The world as it is, is the real world, and it is to that real world that we address ourselves. Striving to be men, and finding no effective aid in government or in politics, the Negro of the Western world must follow the path of the Swadesha movement of India and the Sinn Fein movement of Ireland. The meaning of both these terms is "ourselves first." This is the mental background of the new politics of the New Negro, and we commend it to the consideration of all the political parties. For it is upon this background that we will predicate such policies as shall seem to us necessary and desirable.

In the British Parliament the Irish Home Rule party clubbed its full strength and devoted itself so exclusively to the cause of Free Ireland that it virtually dictated for a time the policies of Liberals and Conservatives alike.

The new Negro race in America will not achieve political self-respect until it is in a position to organize itself as a politically independent party and follow the example of the Irish Home Rulers. This is what will happen in American politics.
—September, 1917.

A NEGRO FOR PRESIDENT

HUBERT H. HARRISON

For many years the Negro has been the football of American politics. Kicked from pillar to post, he goes begging, hat in hand, from a Republican convention to a Democratic one. Always is he asking some one else to do something for him. Always is he begging, pleading, demanding or threatening. In all these cases his dependence is on the good will, sense of justice or gratitude of the other fellow. And in none of these cases is the political reaction of the other fellow within the control of the Negro.

But a change for the better is approaching. Four years ago, the present writer was propounding in lectures, indoors and outdoors, the thesis that the Negro people of America would never amount to anything much politically until they should see fit to imitate the Irish of Britain and to organize themselves into a political party of their own whose leaders, on the basis of this large collective vote, could "hold up" Republicans, Democrats, Socialists or any other political group of American whites. As in many other cases, we have lived to see time ripen the fruits of our own thought for some one else to pluck. Here is the editor of the *Challenge* making a campaign along these very lines. His version of the idea takes the form of advocating the nomination of a Negro for the Presidency of the United States. In this form we haven't the slightest doubt that this idea will meet with a great deal of ridicule and contempt. Nevertheless, we venture to prophesy that, whether in the hands of Mr. Bridges or another, it will come to be ultimately accepted as one of the finest contributions to Negro statesmanship.

No one pretends, of course, that the votes of Negroes can elect a Negro to the high office of President of the United States. Nor would any one expect that the votes of white people will be forthcoming to assist them in such a project. The only way in which a Negro could be elected President of the United States would be by virtue of the voters not knowing that the particular candidate was of Negro ancestry. This, we believe, has already happened within the memory of living men. But, the essential intent of this new plan is to furnish a focussing point around which the ballots of the Negro voters may be concentrated for the realization of racial demands for justice and equality of opportunity and treatment. It would be carrying "Race First" with a vengeance into the arena of domestic politics. It would take the Negro voter out of the ranks of the Republican, Democratic and Socialist parties and would enable their leaders to trade the votes of their followers, openly and above-board, for those things for which masses of men largely exchange their votes.

Mr. Bridges will find that the idea of a Negro candidate for President presupposes the creation of a purely Negro party and upon that prerequisite he will find himself compelled to concentrate. Doubtless, most of the political wise-acres of the Negro race will argue that the idea is impossible because it antagonizes the white politicians of the various parties. They will close their eyes to the fact that politics implies antagonism and a conflict of interest. They will fail to see that the only things which count with politicians are votes, and that, just as one white man will cheerfully cut another white man's throat to get the dollars which a black man has, so will one white politician or party cut another one's throat politically to get the votes which black men may cast at the polls. But these considerations will finally carry the day. Let there be no mistake. The Negro will never be accepted by the white American democracy except in so far as he can by the use of force, financial, political or other, win, seize or maintain in the teeth of opposition that position which he finds necessary to his own security and salvation. And we Negroes may as-well make up our minds now that we can't depend upon the good-will of white men in anything or at any point where our interests and theirs conflict. Disguise it as we may, in business, politics, education or other departments of life, we as Negroes are compelled to fight for what we want to win from the white world.

It is easy enough for those colored men whose psychology is shaped by their white inheritance to argue the ethics of compromise and inter-racial co-operation. But we whose brains are still unbastardized must face the frank realities of this situation of racial conflict and competition. Wherefore, it is well that we marshal our forces to withstand and make head against the constant racial pressure. Action and reaction are equal and opposite. Where there is but slight pressure a slight resistance will suffice. But where, as in our case, that pressure is grinding and pitiless, the resistance that would re-establish equal conditions of freedom must of necessity be intense and radical. And it is this philosophy which must furnish the motive for such a new and radical departure as is implied in the joint idea of a Negro party in American politics and a Negro candidate for the Presidency of these United States.—June, 1920.

THE NEW NEGRO
FACES AMERICA

ERIC D. WALROND's critical assessment of black leadership, "The New Negro Faces America," was published in *The New York Times Current History Magazine* in February 1923. The other more impressionistic essay, "The Black City," is from the January 1924 issue of *The Messenger,* an important socialist-tinged magazine edited by Chandler Owen and A. Philip Randolph that ran from 1917 to 1928.

The leaders of the negro race in the United States
Moton, Du Bois and Marcus Garvey—Industrial
efficiency, political representation and return to
Africa the ends striven for by these men—The
negro's economic progress

The negro is at the crossroads of American life. He is, probably more than any other group within our borders, the most vigorously "led." On the one hand is the old-style leadership of Booker T. Washington's successor, Major Robert Moton, Principal of Tuskegee, who believes, like Christ, in "turning the other cheek," and in a maximum of industrial efficiency. On the other hand is the leadership of W. E. B. Du Bois of the National Association for the Advancement of Colored People, whose idea of salvation is in adequate political representation. This is the organization which is sponsoring the Dyer Anti-Lynching bill.

Towering head and shoulders above these two is Marcus Garvey, "Provisional President of Africa," and President General of the Universal Negro Improvement Association and African Committee League. This organization is otherwise known as the "Back to Africa" movement. It sprang into public notice a few years ago through the appealing oratory and histrionic abilities of its West Indian leader, Marcus Garvey. Garvey is a Jamaican, short, black, swaggering, muscularly built. As a printer and journalist in the West Indies he suffered from the injustices heaped upon members of his race. He went to South America, Europe and Africa. While in London he met Duse Mahomed Ali, the Egyptian editor of The African Times and Orient Review, from whom, it is said, he got his idea of an "Africa for the Africans."

Early in 1915 Garvey came to the United States and with a nucleus of seven formed in a dingy Harlem hall bedroom the most-talked-of negro movement in modern times. Just from the war, thousands of negro ex-service men, bitter, morose, disillusioned fell into it. Stories of negro officers being stripped of their medals and epaulets and Croix de Guerres by "crackers" in the South stimulated recruiting in Garvey's African army. They dumped their money into it. The movement grew beyond Garvey's fondest hopes.

Early this year Garvey made a trip to Atlanta, Georgia, where he interviewed the Imperial Wizard of the Knights of the Ku Klux Klan to find out, he said, "just what the Klan's attitude toward the negro was." Knowing the history of Ku Klux activities in reconstruction days in the South, the bulk of the American negroes who had faith in him, even after the colossal failure of the Black Star Line, viewed this as the last tie that linked them to the "American Emperor."

Just at this point it is well to observe that the negroes of America do not want to go back to Africa. Though Africa, to the thinking ones, means something racial, if not spiritual, it takes the same place in the negro's "colonization" plans as Jerusalem in the Jew's, for instance. This return, however, was the salient feature of Garvey's propaganda. In August of this year, at the Third International Convention of Negroes held at Garvey's Liberty Hall, a delegation of four was appointed, headed by G. O. Marke, a West African lawyer and editor, to go to Geneva to present a petition to the League of Nations asking it to turn over Germany's former African colonies to the Universal Negro Improvement Association. The delegation went and returned, and in glowing rhetoric at a riotously primeval festival at Liberty Hall told of the "impression" it made on the League delegates. The sending of this delegation, like most of Garvey's acts, was for theatrical effect.

Garvey, however, is paying dearly for these preposterous mistakes. A reaction has set in. The crowds who once flocked to hear how he was going to redeem Africa have begun to dwindle. The negroes have lost faith in Garvey. Still, in a thoroughly dispassionate survey of negro progress, one cannot deny that the idea of "Africa for the Africans" means a great deal to negroes in America. Some of them feel that with a strong native Government flourishing on the shores of Africa, evils like lynching in Georgia and exclusion laws in Australia would be dispensed with. Others, and these are in the majority, cannot see beyond the shores of the Hudson. They haven't any international vision. They, for the most part, are negroes of the agricultural regions, the very backbone of the South. To them Africa is a dream— an unrealizable dream. In America, despite its "Jim Crow" laws, they see something beautiful.

On the other hand, there is the foreign negro to be considered. Yearly, a certain percentage of West Indians come to America. On the whole the West Indian is intelligent. He is an indefatigable student. When the epic of the negro in America is written, it will show the West Indian as the stokesman in the furnace of negro ideals. What he lacks in political consciousness he makes up in industrial productivity. He works hard, saves his money, sends his children to the best schools and colleges, and does a little original thinking of his own.

The rank and file of negroes are opposed to Garveyism; dissatisfied with the personal vituperation and morbid satire of Mr. Du Bois, and prone to discount Major Moton's Tuskegee as a monument of respectable reaction. Even before the death of Booker T. Washington, Dr. W. E. B. Du Bois, Harvard Ph.D., was looked upon by the negroes as an intellectual icon. But there is now a revolt against Du Bois. The new negro feels that Mr. Du Bois is too far above the masses to comprehend their desires and aspirations. His *Darkwater*, they feel, is a beautiful book, but it reveals the soul of a man who is sorry and ashamed he is not white. He hates to be black. In his writings there is a stream of endless woe, the sorrow of a mulatto whose white blood hates and despises the black in him. Clearly the issue is pretty well known on the fundamentals of present-day negro leadership. Garvey is a megalomaniac. Du Bois, unlike either Washington or the poet Dunbar, suffers from the "superiority complex."

What, then, is the outlook for the new negro? Despite the handicaps of inadequate leadership, he is making tremendous headway in industry, to say nothing of art and literature. From 1900–1920 the value of farm property owned by negro farmers of the South has rapidly increased. This is true with reference to the value of the live stock, poultry, and implements and machinery owned. The value of land and buildings increased from $69,636,420 in 1900 to $273,501,665 in 1910 or 293 per cent. The value of land and buildings owned by the negro farmers of the South in 1920 was $522,178,137, an increase for the ten years of $248,676,472, or 91 per cent.

In the fifty-six years of emancipation the table on the following page[1] shows the phenomenal progress made.

According to the Negro Year Book for 1922 "negroes in South Carolina paid taxes on a property value of $53,901,018. In Virginia, negroes in 1921 owned 1,911,443 acres of land valued at $17,600,148."

It is estimated that the value of the property now owned by the negroes of the United States is over $1,500,000,000. The lands which they own amount to more than 22,000,000 acres, or more than 34,000 square miles, an area greater than that of the five New England States, New Hampshire, Vermont, Massachusetts, Connecticut and Rhode Island.

With this background of industrial prosperity what is the outlook for the negro? To give an adequate answer to this one must examine the negro's mental state. In the first place, he is race-conscious. He does not want, like the American Indian, to be like the white man. He is coming to realize the great possibilities within himself, and his tendency is to develop those possibilities. He is looking toward a broader leadership. That which he has at present is either old-fashioned, unrepresentative of his spirit and desires, or stupid, corrupt, and hate-mad. Though there are thousands of college-bred negroes working as janitors and bricklayers and railroad porters, there are still more thousands in colleges and universities who are fitting themselves to become architects, engineers, chemists, manufacturers. The new negro, who does not want to go back to Africa, is fondly cherishing an ideal—and that is, that the time will come when America will look upon the negro not as a savage with an inferior mentality, but as a civilized man. The American negro of today believes intensely in America. At times, when the train is whirling him back to dearly loved ones "below the line," he is tempted to be bitter and morose and, perhaps, iconoclastic. But he is hoping and dreaming. He is pinning everything on the hope, illusion or not, that America will some day find its soul, forget the negro's black skin, and recognize him as one of the nation's most loyal sons and defenders.

NEGROS' PROGRESS SINCE THE CIVIL WAR			
	1866	1922	Gain in Fifty-six Yrs.
ECONOMIC PROGRESS			
Homes owned	12,000	650,000	638,000
Farms operated............	20,000	1,000,000	980,000
Businesses conducted	2,100	60,000	57,900
Wealth accumulated	$20,000,000	$1,500,000,000	$1,480,000,000
EDUCATIONAL PROGRESS			
Per cent. literate	10	80	70
Colleges and normal schools...................	15	500	485
Students in public schools	100,000	2,000,000	1,900,000
Teachers in all schools ..	600	44,000	43,400
Property for higher education................	$60,000	$30,000,000	$29,940,000
Annual expend. for education................	$700,000	$28,000,000	$27,300,000
Raised by negroes.........	$80,000	$2,000,000	$1,920,000
RELIGIOUS PROGRESS			
Number of churches	700	45,000	44,300
Number of communicants..........	600,000	4,800,000	4,200,000
Number of Sunday schools...................	1,000	46,000	45,000
Sunday school pupils	500,000	2,250,000	2,200,000
Value of church property	$1,500,000	$90,000,000	$88,500,000

THE BLACK CITY

ERIC D. WALROND

I

N orth of 125th Street and glowing at the foot of Spuyten Duyvil is the sweltering city of Harlem, the "Black Belt" of Greater New York. With Negroes residing on San Juan Hill, on the East Side, in Greenwich Village, Harlem, undoubtedly, is the seething spot of the darker races of the world. As Atlanta, Georgia, is the breeding spot of the American Negro; Chicago, the fulfillment of his industrial hopes; Washington, the intellectual capital of his world; so is Harlem, with its 185,000 beings, the melting pot of the darker races. Here one is able to distinguish the blending of prodigal sons and daughters of Africa and Polynesia and the sun-drenched shores of the Caribbean; of peasant folk from Georgia and Alabama and the marsh lands of Florida and Louisiana. Here is banker and statesman, editor and politician, poet and scholar, scientist and laborer. Here is a world of song and color and emotion. Of life and beauty and majestic somnolence.

It is a sociological *el dorado*. With its rise, its struggles, its beginnings; its loves, its hates, its visionings, its tossings on the crest of the storming white sea; its orgies, its gluttonies; its restraints, its passivities; its spiritual yearnings—it is beautiful. On its bosom is the omnipresent symbol of oneness, of ethnologic oneness. Of solidarity! Hence its striving, its desperate striving, after a pigmentational purity, of distinctiveness of beauty. It is neither white nor black.

It is a city of dualities. Yonder, as the sun shoots its slanting rays across the doorstep of a realtor or banker or capitalist there is a noble son of Africa Redeemed on whose crown it shines. Well groomed, he is monocled or sprayed with a leaf of violet. By way of a boutonniere he sports a white or crimson aster—and in he goes. It is the beginning of his day as merchant or realtor or whatever he is. . . .

Towards sunset, as his pale-faced prototype resigns himself to supper or home or cabaret or adoring wife or chorus girl he is seen, is this black son, this time in denim or gold-braided toga, on his way to that thing that puts bread in his and his wife's and his children's mouths, and steels that silver-like spot glowing at the bottom of him, so that day in and day out he doggedly goes on, striving, conquering, upbuilding.

It is the beginning of his day as a domestic.

II

It is a city of paradoxes. You go to the neighborhood theatre and there is a play of Negro life. It is sharp, true, poignant. In awe you open your mouth at the beauty, the majesty, the sheer Russian-like reality of it. Grateful, the house asks for the author, the creator, the playwright. He is dragged forward; there is an outburst of applause—emotion unleashed. Modestly bowing the young man is slowly enveloped in the descending shadows—and the crowd is no more.

Wonderful! You go home; on a roseate bed you sleep, dream, remember things. In the morning you get up. Slipping into a dressing robe you go down in answer to the postman's shrilling whistle. Out of eyes painted with mist you go and take the letter, take the letter from the postman. Wholly by accident you raise your eyes and find, find yourself looking at—the playwright!

It is a city of paradoxes. Along the avenue you are strolling. It is dusk. Harlem at dusk—is exotic. Music. Song. Laughter. The street is full of people—dark, brown, crimson, pomegranate. Crystal clear is the light that shines in their eyes. It is different, is the light that shines in these black people's eyes. It is a light mirroring the emancipation of a people and still you feel that they are not quite emancipated. It is the light of an unregenerate.

As I say, you are walking along the avenue. There is a commotion. No, it is not really a commotion. Only a gathering together of folk. "Step this way, ladies and gentlemen . . . step, this way. . . . There you are. . . . Now this Coofu medicine is compounded from the best African herbs. . . ." East Fourteenth Street. Nassau Street. The Jewish ghetto. Glimpses of them whirl by you. Not of the Barnum herd, you are tempted to go on, to let the asses gourmandize it. Seized by a fit of reminiscence you pause. Over the heads of the mob you see, not the bushy, black-haired head of the Hindu "fakir," the Ph.D. of Oxford and Cambridge (in reality the blatant son of the acacia soil of Constant Springs, Jamaica, still basking in the shadows of dialectical oppression); not the boomeranging Congo oil magnate; nor the Jew invader with his white, ivory-white cheeks, hungry, Christ-like features, and flowing rabbinical beard. Instead you see a black man, of noble bearing, of intellectual poise, of undefiled English, a university man, selling at 900 per cent profit a beastly concoction that even white barbarians do not hesitate to gobble up.

And there is a reason, a mighty reason, for this, for the conversion, for the triumph of this black charlatan; a reason that goes up into the very warp and woof of American life. Imagine it—think, think about it sometime.

III

It is a house of assignation, a white man's house of assignation, is this black city. It is voluptuously accessible to him. Before cabarets and restaurants, cabarets and restaurants that black folk cannot go into, he stops, draws up his limousine, takes his lady, bathed in shining silk, out; squeezes through the molting, unminding folk, tips the black pyramidal *major domo*, and skips up to the scarlet draped seraglio. Here is white morality, white bestiality, for the Negroes to murmur and shake their bronzing cauliflower heads at.

It is wise, is this black city.

THE BLACK AND TAN CABARET—AMERICA'S MOST DEMOCRATIC INSTITUTION

CHANDLER OWEN (1889–1967) was a journalist, socialist, and ardent union supporter who joined with A. Philip Randolph to publish *The Messenger*, one of the significant black publications of the 1920s and the one of the most significant radical magazines in American history. Owen stayed with *The Messenger* until 1923 when he left for Chicago and other journalistic activities. As the 1920s went on he became a great deal less interested in socialism. "The Black and Tan Cabaret—America's Most Democratic Institution" was published in the February 1925 issue of *The Messenger* and "Bobbed Hair" was in the March 1925 issue of the same magazine. Both are articles that are responding to specific but major social conventions of the urban twenties.

The object of life is happiness—the gratification of desire. Neither money nor education is an end in itself. Both simply serve as means to still further ends. Among all classes, rich and poor, educated or ignorant, the appeal of a prize fight, a football or baseball game, an automobile or horse race is far stronger and more fascinating than the appeal of the school. Education in any true sense of the word must be compulsory since pupils would rather play than study. The returns are too indirect and distant for the young mind to foresee. Even grown-ups respond most readily to the "call of the wild." To read the box holders of the Kentucky Derby, an Indianapolis Speedway or of a Dempsey–Carpentier fight is like scanning the Who's Who of America. The Harvard–Yale game and the World Series Baseball Contest attract all America—cultured and uncultured.

Moreover, the basic pleasures release the true self more than the so-called more highly (?) developed intellectual and alleged cultural enjoyments. At a full-dress feature ball, an honorary dinner, a memorial service, Metropolitan Opera box party, people are on their "dignity." They are formal affairs, and formal is just another term for unnatural. In other words, people are pretending, putting on, feigning, counterfeiting, appearing to be what *they ain't*. Under such circumstances we observe human beings shamming and concealing, hiding their true selves. Not so with a black and tan cabaret. It is here that we see white and colored people mix freely. They dance together not only in the sense of both races being on the floor at the same time, but in the still more poignant and significant sense of white and colored people dancing as respective partners. Nor can it be said that Negroes are pushing themselves on the white people. Just the reverse; the white people are pushing themselves among the colored. There are plenty of other cabarets in the white sections, but none so popular as these marooned in the Negro districts.

Why?

Is it because white people like the Negro music? No. Negro orchestras play in the "lily-white" cabarets, too. Is it because cabarets are lewd and vulgar? This is old stuff. The modern cabaret of New York and Chicago is conducted with almost the decorum of a supervised dance hall in California. No shimmying is allowed. The dancers are not permitted to go to sleep on the floor with cheeks natural pillows as at many private house parties. The entertainment is not unlike a high class vaude-ville; in many instances it is a revue of twenty-five or thirty people, racy, vivacious dancing and thrilling music.

Are the people who attend the cabaret of low moral caliber? Hardly. We go, and large numbers of other respectable people go occasionally. Opera stars go, business men and women, artists, professional men, just the plain everyday forgotten man of whom the late Professor Summers of Yale said "the forgotten man who sometimes prays, but he always pays."

But is the cabaret democratic? All classes of people go there, rich and poor, learned and ignorant, white and colored, prominent and unknown. Besides, they get along. There is no fighting, no hostility, no suspicion, no discrimination. All pay alike and receive alike.

To illustrate. There was a terrible race riot in Chicago in 1919. Civil govern-ment collapsed; the Church fell down on the job; the school shrank away; social service agencies recoiled into their shell; publicists either succumbed to the hysteria or closed their otherwise vigilant eyes; the good church people hied away to their holes of holiness. On either side, the races barricaded themselves for a fight to the death. The dykes were opened and the dark waters rushed in. There was a back-wash in civilization. For a while the great metropolitan city of Chicago harked back to savagery—to the jackal and hyena era when nearly every man of the white race was at his colored brother's throat. The break down in racial brotherhood was well nigh complete except for the black and tan cabarets. Here white and colored men and women still drank, ate, sang and danced together. Smiling faces, light hearts, undulating couples in poetry of motion conspired with syncopated music to convert the hell and death from *without* to a little paradise *within*. Such an accomplishment renders the cabaret an institution at once social and democratic. It also reveals the unveneered American, white and black, as true human beings, kindly, tolerant, fraternal, able and anxious to get along, and able to get along together, if they can just be left alone and freed from the views of vicious Ku Kluxers who are making a business of race hate.

Again, these black and tan cabarets establish the desire of the races to mix and to mingle. They show that there is lurking ever a prurient longing for the prohibited association between the races which should be a matter of personal choice. These cabarets portray even the vanished prejudice of white men lest a Negro man should brush against a white woman. They show as Emerson would say that "every human heart is human; every human heart is big with truth." They prove that the white race is taking the initiative in seeking out the Negro; that in the social equality equation the Negro is the sought, rather than the seeking factor. They prove that there is no sex line in the seeking since both white men and white women attend— attend not only with their own racial mates but with opposite race mates.

The Sunset cabaret of Chicago, Connie's Inn and Happy Rhone's of New York are high types of cabarets in which a person may go without fear of physical or moral contamination. Cabarets, like other institutions, are good or bad according to the use to which they are put. No sane person would condemn houses because some houses are used for prostitution and dope joints. Nor would he destroy the act of writing because some people use it for forgery. To do so would be as illogical as prohibiting the manufacture of automobiles because Leopold and Loeb kidnapped and murdered the little Franks boy in a Willys Knight car.

Fundamentally the cabaret is a place where people abandon their cant and hypocrisy just as they do in going on a hike, a picnic, or a hunting trip. They get close to earth where human nature is more neatly uniform. The little barracks of hypocrisy and the prison bars of prejudice are temporarily at least torn down, and people act like natural plain human beings—kind, cordial, friendly, gentle— bringing with them what Walt Whitman called "a new roughness and a new gladness."

True democracy should teach not only how to tolerate each other but how races and people can understand, adapt themselves to and like each other. Especially necessary is this in the realm of pleasure seeking. Here snobbery runs riot—racial and class. For instance white persons will work *all* day side by side with Negroes in factory, mill and office, and then contend that, *in the evening*, they cannot sit together in restaurant, theatre or public conveyance. This too, in spite of the ridiculous time aspects, since white persons will work eight hours or more with Negroes, yet complain about eating a meal together twenty minutes, riding on a car five or ten, or sitting in a show from two to three hours. The reason for this is because a person who is securing pleasure is supposed to be at leisure. He is aping the leisure class: This raises the question of caste. And if white and colored are having the same kind of amusement, at the same time and place, it suggests equality of social class or caste, and its further and inevitable implication of equality of race.

But the cabaret has broken down even this caste, snobbery and discrimination, so deeply embedded in recreation and amusement. It has broken it not only inter- racially but intra-racially since even all classes of white people congregate here— and congregate voluntarily. The black and tan cabaret is peculiarly fitted for this, since the disintegration of caste which starts on the race question quickly expresses itself as between different social groups inside the white race. The white man of affluence and prestige says, "If I can meet, mix and mingle with colored people then I can afford to be tolerant with poor whites." The poor white says (the lower ever aping the higher): "If rich white people of influence and prominence can associate with Negroes, I too, can certainly afford to." And the Negro who invariably hates the poor whites (his chief competitors) says (also aping his superior rich whites): "If rich white people can afford to associate with these poor whites, then, I, a Negro, will condescend to do likewise."

The result is a tread toward the norm toward common understanding through general contact. All learn with Shakespeare: "If you tickle us we laugh; if you prick us we bleed."

Does anyone know of a more democratic institution in America than the "black and tan cabaret"?

BOBBED HAIR

CHANDLER OWEN

W hy do women bob their hair? Does it make them more beautiful? Is
it more convenient? More hygienic and sanitary? Less expensive?
More attractive to men? Or what?

Probably the original history of bobbing hair reveals about what might be
termed, for the want of a better word, the Greenwich Village and the radical women.
They were not seeking aesthetic effects, convenience, hygiene or economy—but
merely difference. For a long while it was considered a mark of radicalism for a
woman to bob her hair, to wear sandals and to smoke. Here the feminine iconoclasts
were at work trying to go against the established order for no reason other than
revolting against the *status quo*.

We have no prejudices whatever against spontaneous variation whether in the
biological or in the social world. If a thing is useful and desirable, it ought to be
inaugurated; if not, wisdom would dictate rejecting it. When a practice assumes
such a widespread role, one should examine it very painstakingly before condemning
it. This in spite of the fact that the majority is usually wrong, for there is some
modicum of truth and utility in anything so generally received: Let us, therefore,
return to the questions asked at the beginning.

First, does bobbed hair make women more beautiful? Here is a very pertinent
question, since women spare no pains to adopt anything calculated to improve their
looks. Moreover, there is some queer quirk of the cranium which impels, almost
overnight, millions of women to adopt a reverse hair style from one in which they
have been making the third largest expenditure in the United States—hair growing.
Three or four Negro firms like the C. J. Walker, Poro, Overton, Lee and a half
dozen white firms, have made millions on the strength of the mere claim they could
grow hair. All the while it has been possible to make comparisons between long

hair and bobbed hair, since the great majority of people's hair was already bobbed by nature. In fact, length of hair took precedence to quality, since it was possible to improve the quality but impossible to increase the quantity. So long hair was universally regarded as more beautiful—a consummation devoutly to be wished.

Sometimes, however, convenience or utility will take precedence to pulchritude. So we shall inquire whether bobbed hair is more convenient. It is probably more easily combed, but the time spent in the barber's chair for constant recutting, shaving the neck and shaping will easily outdistance the time required for dressing the hair. Especially true is this of people who have long hair, since there is something impressive about the very quantity which enables them to wind and twist it to advantage in almost any way.

Is bobbed hair more hygienic and sanitary? The less hair one has the less he has to keep clean. But if the question of laziness is permitted to run riot one might reduce the human race to lilliputians in order to have less body to bathe; diminish the teeth to one fourth their size to have less to brush; make the eyes the size of a sparrow's (birds can see quicker and farther than men) in order to have less eye to wash, or decrease the ears to the size of a crow's to have less ear to swab. Moreover, the washing of a woman's hair is not what takes so much time, but the drying. Still one half of it will dry as quickly as all, just as a dozen handkerchiefs will dry as quickly as one. The person who cannot grasp this elementary logic is on all fours with the three Irishmen who were thirty miles from town when the evening shadows were falling. Pat said, "Well, we've got thirty miles to go." Mike replied, "That isn't so bad—just ten miles apiece."

Is bobbed hair less expensive? The answer to this would seem to require answering some other questions, namely, do hair dressers charge less for washing a bobbed head than a long one? Does long hair have to be attended to more frequently? And, third, what about the cost of constant bobbing, reshaping, marcelling, waving, straightening? The answer to these questions would seem to be that a woman with bobbed hair has all the expense of one with long hair plus that additional expense which comes around with rhythmic regularity—the reshaping, cutting and trimming.

Is bobbed hair more attractive to men? This question could hardly be ignored, since the great bag of feminine tricks from the making of fine underwear to the creation of fur coats constantly at least gives large consideration to, How will the men like it? Just as men are no little concerned about how their creations please the feminine taste. There are some very comprehensive answers to be made on the relation of the eternal masculine to the persistent feminine. In the Universities of California, Columbia, and Chicago, where the men students took a vote on the most beautiful girl, the model selected each time and in each place was the girl with flowing locks and long. Again, I have never seen a man who really liked bobbed hair. They tolerate it—another evidence of the reviving gynecocracy—the period of female rule or power. Nor is it strange that men don't like bobbed hair. Sex relations proceed from the principle that unlike poles attract. Men like dresses on women better than knickerbockers. They prefer the night gown to pajamas; the petite shoes to the broad; and the gentle hat to the derby or plug. Reverse the order.

How many women would like to see the man they admire with a dress on, in a night gown or with long hair? No sane one. And the reason is that deep philosophic, physical and biological principle that "like poles repel and unlike poles attract." Again, the kind of clothing adapted to each sex was so adapted largely for purposes of discrimination. It is true, however, as Lester Ward points out, that men having the power imposed on women the less utilitarian dress. For instance, trousers are much more hygienic and convenient than dresses and skirts. Skirts hanging from the waist were a strain on the pelvic organs and have given rise to many of the ailments of women. Part of this female revolt then, is directed against a species of masculine tyranny (revolutions usually produce excesses), but like most revolts proceeds beyond the necessary limits. Since then bobbed hair is not so beautiful as long tresses, is no more convenient, hygienic and sanitary, but more expensive and less attractive to men—why do women insist on having it? What is this Prometheus Bound which disregards the call of money and the call of man; which kicks overboard without reserve or pity both economic and biological considerations? The explanation is two-fold. Man has become the slave of his own manufactured god. First, there is the fashion god—a product of man's own mind, a creation which has grown so strong that it can inaugurate the ugly and force its acceptance. Fashion has trained the human mind to accept diametrically reverse styles. To illustrate, one season decrees a hobble skirt clinging so tightly as almost to obstruct walking; the following season will proclaim wide skirts which seem to cooperate with the wind in exposing the woman's legs. One year skirts are trailing two and three feet long with weights to hold them down; the following year the skirts get so short that city councils pass laws to stop them from reaching the hip. One season decrees such wide hats that women may dispense with umbrellas, the next season brackets their heads in little vamp caps which prevent any hair dress at all. One season gives needle toes and high French heels, the next shoes which are so wide and flat that they become veritable sandals. Yesterday the dress necks were so high that the collars had on sharp points which almost touched the ear; today, the top of the waist has gotten so far from the ear that it can not hear the waist rattle. A little while ago women wore so many underskirts, petticoats and alternates that one might have been mistaken for carrying a blanket display; today, the women are showing that history repeats itself as they approximate the no-clothes savage.

Economists recognize that selling hair is a great business, and if most of the women cut off their hair the fashion kings know that by decreeing long hair as a style they will stimulate a titanic hair consumption. A fortune can be made by selling switches, wigs, etc., and since it is easier and quicker to cut off hair than to grow it the only possible way to resecure it in time for the style would be to buy it. It is not amiss here to note that these extremely reverse styles are deliberately decreed to stop the buyer from being able to make slight alterations and use his old clothing. Of course, we can not overlook the hair pedigree argument. When one's hair has been bobbed she can always claim that before she cut it it reached almost to her knees—and most people so claim this when visiting among strangers.

Another reason for so completely disregarding the whims of men on bobbed hair is a subtle, evolutionary, protective force—the recognition that bobbed hair makes a woman look younger. Of all the ravages to which women are subjected, none is so dreaded—and justly dreaded—as the weight of increasing years. Whoever discovers the mythical "fountain of youth" can reap his millions from the persistent feminine. Most goods are sold not on their merits but on their apparent merits. The law even protects this fraud on the theory that the purchaser should beware *caveat emptor*. Bobbed hair enabling women to appear to be what they ain't—also lets them sell, to an extent, apparent youth for real youth.

Is bobbed hair here to stay? I don't know. I do know that it is the style now. As such it is part of one's dress and if it persists, nearly every woman will bob her hair. Men will realize that it is almost as unreasonable to require their wives to wear long hair as it is to require them to wear trailing skirts when everybody else is garbed in smart, short ones. Then, too, people wish to be like others. To be different sets up an impassable chasm. Women will not get outside the pale of society nor will the men who restrain them permit it. So long as a woman has a prominent husband or distinguished sweetheart who prefers a different style she need not capitulate to the bobbed hair and she won't. But this is simply a case where the resultant takes the direction of the greater force. When social pressure, the urgence of companions becomes more powerful and important to her, she will disregard those former whims and wishes.

All in all, the bobbed hair craze seems to be but a reflection of the general tendency of the women to become more masculine and the men to become more feminine, both of which square with the fundamental law that unlike poles attract and like poles repel. The feminine women will like the masculine men, while the masculine men will continue to like the feminine women.

THE MAKING OF HARLEM

JAMES WELDON JOHNSON (1871–1938) was a
novelist, songwriter, poet, school principal, lawyer, Consul to Nicaragua
and Venezuela, newspaper editor, and civil rights leader. Along with his
brother, J. Rosamond, he wrote "Lift Every Voice and Sing," the Negro
National Anthem. He wrote the noted novel, *The Autobiography of an
Ex-Colored Man* (1912; republished in 1927, during the Renaissance);
the famous selection of Negro folk poems, *God's Trombones* (1927); the
fine history of Harlem, *Black Manhattan* (1930), and his autobiography,
Along This Way (1933). "The Making of Harlem" appeared in the
special March 1925 number of *Survey Graphic* as well as in Locke's *The
New Negro*.

In the history of New York, the significance of the name Harlem has changed
from Dutch to Irish to Jewish to Negro. Of these changes, the last has
come most swiftly. Throughout colored America, from Massachusetts to
Mississippi, and across the continent to Los Angeles and Seattle, its name, which
as late as fifteen years ago had scarcely been heard, now stands for the Negro
metropolis. Harlem is indeed the great Mecca for the sight-seer, the pleasure-seeker,
the curious, the adventurous, the enterprising, the ambitious and the talented of
the whole Negro world; for the lure of it has reached down to every island of the
Carib Sea and has penetrated even into Africa.

In the make-up of New York, Harlem is not merely a Negro colony or commu-
nity, it is a city within a city, the greatest Negro city in the world. It is not a slum
or a fringe, it is located in the heart of Manhattan and occupies one of the most
beautiful and healthful sections of the city. It is not a "quarter" of dilapidated
tenements, but is made up of new-law apartments and handsome dwellings, with
well-paved and well-lighted streets. It has its own churches, social and civic centers,

shops, theatres and other places of amusement. And it contains more Negroes to the square mile than any other spot on earth. A stranger who rides up magnificent Seventh Avenue on a bus or in an automobile must be struck with surprise at the transformation which takes place after he crosses 125th Street. Beginning there, the population suddenly darkens and he rides through twenty-five solid blocks where the passers-by, the shoppers, those sitting in restaurants, coming out of theatres, standing in doorways and looking out of windows are practically all Negroes; and then he emerges where the population as suddenly becomes white again. There is nothing just like it in any other city in the country, for there is no preparation for it; no change in the character of the houses and streets; no change, indeed, in the appearance of the people, except their color.

Negro Harlem is practically a development of the past decade, but the story behind it goes back a long way. There have always been colored people in New York. In the middle of the last century they lived in the vicinity of Lispenard, Broome and Spring Streets. When Washington Square and lower Fifth Avenue was the center of aristocratic life, the colored people, whose chief occupation was domestic service in the homes of the rich, lived in a fringe and were scattered in nests to the south, east and west of the square. As late as the eighties the major part of the colored population lived in Sullivan, Thompson, Bleecker, Grove, Minetta Lane and adjacent streets. It is curious to note that some of these nests still persist. In a number of the blocks of Greenwich Village and Little Italy may be found small groups of Negroes who have never lived in any other section of the city. By about 1890 the center of colored population had shifted to the upper Twenties and lower Thirties west of Sixth Avenue. Ten years later another considerable shift northward had been made to West Fifty-third Street.

The West Fifty-third Street settlement deserves some special mention because it ushered in a new phase of life among colored New Yorkers. Three rather well appointed hotels were opened in the street and they quickly became the centers of a sort of fashionable life that hitherto had not existed. On Sunday evenings these hotels served dinner to music and attracted crowds of well-dressed diners. One of these hotels, The Marshall, became famous as the headquarters of Negro talent. There gathered the actors, the musicians, the composers, the writers, the singers, dancers and vaudevillians. There one went to get a close-up of Williams and Walker, Cole and Johnson, Ernest Hogan, Will Marion Cook, Jim Europe, Aida Overton, and of others equally and less known. Paul Laurence Dunbar was frequently there whenever he was in New York. Numbers of those who love to shine by the light reflected from celebrities were always to be found. The first modern jazz band ever heard in New York, or, perhaps anywhere, was organized at The Marshall. It was a playing-singing-dancing orchestra, making the first dominant use of banjos, saxophones, clarinets and trap drums in combination, and was called The Memphis Students. Jim Europe was a member of that band, and out of it grew the famous Clef Club, of which he was the noted leader, and which for a long time monopolized the business of "entertaining" private parties and furnishing music for the new dance craze. Also in the Clef Club was "Buddy" Gilmore who originated trap drumming as it is now practiced, and set hundreds of white men to juggling their sticks and doing acrobatic stunts while they manipulated a dozen other noise-making devices aside from their drums. A good many well-known white performers frequented The Marshall and for seven or eight years the place was one of the sights of New York.

The move to Fifty-third Street was the result of the opportunity to get into newer and better houses. About 1900 the move to Harlem began, and for the same reason. Harlem had been overbuilt with large, new-law apartment houses, but rapid transportation to that section was very inadequate—the Lenox Avenue Subway had not yet been built—and landlords were finding difficulty in keeping houses on the east side of the section filled. Residents along and near Seventh Avenue were fairly well served by the Eighth Avenue Elevated. A colored man, in the real estate business at this time, Philip A. Payton, approached several of these landlords with the proposition that he would fill their empty or partially empty houses with steady colored tenants. The suggestion was accepted, and one or two houses on 134th Street east of Lenox Avenue were taken over. Gradually other houses were filled. The whites paid little attention to the movement until it began to spread west of Lenox Avenue; they then took steps to check it. They proposed through a financial organization, the Hudson Realty Company, to buy in all properties occupied by colored people and evict the tenants. The Negroes countered by similar methods. Payton formed the Afro-American Realty Company, a Negro corporation organized for the purpose of buying and leasing houses for occupancy by colored people. Under this counter stroke the opposition subsided for several years.

But the continually increasing pressure of colored people to the west over the Lenox Avenue dead line caused the opposition to break out again, but in a new and more menacing form. Several white men undertook to organize all the white people of the community for the purpose of inducing financial institutions not to lend money or renew mortgages on properties occupied by colored people. In this effort they had considerable success, and created a situation which has not yet been completely overcome, a situation which is one of the hardest and most unjustifiable the Negro property owner in Harlem has to contend with. The Afro-American Realty Company was now defunct; but two or three colored men of means stepped into the breach. Philip A. Payton and J. C. Thomas bought two five-story apartments, dispossessed the white tenants and put in colored. J. B. Nail bought a row of five apartments and did the same thing. St. Philip's Church bought a row of thirteen apartment houses on 135th Street, running from Seventh Avenue almost to Lenox.

The situation now resolved itself into an actual contest. Negroes not only continued to occupy available apartment houses, but began to purchase private dwellings between Lenox and Seventh Avenues. Then the whole movement, in the eyes of the whites, took on the aspect of an "invasion"; they became panic stricken and began fleeing as from a plague. The presence of one colored family in a block, no matter how well bred and orderly, was sufficient to precipitate a flight. House after house and block after block was actually deserted. It was a great demonstration of human beings running amuck. None of them stopped to reason why they were doing it or what would happen if they didn't. The banks and lending companies holding mortgages on these deserted houses were compelled to take them over. For some time they held these houses vacant, preferring to do that and carry the charges than to rent or sell them to colored people. But values dropped and continued to drop until at the outbreak of the war in Europe property in the northern part of Harlem had reached the nadir.

In the meantime the Negro colony was becoming more stable; the churches were being moved from the lower part of the city; social and civic centers were being formed; and gradually a community was being evolved. Following the outbreak of the war in Europe Negro Harlem received a new and tremendous impetus. Because of the war thousands of aliens in the United States rushed back to their native lands to join the colors and immigration practically ceased. The result was a critical shortage in labor. This shortage was rapidly increased as the United States went more and more largely into the business of furnishing munitions and supplies to the warring countries. To help meet this shortage of common labor Negroes were brought up from the South. The government itself took the first steps, following the practice in vogue in Germany of shifting labor according to the supply and demand in various parts of the country. The example of the government was promptly taken up by the big industrial concerns, which sent hundreds, perhaps thousands, of labor agents into the South who recruited Negroes by wholesale. I was in Jacksonville, Florida, for a while at that time, and I sat one day and watched the stream of migrants passing to take the train. For hours they passed steadily, carrying flimsy suit cases, new and shiny, rusty old ones, bursting at the seams, boxes and bundles and impedimenta of all sorts, including banjos, guitars, birds in cages and what not. Similar scenes were being enacted in cities and towns all over that region. The first wave of the great exodus of Negroes from the South was on. Great numbers of these migrants headed for New York or eventually got there, and naturally the majority went up into Harlem. But the Negro population of Harlem was not swollen by migrants from the South alone; the opportunity for Negro labor exerted its pull upon the Negroes of the West Indies, and those islanders in the course of time poured into Harlem to the number of twenty-five thousand or more.

These new-comers did not have to look for work; work looked for them, and at wages of which they had never even dreamed. And here is where the unlooked for, the unprecedented, the miraculous happened. According to all preconceived notions, these Negroes suddenly earning large sums of money for the first time in their lives should have had their heads turned; they should have squandered it in the most silly and absurd manners imaginable. Later, after the United States had entered the war and even Negroes in the South were making money fast, many stories in accord with the tradition came out of that section. There was the one about the colored man who went into a general store and on hearing a phonograph for the first time promptly ordered six of them, one for each child in the house. I shall not stop to discuss whether Negroes in the South did that sort of thing or not, but I do know that those who got to New York didn't. The Negroes of Harlem, for the greater part, worked and saved their money. Nobody knew how much they had saved until congestion made expansion necessary for tenants and ownership profitable for landlords, and they began to buy property. Persons who would never be suspected of having money bought property. The Rev. W. W. Brown, pastor of the Metropolitan Baptist Church, repeatedly made "Buy property" the text of his sermons. A large part of his congregation carried out the injunction. The church itself set an example by purchasing a magnificent brown stone church building on Seventh Avenue from a white congregation. Buying property became a fever. At the height of this activity, that is, 1920–21, it was not an uncommon thing for a colored washerwoman or cook to go into a real estate office and lay down from one thousand to five thousand dollars on a house. "Pig Foot Mary" is a character in Harlem. Everybody who knows the corner of Lenox Avenue and 135th Street knows "Mary" and her stand and has been tempted by the smell of her pigsfeet, fried chicken and hot corn, even if he has not been a customer. "Mary," whose real name is Mrs. Mary Dean, bought the five-story apartment house at the corner of Seventh Avenue and 137th Street at a price of $42,000. Later she sold it to the Y.W.C.A. for dormitory purposes. The Y.W.C.A. sold it recently to Adolph Howell, a leading colored undertaker, the price given being $72,000. Often companies of a half dozen men combined to buy a house—these combinations were and still are generally made up of West Indians—and would produce five or ten thousand dollars to put through the deal.

When the buying activity began to make itself felt, the lending companies that had been holding vacant the handsome dwellings on and abutting Seventh Avenue decided to put them on the market. The values on these houses had dropped to the lowest mark possible and they were put up at astonishingly low prices. Houses that had been bought at from $15,000 to $20,000 were sold at one-third those figures. They were quickly gobbled up. The Equitable Life Assurance Company held 106 model private houses that were designed by Stanford White. They are built with courts running straight through the block and closed off by wrought iron gates. Every one of these houses was sold within eleven months at an aggregate price of about two million dollars. Today they are probably worth about 100 per cent more. And not only have private dwellings and similar apartments been bought but big elevator apartments have been taken over. Corporations have been organized for this purpose. Two of these, The Antillian Realty Company, composed of West Indian Negroes, and the Sphinx Securities Company, composed of American and West Indian Negroes, represent holdings amounting to approximately $750,000. Individual Negroes and companies in the South have invested in Harlem real estate. About two years ago a Negro institution of Savannah, Georgia, bought a parcel for $115,000 which it sold a month or so ago at a profit of $110,000.

I am informed by John E. Nail, a successful colored real estate dealer of Harlem and a reliable authority, that the total value of property in Harlem owned and controlled by colored people would at a conservative estimate amount to more than sixty million dollars. These figures are amazing, especially when we take into account the short time in which they have been piled up. Twenty years ago Negroes were begging for the privilege of renting a flat in Harlem. Fifteen years ago barely a half dozen colored men owned real property in all Manhattan. And down to ten years ago the amount that had been acquired in Harlem was comparatively negligible. Today Negro Harlem is practically owned by Negroes.

The question naturally arises, "Are the Negroes going to be able to hold Harlem?" If they have been steadily driven northward for the past hundred years and out of less desirable sections, can they hold this choice bit of Manhattan Island? It is hardly probable that Negroes will hold Harlem indefinitely, but when they are forced out it will not be for the same reasons that forced them out of former quarters in New York City. The situation is entirely different and without precedent. When colored people do leave Harlem, their homes, their churches, their investments and their businesses, it will be because the land has become so valuable they can no longer afford to live on it. But the date of another move northward is very far in the future. What will Harlem be and become in the meantime? Is there danger that the Negro may lose his economic status in New York and be unable to hold his property? Will Harlem become merely a famous ghetto, or will it be a center of intellectual, cultural and economic forces exerting an influence throughout the world, especially upon Negro peoples? Will it become a point of friction between the races in New York?

I think there is less danger to the Negroes of New York of losing out economically and industrially than to the Negroes of any large city in the North. In most of the big industrial centers Negroes are engaged in gang labor. They are employed by thousands in the stockyards in Chicago, by thousands in the automobile plants in Detroit; and in those cities they are likely to be the first to be let go, and in thousands, with every business depression. In New York there is hardly such a thing as gang labor among Negroes, except among the longshoremen, and it is in the longshoremen's unions, above all others, that Negroes stand on an equal footing. Employment among Negroes in New York is highly diversified; in the main they are employed more as individuals than as non-integral parts of a gang. Furthermore, Harlem is gradually becoming more and more a self-supporting community. Negroes there are steadily branching out into new businesses and enterprises in which Negroes are employed. So the danger of great numbers of Negroes being thrown out of work at once, with a resulting economic crisis among them, is less in New York than in most of the large cities of the North to which Southern migrants have come.

These facts have an effect which goes beyond the economic and industrial situation. They have a direct bearing on the future character of Harlem and on the question as to whether Harlem will be a point of friction between the races in New York. It is true that Harlem is a Negro community, well defined and stable; anchored to its fixed homes, churches, institutions, business and amusement places; having its own working, business and professional classes. It is experiencing a constant growth of group consciousness and community feeling. Harlem is therefore, in many respects, typically Negro. It has many unique characteristics. It has movement, color, gaiety, singing, dancing, boisterous laughter and loud talk. One of its outstanding features is brass band parades. Hardly a Sunday passes but that there are several of these parades of which many are gorgeous with regalia and insignia. Almost any excuse will do—the death of an humble member of the Elks, the laying of a corner stone, the "turning out" of the order of this or that. In many of these characteristics it is similar to the Italian colony. But withal, Harlem grows more metropolitan and more a part of New York all the while. Why is it then that its tendency is not to become a mere "quarter"?

I shall give three reasons that seem to me to be important in their order. First, the language of Harlem is not alien; it is not Italian or Yiddish; it is English. Harlem talks American, reads American, thinks American. Second, Harlem is not physically a "quarter." It is not a section cut off. It is merely a zone through which four main arteries of the city run. Third, the fact that there is little or no gang labor gives Harlem Negroes the opportunity for individual expansion and individual contacts with the life and spirit of New York. A thousand Negroes from Mississippi put to work as a gang in a Pittsburgh steel mill will for a long time remain a thousand Negroes from Mississippi. Under the conditions that prevail in New York they would all within six months become New Yorkers. The rapidity with which Negroes become good New Yorkers is one of the marvels to observers.

These three reasons form a single reason why there is small probability that Harlem will ever be a point of race friction between the races in New York. One of the principal factors in the race riot in Chicago in 1919 was the fact that at that time there were twelve thousand Negroes employed in gangs in the stock yards. There was considerable race feeling in Harlem at the time of the hegira of white residents due to the "invasion," but that feeling, of course, is no more. Indeed, a number of the old white residents who didn't go or could not get away before the housing shortage struck New York are now living peacefully side by side with colored residents. In fact, in some cases white and colored tenants occupy apartments in the same house. Many white merchants still do business in thickest Harlem. On the whole, I know of no place in the country where the feeling between the races is so cordial and at the same time so matter-of-fact and taken for granted. One of the surest safeguards against an outbreak in New York such as took place in so many Northern cities in the summer of 1919 is the large proportion of Negro police on duty in Harlem.

To my mind, Harlem is more than a Negro community; it is a large scale laboratory experiment in the race problem. The statement has often been made that if Negroes were transported to the North in large numbers the race problem with all of its acuteness and with new aspects would be transferred with them. Well, 175,000 Negroes live closely together in Harlem, in the heart of New York, 75,000 more than live in any Southern city, and do so without any race friction. Nor is there any unusual record of crime. I once heard a captain of the 38th Police Precinct (the Harlem precinct) say that on the whole it was the most law-abiding precinct in the city. New York guarantees its Negro citizens the fundamental rights of American citizenship and protects them in the exercise of those rights. In return the Negro loves New York and is proud of it, and contributes in his way to its greatness. He still meets with discriminations, but possessing the basic rights, he knows that these discriminations will be abolished.

I believe that the Negro's advantages and opportunities are greater in Harlem than in any other place in the country, and that Harlem will become the intellectual, the cultural and the financial center for Negroes of the United States, and will exert a vital influence upon all Negro peoples.

NEGRO LIFE IN
NEW YORK'S HARLEM

WALLACE THURMAN (1902–1934) was a voracious reader and apparently a man of great intellect and literary promise that was never fulfilled. He wrote two novels, *The Black the Berry* (1929), a compelling account of the despair and discrimination a black-skinned girl faces from her own group; and *The Infants of the Spring* (1932), a less than successful satire of the Harlem Renaissance. He also wrote Hollywood screenplays and for potboiler and romance magazines, often under pseudonyms. He, along with Langston Hughes and Zora Neale Hurston, was editor and publisher of *Fire!!*, a magazine that was devoted to the work of the young radicals of the Renaissance. It lasted only one issue. "Negro Life in New York's Harlem," a small pamphlet, or chapbook of a sort, was published in 1928. Despite its factual and objective veneer, a satirical undertone can be detected throughout the piece.

I. A LIVELY PICTURE OF A POPULAR AND INTERESTING SECTION

Harlem has been called the Mecca of the New Negro, the center of black America's cultural renaissance, Nigger Heaven, Pickaninny Paradise, Capital of Black America, and various other things. It has been surveyed and interpreted, explored and exploited. It has had its day in literature, in the drama, even in the tabloid press. It is considered the most popular and interesting section of contemporary New York. Its fame is international; its personality individual and inimitable. There is no Negro settlement anywhere comparable to Harlem, just as there is no other metropolis comparable to New York. As the great south side black belt of Chicago spreads and smells with the same industrial clumsiness and stockyardish vigor of Chicago, so does the black belt of New York teem and rhyme with the cosmopolitan cross currents of the world's greatest city. Harlem is Harlem because it is part and parcel of greater New York. Its rhythms are the lackadaisical rhythms of a transplanted minority group caught up and rendered half mad by the more speedy rhythms of the subway, Fifth Avenue and the Great White Way.

Negro Harlem is located on one of the choice sites of Manhattan Island. It covers the greater portion of the northwestern end, and is more free from grime, smoke and oceanic dampness than the lower eastside where most of the hyphenated American groups live. Harlem is a great black city. There are no shanty-filled, mean streets. No antiquated cobble-stoned pavement; no flimsy frame fire-traps. Little Africa has fortressed itself behind brick and stone on wide important streets where the air is plentiful and sunshine can be appreciated.

There are six main north and south thoroughfares streaming through Negro Harlem—Fifth Avenue, Lenox Avenue, Seventh Avenue, Eighth Avenue, Edgecombe and St. Nicholas. Fifth Avenue begins prosperously at 125th Street, becomes a slum district above 131st Street, and finally slithers off into a warehouse-lined, dingy alleyway above 139th Street. The people seen on Fifth Avenue are either sad or nasty looking. The women seem to be drudges or drunkards, the men pugnacious and loud—petty thieves and vicious parasites. The children are pitiful specimens of ugliness and dirt.

The tenement houses in this vicinity are darkened dungheaps, festering with poverty-stricken and crime-ridden step-children of nature. This is the edge of Harlem's slum district; Fifth Avenue is its board-walk. Push carts line the curbstone, dirty push carts manned by dirtier hucksters, selling fly-specked vegetables and other cheap commodities. Evil faces leer at you from doorways and windows. Brutish men elbow you out of their way, dreary looking women scowl at and curse children playing on the sidewalk. That is Harlem's Fifth Avenue.

Lenox Avenue knows the rumble of the subway and the rattle of the crosstown street car. It is always crowded, crowded with pedestrians seeking the subway or the street car, crowded with idlers from the many pool halls and dives along its line of march, crowded with men and women from the slum district which it borders on the west and Fifth Avenue borders on the east. Lenox Avenue is Harlem's Bowery. It is dirty and noisy, its buildings ill-used, and made shaky by the subway underneath. At 140th Street it makes its one bid for respectability. On one corner there is Tabb's Restaurant and Grill, one of Harlem's most delightful and respectable eating houses; across the street is the Savoy building, housing a first-class dance hall, a motion picture theater and many small business establishments behind its stucco front. But above 141st Street Lenox Avenue gets mean and squalid, deprived of even its crowds of people, and finally peters out into a dirt pile, before leading to a car-barn at 147th St.

Seventh Avenue—Black Broadway—Harlem's main street, a place to promenade, a place to loiter, an avenue spacious and sleek with wide pavement, modern well-kept buildings, theaters, drug stores and other businesses. Seventh Avenue, down which no Negro dared walk twenty years ago unless he was prepared to fight belligerent Irishmen. Seventh Avenue, teeming with life and ablaze with color, the most interesting and important street in one of the most interesting and important city sections of greater New York.

Negro Harlem is best represented by Seventh Avenue. It is not, like Fifth Avenue, filthy and stark, nor like Lenox, squalid and dirty. It is a grand thoroughfare into which every element of Harlem population ventures either for reasons of pleasure or of business. From 125th Street to 145th Street, Seventh Avenue is a stream of dark people going to churches, theaters, restaurants, billiard halls, business offices, food markets, barber shops and apartment houses. Seventh Avenue is majestic yet warm, and it reflects both the sordid chaos and the rhythmic splendor of Harlem.

From five o'clock in the evening until way past midnight, Seventh Avenue is one electric-lit line of brilliance and activity, especially during the spring, summer and early fall months. Dwelling houses are close, overcrowded and dark. Seventh Avenue is the place to seek relief. People everywhere. Lines of people in front of the box offices of the Lafayette Theater at 132d Street, the Renaissance motion picture theater at 138th Street and the Roosevelt Theater at 145th Street. Knots of people in front of the Metropolitan Baptist Church at 129th Street and Salem M. E. Church, which dominates the corner at 129th Street.

People going into the cabarets. People going into speak-easies and saloons. Groups of boisterous men and boys, congregated on corners and in the middle of the blocks, making remarks about individuals in the passing parade. Adolescent boys and girls flaunting their youth. Street speakers on every corner. A Hindoo faker here, a loud-voiced Socialist there, a medicine doctor ballyhooing, a corn doctor, a blind musician, serious people, gay people, philanderers and preachers. Seventh Avenue is filled with deep rhythmic laughter. It is a civilized lane with primitive traits, Harlem's most representative street.

Eighth Avenue supports the elevated lines. It is noticeably negroid only from 135th Street to 145th Street. It is packed with dingy, cheap shops owned by Jews. Above 139th Street the curbstone is lined with push-cart merchants selling everything from underwear to foodstuffs. Eighth Avenue is dark and noisy. The elevated trestle and its shadows dominate the street. Few people linger along its sidewalks. Eighth Avenue is a street for business, a street for people who live west of it to cross hurriedly in order to reach places located east of it.

Edgecombe, Brandhurst and St. Nicholas Avenues are strictly residential thoroughfares of the better variety. Expensive modern apartment houses line these streets. They were once occupied by well-to-do white people who now live on Riverside Drive, West End Avenue and in Washington Heights. They are luxuriously appointed with imposing entrances, elevator service, disappearing garbage cans, and all the other appurtenances that make a modern apartment house convenient. The Negroes who live in these places are either high-salaried workingmen or professional folk.

Most of the cross streets in Harlem, lying between the main north and south thoroughfares, are monotonous and overcrowded. There is little difference between any of them save that some are more dirty and more squalid than others. They are lined with ordinary, undistinguished tenement and apartment houses. Some are well kept, others are run down. There are only four streets that are noticeably different, 136th Street, 137th Street, 138th Street and 139th Street west of Seventh Avenue and these are the only blocks in Harlem that can boast of having shade trees. An improvement association organized by people living in these streets, strives to keep them looking respectable.

Between Seventh and Eighth Avenues, is 139th Street, known among Harlemites as "strivers' row." It is the most artistocratic street in Harlem. Stanford White designed the houses for a wealthy white clientele. Moneyed Negroes now own and inhabit them. When one lives on "strivers' row" one has supposedly arrived. Harry Wills resides there, as do a number of the leading Babbitts and professional folk of Harlem.

II. 200,000 NEGROES IN HARLEM

There are approximately 200,000 Negroes in Harlem. Two hundred thousand Negroes drawn from all sections of America, from Europe, the West Indies, Africa, Asia, or where you will. Two hundred thousand Negroes living, loving, laughing, crying, procreating and dying in the segregated city section of Greater New York, about twenty-five blocks long and seven blocks wide. Like all of New York, Harlem is overcrowded. There are as many as 5,000 persons living in some single blocks; living in dark, mephitic tenements, jammed together, brownstone fronts, dingy elevator flats and modern apartment houses.

Living conditions are ribald and ridiculous. Rents are high and sleeping quarters at a premium. Landlords profiteer and accept bribes, putting out one tenant in order to house another willing to pay more rent. Tenants, in turn, sublet and profiteer on roomers. People rent a five-room apartment, originally planned for a small family, and crowd two over-sized families into it. Others lease or buy a private house and partition off spacious front and back rooms into two or three parts. Hallways are curtained off and lined with cots. Living rooms become triplex apartments. Clothes closets and washrooms become kitchenettes. Dining rooms, parlors, libraries, drawing rooms are all profaned by cots, day beds and snoring sleepers.

There is little privacy, little unused space. The man in the front room of a railroad flat, so called because each room opens into the other like coaches on a train, must pass through three other bedrooms in order to reach the bathroom stuck on the end of the kitchen. He who works nights will sleep by day in the bed of one who works days, and vice versa. Mother and father sleep in a three-quarter bed. Two adolescent children sleep on a portable cot set up in the parent's bedroom. Other cots are dragged by night from closets and corners to be set up in the dining room, in the parlor, or even in the kitchen to accommodate the remaining members of the family. It is all disconcerting, mad. There must be expansion. There is expansion, but it is not rapid enough or continuous enough to keep pace with the ever-growing population of Negro Harlem.

The first place in New York where Negroes had a segregated community was in Greenwich Village, but as the years passed and their numbers increased they soon moved northward into the twenties and lower thirties west of Sixth Avenue until they finally made one big jump and centered around west Fifty-third Street. About 1900, looking for better housing conditions, a few Negroes moved to Harlem. The Lenox Avenue subway had not yet been built and white landlords were having difficulty in keeping white tenants east of Seventh Avenue because of the poor transportation facilities. Being good businessmen they eagerly accepted the suggestion of a Negro real estate agent that these properties be opened to colored tenants. Then it was discovered that the few houses available would not be sufficient to accommodate the sudden influx. Negroes began to creep west of Lenox Avenue. White property owners and residents began to protest and tried to find means of checking or evicting unwelcome black neighbors. Negroes kept pouring in. Negro capital, belligerently organized, began to buy all available properties.

Then, to quote James Johnson:

> The whole movement, in the eyes of the whites, took on the aspect of an "invasion"; they became panic stricken and began fleeing as from a plague. The presence of one colored family in a block, no matter how well-bred and orderly, was sufficient to precipitate a flight. House after house and block after block was actually deserted. It was a great demonstration of human beings running amuck. None of them stopped to reason why they were doing it or what would happen if they didn't. The banks and the lending companies holding mortgages on these deserted houses were compelled to take them over. For some time they held these houses vacant, preferring to do that and carry the charges than to rent or sell them to colored people. But values dropped and continued to drop until at the outbreak of the war in Europe property in the northern part of Harlem had reached the nadir.

With the war came a critical shortage of common labor and the introducing of thousands of southern Negroes into northern industrial and civic centers. A great migration took place. Negroes were in search of a holy grail. Southern Negroes, tired of moral and financial blue days, struck out for the promised land, to seek adventure among factories, subways and skyscrapers. New York, of course, has always been a magnet for ambitious and adventurous Americans and foreigners. New York to the Negro meant Harlem, and the great influx included not only thousands of Negroes from every state in the Union, but also over thirty thousand immigrants from the West Indian Islands and the Caribbean regions. Harlem was the promised land.

Thanks to New York's many and varied industries, Harlem Negroes have been able to demand and find much work. There is a welcome and profitable diversity of employment. Unlike Negroes in Chicago, or in Pittsburgh, or in Detroit, no one industry is called upon to employ the greater part of their population. Negroes have made money in New York; Negroes have brought money to New York with them, and with this money they have bought property, built certain civic institutions and increased their business activities until their real estate holdings are now valued at more than sixty million dollars.

III. THE SOCIAL LIFE OF HARLEM

The social life of Harlem is both complex and diversified. Here you have two hundred thousand people collectively known as Negroes. You have pure-blooded Africans, British Negroes, Spanish Negroes, Portuguese Negroes, Dutch Negroes, Danish Negroes, Cubans, Puerto Ricans, Arabians, East Indians and black Abyssinian Jews in addition to the racially well-mixed American Negro. You have persons of every conceivable shade and color. Persons speaking all languages, persons representative of many cultures and civilizations. Harlem is a magic melting pot, a modern Babel mocking the gods with its cosmopolitan uniqueness.

The American Negro predominates and, having adopted all of white America's prejudices and manners, is inclined to look askance at his little dark-skinned brothers from across the sea. The Spanish Negro, i.e., those Negroes hailing from Spanish possessions, stays to himself and has little traffic with the other racial groups in his environment. The other foreigners, with the exception of the British West Indians are not large enough to form a separate social group and generally become quickly identified with the regulation social life of the community.

It is the Negro from the British West Indies who creates and has to face a disagreeable problem. Being the second largest Negro Group in Harlem, and being less susceptible to American manners and customs than others, he is frowned upon and berated by the American Negro. This intraracial prejudice is an amazing though natural thing. Imagine a community made up of people universally known as oppressed, wasting time and energy trying to oppress others of their kind, more recently transplanted from a foreign clime. It is easy to explain. All people seem subject to prejudice, even those who suffer from it most, and all people seem inherently to dislike other folk who are characterized by cultural and lingual differences. It is a failing of man, a curse of humanity, and if these differences are accompanied, as they usually are, by quarrels concerning economic matters, there is bound to be an intensifying of the bitter antagonism existent between the two groups. Such has been the case with the British West Indian in Harlem. Because of his numerical strength, because of his cockney English inflections and accent, because of his unwillingness to submit to certain American do's and don'ts, and because he, like most foreigners, has seemed willing to work for low wages, he has been hated and abused by his fellow-Harlemites. And, as a matter of protection, he has learned to fight back.

It has been said that West Indians are comparable to Jews in that they are "both ambitious, eager for education, willing to engage in business, argumentative, aggressive, and possess a great proselytizing zeal for any cause they espouse." Most of the retail business in Harlem is owned and controlled by West Indians. They are also well represented and often officiate as provocative agents and leaders in radical movements among Harlem Negroes. And it is obvious that the average American Negro, in manifesting a dislike for the West Indian Negro, is being victimized by that same delusion which he claims blinds the American white man; namely, that all Negroes are alike. There are some West Indians who are distasteful; there are some of all people about whom one could easily say the same thing.

It is to be seen then that all this widely diversified population would erect an elaborate social structure. For instance, there are thousands of Negroes in New York from Georgia. These have organized themselves into many clubs, such as the Georgia Circle or the Sons of Georgia. People from Virginia, South Carolina, Florida and other states do likewise. The foreign contingents also seem to have a mania for social organization. Social clubs and secret lodges are legion. And all of them vie with one another in giving dances, parties, entertainments and benefits in addition to public turnouts and parades.

Speaking of parades, one must mention Marcus Garvey. Garvey, a Jamaican, is one of the most widely known Negroes in contemporary life. He became notorious because of his Back-to-Africa campaign. With the West Indian population of Harlem as a nucleus, he enlisted the aid of thousands of Negroes all over America in launching the Black Star Line, the purpose of which was to establish a trade and travel route between America and Africa by and for Negroes. He also planned to establish a black empire in Africa of which he was to be emperor. The man's imagination and influence were colossal; his manifestations of these qualities often ridiculous and adolescent, though they seldom lacked color and interest.

Garvey added much to the gaiety and life of Harlem with his parades. Garmented in a royal purple robe with crimson trimmings and an elaborate headdress, he would ride in state down Seventh Avenue in an open limousine, surrounded and followed by his personal cabinet of high chieftains, ladies in waiting and protective legion. Since his incarceration in Atlanta Federal prison on a charge of having used the mails to defraud, Harlem knows no more such spectacles. The street parades held now are uninteresting and pallid when compared to the Garvey turnouts, brilliantly primitive as they were.

In addition to the racial and territorial divisions of the social structure there are also minor divisions determined by color and wealth. First there are the "dictys," that class of Negroes who constitute themselves as the upper strata and have lately done much wailing in the public places because white and black writers have seemingly overlooked them in their delineations of Negro life in Harlem. This upper strata is composed of the more successful and more socially inclined professional folk—lawyers, doctors, dentists, druggists, politicians, beauty parlor proprietors and real estate dealers. They are for the most part mulattoes of light brown skin and have succeeded in absorbing all the social mannerisms of the white American middle class. They live in the stately rows of houses on 138th and 139th Streets between Seventh and Eighth Avenues or else in the "high-tone" apartment houses on Edgecombe and St. Nicholas. They are both stupid and snobbish as is their class in any race. Their most compelling if sometimes unconscious ambition is to be as near white as possible, and their greatest expenditure of energy is concentrated on eradicating any trait or characteristic commonly known as negroid.

Their homes are expensively appointed and comfortable. Most of them are furnished in good taste, thanks to the interior decorator who was hired to do the job. Their existence is one of smug complacence. They are well satisfied with themselves and with their class. They are without a doubt the basic element from which the Negro aristocracy of the future will evolve. They are also good illustrations, mentally, sartorially and socially, of what the American standardizing machine can do to susceptible material.

These people have a social life of their own. They attend formal dinners and dances, resplendent in chic expensive replicas of Fifth Avenue finery. They arrange suitable intercoterie weddings, preside luxuriously at announcement dinners, prenuptial showers, wedding breakfasts and the like. They attend church socials, fraternity dances and sorority gatherings. They frequent the downtown theaters, and occasionally, quite occasionally, drop into one of the Harlem night clubs which certain of their lower caste brethren frequent and white downtown excursionists make wealthy.

Despite this upper strata which is quite small, social barriers among Negroes are not as strict and well regulated in Harlem as they are in other Negro communities. Like all cosmopolitan centers Harlem is democratic. People associate with all types should chance happen to throw them together. There are a few aristocrats, a plethora of striving bourgeoisie, a few artistic spirits and a great proletarian mass, which constitutes the most interesting and important element in Harlem, for it is this latter class and their institutions that gives the community its color and fascination.

IV. NIGHT LIFE IN HARLEM

Much has been written and said about night life in Harlem. It has become the *leit motif* of sophisticated conversation and shop girl intimacies. To call yourself a New Yorker you must have been to Harlem at least once. Every up-to-date person knows Harlem, and knowing Harlem generally means that one has visited a night club or two. These night clubs are now enjoying much publicity along with the New Negro and Negro art. They are the shrines to which white sophisticates, Greenwich Village artists, Broadway revellers and provincial commuters make eager pilgrimage. In fact, the white patronage is so profitable and so abundant that Negroes find themselves crowded out and even segregated in their own places of jazz.

There are, at the present time, about one dozen of these night clubs in Harlem—Bamville, Connie's Inn, Baron Wilkins, The Nest, Small's Paradise, The Capitol, The Cotton Club, The Green Cat, The Sugar Cane Club, Happy Rhones, The Hoofers Club and the Little Savoy. Most of these generally have from two to ten white persons for every black one. Only The Hoofers, The Little Savoy, and The Sugar Cane Club seem to cater almost exclusively to Negro trade.

At the Bamville and at Small's Paradise, one finds smart white patrons, the type that reads the ultrasophisticated *New Yorker*. Indeed, that journal says in its catalogue of places to go—"Small's and Bamville are the show places of Harlem for downtowners on their first excursion. Go late. Better not to dress." And so the younger generation of Broadway, Park Avenue, Riverside Drive, Third Avenue and the Bronx go late, take their own gin, applaud the raucous vulgarity of the entertainers, dance with abandon and go home with a headache. They have seen Harlem.

The Cotton Club and Connie's Inn make a bid for theatrical performers and well-to-do folk around town. The Nest and Happy Rhones attract traveling salesmen, store clerks and commuters from Jersey and Yonkers. The Green Cat has a large Latin clientele. Baron Wilkins draws glittering ladies from Broadway with their sleek gentlemen friends. Because of these conditions of invasion, Harlem's far-famed night clubs have become merely side shows staged for sensation-seeking whites. Nevertheless, they are still an egregious something to experience. Their smoking cavernous depths are eerie and ecstatic. Patrons enter, shiver involuntarily, then settle down to be shoved about and scared by the intangible rhythms that surge all around them. White night clubs are noisy. White night clubs affect weird music, soft light, Negro entertainers and dancing waiters, but, even with all these contributing elements, they cannot approximate the infectious rhythm and joy always found in a Negro cabaret.

Take the Sugar Cane Club on Fifth Avenue near 135th Street, located on the border of the most "low-down" section of Harlem. This place is visited by few whites or few "dicty" Negroes. Its customers are the rough-and-ready, happy-go-lucky more primitive type—street walkers, petty gamblers and pimps, with an occasional adventurer from other strata of society.

The Sugar Cane Club is a narrow subterranean passageway about twenty-five feet wide and 125 feet long. Rough wooden tables, surrounded by rough wooden chairs, and the orchestra stands, jammed into the right wall center, use up about three-quarters of the space. The remaining rectangular area is bared for dancing. With a capacity for seating about one hundred people, it usually finds room on gala nights for twice that many. The orchestra weeps and moans and groans as only an unsophisticated Negro jazz orchestra can. A blues singer croons vulgar ditties over the tables to individual parties or else wah-wahs husky syncopated blues songs from the center of the floor. Her act over, the white lights are extinguished, red and blue spot lights are centered on the diminutive dancing space, couples push back their chairs, squeeze out from behind the tables and from against the wall, then finding one another's bodies, sweat gloriously together, with shoulders hunched, limbs obscenely intertwined and hips wiggling; animal beings urged on by liquor and music and physical contact.

Small's Paradise, on Seventh Avenue near 135th Street, is just the opposite of the Sugar Cane Club. It caters almost exclusively to white trade with just enough Negroes present to give the necessary atmosphere and "difference." Yet even in Small's with its symphonic orchestra, full-dress appearance and dignified onlookers, there is a great deal of that unexplainable, intangible rhythmic presence so character-istic of a Negro cabaret.

In addition to the well-known cabarets, which are largely show places to curious whites, there are innumerable places—really speak-easies—which are open only to the initiate. These places are far more colorful and more full of spontaneous joy than the larger places to which one has ready access. They also furnish more thrills to the spectator. This is possible because the crowd is more select, the liquor more fiery, the atmosphere more intimate and the activities of the patrons not subject to be watched by open-mouthed white people from downtown and the Bronx.

One particular place known as the Glory Hole is hidden in a musty damp basement behind an express and trucking office. It is a single room about ten feet square and remains an unembellished basement except for a planed down plank floor, a piano, three chairs and a library table. The Glory Hole is typical of its class. It is a social club, commonly called a dive, convenient for the high times of a certain group. The men are unskilled laborers during the day, and in the evenings they round up their girls or else meet them at the rendezvous in order to have what they consider and enjoy as a good time. The women, like the men, swear, drink and dance as much and as vulgarly as they please. Yet they do not strike the observer as being vulgar. They are merely being and doing what their environment and their desire for pleasure suggest.

Such places as the Glory Hole can be found all over the so-called "bad lands" of Harlem. They are not always confined to basement rooms. They can be found in apartment flats, in the rear of barber shops, lunch counters, pool halls, and other such conveniently blind places. Each one has its regular quota of customers with just enough new patrons introduced from time to time to keep the place alive and prosperous. These intimate, lowdown civic centers are occasionally misjudged. Social service reports damn them with the phrase "breeding places of vice and crime." They may be. They are also good training grounds for prospective pugilists. Fights are staged with regularity and with vigor. And most of the regular customers have some mark on their faces or bodies that can be displayed as having been received during a battle in one of the glory holes.

The other extreme of amusement places in Harlem is exemplified by the Bamboo Inn, a Chinese-American restaurant that features Oriental cuisine, a jazz band and dancing. It is the place for select Negro Harlem's night life, the place where debutantes have their coming out parties, where college lads take their co-eds and society sweethearts and where dignified matrons entertain. It is a beautifully decorated establishment, glorified by a balcony with booths, and a large gyroflector, suspended from the center of the ceiling, on which colored spotlights play, flecting the room with triangular bits of vari-colored light. The Bamboo Inn is *the* place to see "high Harlem," just like the Glory Hole is *the* place to see "low Harlem." Well-dressed men escorting expensively garbed women and girls; models from Vanity Fair with brown, yellow and black skins. Doctors and lawyers, Babbitts and their ladies with fine manners (not necessarily learned through Emily Post), fine clothes and fine homes to return to when the night's fun has ended.

The music plays. The gyroflector revolves. The wellbred, polite dancers mingle on the dance floor. There are a few silver hip flasks. There is an occasional burst of too-spontaneous-for-the-environment laughter. The Chinese waiters slip around, quiet and bored. A big black-face bouncer, arrayed in tuxedo, watches eagerly for some too boisterous, too unconventional person to put out. The Bamboo Inn has only one blemishing feature. It is also the rendezvous for a set of oriental men who favor white women, and who, with their pale face partners, mingle with Harlem's four hundred.

When Harlem people wish to dance, without attending a cabaret, they go to the Renaissance Casino or to the Savoy, Harlem's two most famous public dance halls. The Savoy is the pioneer in the field of giving dance-loving Harlemites some place to gather nightly. It is an elaborate ensemble with a Chinese garden (Negroes seem to have a penchant for Chinese food—there are innumerable Chinese restaurants all over Harlem), two orchestras that work in relays, and hostesses provided at twenty-five cents per dance for partnerless young men. The Savoy opens at three in the afternoon and closes at three in the morning. One can spend twelve hours in this jazz palace for sixty-five cents, and the price of a dinner or an occasional sustaining sandwich and drink. The music is good, the dancers are gay, and the setting is conducive to joy.

The Renaissance Casino was formerly a dance hall, rented out only for social affairs, but when the Savoy began to flourish, the Renaissance, after closing a while for redecorations, changed its policy and reopened as a public dance hall. It has no lounging room or Chinese garden, but it stages a basket ball game every Sunday night that is one of the most popular amusement institutions in Harlem, and it has an exceptionally good orchestra, comfortable sitting-out places and a packed dance floor nightly.

Then, when any social club wishes to give a dance at the Renaissance, the name of the organization is flashed from the electric signboard that hangs above the entrance and in return for the additional and assured crowd, some division of the door receipts is made. The Renaissance is, I believe, in good Harlemese, considered more "dicty" than the Savoy. It has a more regulated and more dignified clientele, and almost every night in the week the dances are sponsored by some well-known social group.

In addition to the above two places, the Manhattan Casino, an elaborate dance palace, is always available for the more de luxe gatherings. It is at the Manhattan Casino that the National Association for the Advancement of Colored People has its yearly whist tournament and dance, that Harlem society folk have their charity balls, and select formals, and that the notorious Hamilton Lodge holds its spectacular masquerade each year.

All of the dances held in this Casino are occasions never to be forgotten. Hundreds of well-dressed couples dancing on the floor. Hundreds of Negroes of all types and colors, mingling together on the dance floor, gathering in the boxes, meeting and conversing on the promenade. And here and there an occasional white person, or is it a Negro who can "pass"?

Negroes love to dance, and in Harlem where the struggle to live is so intensely complex, the dance serves as a welcome and feverish outlet. Yet it is strange that none of these dance palaces are owned or operated by Negroes. The Renaissance Casino was formerly owned by a syndicate of West Indians, but has now fallen into the hands of a Jewish group. And despite the thousands of dollars Negroes spend in order to dance, the only monetary returns in their own community are the salaries paid to the Negro musicians, ushers, janitors and door-men. The rest of the profits are spent and exploited outside of Harlem.

This is true of most Harlem establishments. The Negro in Harlem is not, like the Negro in Chicago and other metropolitan centers, in charge of the commercial enterprises located in his community. South State Street in Chicago's great Black belt, is studded with Negro banks, Negro office buildings, housing Negro insurance companies, manufacturing concerns, and other major enterprises. There are no Negro controlled banks in Harlem. There are only branches of downtown Manhattan's financial institutions, manned solely by whites and patronized almost exclusively by Negroes. Harlem has no outstanding manufacturing concern like the

Overton enterprises in Chicago, the Poro school and factory in St. Louis, or the Madame Walker combine in Indianapolis. Harlem Negroes own over sixty million dollars worth of real estate, but they neither own nor operate one first-class grocery store, butchershop, dance hall, theater, clothing store or saloon. They do invest their money in barber shops, beauty parlors, pool halls, tailor shops, restaurants and lunch counters.

V. THE AMUSEMENT LIFE OF HARLEM

Like most good American communities the movies hold a primary position in the amusement life of Harlem. There are seven neighborhood motion picture houses in Negro Harlem proper, and about six big time cinema palaces on 125th Street that have more white patronage than black, yet whose audiences are swelled by movie fans from downtown.

The picture emporiums of Harlem are comparable to those in any residential neighborhood. They present second and third run features with supporting bills of comedies, novelties, and an occasional special performance when the management presents a bathing beauties contest, a plantation jubilee, an amateur ensemble and other vaudeville stunts. The Renaissance Theater, in the same building with the Renaissance Casino, is the cream of Harlem motion picture houses. It, too, was formerly owned and operated by Negroes, the only one of its kind in Harlem. Now Negroes only operate it. The Renaissance attracts the more select movie audiences; it has a reputable symphony orchestra, a Wurlitzer organ, and presents straight movies without vaudeville flapdoodle. It is spacious and clean and free from disagreeable odors.

The Roosevelt Theater, the New Douglas, and the Savoy are less aristocratic competitors. They show the same pictures as the Renaissance, but seem to be patronized by an entirely different set of people, and, although their interiors are more spacious, they are not as well decorated or as clean as the Renaissance. They attract a set of fresh youngsters, smart aleck youths and lecherous adult males who attend, not so much to see the picture as to pick up a susceptible female or to spoon with some girl they have picked up elsewhere. The places are also frequented by family groups, poor but honest folk, who cannot afford other forms or places of amusement.

The Franklin and the Gem are the social outcasts of the group. Their audiences are composed almost entirely of loafers from the low-grade pool rooms and dives in their vicinity, and tenement-trained drudges from the slums. The stench in these two places is nauseating. The Board of Health rules are posted conspicuously, admonishing patrons not to spit on the floor or to smoke in the auditorium, but the aisle is slippery with tobacco spew and cigarette smoke adds to the density of the foul air. The movies flicker on the screen, some wild west picture three or four years old, dirty babies cry in time with the electric piano that furnishes the music, men talk out loud, smoke, spit, and drop empty gin or whiskey bottles on the floor when emptied.

All of these places from the Renaissance to the Gem are open daily from two in the afternoon until eleven at night, and save for a lean audience during the supper hour are usually filled to capacity. Saturdays, Sundays and holidays are harvest times, and the Jewish representatives of the chain to which a theater belongs walk around excitedly and are exceedingly gracious, thinking no doubt of the quarters that are being deposited at the box office.

The Lafayette and Lincoln theaters are three-a-day combination movie and musical comedy revue houses. The Lafayette used to house a local stock company composed of all Negro players, but it has now fallen into less dignified hands. Each week it presents a new revue. These revues are generally weak-kneed, watery variations on downtown productions. If Earl Carroll is presenting Artists and Models on Broadway, the Lafayette presents Brown Skin Models in Harlem soon afterwards. Week after week one sees the same type of "high yaller" chorus, hears the same blues songs, and applauds different dancers doing the same dance steps. There is little originality on the part of the performers, and seldom any change of fare. Cheap imitations of Broadway successes, nudity, vulgar dances and vulgar jokes are the box office attractions.

On Friday nights there is a midnight show, which is one of the most interesting spectacles in Harlem. The performance begins some time after midnight and lasts until four or four-thirty the next morning. The audience is as much if not more interesting and amusing than the performers on the stage. Gin bottles are carried and passed among groups of friends. Cat calls and hisses attend any dull bit. Outspoken comments punctuate the lines, songs and dances of the performers. Impromptu acts are staged in the orchestra and in the gallery. The performers themselves are at their best and leave the stage to make the audience a part of their act. There are no conventions considered, no reserve is manifested. Everyone has a jolly good time, and after the theater there are parties or work according to the wealth and inclinations of the individual.

The Lincoln theater is smaller and more smelly than the Lafayette, and most people who attend the latter will turn up their noses at the Lincoln. It too has revues and movies, and its only distinguishing feature is that its shows are even worse than those staged at the Lafayette. They are so bad that they are ludicrously funny. The audience is comparable to that found in the Lafayette on Friday nights at the midnight jamboree. Performers are razzed. Chorus girls are openly courted or damned, and the spontaneous utterances of the patrons are far more funny than any joke the comedians ever tell. If one can stand the stench, one can have a good time for three hours or more just by watching the unpredictable and surprising reactions of the audience to what is being presented on the stage.

VI. HOUSE RENT PARTIES, NUMBERS
AND HOT MEN

The Harlem institutions that intrigue the imagination and stimulate the most interest on the part of an investigator are House Rent Parties, Numbers and Hot Men. House Rent parties are the result of high rents. Private houses containing nine or ten or twelve rooms rent from $185 up to $250 per month. Apartments are rated at $20 per room or more, according to the newness of the building and the conveniences therein. Five-room flats, located in walk-up tenements, with inside rooms, dark hallways and dirty stairs rent for $10 per room or more. It can be seen then that when the average Negro workingman's salary is considered (he is often paid less for his labors than a white man engaged in the same sort of work), and when it is also considered that he and his family must eat, dress and have some amusements and petty luxuries, these rents assume a criminal enormity. And even though every available bit of unused space is sub-let at exorbitant rates to roomers, some other source of revenue is needed when the time comes to meet the landlord.

Hence we have hundreds of people opening their apartments and houses to the public, their only stipulation being that the public pay twenty-five cents admission fee and buy plentifully of the food and drinks offered for sale. Although one of these parties can be found any time during the week, Saturday night is favored. The reasons are obvious; folk don't have to get up early on Sunday morning and most of them have had a pay day.

Of course, this commercialization of spontaneous pleasure in order to pay the landlord has been abused, and now there are folk who make their living altogether by giving alleged House Rent Parties. This is possible because there are in Harlem thousands of people with no place to go, thousands of people lonesome, unattached and cramped, who stroll the streets eager for a chance to form momentary contacts, to dance, to drink and make merry. They willingly part with more of the week's pay than they should just to enjoy an oasis in the desert of their existence and a joyful intimate party, open to the public yet held in a private home, is, as they say, "their meat."

So elaborate has the technique of these parties and their promotion become that great competition has sprung up between prospective party givers. Private advertising stunts are resorted to, and done quietly so as not to attract too much attention from the police, who might want to collect a license fee or else drop in and search for liquor. Cards are passed out in pool halls, subway stations, cigar stores, and on the street. This is an example:

> Hey! Hey!
> Come on boys and girls let's shake
> that thing
> Where?
> At
> Hot Poppa Sam's
> West 134th Street, three flights up.
> Jelly Roll Smith at the piano
> Saturday night, May 7, 1927
> Hey! Hey!

Saturday night comes. There may be only piano music, there may be a piano and drum, or a three or four-piece ensemble. Red lights, dim and suggestive, are in order. The parlor and the dining room are cleared for the dance, and one bedroom is utilized for hats and coats. In the kitchen will be found boiled pigs feet, ham hock and cabbage, hopping John (a combination of peas and rice), and other proletarian dishes.

The music will be barbarous and slow. The dancers will use their bodies and the bodies of their partners without regard to the conventions. There will be little restraint. Happy individuals will do solo specialties, will sing, dance—have Charleston and Black Bottom contests and breakdowns. Hard little tenement girls will flirt and make dates with Pool Hall Johnnies and drug store cowboys. Prostitutes will drop in and slink out. And in addition to the liquor sold by the house, flasks of gin, and corn and rye will be passed around and emptied. Here "low" Harlem is in its glory, primitive and unashamed.

I have counted as many as twelve such parties in one block, five in one apartment house containing forty flats. They are held all over Harlem with the possible exception of 137th, 138th and 139th Streets between Seventh and Eighth Avenues where the bulk of Harlem's upper class lives. Yet the house rent party is not on the whole a vicious institution. It serves a real and vital purpose, and is as essential to "low Harlem" as the cultured receptions and soirees held on "strivers' row" are to "high Harlem."

House rent parties have their evils; it is an economic evil and a social evil that makes them necessary, but they also have their virtues. Like all other institutions of man it depends upon what perspective you view them from. But regardless of abstract matters, house rent parties do provide a source of revenue to those in difficult financial straits, and they also give lonesome Harlemites, caged in by intangible bars, some place to have their fun and forget problems of color, civilization and economics.

Numbers, unlike house rent parties, is not an institution confined to any one class of Harlem folk. Almost everybody plays the numbers, a universal and illegal gambling pastime, which has become Harlem's favorite indoor sport.

Numbers is one of the most elaborate, big-scale lottery games in America. It is based on the digits listed in the daily reports of the New York stock exchange. A person wishing to play the game places a certain sum of money, from one penny up, on a number composed of three digits. This number must be placed in the hands of a runner before ten o'clock in the morning as the reports are printed in the early editions of the afternoon papers. The clearing house reports are like this:

Exchanges $1,023,000,000
Balances   128,000,000
Credit Bal.   98,000,000

The winning number is composed from the second and third digits in the millionth figures opposite exchanges and from the third figure in the millionth place opposite the balances. Thus if the report is like the example above, the winning number for that day will be 238.

An elaborate system of placement and paying off has grown around this game. Hundreds of persons known as runners make their rounds daily, collecting number slips and cash placements from their clients. These runners are the middle men between the public and the banker, who pays the runner a commission on all collections, reimburses winners, if there are any, and also gives the runner a percentage of his client's winnings.

These bankers and runners can well afford to be and often are rogues. Since numbers is an illegal pastime, they can easily disappear when the receipts are heavy or a number of people have chosen the correct three digits and wish their winnings. The police are supposed to make some effort to enforce the law and check the game. Occasionally a runner or a banker is arrested, but this generally occurs only when some irate player notifies the police that he "ain't been done right by." Numbers can be placed in innumerable ways, the grocer, the butcher, the confectioner, the waitress at the lunch counter, the soda clerk, and the choir leader all collect slips for the number bankers.

People look everywhere for a number to play. The postman passes, some addict notes the number on his cap and puts ten cents on it for that day. A hymn is announced by the pastor in church and all the members in the congregation will note the number for future reference. People dream, each dream is a symbol for a number that can be ascertained by looking in a dream book for sale at all Harlem newsstands. Street car numbers, house numbers, street numbers, chance calculations—anything that has figures on it or connected with it will give some player a good number, and inspire him to place much money on it.

There is slight chance to win, it is a thousand to one shot, and yet this game and its possible awards have such a hold on the community that it is often the cause for divorce, murder, scanty meals, dispossess notices and other misfortunes. Some player makes a "hit" for one dollar, and receives $540. Immediately his acquaintances and neighbors are in a frenzy and begin staking large sums on any number their winning friend happens to suggest.

It is all a game of chance. There is no way to figure out scientifically or otherwise what digits will be listed in the clearing house reports. Few people placing fifty cents on No. 238 stop to realize now many other combinations of three digits are liable to win. One can become familiar with the market's slump days and fat days, but even then the digits which determine the winning number could be almost anything.

People who are moral in every other respect, church going folk, who damn drinking, dancing, or gambling in any other form, will play the numbers. For some vague reason this game is not considered as gambling, and its illegality gives little concern to any one—even to the Harlem police, who can be seen slipping into a corner cigar store to place their number for the day with an obliging and secretive clerk.

As I write a friend of mine comes in with a big roll of money, $540. He has made a "hit." I guess I will play fifty cents on the number I found stamped inside the band of my last year's straw hat.

Stroll down Seventh Avenue on a spring Sunday afternoon. Everybody seems to be well dressed. The latest fashions prevail, and though there are the usual number of folk attired in outlandish color combinations and queer styles, the majority of the promenaders are dressed in good taste. In the winter, expensive fur coats swathe the women of Harlem's Seventh Avenue as they swathe the pale face fashionplates on Fifth Avenue down town, while the men escorting them are usually sartorially perfect.

How is all this well-ordered finery possible? Most of these people are employed as menials—dish washers, elevator operators, porters, waiters, red caps, longshore-men, and factory hands. Their salaries are notoriously low, not many men picked at random on Seventh Avenue can truthfully say that they regularly earn more than $100 per month, and from this salary must come room rent, food and other of life's necessities and luxuries. How can they dress so well?

There are, of course, the installment houses, considered by many authorities one of the main economic curses of our present day civilization, and there are numerous people who run accounts at such places just to keep up a front, but these folk have little money to jingle in their pockets. All of it must be dribbled out to the installment collectors. There was even one chap I knew, who had to pawn a suit he had bought on the installment plan in order to make the final ten dollar payment and prevent the credit house collector from garnisheeing his wages. And it will be found that the majority of the Harlemites, who must dress well on a small salary, shun the installment house leechers and patronize the "hot men."

"Hot men" sell "hot stuff," which when translated from Harlemese into En-glish, means merchandise supposedly obtained illegally and sold on the q.t. far below par. "Hot men" do a big business in Harlem. Some have apartments fitted out as showrooms, but the majority peddle their goods piece by piece from person to person.

"Hot stuff" is supposedly stolen by shoplifters or by store employes or by organized gangs, who raid warehouses and freight yards. Actually, most of the "hot stuff" sold in Harlem originally comes from bankrupt stores. Some ingenious group of people make a practice of attending bankruptcy sales and by buying blocks of merchandise get a great deal for a small sum of money. This merchandise is then given in small lots to various agents in Harlem, who secretly dispose of it.

There is a certain glamour about buying stolen goods aside from their cheapness. Realizing this, "hot men" and their agents maintain that their goods are stolen whether they are or not. People like to feel that they are breaking the law and when they are getting undeniable bargains at the same time, the temptation becomes twofold. Of course, one never really knows whether what they are buying has been stolen from a neighbor next door or bought from a defunct merchant. There have been many instances when a gentleman, strolling down the avenue in a newly acquired overcoat, has had it recognized by a former owner, and found himself either beaten up or behind the bars. However, such happenings are rare, for the experienced Harlemite will buy only that "hot stuff" which is obviously not secondhand.

One evening I happened to be sitting in one of the private reception rooms of the Harlem Y.W.C.A. There was a great commotion in the adjoining room, a great coming in and going out. It seemed as if every girl in the Y.W.C.A. was trying to crowd into that little room. Finally the young lady I was visiting went to investigate. She was gone for about fifteen minutes. When she returned she had on a new hat, which she informed me, between laughs at the bewildered expressions on my face, she had obtained from a "hot man" for two dollars. This same hat, according to her, would cost $10 downtown and $12 on 125th Street.

I placed my chair near the door and watched the procession of young women entering the room bareheaded and leaving with new head gear. Finally the supply was exhausted and a perspiring little Jew emerged, his pockets filled with dollar bills. I discovered later that this man was a store keeper in Harlem, who had picked up a large supply of spring hats at a bankruptcy sale and stating that it was "hot stuff" had proceeded to sell it not openly in his store, but sub rosa in private places.

There is no limit to the "hot man's" supply or the variety of goods he offers. One can, if one knows the ropes, buy any article of wearing apparel from him. And in addition to the professional "hot man" there are always the shoplifters and thieving store clerks, who accost you secretly and eagerly place at your disposal what they have stolen.

Hence low salaried folk in Harlem dress well, and Seventh Avenue is a fashionable street crowded with expensively dressed people, parading around in all their "hot" finery. A cartoonist in a recent issue of one of the Negro monthlies depicted the following scene: A number of people at a fashionable dance are informed that the police have come to search for some individual known to be wearing stolen goods. Immediately there is a confused and hurried exodus from the room because all of the dancers present were arrayed in "hot stuff."

This, of course, is exaggerated. There are thousands of well-dressed people in Harlem able to be well-dressed not because they patronize a "hot man," but because their incomes make it possible. But there are a mass of people, working for small wages, who make good use of the "hot man," for not only can they buy their much wanted finery cheaply, but, thanks to the obliging "hot man," can buy it on the installment plan. Under the circumstances, who cares about breaking the law?

VII. THE NEGRO AND THE CHURCH

The Negro in America has always supported his religious institutions even though he would not support his schools or business enterprises. Migrating to the city has not lessened his devotion to religious institutions even if it has lessened his religious fervor. He still donates a portion of his income to the church, and the church is still a major social center in all Negro communities.

Harlem is no exception to this rule, and its finest buildings are the churches. Their attendance is large, their prosperity amazing. Baptist, Methodist, Episcopal, Catholic, Presbyterian, Seventh Day Adventist, Spiritualist, Holy Roller and Abyssinian Jew—every sect and every creed with all their innumerable subdivisions can be found in Harlem.

The Baptist and the Methodist churches have the largest membership. There are more than a score of each. St. Phillips Episcopal Church is the most wealthy as well as one of the oldest Negro churches in New York. It owns a great deal of Harlem real estate and was one of the leading factors in urging Negroes to buy property in Harlem.

There are few new church buildings, most of them having been bought from white congregations when the Negro invaded Harlem and claimed it for his own. The most notable of the second-hand churches are the Metropolitan Baptist Church at 128th Street and Seventh Avenue, Salem M.E. Church at 129th Street and

Seventh Avenue, and Mt. Olive Baptist Church at 120th Street and Lenox Avenue. This latter church has had a varied career. It was first a synagogue, then it was sold to white Seventh Day Adventists and finally fell into its present hands.

The most notable new churches are the Abyssinian Baptist Church on 138th Street, Mother Zion on 137th Street, and St. Marks. The latter church has just recently been finished. It is a dignified and colossal structure occupying a triangular block on Edgecombe and St. Nicholas Avenues between 137th and 138th Streets. It is the latest thing in churches, with many modern attachments—gymnasium, swimming pool, club rooms, Sunday school quarters, and other sub-auditoriums. When it was formally opened there was a gala dedication week to celebrate the occasion. Each night services were held by the various secret societies, the Elks, the Masons, the Knights of Pythias, the Odd Fellows, and others. The members of every local chapter of the various orders turned out to do homage to the new edifice. The collection proceeds were donated to the church.

St. Marks goes in for elaborate ceremony quite reminiscent of the Episcopal or Roman Catholic service. The choir is regaled in flowing robes and chants hymns by Handel. The pulpit is a triumph of carving and wood decoration. There is more ceremony than sermon.

The better class of Harlemites attends the larger churches. Most of the so-called "dictys" are registered as "Episcopalians at St. Phillips," which is the religious sanctum of the socially elect and wealthy Negroes of Harlem. The congregation at St. Phillips is largely mulatto. This church has a Parish House that serves as one of the most ambitious and important social centers in Harlem. It supports a gymnasium that produces annually a first-class basket ball team, an art sketch class that is both large and promising, and other activities of interest and benefit to the community.

Every Sunday all of the churches are packed, and were they run entirely on the theatrical plan they would hang out the S.R.O. sign. No matter how large they are they do not seem to be large enough. And in addition to these large denominational churches there are many smaller ones also crowded, and a plethora of outlaw sects, ranging from Holy Rollers to Black Jews and Moslems.

The Holy Rollers collect in small groups of from twenty-five to one hundred and call themselves various things. Some are known as the Saints of God in Christ, others call themselves members of the Church of God and still others call themselves Sanctified Children of the Holy Ghost. Their meetings are primitive performances. Their songs and chants are lashing to the emotions. They also practice healing, and, during the course of their services, shout and dance as erotically and sincerely as savages around a jungle fire.

The Black Jews are a sect migrated from Abyssinia. Their services are similar to those in a Jewish Synagogue only they are of a lower order, for these people still believe in alchemy and practice polygamy when they can get away with it. Just recently a group of them were apprehended by agents from the Department of Justice for establishing a free love farm in the State of New Jersey. They were all citizens of Harlem and had induced many young Negro girls to join them.

The Mohammedans are beginning to send missionaries to work among Negroes in America. Already they have succeeded in getting enough converts in Harlem, Chicago, St. Louis and Detroit to establish mosques in these cities. There are about one hundred and twenty-five active members of the Mohammedan church in Harlem, practicing the precepts of the Koran under the leadership of an Islamic missionary.

The Spiritualist churches also thrive in Harlem. There are about twenty-five or more of their little chapels scattered about. They enjoy an enormous patronage from the more superstitious, ignorant classes. The leaders of the larger ones make most of their money from white clients, who drop in regularly for private sessions.

VIII. NEGRO JOURNALISM IN HARLEM

The Harlem Negro owns, publishes, and supports five local weekly newspapers. These papers are just beginning to influence Harlem thought and opinion. For a long time they were merely purveyors of local gossip and scandal. Now some of them actually have begun to support certain issues for the benefit of the community and to cry out for reforms in the regulation journalistic manner.

For instance, *The New York Age*, which is the oldest Negro weekly in New York, has been conducting a publicity campaign against numbers and saloons. These saloons are to this paper as unwelcome a Harlem institution as the numbers. Each block along the main streets has at least one saloon, maybe two or three. They are open affairs, save instead of calling themselves saloons, they call themselves cafés. To get in is an easy matter. One has only to approach the door and look at a man seated on a box behind the front window, who acknowledges your look by pulling a chain which releases a bolt on the door. Once in you order what you wish from an old-fashioned bartender and stand before an old-fashioned bar with a brass rail, mirrors, pictures, spittoons, and everything. What is more, they even have ladies' rooms in the rear.

The editor of *The New York Age*, in the process of conducting his crusade, published the addresses of all these saloons and urged that they be closed. The result of his campaign was that they are still open and doing more business than ever, thanks to his having informed people where they were located.

At first glance any of the Harlem newspapers gives one the impression that Harlem is a hotbed of vice and crime. They smack of the tabloid in this respect and should be considered accordingly. True, there is vice and crime in Harlem as there is in any community where living conditions are chaotic and crowded.

For instance, there are 110 Negro women in Harlem for every 100 Negro men. Sixty and six-tenths percent of them are regularly employed. This, according to social service reports, makes women cheap, and conversely I suppose makes men expensive. Anyway there are a great number of youths and men who are either wholly or partially supported by single or married women. These male parasites, known as sweetbacks, dress well and spend their days standing on street corners, playing pool, gambling and looking for some other "fish" to aid in their support. This is considered by some an alarming condition inasmuch as many immigrant youths from foreign countries and rural southern American districts naturally inclined to be lazy, think that it is smart and citified to be a parasite and do almost anything in order to live without working.

The newspapers of Harlem seldom speak of this condition, but their headlines give eloquent testimony to the results, with their reports of gun play, divorce actions (and in New York State there is only one ground for divorce) and brick-throwing parties. These conditions are magnified, of course, by proximity, and really are not important at all when the whole vice and crime situation in greater New York is taken under consideration.

To return to the newspapers, *The Negro World* is the official organ of the Garvey Movement. At one time it was one of the most forceful weeklies among Negroes. Now it has little life or power; its life-giving mentor, Marcus Garvey, being in Atlanta Federal Prison. Its only interesting feature is the weekly manifesto Garvey issues from his prison sanctum, urging his followers to remain faithful to the cause and not fight among themselves while he is kept away from them.

The Amsterdam News is the largest and most progressive Negro weekly published in Harlem. It, like all of its contemporaries, is conservative in politics and policy, but it does feature the work of many of the leading Negro journalists and has the most forceful editorial page of the group, even if it does believe that most of the younger Negro artists are "bad New Negroes."

The New York News is a political sheet, affecting the tabloid form. The *Tattler* is a scandal sheet. It specializes in personalities and theatrical and sport news.

IX. THE NEW NEGRO

Harlem has been called the center of the American Negroes' cultural renaissance and the mecca of the New Negro. If this is so, it is so only because Harlem is a part of New York, the cultural and literary capital of America. And Harlem becomes the mecca of the so-called New Negro only because he imagines that once there he can enjoy the cultural contact and intellectual stimulation necessary for his growth.

This includes the young Negro writer who comes to Harlem in order to be near both patrons and publishers of literature, and the young Negro artist and musician who comes to Harlem in order to be near the most reputable artistic and musical institutions in the country.

These folk, along with the librarians employed at the Harlem Branch of the New York Public Library, a few of the younger, more cultured professional men and women and the school teachers, who can be found in the grammar and high schools all over the city, constitute the Negro intelligentsia. This group is sophisticated and small and more a part of New York's life than of Harlem's. Its members are accepted as social and intellectual equals among whites downtown, and can be found at informal and formal gatherings in any of the five boroughs that compose greater New York. Harlem to most of them is just a place of residence; they are not "fixed" there as are the majority of Harlem's inhabitants.

Then there are the college youngsters and local intellectuals, whose prototypes can be found in any community. These people plan to attend lectures and concerts, given under the auspices of the Y.M.C.A., Y.W.C.A., churches, and public school civic centers. They are the people who form intercollegiate societies, who stage fraternity go-to-school campaigns, who attend the course of lectures presented by the Harlem Branch of the New York Public Library, during the winter months, and who frequent the many musical and literary entertainments given by local talent in Harlem auditoriums.

Harlem is crowded with such folk. The three great major educational institutions of New York, Columbia, New York University and the College of the City of New York, have a large Negro student attendance. Then there are many never-will-be-top-notch literary, artistic and intellectual strivers in Harlem as there are all over New York. Since the well advertised "literary renaissance," it is almost a Negro Greenwich Village in this respect. Every other person one meets is writing a novel, a poem or a drama. And there is seemingly no end to artists who do oils, pianists who pound out Rachmaninoff's Prelude in C Sharp Minor, and singers, with long faces and rolling eyes, who sing spirituals.

X. HARLEM—MECCA OF THE NEW NEGRO

Harlem, the so-called citadel of Negro achievement in the New World, the alleged mecca of the New Negro and the advertised center of colored America's cultural renaissance. Harlem, a thriving black city, pulsing with vivid passions, alive with colorful personalities, and packed with many types and classes of people.

Harlem is a dream city pregnant with wide-awake realities. It is a masterpiece of contradictory elements and surprising types. There is no end to its versatile presentation of people, personalities and institutions. It is a mad medley.

There seems to be no end to its numerical and geographical growth. It is spreading north, east, south and west. It is slowly pushing beyond the barriers imposed by white people. It is slowly uprooting them from their present homes in the near vicinity of Negro Harlem as it has uprooted them before. There must be expansion and Negro Harlem is too much a part of New York to remain sluggish and still while all around is activity and expansion. As New York grows, so will Harlem grow. As Negro America progresses, so will Negro Harlem progress.

New York is now most liberal. There is little racial conflict, and there have been no inter-racial riots since the San Juan Hill days. The question is will the relations between New York Negro and New York white man always remain as tranquil as they are today? No one knows, and once in Harlem one seldom cares, for the sight of Harlem gives any Negro a feeling of great security. It is too large and too complex to seem to be affected in any way by such a futile thing as race prejudice.

There is no typical Harlem Negro as there is no typical American Negro. There are too many different types and classes. White, yellow, brown and black and all the intervening shades. North American, South American, African and Asian; Northerner and Southerner; high and low; seer and fool—Harlem holds them all, and strives to become a homogeneous community despite its motley hodge-podge of incompatible elements, and its self-nurtured or outwardly imposed limitations.

DOWN UNDER IN HARLEM

LANGSTON HUGHES (1902–1967) was probably one of the most famous black poets produced in America. He was also a prolific writer in a number of genres, including translations, plays, fiction, articles and essays, children's books, autobiographies, and songs. He was one of the leading literary lights of the Harlem Renaissance. He wrote "Down Under in Harlem," about conditions in Harlem during the Second World War, for the March 27, 1944 issue of the *New Republic*.

If you are white and are reading this vignette, don't take it for granted that all Harlem is a slum. It isn't. There are big apartment houses up on the hill, Sugar Hill, and up by City College—nice high-rent houses with elevators and doormen, where Canada Lee lives, and W.C. Handy, and the George S. Schuylers, and the Walter Whites, where colored families send their babies to private kindergartens and their youngsters to Ethical Culture School. And, please, white people, don't think that all Negroes are the same. They aren't.

Last year's Harlem riots demonstrated this clearly. Most of the people on Sugar Hill were just as indignant about the riots as was Mayor LaGuardia. Some of them even said the riots put the Negro race back fifty years. But the people who live in the riot area don't make enough money really to afford the high rents and the high prices merchants and landlords charge in Harlem, and most of them are not acquainted personally—as are many Sugar Hillites—with liberals like Pearl Buck and John Haynes Holmes. They have not attended civic banquets at the Astor, or had luncheon with emancipated movie stars at Sardi's. Indeed, the average Harlemite's impression of white folks, democracy and life in general is rather bad.

Naturally, if you live on nice, tree-lined, quiet Convent Avenue, even though you are colored, it would never occur to you to riot and break windows. When some of the colored leaders whose names are often in the white newspapers, came out of their elevator houses and down into Harlem during the riots, to urge, with the best intentions in the world, that the mobs stop breaking windows and go home, lots of the rioters did not even know who they were. And others of them said, "Boo-oo-o! Go home yourself."

It is, I should imagine, nice to be smart enough and lucky enough to be among Dr. Du Bois' "talented tenth" and be a race leader and go to the symphony concerts and live on that attractive rise of bluff and parkway along upper Edgecombe Avenue overlooking the Polo Grounds, where the plumbing really works and the ceilings are high and airy. For just a few thousands a year one can live very well on Sugar Hill in a house with a white-tiled hall.

But under the hill on Eighth Avenue, on Lenox, and on Fifth there are places like this—dark, unpleasant houses with steep stairs and narrow halls, where the rooms are too small, the ceilings too low and the rents too high. There are apartments with a dozen names over each bell. The house is full of roomers. Papa and mama sleep in the living room, the kids in the dining room, lodgers in every alcove, and everything but the kitchen is rented out for sleeping. Cooking and meals are rotated in the kitchen.

In vast sections below the hill, neighborhood amusement centers after dark are gin mills, candy stores that sell King Kong (and maybe reefers), drug stores that sell geronimoes—dope tablets—to juveniles for pepping up cokes, pool halls where gambling is wide open and barbecue stands that book numbers. Sometimes, even the grocery stores have their little side rackets without the law. White men, more often than Negroes, own these immoral places where kids as well as grown-ups come.

The kids and the grown-ups are not criminal or low by nature. Poverty, however, and frustration have made some of them too desperate to be decent. Some of them don't try any more. Slum-shocked, I reckon.

One Saturday night last winter, I went into a barbecue stand where the juke-box was loud and the air thick with smoke. At the tables there were mostly young folks—nice, not very pretty girls dressed in their best, with young men who had cleaned up after work. Some of the young men still wore their last spring's artificial camel's-hair coats—a top coat in winter with the snow outside—but they were trying to look nice, to be nice in the Harlem slums.

A half-dozen teen-age boys came in and stood around listening to the records on the juke-box. Shortly, a quarrel began among them. Almost immediately knives were drawn and switch-blades flashed, and one youngster let a blackjack a foot long slide out of his sleeve.

The woman at the counter who served my sandwich said, "Somebody ought to call the cops." (As though cops could solve the problems of poverty and delinquency in Harlem.) The white proprietor behind the beer bar paid no attention to the turmoil. Short of murder or destruction, white proprietors in Harlem seldom mix in Negro squabbles—just as they never belong to neighborhood committees to improve conditions, either.

"I just don't want 'em to fight in here," the woman said, "that's all!"

The boys didn't fight. They simply milled around, showed their weapons, bluffed and cursed each other. But their language frightened some of the quiet, not-very-pretty girls at the tables with the young men in their thin near-camel's-hair coats, out on a Saturday night trying to look nice and have a nice quiet time.

Louis Jordan on the juke-box, loud. Over the music the woman behind the counter said, "This time of night, all these young boys ought to be home."

"That's right," I said.

Home. A dozen names on the bell. Roomers all over the house. No place for a kid to bring his friends. Only the pool halls open, the candy stores that boot-leg liquor, the barbecue stands where you can listen to the juke-box even if you're broke and don't want to buy anything, and the long Harlem streets outside dimmed out because Hitler might send his planes overhead some dark night.

Should the planes come, their bombs most certainly would be louder than the juke-boxes, and their flying fragments of metal sharper than the cheap steel of drug-store switch-blades in the hands of kids who have no homes where they can bring their friends. A piece of bomb can hit harder than a boy with a blackjack up his sleeve.

Hitler in Berlin. Bad kids in Harlem. Indignation in the Mayor's office. Also on Sugar Hill. Louis Jordan's records:

I'm gonna move . . .
. . . outskirts of town . . .

Barbecued ribs, a quarter. Sign:

DON'T ASK FOR CREDIT—HE'S DEAD!!!

Riots. Long discussions downtown about forming more committees to make more surveys for more reports for more detailed study by more politicians before taking action on conditions in Harlem.

Sign over the barbecue counter:

WE CAN'T PAY OUR BILLS WITH TRUST! CAN YOU?

That sign, of course, is in reference to credit for sandwiches. It has nothing to do with the democratic system. It simply means that if you haven't got a quarter, you don't eat. There has been a sort of permanent scarcity of quarters in Harlem, so that sign might very well serve the committees as a motto for their surveys.

THE HARLEM
RENAISSANCE

ARNA BONTEMPS (1902–1973) was a novelist, essayist, poet, and a general man of letters who cut his literary teeth as a young man during the Renaissance. He was very good friends with Langston Hughes and their correspondence, collected in *The Langston Hughes–Arna Bontemps Letters* (1980, edited by Charles H. Nichols), constituted a series of important documents about the shape of black literary history in the United States. Bontemps wrote this piece on the Renaissance long after it had ended, blending the stances of objective observer and inside participant and witness. "The Harlem Renaissance" appeared in *The Saturday Review* on March 22, 1947 and deals with the careers of Hughes and Countee Cullen.

New books of poems by Langston Hughes and Countée Cullen have appeared this year. Some readers, no doubt, will be reminded of the shy, disarming bows made by these new writers before literary circles back in the twenties, when neither of them had yet finished college. In the case of Cullen, who died a year ago January, there will be a tendency to summarize as well as reflect. His stature as a poet will be estimated. With Hughes, of course, only a tentative and partial measurement can be attempted. But whatever evaluations may follow, whatever ranks and positions may finally fall to them in American literature, there isn't likely to be much question about their importance to the Harlem renaissance, so well remembered by many. They were its heralds and its brightest stars.

Except for their ages (there was a difference of about a year) and the fact that each was a Negro American, they were not much alike. An observer got the impression that while they were drawn together by the common experience of writing poetry, they actually had remarkably little in common. Their personal backgrounds, their reading, their moods, their attitudes, their tastes and preferences—everything one saw in their personalities was different. Even when they wrote poems on identical subjects, as in Cullen's "Epitaph for a Poet" and Hughes's "The Dreamkeeper," the contrast was striking. Cullen's stanza goes:

> I have wrapped my dreams in a silken cloth.
> And laid them away in a box of gold!
> Where long will cling the lips of the moth,
> I have wrapped my dreams in a silken cloth;
> I hide no hate; I am not even wroth
> Who found earth's breath so keen and cold.
> I have wrapped my dreams in a silken cloth,
> And laid them away in a box of gold.

Hughes put the same idea in these words:

> Bring me all of your dreams,
> You dreamers,
> Bring me all of your
> Heart melodies
> That I may wrap them
> In a blue cloud-cloth
> Away from the too-rough fingers
> Of the world.

Cullen's verses skip; those by Hughes glide. But in life Hughes is the merry one. Cullen was a worrier. If these traits in the two poets stood out with less emphasis in the days of cultural and artistic awakening among Negroes, twenty-odd years ago, they were nevertheless present. Equally evident, then as later, was Cullen's tendency to get his inspiration, his rhythms and patterns as well as much of his substance from books and the world's lore of scholarship; while Hughes made a ceremony of standing on the deck of a tramp steamer and tossing into the sea, one by one, all the books he had accumulated before his twenty-first birthday. He need not have done it, of course, for he had never been chained to any tradition, and there isn't the least danger that he ever will be; yet this stern renunciation was in keeping with his old habit of using living models and taking poetic forms as well as content from folk sources.

Cullen was in many ways an old-fashioned poet. He never ventured very far from the Methodist parsonage in which he grew up in New York. A foster child, drawn into this shelter at an early age, he continued to cherish it gratefully. He paid his adopted parents a devotion, one is almost inclined to say a submission, only rarely rendered by natural sons. But it was all a part of his own choice. He did not stand in fear of his foster parents. He simply preferred pleasing them to having his own way. It is possible that he felt or imagined the cords of this relationship to be the kind that would not stand strain, but the decisions he made later do not seem to support such an idea.

By the time he was half way through DeWitt Clinton High School, Countée Cullen had written at least one of the poems on which his reputation was to be built. Those readers who now complain of Pre-Raphaelite Victorian echoes in his work, perhaps find significance in the fact that the composition was called "I Have a Rendezvous with Life" and that it was offered by the eager youngster "with apologies to the memory of Alan Seeger." At the time it came to notice, however, after winning a city-wide poetry prize for high school students, most responses were enthusiastic. Ministers in prominent pulpits took the poem as a text and preached sermons on it. Editorials quoted it. A cheerful shout went up.

Here, some voices cried, was a poetic voice—a Negro at that—who thought that life was good. Here was a fledgling singer, praise God, who gave you a tune you could hum. A Cullen rooting section, consisting mainly of readers who had little truck with most of the new poetry, stood by anxiously. A year or two passed. Cullen became a conspicuous high school graduate, took home medals and ribbons galore, and went to college fully dedicated to literature. He continued to be a good student—good enough, in fact, for Phi Beta Kappa—but his pride was in his poetry.

About half of his "best poems" were written while he was a student of New York University, and it was during these years that he first came up for consideration as an authentic American writer, the goal to which he aspired. Up at "The Dark Tower," a gathering place of awakened Harlem, the very name of which was taken from one of Cullen's sonnets, there was never any doubt that he would make it. At the *Opportunity* banquets, where prizes were awarded by that once-influential magazine in order to encourage the efforts of new Negro writers, it was taken for granted that Cullen was in. Before he finished college, his poems had been published in a dozen or more magazines, including *The Nation, Poetry, The American Mercury,* and *Harper's.* "Color," the first collection of these lyrics, made a solid impression in 1925, the year in which Cullen celebrated his twenty-second birthday, and "Copper Sun" and "The Ballad of the Brown Girl," both presenting more of his undergraduate output, followed in 1926 and 1928. Meanwhile, the young poet went abroad on a Guggenheim Fellowship, perhaps, as much as anything else, to take stock.

His stay in France was extended a year beyond his original plans, but even that wasn't long enough. His springtime leaves had fallen, and he was still waiting for a new season to bring another yield. He kept writing as a matter of habit, and the little shelf of his books increased steadily, but that wasn't the real thing; that wasn't what he was waiting for. A decade later he wrote to a friend: "My muse is either dead or taking a twenty-year sleep."

Notice was paid, on a more limited scale, to the adolescent writing of Langston Hughes. In his case this happened to consist of delightfully innocent little pieces like "Dressed Up," perhaps inspired by a childhood fondness for the work of Paul Laurence Dunbar. They appeared in the school publications of Central High in Cleveland, and it is unlikely that anyone used them as texts for sermons in those days. To achieve that special distinction, Hughes had to wait until a number of years later when, in a moment of puzzlement, no doubt, he composed and allowed to be published a little item called "Good-bye, Christ," which not only misrepresented himself, in the light of his total writing, but caused him to be misinterpreted, denounced, and abused from dozens of rostrums and platforms, picketed by the followers of Amy McPherson and the supporters of Gerald L. K. Smith, and derided before the nation in newspapers and magazines.

Mainly, however, the response to Hughes's early writing was neither sudden nor spontaneous. Even "The Negro Speaks of Rivers," a poem written in the weeks following his graduation from high school and which few people in any part of the world have been able to read without feeling, caught on slowly. It was hard for those readers who noticed a new Negro poet at that time to know what to make of a young man who wrote what he called a "Suicide's Note," saying:

> The calm,
> Cool face of the river
> Asked me for a kiss.

Was this a poem or not? There was another one that said only:

> I loved my friend.
> He went away from me.
> There is nothing more to say.

If these were puzzling to people whose reading experiences had been formal and conservative, the one which began:

> My old man's a white old man
> And my old mother's black,

was downright shocking. So was the free verse work in which Hughes insisted that a clean spittoon is "beautiful to the Lord." His preoccupation with low life, with the singers of blues, with rounders and cabaret girls, with the misery and exaltation of road workers and of shouting church folk bothered even those who had found something which they could admire in his "Fantasy in Purple" or his "Dream Variation." Nevertheless there were those who felt, even then, that this poet of broad human sympathies, this writer of effortless, almost casual, verses, this singer with an ear for street music and for the folk idioms of our modern urbanization was indeed an American original.

The career which began with the magazine publication of "The Negro Speaks of Rivers" in 1921 yielded "The Weary Blues," a first book of poems, in 1926, and Langston Hughes, home from world wanderings, found his lines being used as touchstones of an awakening movement. His poems were set to music, they were painted, they were danced. They were recited, they were interpreted, they were translated—the Latin Americans are particularly fond of them. They were drama- tized, they were recorded, they were imitated. To rest and perhaps recuperate from too much excitement—and perhaps to take stock—the poet went back to college and completed his interrupted schooling. The experience did him no more harm than had been done by the books he discarded at sea. On the other hand, it provided the calm security necessary to write his first novel. What he did about the curriculum is something of a mystery, but obviously he satisfied the requirements, for Lincoln University not only gave him a bachelor's degree but an honorary doctorate.

The literary and artistic movement which Cullen and Hughes highlighted was regarded sympathetically, but it was never quite certified or approved as a phase of America's cultural growth. In the twenties the Negro's gifts were still departmental- ized. There were poets in the United States, and there were Negro poets. There were musicians, and there were Negro musicians. There were painters, and there were Negro painters. Cullen abhorred this attitude. Almost his only public com- ments about the art in which he expressed himself were pleas for an evaluation of his work strictly on its merits, without racial considerations. He was to learn, however, that this was no small matter.

Cullen did not live to see another springtime resurgence of his own creative powers comparable with the impulse that produced his first three books of poetry, the books which give his selected poems most of their lilt and brightness. He did live to see young poets like Gwendolyn Brooks and Robert E. Hayden coming up for the kind of evaluation he had hoped to receive. Before he was forty, a second generation of the renaissance, owing much to him and to Langston Hughes, was on the way.

A curious footnote to these events now reveals that Langston Hughes, whose work seemed to have such a definite Negro flavor in the days of the Dark Tower, has not only written the lyrics for the successful musical adaptation of "Street Scene" but has also published "Fields of Wonder," a volume of poems which contains not a single blue note. The renaissance isn't over yet.

THE HARLEM GHETTO

JAMES BALDWIN (1924–1988) was one of most renowned black writers in American literary history. He achieved critical and commercial success through his plays and novels but was particularly admired for his essays. He was probably one of the finest essayists of his generation and his collections, *Notes of a Native Son* (1955), *Nobody Knows My Name* (1961), and *The Fire Next Time* (1963) were not only best sellers but were tremendously influential works in literary and political circles both then and now. Baldwin grew up in Harlem and his essay, "The Harlem Ghetto," reflects the insider's intimacy. The essay appeared in the February 1948 issue of *Commentary* and was republished in *Notes of a Native Son*.

Harlem, physically at least, has changed very little in my parents' lifetime or in mine. Now as then the buildings are old and in desperate need of repair, the streets are crowded and dirty, there are too many human beings per square block. Rents are 10 to 58 per cent higher than anywhere else in the city; food, expensive everywhere, is more expensive here and of an inferior quality; and now that the war is over and money is dwindling, clothes are carefully shopped for and seldom bought. Negroes, traditionally the last to be hired and the first to be fired, are finding jobs harder to get, and, while prices are rising implacably, wages are going down. All over Harlem now there is felt the same bitter expectancy with which, in my childhood, we awaited winter: it is coming and it will be hard; there is nothing anyone can do about it.

All of Harlem is pervaded by a sense of congestion, rather like the insistent, maddening, claustrophobic pounding in the skull that comes from trying to breathe in a very small room with all the windows shut. Yet the white man walking through Harlem is not at all likely to find it sinister or more wretched than any other slum.

Harlem wears to the casual observer a casual face; no one remarks that—considering the history of black men and women and the legends that have sprung up about them, to say nothing of the ever-present policemen, wary on the street corners—the face is, indeed, somewhat excessively casual and may not be as open or as careless as it seems. If an outbreak of more than usual violence occurs, as in 1935 or in 1943, it is met with sorrow and surprise and rage; the social hostility of the rest of the city feeds on this as proof that they were right all along, and the hostility increases; speeches are made, committees are set up, investigations ensue. Steps are taken to right the wrong, without, however, expanding or demolishing the ghetto. The idea is to make it less of a social liability, a process about as helpful as make-up to a leper. Thus, we have the Boys' Club on West 134th Street, the playground at West 131st and Fifth Avenue; and, since Negroes will not be allowed to live in Stuyvesant Town, Metropolitan Life is thoughtfully erecting a housing project called Riverton in the center of Harlem; however, it is not likely that any but the professional class of Negroes—and not all of them—will be able to pay the rent.

Most of these projects have been stimulated by perpetually embattled Negro leaders and by the Negro press. Concerning Negro leaders, the best that one can say is that they are in an impossible position and that the handful motivated by genuine concern maintain this position with heartbreaking dignity. It is unlikely that anyone acquainted with Harlem seriously assumes that the presence of one playground more or less has any profound effect upon the psychology of the citizens there. And yet it is better to have the playground; it is better than nothing; and it will, at least, make life somewhat easier for parents who will then know that their children are not in as much danger of being run down in the streets. Similarly, even though the American cult of literacy has chiefly operated only to provide a market for the *Reader's Digest* and the *Daily News*, literacy is still better than illiteracy; so Negro leaders must demand more and better schools for Negroes, though any Negro who takes this schooling at face value will find himself virtually incapacitated for life in this democracy. Possibly the most salutary effect of all this activity is that it assures the Negro that he is not altogether forgotten: people *are* working in his behalf, however hopeless or misguided they may be; and as long as the water is troubled it cannot become stagnant.

The terrible thing about being a Negro leader lies in the term itself. I do not mean merely the somewhat condescending differentiation the term implies, but the nicely refined torture a man can experience from having been created and defeated by the same circumstances. That is, Negro leaders have been created by the American scene, which thereafter works against them at every point; and the best that they can hope for is ultimately to work themselves out of their jobs, to nag contemporary American leaders and the members of their own group until a bad situation becomes so complicated and so bad that it cannot be endured any longer. It is like needling a blister until it bursts. On the other hand, one cannot help observing that some Negro leaders and politicians are far more concerned with their careers than with the welfare of Negroes, and their dramatic and publicized battles are battles with the wind. Again, this phenomenon cannot be changed without a change in the

American scene. In a land where, it is said, any citizen can grow up and become president, Negroes can be pardoned for desiring to enter Congress.

The Negro press, which supports any man, provided he is sufficiently dark and well-known—with the exception of certain Negro novelists accused of drawing portraits unflattering to the race—has for years received vastly confusing criticism based on the fact that it is helplessly and always exactly what it calls itself, that is, a press devoted entirely to happenings in or about the Negro world. This preoccupation can probably be forgiven in view of the great indifference and frequent hostility of the American white press. The Negro press has been accused of not helping matters much—as indeed, it has not, nor do I see how it could have. And it has been accused of being sensational, which it is; but this is a criticism difficult to take seriously in a country so devoted to the sensational as ours.

The best-selling Negro newspaper, I believe, is the *Amsterdam Star-News*, which is also the worst, being gleefully devoted to murders, rapes, raids on love-nests, interracial wars, any item—however meaningless—concerning prominent Negroes, and whatever racial gains can be reported for the week—all in just about that order. Apparently, this policy works well; it sells papers—which is, after all, the aim; in my childhood we never missed an edition. The day the paper came out we could hear, far down the street, the news vendor screaming the latest scandal and people rushing to read about it.

The *Amsterdam* has been rivaled, in recent years, by the *People's Voice*, a journal, modeled on *PM* and referred to as *PV*. *PV* is not so wildly sensational a paper as the *Amsterdam*, though its coverage is much the same (the news coverage of the Negro press is naturally pretty limited). *PV*'s politics are less murky, to the left of center (the *Amsterdam* is Republican, a political affiliation that has led it into some strange doubletalk), and its tone, since its inception, has been ever more hopelessly militant, full of warnings, appeals, and open letters to the government— which, to no one's surprise, are not answered—and the same rather pathetic preoccupation with prominent Negroes and what they are doing. Columns signed by Lena Horne and Paul Robeson appeared in *PV* until several weeks ago, when both severed their connections with the paper. Miss Horne's column made her sound like an embittered Eleanor Roosevelt, and the only column of Robeson's I have read was concerned with the current witch-hunt in Hollywood, discussing the kind of movies under attack and Hollywood's traditional treatment of Negroes. It is personally painful to me to realize that so gifted and forceful a man as Robeson should have been tricked by his own bitterness and by a total inability to understand the nature of political power in general, or Communist aims in particular, into missing the point of his own critique, which is worth a great deal of thought: that there are a great many ways of being un-American, some of them nearly as old as the country itself, and that the House Un-American Activities Committee might find concepts and attitudes even more damaging to American life in a picture like *Gone With the Wind* than in the possibly equally romantic but far less successful *Watch on the Rhine*.

The only other newspapers in the field with any significant sale in Harlem are the Pittsburgh *Courier*, which has the reputation of being the best of the lot, and the *Afro-American*, which resembles the *New York Journal-American* in layout and type and seems to make a consistent if unsuccessful effort to be at once readable, intelligent, and fiery. The *Courier* is a high-class paper, reaching its peak in the handling of its society news and in the columns of George S. Schuyler, whose Olympian serenity infuriates me, but who, as a matter of fact, reflects with great accuracy the state of mind and the ambitions of the professional, well-to-do Negro who has managed to find a place to stand. Mr. Schuyler, who is remembered still for a satirical novel I have not read, called *Black No More*, is aided enormously in this position by a genteel white wife and a child-prodigy daughter—who is seriously regarded in some circles as proof of the incomprehensible contention that the mating of white and black is more likely to produce genius than any other combination. (The *Afro-American* recently ran a series of articles on this subject, "The Education of a Genius," by Mrs. Amarintha Work, who recorded in detail the development of her mulatto son, Craig.)

Ebony and *Our World* are the two big magazines in the field, *Ebony* looking and sounding very much like *Life*, and *Our World* being the black man's *Look*. *Our World* is a very strange, disorganized magazine indeed, sounding sometimes like a college newspaper and sometimes like a call to arms, but principally, like its more skillful brothers, devoted to the proposition that anything a white man can do a Negro can probably do better. *Ebony* digs feature articles out of such things as the "real" Lena Horne and Negro FBI agents, and it travels into the far corners of the earth for any news, however trivial, concerning any Negro or group of Negroes who are in any way unusual and/or newsworthy. The tone of both *Ebony* and *Our World* is affirmative; they cater to the "better class of Negro." *Ebony*'s November 1947 issue carried an editorial entitled "Time To Count Our Blessings," which began by accusing Chester Himes (author of the novel *Lonely Crusade*) of having a color psychosis, and went on to explain that there are Negro racists also who are just as blind and dangerous as Bilbo, which is incontestably true, and that, compared to the millions of starving Europeans, Negroes are sitting pretty—which comparison, I hazard, cannot possibly mean anything to any Negro who has not seen Europe. The editorial concluded that Negroes had come a long way and that "as patriotic Americans" it was time "we" stopped singing the blues and realized just how bright the future was. These cheering sentiments were flanked—or underscored, if you will—by a photograph on the opposite page of an aging Negro farm woman carrying home a bumper crop of onions. It apparently escaped the editors of *Ebony* that the very existence of their magazine, and its table of contents for any month, gave the lie to this effort to make the best of a bad bargain.

The true *raison d'être* of the Negro press can be found in the letters-to-the-editor sections, where the truth about life among the rejected can be seen in print. It is the terrible dilemma of the Negro press that, having no other model, it models itself on the white press, attempting to emulate the same effortless, sophisticated tone—a tone its subject matter renders utterly unconvincing. It is simply impossible not to sing the blues, audibly or not, when the lives lived by Negroes are so inescapably harsh and stunted. It is not the Negro press that is at fault: whatever contradictions, inanities, and political infantilism can be charged to it can be charged equally to the American press at large. It is a black man's newspaper straining for recognition and a foothold in the white man's world. Matters are not helped in the least by the fact that the white man's world, intellectually, morally, and spiritually, has the meaningless ring of a hollow drum and the odor of slow death. Within the body of the Negro press all the wars and falsehoods, all the decay and dislocation and struggle of our society are seen in relief.

The Negro press, like the Negro, becomes the scapegoat for our ills. There is no difference, after all, between the *Amsterdam*'s handling of a murder on Lenox Avenue and the *Daily News*' coverage of a murder on Beekman Hill; nor is there any difference between the chauvinism of the two papers, except that the *News* is smug and the *Amsterdam* is desperate. Negroes live violent lives, unavoidably; a Negro press without violence is therefore not possible; and, further, in every act of violence, particularly violence against white men, Negroes feel a certain thrill of identification, a wish to have done it themselves, a feeling that old scores are being settled at last. It is no accident that Joe Louis is the most idolized man in Harlem. He has succeeded on a level that white America indicates is the only level for which it has any respect. We (Americans in general, that is) like to point to Negroes and to most of their activities with a kind of tolerant scorn; but it is ourselves we are watching, ourselves we are damning, or—condescendingly—bending to save.

I have written at perhaps excessive length about the Negro press, principally because its many critics have always seemed to me to make the irrational demand that the nation's most oppressed minority behave itself at all times with a skill and foresight no one ever expected of the late Joseph Patterson or ever expected of Hearst; and I have tried to give some idea of its tone because it seems to me that it is here that the innate desperation is betrayed. As for the question of Negro advertising, which has caused so much comment, it seems to me quite logical that any minority identified by the color of its skin and the texture of its hair would eventually grow self-conscious about these attributes and avoid advertising lotions that made the hair kinkier and soaps that darkened the skin. The American ideal, after all, is that everyone should be as much alike as possible.

It is axiomatic that the Negro is religious, which is to say that he stands in fear of the God our ancestors gave us and before whom we all tremble yet. There are probably more churches in Harlem than in any other ghetto in this city and they are going full blast every night and some of them are filled with praying people every day. This, supposedly, exemplifies the Negro's essential simplicity and goodwill; but it is actually a fairly desperate emotional business.

These churches range from the august and publicized Abyssinian Baptist Church on West 138th Street to resolutely unclassifiable lofts, basements, storefronts, and even private dwellings. Nightly, Holyroller ministers, spiritualists, self-appointed prophets and Messiahs gather their flocks together for worship and for strength through joy. And this is not, as *Cabin in the Sky* would have us believe, merely a childlike emotional release. Their faith may be described as childlike, but the end it serves is often sinister. It may, indeed, "keep them happy"—a phrase carrying the inescapable inference that the way of life imposed on Negroes makes them quite actively unhappy—but also, and much more significantly, religion operates here as a complete and exquisite fantasy revenge: white people own the earth and commit all manner of abomination and injustice on it; the bad will be punished and the good rewarded, for God is not sleeping, the judgment is not far off. It does not require a spectacular degree of perception to realize that bitterness is here neither dead nor sleeping, and that the white man, believing what he wishes to believe, has misread the symbols. Quite often the Negro preacher descends to levels less abstract and leaves no doubt as to what is on his mind: the pressure of life in Harlem, the conduct of the Italian-Ethiopian war, racial injustice during the recent war, and the terrible possibility of yet another very soon. All these topics provide excellent springboards for sermons thinly coated with spirituality but designed mainly to illustrate the injustice of the white American and anticipate his certain and long overdue punishment.

Here, too, can be seen one aspect of the Negro's ambivalent relation to the Jew. To begin with, though the traditional Christian accusation that the Jews killed Christ is neither questioned nor doubted, the term "Jew" actually operates in this initial context to include all infidels of white skin who have failed to accept the Savior. No real distinction is made: the preacher begins by accusing the Jews of having refused the light and proceeds from there to a catalog of their subsequent sins and the sufferings visited on them by a wrathful God. Though the notion of the suffering is based on the image of the wandering, exiled Jew, the context changes imperceptibly, to become a fairly obvious reminder of the trials of the Negro, while the sins recounted are the sins of the American republic.

At this point, the Negro identifies himself almost wholly with the Jew. The more devout Negro considers that he *is* a Jew, in bondage to a hard taskmaster and waiting for a Moses to lead him out of Egypt. The hymns, the texts, and the most favored legends of the devout Negro are all Old Testament and therefore Jewish in origin: the flight from Egypt, the Hebrew children in the fiery furnace, the terrible jubilee songs of deliverance: *Lord, wasn't that hard trials, great tribulations, I'm bound to leave this land!* The covenant God made in the beginning with Abraham and which was to extend to his children and to his children's children forever is a covenant made with these latter-day exiles also: as Israel was chosen, so are they. The birth and death of Jesus, which adds a non-Judaic element, also implements this identification. It is the covenant made with Abraham again, renewed, signed with his blood. ("Before Abraham was, I am.") Here the figure of Jesus operates as the intercessor, the bridge from earth to heaven; it was Jesus who made it possible, who made salvation free to all, "to the Jew first and afterwards the Gentile." The images of the suffering Christ and the suffering Jew are wedded with the image of the suffering slave, and they are one: the people that walked in darkness have seen a great light.

But if the Negro has bought his salvation with pain and the New Testament is used to prove, as it were, the validity of the transformation, it is the Old Testament which is clung to and most frequently preached from, which provides the emotional fire and anatomizes the path of bondage; and which promises vengeance and assures the chosen of their place in Zion. The favorite text of my father, among the most earnest of ministers, was not "Father, forgive them, for they know not what they do," but "How can I sing the Lord's song in a strange land?"

This same identification, which Negroes, since slavery, have accepted with their mother's milk, serves, in contemporary actuality, to implement an involved and specific bitterness. Jews in Harlem are small tradesmen, rent collectors, real estate agents, and pawnbrokers; they operate in accordance with the American business tradition of exploiting Negroes, and they are therefore identified with oppression and are hated for it. I remember meeting no Negro in the years of my growing up, in my family or out of it, who would really ever trust a Jew, and few who did not, indeed, exhibit for them the blackest contempt. On the other hand, this did not prevent their working for Jews, being utterly civil and pleasant to them, and, in most cases, contriving to delude their employers into believing that, far from harboring any dislike for Jews, they would rather work for a Jew than for anyone else. It is part of the price the Negro pays for his position in this society that, as Richard Wright points out, he is almost always acting. A Negro learns to gauge precisely what reaction the alien person facing him desires, and he produces it with disarming artlessness. The friends I had, growing up and going to work, grew more bitter every day; and, conversely, they learned to hide this bitterness and to fit into the pattern Gentile and Jew alike had fixed for them.

The tension between Negroes and Jews contains an element not characteristic of Negro-Gentile tension, an element which accounts in some measure for the Negro's tendency to castigate the Jew verbally more often than the Gentile, and which might lead one to the conclusion that, of all white people on the face of the earth, it is the Jew whom the Negro hates most. When the Negro hates the Jew *as a Jew* he does so partly because the nation does and in much the same painful fashion that he hates himself. It is an aspect of his humiliation whittled down to a manageable size and then transferred; it is the best form the Negro has for tabulating vocally his long record of grievances against his native land.

At the same time, there is a subterranean assumption that the Jew should "know better," that he has suffered enough himself to know what suffering means. An understanding is expected of the Jew such as none but the most naïve and visionary Negro has ever expected of the American Gentile. The Jew, by the nature of his own precarious position, has failed to vindicate this faith. Jews, like Negroes, must use every possible weapon in order to be accepted, and must try to cover their vulnerability by a frenzied adoption of the customs of the country; and the nation's treatment of Negroes is unquestionably a custom. The Jew has been taught—and, too often, accepts—the legend of Negro inferiority; and the Negro, on the other hand, has found nothing in his experience with Jews to counteract the legend of Semitic greed. Here the American white Gentile has two legends serving him at once: he has divided these minorities and he rules.

It seems unlikely that within this complicated structure any real and systematic cooperation can be achieved between Negroes and Jews. (This is in terms of the over-all social problem and is not meant to imply that individual friendships are impossible or that they are valueless when they occur.) The structure of the American commonwealth has trapped both these minorities into attitudes of perpetual hostility. They do not dare trust each other—the Jew because he feels he must climb higher on the American social ladder and has, so far as he is concerned, nothing to gain from identification with any minority even more unloved than he; while the Negro is in the even less tenable position of not really daring to trust anyone.

This applies, with qualifications and yet with almost no exceptions, even to those Negroes called progressive and "unusual." Negroes of the professional class (as distinct from professional Negroes) compete actively with the Jew in daily contact; and they wear anti-Semitism as a defiant proof of their citizenship; their positions are too shaky to allow them any real ease or any faith in anyone. They do not trust whites or each other or themselves; and, particularly and vocally, they do not trust Jews. During my brief days as a Socialist I spent more than one meeting arguing against anti-Semitism with a Negro college student, who was trying to get into civil service and was supporting herself meanwhile as a domestic. She was by no means a stupid girl, nor even a particularly narrow-minded one: she was all in favor of the millennium, even to working with Jews to achieve it; but she was not prepared ever to accept a Jew as a friend. It did no good to point out, as I did, that the exploitation of which she accused the Jews was American, not Jewish, that in fact, behind the Jewish face stood the American reality. And *my* Jewish friends in high school were not like that, I said, they had no intention of exploiting *me*, we did not hate each other. (I remember, as I spoke, being aware of doubt crawling like fog in the back of my mind.) This might all be very well, she told me, we were children now, with no need to earn a living. Wait until later, when your friends go into business and you try to get a job. You'll see!

It is this bitterness—felt alike by the inarticulate, hungry population of Harlem, by the wealthy on Sugar Hill, and by the brilliant exceptions ensconced in universities—which has defeated and promises to continue to defeat all efforts at interracial understanding. I am not one of the people who believe that oppression imbues a people with wisdom or insight or sweet charity, though the survival of the Negro in this country would simply not have been possible if this bitterness had been all he felt. In America, though, life seems to move faster than anywhere else on the globe and each generation is promised more than it will get: which creates, in each generation, a furious, bewildered rage, the rage of people who cannot find solid ground beneath their feet. Just as a mountain of sociological investigations, committee reports, and plans for recreational centers have failed to change the face of Harlem or prevent Negro boys and girls from growing up and facing, individually and alone, the unendurable frustration of being always, everywhere, inferior—until finally the cancer attacks the mind and warps it—so there seems no hope for better Negro-Jewish relations without a change in the American pattern.

Both the Negro and the Jew are helpless; the pressure of living is too immediate and incessant to allow time for understanding. I can conceive of no Negro native to this country who has not, by the age of puberty, been irreparably scarred by the conditions of his life. All over Harlem, Negro boys and girls are growing into stunted maturity, trying desperately to find a place to stand; and the wonder is not that so many are ruined but that so many survive. The Negro's outlets are desperately constricted. In his dilemma he turns first upon himself and then upon whatever most represents to him his own emasculation. Here the Jew is caught in the American crossfire. The Negro, facing a Jew, hates, at bottom, not his Jewishness but the color of his skin. It is not the Jewish tradition by which he has been betrayed but the tradition of his native land. But just as a society must have a scapegoat, so hatred must have a symbol. Georgia has the Negro and Harlem has the Jew.

IIII

ON BEING

SUBVERSIVE

Although few blacks ever became card-carrying communists, leftist and Marxist thought was a big influence among several black intellectual figures, most notably Langston Hughes, Richard Wright, Angela Davis, Eldridge Cleaver, Amiri Baraka, W. E. B. Du Bois and Paul Robeson. Ironically, one of the most intellectual black figures and political activists of the 20th century, A. Philip Randolph, was a socialist and a radical yet fiercely denounced communism. A discussion of communism figured importantly in Harold Cruse's seminal work, *The Crisis of the Negro Intellectual* (1967), and the denouncement of radical leftist (that is, assimilationist) politics was what estranged black cultural nationalists of the late 1960s from not only white sympathizers like SDS but also black radical groups like the Black Panthers. The reasons why communism never succeeded among blacks in the 1920s and 1930s when the opportunity was most ripe for such conversion are well-known now: first, the communists themselves were inept at pushing their cause among the black masses, having difficulty even understanding what sort of group they were dealing with, a peasantry, a proletariat, a nation, a sub-culture (a difficulty in structuring an ideology for a group identity which in fact has beset and continues to beset blacks themselves in a different way); second, a political ideology that denied religion and God was not likely to succeed among a people who had strong religious faith and who tended to see the world in spiritual, often even mystical terms; third, paradoxically, despite their strong religious faith, blacks as a group, especially underclass blacks, exhibit a strong fatalism and resignation to the way the world is (this impulse is the sociological and psychological origins of blues music, an art form that most radical blacks find to be "counterrevolutionary"); fourth, the white communists could not purge themselves of a racism that was apparent to most blacks who became involved with communism. The following essays examine various facets of the black experience with radical politics or radical leftist political expression.

WHY I AM A COMMUNIST

BENJAMIN J. DAVIS, JR. (1903–1964) was a
brilliant lawyer and one of the Communist party's ablest leaders during
the 1930s and 1940s. He was the editor of the *Harlem Liberator*, an
important communist publication aimed at the black masses. Davis, born
into a well-to-do black family, and educated at Amherst and Harvard,
first came to notice in the early thirties as the lawyer of Angelo Herndon,
a black organizer who faced the death penalty under a slave insurrection
act in Georgia because of his activities. Davis was a patron and supporter
of Richard Wright during the famed black novelist's early days as a
communist and a writer. Davis even praised Wright's *Native Son* when it
was first published in 1940 although party leaders generally despised it.
"Why I Am a Communist" was published in *Phylon*, Second Quarter,
1947, at a time when anti-communist feeling in America was running
high.

When, a few weeks ago, *Phylon* invited me to write an article on "Why
I am a Communist," I accepted with pleasure and humility. It is not
often that one has the opportunity to contribute to a publication that
stands its ground for the good old American principle of free speech against the
present reactionary storms that threaten to obliterate this and all other democratic
liberties.

In the midst of the basest campaign of calumny against the Communist Party—
which is, by no means, directed exclusively at the Communists—this is as good a
time as any to recall once more the truths about the Communists, even though
these truths are evident in the deeds of the Communists, as well as in their publicly-
accessible literature and program. In fact, the drive against the Communists is
aimed, above all, against the labor movement, against all anti-fascists, liberals, and

progressives, against democracy—and against truth itself. Whether one agrees with the Communist Party or not, one must at least know the truth about it. One must not permit his ideas to be shaped by the hysteria which now passes as a "crusade against Communism."

Everywhere one turns today—over the big business-controlled radio and the monopoly press—it is "Communist this" and "Communist that." In most cases, it is neither "this" nor "that." Quite the contrary. The big gobs of mud thrown in the direction of the Communists inevitably splash their filth upon everything else decent and forward-looking in American life. This, of course, is not difficult for the Negro people to understand. For, of all the minority groups in the United States, none have been splashed with more mud than the Negro, at the hands of the monopoly-press and other big-money controlled avenues of propaganda and information.

Anti-Communism has its source in the ruling circles of big business and domestic fascism within our country. But it would be a major error to identify with these sinister circles the millions of workers and common people—Negro and white—who are not Communists or who do not accept the Communist program. For they are, like the Communists, victimized by these same groups. Their failure to accept or to know the truth about the Communists is due to honest misconceptions, lack of information and serious questions which they have not yet been able to answer to their satisfaction. This is true even though the contributory conditions of their misconceptions are created by the high-powered anti-Communist campaign of reaction.

It is not the purpose of this article to answer seriatim all the assaults upon common sense and upon the Communist Party, which are being feverishly promoted by reaction. There is no space for that. Besides, to attempt to reply to some of the unbelievable accusations against Communists would be an insult to the average American's intelligence. We are being deluged with the teachings of the "Hitler Big Lie." For example, the canard that every Communist has his pockets lined with "Moscow gold." If that were true, one could be sure that there would scarcely be any room in our party for workers. The capitalists, to whom gold is god of the universe, would crowd them out. Of all the weaknesses that the Communist Party possesses, and we have our share, that of being a haven for the lords of the monopolies and trusts is not one of them.

The choice invective being hurled upon the Communist Party by the reactionaries and the home-grown Hitlerites constitutes one of the many sound reasons why I am a Communist. After all, is it not an honor—better still, isn't it a sign of treading the correct path—to be assailed by the two most notorious un-American characters in political life, Bilbo and Rankin? In fact, those upholders of American democracy who, for one reason or another, have never been assailed by Bilbo or Rankin or have never been called a Communist had better self-critically examine the quality of their pro-democratic activity.

There are many approaches to answering the question of "Why I am a Communist," all of which are interconnected and which enter into my convictions. Obviously, one cannot go into the whole range of them here. For purposes of this paper, I shall limit myself principally to explaining briefly why, as a Negro American, I am a Communist.

As a Negro American, I want to be free. I want equal opportunities, equal rights; I want to be accorded the same dignity as a human being and the same status as a citizen as any other American. This is my constitutional right. I want first-class, unconditional citizenship. I want it, and am entitled to it, now.

I want to be free of discrimination, Jim Crow, segregation, lynch law; I want to be free of second-class citizenship. In short, I want, as an American citizen, to enjoy the four freedoms which were proclaimed by the late Franklin D. Roosevelt, and which the State Department is interested hypocritically in prating about for every place except America.

This is the deepest and most determined desire of the fifteen million Negro citizens of America. All Negroes, in one form or another—or to one degree or another—are affected by Jim Crow, segregation and discrimination. The Negro workers, that is, the great mass of Negroes, bear the heaviest brunt of the national Jim Crow system. But the relatively tiny Negro upper class, as well as the middle class, are also hit by discrimination. They have neither political, social nor economic equality, and they are confined almost exclusively to the Negro market, which they must share with the white ruling class, without being able to share equally the general market of white consumers over which Wall Street maintains undisputed sway.

On the elementary issues of democracy in the deep South, where the great majority of the Negro people live, the white primary, injustice in the courts, lynch terror, lack of educational facilities, Jim Crow are endured by the Negro from top to bottom. I, for example, through no virtue of my own, was born into a middle class family, and received essentially the same educational advantages of one from a white middle class family. But when I board the trolley in Atlanta or Birmingham, I am not asked my class origin among the Negroes, nor are my university degrees inquired about. I must still sit in the Jim Crow section of the car. Discrimination cuts across all sections and classes of the Negro people. So with other walks of life. The white citizen of any class does not have that additional indignity to undergo, even though he may be exploited as a worker.

The Jim Crow system has its sharpest expressions in the South. But it spreads its tentacles all over America, including New York, where I share in common with all other Negroes the denial of my constitutional right to live, for example, at 72nd Street and Fifth Avenue, an exclusive lily-white area. The restrictive covenant, against which the Negro people, their labor and progressive white allies are fighting, makes quite immaterial any Negro's ability to pay the high rent at 72nd Street. That, too, is Jim Crow à la New York, and it works its ways not only in housing but in jobs, civil rights, the slum-infested ghetto, education and in other fields— sometimes covertly and subtly, but, nevertheless, it is there.

My personal daily experience with Jim Crow—which experiences need no detailing because they are universally recognized as the basic experience of the Negro people—confronted me all the way from my native state of Georgia to Massachusetts, where I attended Amherst College and Harvard Law School.

It is certainly ludicrous to observe the imperialist troubadours of a World War III—together with the monopoly press and radio—attacking the Soviet Union by referring to an "iron curtain" allegedly maintained by the Soviets against the world.

For the real "iron curtain," which becomes at times cruelly literal, is the one maintained in our country, separating the Negro Americans from their birthright—their constitutional rights as free and equal citizens. Such is life for the Negro people in the United States—such are the facts—without any "ifs," "ands" or "buts" or so-called "political propaganda."

I am a typical American, who loves liberty and freedom—the same liberty and freedom that a Dewey and a Truman would sacrifice to the golden altar of American imperialism, in the name of "fighting Communism."

Out of my personal experiences as a Negro American, and in quest of the liberty, freedom and equal rights proclaimed in the Constitution, the Bill of Rights and the Declaration of Independence, I, like thousands of other Negroes—and white citizens—joined the Communist Party.

I became a member of the Party in January, 1933, in the heat of battle. At the time, I was serving as defense attorney for Angelo Herndon in Atlanta, Georgia, where Herndon, an eighteen-year-old Negro youth, had been framed on a charge of inciting to insurrection—a charge based on an antiquated and outmoded statute. The charge carried with it the death penalty, but the jury "mercifully"—as I was given to understand by the judge—recommended twenty years for young Herndon on the Georgia chaingang! Such "mercy," of course, meant a living death instead of an instantaneous death in the electric chair.

Of what was Herndon "guilty"? He had led a demonstration of unemployed Negro and white workers to City Hall, had been found with a couple of Communist pamphlets in his possession, and possessed a firm and inspiringly defiant advocacy of the freedom of Negroes and of the liberation of the white masses from exploitation. The "dangerous" policy he then espoused as a Communist, was the unity of the Negroes in the South with the impoverished white workers and poor farmers. His sentence was so raw that, after an extended campaign of mass pressure and public opinion led principally by the Communist Party and International Labor Defense, he was finally freed.

My direct participation in the Herndon case came upon seeing a brief callous news account of his indictment in the *Atlanta Constitution* and I offered my legal services gratis, so intense was my outrage and indignation. In the course of my association and discussion with the Communists, I found the only rational and realistic path to the freedom which burns in the breast of every Negro. It required only a moment to join, but my whole lifetime as a Negro American prepared me for the moment.

Credit for recruiting me into the Communist Party goes to Judge Lee B. Wyatt, who had been summoned from the backwoods hinterland of the state to hear the case. So crude and viciously unconstitutional and anti-Negro were his rulings (rulings which were negated when Herndon was freed), that my instant joining of the Communist Party was the only effective reply I could give. It is fashionable among the lunatic elements of the domestic fascists to say that "the long arm of Moscow reaches into America and does the recruiting." But Judge Wyatt came from LaGrange, Georgia. He would resent, I'm sure, any imputation that he came from Moscow and his resentment would be exceeded only by the protestations from

Moscow. (As for me, I've never been to the Soviet Union, but I'm looking forward with great eagerness and pleasure to that experience.) The point is that the Communist Party arises out of the conditions of life in the country where it exists and the struggle for a better life.

In joining the Communist Party, I was first impressed with the militant, uncompromising fight of its members for the freedom and equal rights of Negro Americans, with its devoted conduct of this fight in the Southern heart of Jim Crowism, with its practice of the equality it preaches, with its policy of unity between Negro and white on the lowest economic level, and with its scientific program of struggle for the immediate needs of the people, while simultaneously pursuing the goal of Socialism. It is folly to assume that either of the two major parties could make such an impression on an average Negro. My impression of the Communists was formed during the period of Scottsboro—the case which epitomized in all its horrible completeness the plight of the Negro and at the same time symbolized the zealously-executed and correct policy of the Communist Party, in the struggle for the full political, economic and social liberation of the Negro people.

My first impression was correct; but it didn't go far enough. Like the thousands of other members of the Communist Party, I was to learn further through activity, struggle and personal application to the study of Marxism-Leninism as it relates to the specific conditions and historical development of our country. Above all, Communists learn from the people, of whom they are flesh and bone.

The struggles of the Negro people are an inseparable part of the struggles of the working class of America, and of the workers, common people and colonials all over the world. We Communists agree with Abraham Lincoln that "the strongest bond of human sympathy, outside of the family relation, should be one uniting all working people, of all nations and tongues and kindreds." If that is "subversive," then the Communists are in mighty good company.

Capitalism is the main and root cause of the discrimination against Negroes, Jews, the foreign-born, Catholics and other minorities. Under capitalism, a tiny minority of the population—the capitalist class which owns the country's basic means of production and natural resources—operates the social system for its profit which it takes out of the hides of the working class, the source of all the country's wealth. The working people, for their very existence, are compelled to struggle against the capitalist class. The basic contradiction between these two classes under capitalism, is known as the class struggle, which neither Marx, Engels, Lenin nor Stalin, invented or created, but which existed prior to them in former societies and takes place irrespective of them. The conclusions and principles which they drew and developed from capitalist development constitute the fund of the science known as Marxism-Leninism, the only social science known to man. The only solution to the class struggle is the establishment of socialism, the highest form of democracy, which entails the common ownership and operation of the national economy under a government of the people led by the working class. Since the working class constitutes the overwhelming majority of the people, when it achieves its own liberation, the masses of people will be liberated and a classless society can be established, with free and equal citizenship to all Americans regardless of race, color, creed, birth or political affiliation.

Racial, religious and other discriminations are weapons of capitalism to intensify its exploitation of certain sections of the population, to keep down the wages and working conditions of the working class, and to prevent the working people from uniting against the common foe—capitalism. Against the Negro people, capitalism has developed the so-called theory of "white supremacy" and "racial inferiority," against the Jews "anti-Semitism" on account of their religion, against Catholics "taking orders from Rome" on account of the central head of their church in the Vatican—and so on. Systematically, capitalism breeds and fans in Hitler-like fashion religious, national, and racial antagonisms because these antagonisms can be used to coin gold. The Negro people constitute the most oppressed section of the population, and in the Black Belt of the deep South, where they're in the majority, they constitute a source of super-profits for Wall Street—the brain center of American capitalism. The Negro's oppression, which is double—both as a worker and as a Negro—is also more intense in the northern Harlems and Southside ghettoes than that of the whites.

In order to achieve its historic destiny, the working class of America needs its own political party—which is the Communist Party. For both of the two major parties are today dominated by the exploiting class—that is, Wall Street—although there are many leaders in both parties who oppose the more pro-fascist sections of Wall Street.

When capitalism is abolished—as it will be when the majority of American people so decide—the basis will have been laid for the real brotherhood of man, implicit in the Declaration of Independence. The only place where there is such brotherhood is in the Soviet Union, which, in 1917, abolished capitalism, and now more than fifty nationalities, many of them darker peoples, live in freedom and equality. Can there be any wonder that political minions of Wall Street rave against the Soviets? And is there a sounder reason for the closest collaboration between the United States and Russia?

The basis of the special, double exploitation of Negro Americans all over the country is the intense lynch-oppression of the Negro people in the Black Belt area of the South where they constitute a numerical majority and are the foundation of the Wall Street–plantation owner economy of the South. From here, capitalism has constructed an elaborate, barbarous and unscientific myth of "white supremacy" and "racial inferiority." This false ideology is an attempt by capitalism to give a theoretical basis to the vicious oppression of the Negro. But in constructing this Frankenstein monster of super-exploitation and racial hatred—which will help destroy the Jim Crow system—the capitalists have created a condition of life that also has given rise to the development of the Negroes as a people—having all the essential characteristics of nationhood. These people are moving in the direction of full consciousness of their nationhood and will, side by side with the poor white workers and sharecroppers, demand the right to determine their own destiny, thus establishing the highest guarantee of the development of their freedom and culture. The white masses will support them, because they, for the first time, will have thrown off their backs the Wall Street–plantation owner combine. The Negro people will then realize their age-old unfulfilled dream, and we shall thus have a higher level of democracy than this country has ever known.

The issue of the Negro people determining their own destiny in their heartland in the Black Belt is not now the order of the day. The immediate issues in the South are the right of the Negro people to vote, equal justice in the courts, adequate housing and educational facilities, abolition of semi-feudal peonage and lynch-discriminating, and land reform—all of which are to the highest benefit of the white southern working people.

What then is the major all-inclusive issue before the American people in the present post-war period? Democracy and progress, on the one hand, versus imperialist reaction and fascism, on the other. On the foreign field, it means that our country should throw its weight, within the framework of the United Nations, on the side of the democratic anti-fascist forces, for the purpose of extirpating the remnants of fascism and securing freedom for colonial and semi-colonial peoples, and establishing international security and an enduring peace.

At home, the issue is to check and defeat the ever-growing menace of fascism in our country (which has already witnessed its first pro-fascist coup, namely, the thuggish, if abortive, seizure of power by Talmadge in Georgia). Positively, the issue before the American people is to advance the cause of democracy and progress in all walks of life, against the pro-fascist monopolists who would take the country down the ruinous and bloody path of Nazi Germany. First swallows of the drive toward fascism in the United States is the unprecedented and multiple campaign of Big Business (principally the National Association of Manufacturers and the U.S. Chamber of Commerce) against the Communist Party, the trade unions, mass living standards and political liberties, against minority groups, among whom the Negro bears the heaviest blows of reaction. The impending economic crisis—a natural concomitant of the capitalist system—will intensify every one of the political, economic and social ills from which the American people suffer today. Unless cushioned by advancing the interests of labor and the people, a great deterioration of conditions for the majority of the people will result that will put the Hoover days "in the shade."

The issue is not Communism versus capitalism or fascism. The fascists use this posing of the issue in order to confuse the people and to extinguish democracy, whether capitalist, as in our country, or the higher socialist form as in the Soviet Union. Hitler's anti-Communist crusade was a smokescreen behind which he extinguished democracy in the seventeen countries conquered by Nazism. None of these countries were Communist or Socialist. On the international front, the Soviet Union—because Wall Street, through the Truman Administration and its Republican backers insist on bolstering world reaction as in Greece, Turkey and China—is now leading the camp of democracy.

The Communists, in America, as all over the world, who gave their lives for the independence of their countries against the Hitler conquerors, are among the staunchest defenders of democracy in the present postwar period.

The terrifying experience of minority groups under fascism, all over the earth, is but a comparatively mild example of what would happen to the Negro people in America, where capitalist reaction has already given fascism a head start by spawning the national system of Jim Crow and "white supremacy" upon the entire body politic of American democracy. The uprooting of the Jim Crow system is a part of the battle to turn back the danger of fascism in America. Conversely, the rights of the Negro people are the acid test of democracy.

Within the framework of the overall issue of democracy versus fascism, the character of the struggle for the full citizenship of the Negro is the defense and extension of their gains over the last years, particularly during the Franklin D. Roosevelt era. Principally, the major issues of this moment are jobs and the establishment of an effective FEPC; the right to vote, abolition of the poll tax and the white primary; anti-lynching legislation; the unseating of Bilbo; and the outlawing of the Ku Klux Klan.

How is this urgently necessary and minimum program of action to be achieved? First, there must be struggle, resolute and unflinching, because American imperialism is the most powerful in the world. And struggle there is and will be among the Negro people, who will find at their side increasing thousands of white workers and progressives in their own self-interest—a repetition of the Fred Douglass–Abe Lincoln Negro and white unity in modern America. The Negro people are a people of struggle, having shed their blood, sweat and tears for every gain. And struggle is the tradition of America, from the time of its birth.

In these critical times, struggle, in order to be effective, cannot be blind, but must be united and based upon correct policy, the necessary prerequisites for success. The Communist Party, with an increasingly large section of white workers and progressives, as well as with a considerable proportion of the Negro people, advocates that this struggle must take place principally against the lily-white trusts, monopolies and big corporations—and their political hirelings—on every front, international and domestic.

Essential to the struggle for Negro rights is that it must be based first of all upon the alliance of the Negro people with the organized labor movement. During the whole Roosevelt era, this alliance, now under serious attack, was the very basis of the limited gains by the Negro people. The Negro people are an indispensable and long-term ally of the labor movement. Conversely, the Negro people must defend, build and strengthen the labor movement as the apple of their eye; for the trade unions, the organized symbol of the working class, are the staunchest supporter and backbone of the struggle for Negro rights. No section of the population has a greater interest in seeing one united labor movement in America than the Negro, who, like labor itself, has been constantly victimized by this split. While labor has the responsibility of taking the lead in wiping the stench of the slave market out of American life, the Negro workers have the job of combating the forces of disunity among certain Negro circles and winning the Negro people to a closer solidarity with labor. "Negro and white, unite and fight the common oppressor" must be transformed into reality wherever man is exploited or oppressed.

Simultaneously, the broadest unity of the Negro people's movement on a local and national scale, is not only crucial but it is the deepest desire of the Negro people. What a more powerful force the Negro people could become if their major people's organizations—the half-million strong and anti-fascist National Association for the Advancement of Colored People, the National Negro Congress, the National Urban League, the National Council of Negro Women, the national church bodies and faiths, the United Negro and Allied Veterans, the fraternal and Greek letter groups and, above all, the Negro workers—could move together on a minimum program to advance the free and equal citizenship of the Negro people! Just as oppression of the Negro people cuts across their political faiths and religious convictions, so should the Negro people unite—Republicans, Democrats, Laborites, Communists, Socialists and Independents—to press, with the support of labor and white progressives, for constructive, progressive legislation in Washington and the states and cities to promote equal rights for the Negro, defense of the trade unions, and the democratic welfare of the American people.

Finally, it is essential that the Negro people take their place on the basis of equality in the growing movement in America for independent political action—for the creation of a national third party, based upon the labor movement, the poor farmers, the middle class and the anti-Fascist majority of the American people. It is quite clear that the coalition of the Roosevelt era, in which the administration in Washington was a part of the people's coalition, no longer exists. President Truman is not just yielding to the Hoover-Dewey-Taft Republicans but is seeking to outstrip them in reaction. Truman has completely betrayed the Roosevelt program. It is almost Republican tweedle-dee, and Democrat tweedle-dum.

What this country needs is a new political party in which labor and the people—Negro and white—will be the dominant force in its policies, instead of the National Association of Manufacturers and the U.S. Chamber of Commerce and assorted Wall Street pirates. Not only can the Negro people make a vital and necessary contribution to such a new party, but only such a party, projected for the 1948 elections, can give full hope of fulfilling some of the promises which the Republican and Democratic national leadership has been hypocritically making since the Civil War.

It would be impossible to conclude this article without mentioning a couple of the main characteristics of the Communist Party itself in its structure and operation. First the Communists fight for the political, economic and social equality of the Negro people now in all aspects of American endeavor. The Party's great contribution to American democracy was first dramatized in the celebrated Scottsboro case, where it not only burned the plight of the Negro into the conscience of America for the first time since the Civil War, but it did something entirely new. It brought for the first time the struggle for Negro rights to the labor movement, and gave flesh and blood to the Marxist classic that "labor in a white skin can never be free while labor in a black skin is branded."

On a thousand fronts the Communists at the side of the Negro people have battled and do battle daily for equal rights. The Communist Party places upon its white members, and seeks to convince all white workers, that they should be in the front ranks against white chauvinism, the main ideology and practice of the monopolist class, not only for enslaving the Negro people, but for exploiting the white masses. White chauvinism is not tolerated in the Communist Party. This makes it possible for the Negro Communists, and other advanced forces among the Negro people, to combat the reactionary nationalism, espoused often by certain Negro leaders, to prevent the unity of the Negro people with their natural white allies in the labor and progressive movement.

The Communist Party recognizes Negro ability and uses it. No other political party in America, while prating about Negro rights in words, has seen fit to elevate a Negro to such a post of honor and responsibility as that held by the young Negro veteran and leader, Henry Winston, Administrative Secretary of the Communist Party. On the 12-man national board of the Communist Party are three Negroes; and on the national Committee of the Communist Party, Negro men and women are in larger proportion than the Negro membership. The Communist Party is the Party of the Negro people, which it must, and can only, be by virtue of being the Party of the white workers. Examples of equal rights for the Negro set by the Communist Party inspire emulation among all organizations in the country. Communists are modestly proud of the warm regard of the Negro people, and seek always to be ever more worthy of this honor.

Can the struggle for peace, democracy, freedom and security, be won in the postwar world? Can the battle for the Negro's full citizenship be won? To be sure! and this requires, besides struggle, unity and correct policy, an abiding faith in the people of America, Negro and white, and of the world. It is the fear of this victory of the people that causes the frightened men of the trusts to wallow in an orgy of red-baiting, labor-baiting and Negro-baiting. They see the forces of democracy— of labor and the people—growing all over the world, including our own land.

The future belongs to the people. Whether one is a member of the Communist Party or not—or agrees in toto with it—one must recognize that the future is not assured without a strong and ever-expanding Communist Party here, as in the other countries of the world. I want that future as quickly as possible—that's why I am a Communist.

MY ADVENTURES
AS A SOCIAL POET

LANGSTON HUGHES's second autobiography, *I Wonder as I Wander* (1956), gives a considerable number of his adventures as a social poet. But some of the incidents in this essay, particularly the last one, were not related in the later book. "My Adventures as a Social Poet" was published in *Phylon*, Third Quarter, 1947.

Poets who write mostly about love, roses and moonlight, sunsets and snow, must lead a very quiet life. Seldom, I imagine, does their poetry get them into difficulties. Beauty and lyricism are really related to another world, to ivory towers, to your head in the clouds, feet floating off the earth.

Unfortunately, having been born poor—and also colored—in Missouri, I was stuck in the mud from the beginning. Try as I might to float off into the clouds, poverty and Jim Crow would grab me by the heels, and right back on earth I would land. A third floor furnished room is the nearest thing I have ever had to an ivory tower.

Some of my earliest poems were social poems in that they were about people's problems—whole groups of people's problems—rather than my own personal difficulties. Sometimes, though, certain aspects of my personal problems happened to be also common to many other people. And certainly, racially speaking, my own problems of adjustment to American life were the same as those of millions of other segregated Negroes. The moon belongs to everybody, but not this American earth of ours. That is perhaps why poems about the moon perturb no one, but poems about color and poverty do perturb many citizens. Social forces pull backwards or forwards, right or left, and social poems get caught in the pulling and hauling. Sometimes the poet himself gets pulled and hauled—even hauled off to jail.

I have never been in jail but I have been detained by the Japanese police in Tokyo and by the immigration authorities in Cuba—in custody, to put it politely—due, no doubt, to their interest in my written words. These authorities would hardly have detained me had I been a writer of the roses and moonlight school. I have never known the police of any country to show an interest in lyric poetry as such. But when poems stop talking about the moon and begin to mention poverty, trade unions, color lines, and colonies, somebody tells the police. The history of world literature has many examples of poets fleeing into exile to escape persecution, of poets in jail, even of poets killed like Placido or, more recently, Lorca in Spain.

My adventures as a social poet are mild indeed compared to the body-breaking, soul-searing experiences of poets in the recent fascist countries or of the resistance poets of the Nazi invaded lands during the war. For that reason, I can use so light a word as "adventure" in regard to my own skirmishes with reaction and censorship.

My adventures as a social poet began in a colored church in Atlantic City shortly after my first book, *The Weary Blues*, was published in 1926. I had been invited to come down to the shore from Lincoln University where I was a student, to give a program of my poems in the church. During the course of my program I read several of my poems in the form of the Negro folk songs, including some blues poems about hard luck and hard work. As I read I noticed a deacon approach the pulpit with a note which he placed on the rostrum beside me, but I did not stop to open the note until I had finished and had acknowledged the applause of a cordial audience. The note read, "Do not read any more blues in my pulpit." It was signed by the minister. That was my first experience with censorship.

The kind and generous woman who sponsored my writing for a few years after my college days did not come to the point quite so directly as did the minister who disliked blues. Perhaps, had it not been in the midst of the great depression of the late '20s and early '30s, the kind of poems that I am afraid helped to end her patronage might not have been written. But it was impossible for me to travel from hungry Harlem to the lovely homes on Park Avenue without feeling in my soul the great gulf between the very poor and the very rich in our society. In those days, on the way to visit this kind lady I would see the homeless sleeping in subways and the hungry begging in doorways on sleet-stung winter days. It was then that I wrote a poem called "An Ad for the Waldorf-Astoria," satirizing the slick-paper magazine advertisements of the opening of that de luxe hotel. Also I wrote:

PARK BENCH

I live on a park bench.
You, Park Avenue.
Hell of a distance
Between us two.

I beg a dime for dinner—
You got a butler and maid.
But I'm wakin' up!
Say, ain't you afraid

That I might, just maybe,
In a year or two,
Move on over
To Park Avenue?

In a little while I did not have a patron any more.

But that year I won a prize, the Harmon Gold Award for Literature, which consisted of a medal and four hundred dollars. With the four hundred dollars I went to Haiti. On the way I stopped in Cuba where I was cordially received by the writers and artists. I had written poems about the exploitation of Cuba by the sugar barons and I had translated many poems of Nicholas Guillen such as:

CANE

Negro
In the cane fields.
White man
Above the cane fields.
Earth
Beneath the cane fields.
Blood
That flows from us.

This was during the days of the dictatorial Machado regime. Perhaps someone called his attention to these poems and translations because, when I came back from Haiti weeks later, I was not allowed to land in Cuba, but was detained by the immigration authorities at Santiago and put on an island until the American consul came, after three days, to get me off with the provision that I cross the country to Havana and leave Cuban soil at once.

That was my first time being put out of any place. But since that time I have been put out of or barred from quite a number of places, all because of my poetry— not the roses and moonlight poems (which I write, too) but because of poems about poverty, oppression, and segregation. Nine Negro boys in Alabama were on trial for their lives when I got back from Cuba and Haiti. The famous Scottsboro "rape" case was in full session. I visited those boys in the death house at Kilby Prison, and I wrote many poems about them. One of these poems was:

CHRIST IN ALABAMA

Christ is a Nigger,
Beaten and black—
O, bare your back.

Mary is His Mother—
Mammy of the South.
Silence your mouth.

God's His Father—
White Master above,
Grant us your love.

Most holy bastard
Of the bleeding mouth:
Nigger Christ
On the cross of the South.

Contempo, a publication of some of the students at the University of North Carolina, published the poem on its front page on the very day that I was being presented in a program of my poems at the University in Chapel Hill. That evening there were police outside the building in which I spoke, and in the air the rising tension of race that is peculiar to the South. It had been rumored that some of the local citizenry were saying that I should be run out of town, and that one of the sheriffs agreed, saying, "Sure, he ought to be run out! It's bad enough to call Christ a *bastard*. But when he calls him a *nigger*, he's gone too far!"

The next morning a third of my fee was missing when I was handed my check. One of the departments of the university jointly sponsoring my program had refused to come through with its portion of the money. Nevertheless, I remember with pleasure the courtesy and kindness of many of the students and faculty at Chapel Hill and their lack of agreement with the anti-Negro elements of the town. There I began to learn at the University of North Carolina how hard it is to be a white liberal in the South.

It was not until I had been to Russia and around the world as a writer and journalist that censorship and opposition to my poems reached the point of completely preventing me from appearing in public programs on a few occasions. It happened first in Los Angeles shortly after my return from the Soviet Union. I was to have been one of several speakers on a memorial program to be held at the colored branch Y.M.C.A. for a young Negro journalist of the community. At the behest of white higher-ups, no doubt, some reactionary Negro politicians informed the Negro Y.M.C.A. that I was a Communist. The secretary of the Negro Branch Y then informed the committee of young people in charge of the memorial that they could have their program only if I did not appear.

I have never been a Communist, but I soon learned that anyone visiting the Soviet Union and speaking with favor of it upon returning is liable to be so labeled. Indeed when Mrs. Roosevelt, Walter White, and so Christian a lady as Mrs. Bethune who has never been in Moscow, are so labeled, I should hardly be surprised! I wasn't surprised. And the young people's committee informed the Y secretary that since the Y was a public community center which they helped to support, they saw no reason why it should censor their memorial program to the extent of eliminating any speaker.

Since I had been allotted but a few moments on the program, it was my intention simply to read this short poem of mine:

Dear lovely death
That taketh all things under wing,
Never to kill,
Only to change into some other thing
This suffering flesh—

To make it either more or less
But not again the same,
Dear lovely death,
Change is thy other name.

But the Negro branch Y, egged on by the reactionary politicians (whose incomes, incidentally, were allegedly derived largely from gambling houses and other underworld activities), informed the young people's committee that the police would be at the door to prevent my entering the Y on the afternoon of the scheduled program. So when the crowd gathered, the memorial was not held that Sunday. The young people simply informed the audience of the situation and said that the memorial would be postponed until a place could be found where all the participants could be heard. The program was held elsewhere a few Sundays later.

Somebody with malice aforethought (probably the Negro politicians of Uncle Tom vintage) gave the highly publicized California evangelist, Aimee Semple McPherson, a copy of a poem of mine, "Goodbye, Christ." This poem was one of my least successful efforts at poetic communication, in that many persons have misinterpreted it as an anti-Christian poem. I intended it to be just the opposite. Satirical, even ironic, in style, I meant it to be a poem against those whom I felt were misusing religion for worldly or profitable purposes. In the poem I mentioned Aimee Semple McPherson. This apparently made her angry. From her Angelus Temple pulpit she preached against me, saying, "There are many devils among us, but the most dangerous of all is the red devil. And now there comes among us a red devil *in a black skin!*"

She gathered her followers together and sent them to swoop down upon me one afternoon at an unsuspecting and innocent literary luncheon in Pasadena's Vista del Arroyo Hotel. Robert Nathan, I believe, was one of the speakers, along with a number of other authors. I was to have five minutes on the program to read a few poems from my latest collection of folk verses, *Shakespeare in Harlem*, hardly a radical book.

When I arrived at the hotel by car from Los Angeles, I noticed quite a crowd in the streets where the traffic seemed to be tangled. So I got out some distance from the front of the hotel and walked through the grounds to the entrance, requesting my car to return at three o'clock. When I asked in the lobby for the location of the luncheon, I was told to wait until the desk clerk sent for the chairman, George Palmer Putnam. Mr. Putnam arrived with the manager, both visibly excited. They informed me that the followers of Aimee McPherson were vehemently picketing the hotel because of my appearance there. The manager added with an aggrieved look that he could not have such a commotion in front of his hotel. Either I would have to go or he would cancel the entire luncheon.

Mr. Putnam put it up to me. I said that rather than inconvenience several hundred guests and a half dozen authors, I would withdraw—except that I did not know where my car had gone, so would someone be kind enough to drive me to the station. Just then a doorman came in to inform the manager that traffic was completely blocked in front of the hotel. Frantically the manager rushed out. About that time a group of Foursquare Gospel members poured into the lobby in uniforms and armbands and surrounded me and George Palmer Putnam, demanding to know if we were Christians. Before I could say anything, Mr. Putnam lit into them angrily, saying it was none of their business and stating that under our Constitution a man could have any religion he chose, as well as freedom to express himself.

Just then an old gentleman about seventy-two who was one of the organizers of the literary luncheon came up, saying he had been asked to drive me to the station and get me out of there so they could start the luncheon. Shaking hands with Mr. Putnam, I accompanied the old gentleman to the street. There Aimee's sound truck had been backed across the roadway blocking all passage so that limousines, trucks, and taxis were tangled up in all directions. The sound truck was playing "God Bless America" while hundreds of pickets milled about with signs denouncing Langston Hughes—atheistic Red. Rich old ladies on the arms of their chauffeurs were trying to get through the crowd to the luncheon. Reporters were dashing about.

None of the people recognized me, but in the excitement the old gentleman could not find his car. Finally he hailed a taxi and nervously thrust a dollar into the driver's hand with the request that I be driven to the station. He asked to be excused himself in order to get back to the luncheon. Just as I reached out the door to shake hands in farewell, three large white ladies with banners rushed up to the cab. One of them screamed, "We don't shake hands with niggers where we come from!"

The thought came over me that the picketing might turn into a race riot, in which case I did not wish to be caught in a cab in a traffic jam alone. I did not turn loose the old gentleman's hand. Instead of shaking it in farewell, I simply pulled him into the taxi with me, saying, "I thought you were going to the station, too."

As the pickets snarled outside, I slammed the door. The driver started off, but we were caught in the traffic blocked by the sound truck lustily playing "God Bless America." The old gentleman trembled beside me, until finally we got clear of the mob. As we backed down a side street and turned to head for the station, the sirens of approaching police cars were heard in the distance.

Later I learned from the afternoon papers that the whole demonstration had been organized by Aimee McPherson's publicity man, and that when the police arrived he had been arrested for refusing to give up the keys to the sound truck stalled midway the street to block the traffic. This simply proved the point I had tried to make in the poem—that the church might as well bid Christ goodbye if his gospel were left in the hands of such people.

Four years later I was to be picketed again in Detroit by Gerald L. K. Smith's Mothers of America—for ever since the Foursquare Gospel demonstration in California, reactionary groups have copied, used and distributed this poem. Always they have been groups like Smith's, never known to help the fight for democratic Negro rights in America, but rather to use their energies to foment riots such as that before Detroit's Sojourner Truth housing project where the Klan-minded tried to prevent colored citizens from occupying government homes built for them.

I have had one threatening communication signed A *Klansman*. And many scurrilous anonymous anti-Negro letters from persons whose writing did not always indicate illiteracy. On a few occasions, reactionary elements have forced liberal sponsors to cancel their plans to present me in a reading of my poems. I recall that in Gary, Indiana, some years ago the colored teachers were threatened with the loss of their jobs if I accepted their invitation to appear at one of the public schools. In another city a white high school principal, made apprehensive by a small group of reactionary parents, told me that he communicated with the F.B.I at Washington to find out if I were a member of the Communist Party. Assured that I was not, with the approval of his school board, he presented me to his student body. To further fortify his respectability, that morning at assembly, he had invited all of the Negro ministers and civic leaders of the town to sit on the stage in a semi-circle behind me. To the students it must have looked like a kind of modern minstrel show as it was the first time any Negroes at all had been invited to their assembly.

So goes the life of a social poet. I am sure none of these things would ever have happened to me had I limited the subject matter of my poems to roses and moonlight. But, unfortunately, I was born poor—and colored—and almost all the prettiest roses I have seen have been in rich white people's yards—not in mine. That is why I cannot write exclusively about roses and moonlight—for sometimes in the moonlight my brothers see a fiery cross and a circle of Klansmen's hoods. Sometimes in the moonlight a dark body swings from a lynching tree—but for his funeral there are no roses.

THE NEGRO AND
THE COMMUNISTS

WALTER WHITE (1893–1955) was assistant executive
secretary of the NAACP from 1918 to 1930 and executive secretary from
1930 until his death from a heart attack in 1955. Born and bred in the
South, he was an investigator of lynchings (his fair skin making it possible
for him to pass for white on these occasions), a novelist, a tireless
polemicist and essayist. His essay on blacks and communism, including
his vehemently anti-communist account of communist involvement in
the famed Scottsboro case, appeared in *Harper's* in December 1931.

I

About noon of a late March day of this year two white women mill workers
clambered aboard a freight train at Chattanooga with seven white men
to hobo their way back home to Huntsville, Alabama. In doing this these
two women started something—something that has had its repercussions in every
part of the civilized world. Thomas Mann and Albert Einstein, H. G. Wells and
Theodore Dreiser and thousands of lesser luminaries of the world of letters, politics,
religion, and business have had something to say on the matter. The events which
flowed with such startling rapidity from that March day have moved Negro thought
as has nothing else within recent years. For this series of episodes growing out of
the stealing of rides in a "side-door Pullman" has given a new significance to the
race question and forced it into the consciousness of the United States and of the
world at large.

What happened? Pieced together from the official transcript of the court trials
which grew out of the episode and from the enormous mass of rumor which
inevitably accompanies such a case, the facts are these. The freight train, half a
mile or so in length, sped along westward from Chattanooga towards Memphis.

The two girls, dressed in men's overalls, and their seven white male companions occupied a gondola—a freight car with sides but no top—filled to two-thirds of its capacity with crushed gravel. One of the girls declares that in all the journey of thirty odd miles to Stevenson, Alabama, neither she nor her companion paid any attention to their companions nor spoke to them. The other girl told the more probable story that they laughed, joked, sang, and had a generally pleasant time with the seven men who shared the gondola with them.

At Stevenson the human cargo of the freight train was materially augmented when twenty or thirty Negroes clambered aboard. The whites assert that all of them entered the gondola. A quarrel arose when, according to some of the Negroes, one of the white men angrily shouted, "You niggers get out of here!" So thoroughly is the principle and practice of "Jim Crow" embedded in the Southern consciousness, apparently, that the white hoboes felt there ought even to be "Jim Crow" freight cars as well as passenger ones. The whites allege they were overpowered by the larger number of Negroes and thrown from the train; another story has it that there was no fight but that the white men hastily quitted the train, leaving the girls to whatever fate should befall them. One of the white men in his haste to get off fell between two cars and, about to be injured or killed, was pulled back to safety by two of the Negro boys. The press, however, declared he was forced out of sheer viciousness to remain as a witness to the alleged attacks. One of the whites who fled the train hurried back to Stevenson and telephoned the sheriff at Paint Rock, the next town, of what had happened and asked that he stop the train and arrest the Negroes.

All this, together with six alleged criminal attacks upon each girl, happened in the time it took the train to make the run from Stevenson to Paint Rock, a distance of thirty-eight miles. A harrowing tale was related by the older girl of knives held at the throats of her companion and herself while the assaults took place.

The sheriff and an armed posse halted the train at Paint Rock. Only nine of the twenty to thirty Negroes who had boarded the train remained on it. These nine were scattered along the length of the train. They were arrested and placed in jail at Scottsboro, the county seat of Jackson County, as were the two girls and two white men found on the train, one of them being the one who was rescued by the Negroes. Significantly enough, this man who was the only known eyewitness to the alleged attacks other than the plaintiffs and defendants, was placed on the witness stand by the prosecution only in rebuttal. The prosecutor of Jackson County is reported to have attributed this to the fact that this white man was incapable of comprehending that "having sexual intercourse" is synonymous with a short, less literary, Anglo-Saxon word not used in polite society.

It seems clear that the officials of the law at Scottsboro intended at first only to charge the nine Negro defendants, who ranged in age from fourteen to twenty years, with the crimes of fighting and stealing a ride. But when it was discovered that two of the four white "men" were women in men's clothing, the girls were vigorously questioned as to whether or not sex offenses had been committed on them by the Negroes. It is reported reliably that for some time they asserted that none had been committed. Meantime news of the arrest and especially of discovery of the sex of two of the whites had spread through the vicinity. A crowd which grew rapidly gathered about the jail, ominously working up its rage and seeking a leader to stage a wholesale lynching. Two white local physicians were summoned to examine the girls. They later testified that they found the girls "in normal condition, mentally and physically." One of the girls had a slight abrasion which, one of the doctors admitted, might easily have been caused by riding in a springless freight car fifty miles with crushed gravel as a resting place, or in clambering over the side of the car in boarding or getting down from it. There was evidence that both girls had had sexual relations at some time prior to the examination, but further questioning established strongly the likelihood that these relations had occurred some hours previous to their entering the freight car at Chattanooga. There was no evidence of assault.

An infinite number of rumors (none the less potent because many of them untrue) swept through the town like a prairie fire. All manner of unbelievable atrocities had been perpetrated upon the two girls which, with each retelling, became more fiendish. At the same rate the reputations of the girls grew speedily more pure and unblemished. Huddled in terror inside the tiny country jail, the nine Negro lads, only two of whom, according to their story, had even so much as seen each other until they met in the Scottsboro jail, listened to the steadily mounting roar of the blood-hungry mob outside.

So ominous did it become that officers after nightfall bundled the boys into motor cars and hurried them away to a stronger jail at Gadsden.

A week later the defendants were returned to Scottsboro and speedily indicted on charges of rape; a fortnight later they went on trial. One hundred and three national guardsmen with drawn bayonets, tear-gas bombs, and machine guns surrounded the Jackson County courthouse to prevent lynchings; they were sent there through the intercession with the governor by the Alabama Commission on Interracial Co-operation. The courtroom and the space outside for a great distance around the courthouse were packed tight with ten thousand people, many of them armed, according to conservative estimates. Scottsboro's merchants, who catered on ordinary days to the simple needs of fifteen hundred souls, did a thriving business with the quintupled population.

As required by law when penniless defendants face trial where death is a possible verdict, Judge A. J. Hawkins assigned to the defense the entire Jackson County bar, consisting of seven lawyers. Six hastily made excuses and were relieved by the court from the obligation of serving. One remained on the case—Milo Moody, getting along in years but true to his reputation of being a mild village iconoclast, willing to take hopeless cases.

Into the courtroom walked a white lawyer from Chattanooga to ask permission of the court to assist in the defense. A group of Negro ministers and members of the National Association for the Advancement of Colored People had been stirred to action by the impending danger to the youthful defendants and by the far from groundless fear that their constitutional rights would be gravely endangered in such an atmosphere when charged with such an offense. These Chattanooga Negro leaders had raised about a hundred dollars to employ a lawyer. Knowing it would have been useless if not suicidal for a Negro lawyer to have appeared at Scottsboro, they retained Stephen R. Roddy, the only white lawyer in Chattanooga who, so far as they knew, dared face the hostile mob.

Judge Hawkins challenged Roddy at once, declaring that if the Chattanooga lawyer had been retained to defend the nine boys, he would relieve the Scottsboro Bar from its responsibility. Knowing the hostility any lawyer from outside the town and State would encounter, and being himself unfamiliar with Alabama legal procedure, Roddy explained to the judge that he had not "exactly been retained" but would like permission to assist Mr. Moody. After some discussion this was permitted, and the trials proceeded.

The defense provided the nine boys fell considerably short of perfection. It is difficult, however, months afterward and miles away to picture the thoughts and emotions which went through the minds of the two defense attorneys. Inside the dingy courtroom men with grim, hard faces pressed close to them as they sat at the counsel table. When Victoria Price jauntily told her story, reveling in the exciting spotlight so utterly different from the accustomed dreariness of her work in an antiquated cotton mill, out of the crowd came a roar which repeated banging of the judge's gavel could not suppress. Outside, tightly packed thousands sent their message of venom and hatred through the windows, opened in the sultry heat of a prematurely warm spring day. Appallingly hostile was the atmosphere already. But that hostility knew no bounds, and the faint chance of getting into the official record of the trial sufficient basis for appeal to a higher court went glimmering when it became known that Judge Hawkins had received a bombastic telegraphic threat from a Communist organization in New York City, the International Labor Defense, which intemperately asserted that the presiding judge "would be held personally responsible unless the nine defendants are immediately released."

With sickening rapidity one after another of the boys was found guilty and sentenced to death. Only one escaped the death penalty. The prosecutor asked only for life imprisonment for him because the defendant had just then attained his fourteenth birthday. But seven jurors were adamant for the death penalty for him as well.

The prospect of early deaths for the other eight appeased the crowd. Taking advantage of the subsiding of the lynching atmosphere, the defense attorneys encountered no objection when they placed on the witness stand the officer in charge of the national guardsmen and a local court official. From these the admission was gained for the record that the roar of approbation which greeted announcement of the verdicts of guilty of the first two boys tried had unquestionably been sufficient to penetrate to the room where jurors deliberated over the cases of the others. Such admissions are of vital importance in appealing the cases to a higher court, for the United States Supreme Court ruled in 1915 in the famous Arkansas Riot Cases (Moore vs. Dempsey, 261 U. S. 86) that trial in a court dominated by a mob is not due process of law.

II

Steps were promptly taken by the National Association for the Advancement of Colored People, aided by the Commission on Interracial Co-operation and other bodies, to appeal the case to the Alabama Supreme Court, since careful investigation had established more than reasonable doubts of the innocence of most if not all of the defendants. When the boys were safely incarcerated in the stout Kilby State Prison, near Montgomery, two of them who had testified against several of their co-defendants now declared in affidavits that they had been induced to do so by beatings and by threats that they would be shot down in the courtroom if they varied in the slightest from the stories they were forced to tell. All nine of the boys vehemently protested their innocence, declaring that had they had the faintest notion they were to be accused of any crime, however trivial, they too would have fled the train between Stevenson and Paint Rock as did others of the original twenty to thirty Negroes who had boarded the ill-fated train at Stevenson.

Exhaustive investigations vitally necessary to successful action to obtain a new trial or rehearing in a less mob-charged atmosphere were begun. A highly competent newspaper woman and investigator sent to the scene by the American Civil Liberties Union revealed that the reputation of the two girls was far from savory. Conversation with one of the plaintiffs, according to this investigator, "convinced me that she was the type who welcomes attention and publicity at any price. The price in this case means little to her. . . . Having been in direct contact from the cradle with the institution of prostitution as a sideline necessary to make the meager wages of a mill worker pay the rent and buy the groceries, she has no feeling of revulsion against promiscuous sexual intercourse such as women of easier lives might suffer. . . . The younger girl found herself from the beginning pushed into the background by the more bubbling, pert personality" of the older girl, and resented the monopoly of the spotlight her companion had obtained.

The Advancement Association sent its secretary to the scene to co-operate with its branches in Chattanooga and Alabama and to select counsel to perfect appeals. He retained the outstanding criminal law firm of the State, one of whose members had for fourteen years served on the bench. Another member of the firm is generally reputed to be the ablest trial lawyer in the State, whose father before him had been a distinguished member of the Alabama bar. All the members of the firm are representative of the new South which is valiantly struggling to free that section of the country from the stigma of prejudice and oppression. Later, Clarence Darrow agreed to join counsel retained by the N.A.A.C.P. for the defense.

When a motion for a new trial was denied, appeal was taken to the Alabama Supreme Court, where arguments will be held during the third week in January.

III

But while these investigations and negotiations were proceeding, a new element entered the cases which simultaneously complicated them to an unbelievable degree and, at the same time, made them the most notable test of strength to date between those who seek justice for the Negro through American forms of government and those who seek to spread Communist propaganda among American Negroes.

With a blare of trumpets the Communists seized upon the Scottsboro convictions. It was, they realized, a golden opportunity to put into effect the plan decided upon by the Third Internationale and upon which they had been assiduously working but with only a modicum of success—to capitalize Negro unrest in the United States against lynching, jim crowism, proscription, and insult. As far back as 1925 a segregated wing of Communism, "The American Negro Labor Congress," which later became "The League of Struggle for Negro Rights," had held at Chicago a convention to win Negroes to the cause of Communism. In October, 1928, there was issued in Moscow a lengthy resolution on the Negro question in the United States, urging the Negro working class to form organizations which "if properly organized and well led" could "play a considerable role in the class struggle against American imperialism" and in leading "the movement of the oppressed masses of the Negro populace."

These efforts at organization were based upon the theory that the Negroes are the most oppressed group in the United States and, therefore, should be the most fertile field for revolutionary propaganda. The Scottsboro case offered the most dramatic opportunity yet afforded for this campaign.

Representatives of the International Labor Defense called on Mr. Roddy and sought to get him away from those who had retained him prior to the trial at Scottsboro. Edmund Wilson thus describes in the *New Republic* the offer: "According to Mr. Roddy, they went through all the gestures of taking him up into a high place and showing him the kingdoms of the earth. They told him he had the opportunity of becoming a national figure, a second Clarence Darrow—a dream, one gathers, entirely alien to Mr. Roddy's ambitions. He asked how they proposed to pay him. They explained that they would raise the money by holding meetings among the Negroes and getting them to contribute to a defense fund. This idea seemed distasteful to Mr. Roddy—and the I.L.D. representatives had begun to arouse his suspicions: one of them, who had said he was a lawyer, had in the course of a discussion of the trials, inquired whether the defendants had been 'arraigned' yet. Mr. Roddy refused to have anything to do with the International Labor Defense."

Immediately all the floods of American Communist billingsgate were loosed upon the Chattanooga lawyer. He was accused in the *Daily Worker*, the Communist organ, of being a member of the Ku Klux Klan, of having conspired with the prosecution to electrocute the nine boys, of having been the inmate of an insane asylum. Later on a story was sent to the Negro press that Roddy had gone violently insane on the streets of Birmingham, attempted to kill his wife with an axe, and had been incarcerated by his own father in a Missouri asylum. No distortion of the truth, however libelous, which could be conjured up to deprecate Roddy's modest talents and reputation was considered unworthy of use in the Communist attempt to whip up enthusiasm for themselves among Negroes and whites who were stirred by the Scottsboro verdicts.

A special committee to raise funds for defense was organized by the I.L.D. among well-known writers of liberal tendencies such as Theodore Dreiser, Lincoln Steffens, John Dos Passos, Burton Rascoe, Lola Ridge, and Floyd Dell. Many thousands of letters appealing for funds to aid in defense were sent to white and colored individuals. With remarkable efficiency a house-to-house canvass was made of practically every Negro community, especially in the larger cities of the country, and leaflets, magazines, and copies of the *Daily Worker* were deposited in each home or apartment. Negro ministers were asked to permit Communist speakers to address their congregations and solicit funds for defense. Such permission was in many cases granted until these ministers became suspicious because of the Communist attacks on the N.A.A.C.P. Mothers of some of the defendants were convinced that every hand was turned against their boys save those of the Communists, that everyone else was "a tool of the capitalists" and was seeking to have their boys electrocuted or hanged. Some of the parents and relatives, carried about the country to address meetings with speeches written for them, were insulated carefully from contact with any persons who might be of other than Communist opinions. A few of them, of humble background and with meager educational and other advantages, still believe the only way their boys can be saved from the electric chair will be through Communist "mass action." One of them is reported by the warden of Kilby Prison as having been so thoroughly convinced of this fact that she stood, arms akimbo, in the foyer of the prison and loudly asserted of the secretary of the National Association for the Advancement of Colored People that "I just wish I could get my hands on him—I'd wring his neck—trying to get my boy electrocuted!"

Particularly determined was the Communist assault on that organization which, for twenty-two years, has had a notable record of victories in State and Federal courts in protecting the Negro's constitutional rights. It numbers among the members of its Board of Directors distinguished white and Negro Americans of varying shades of political opinion, including such lawyers as the late Moorfield Storey of Boston, former president of the American Bar Association, Clarence Darrow, Arthur B. Spingarn, Felix Frankfurter of the Harvard University Law School, the late Louis Marshall, his son, James Marshall; such public figures as the Senior Senator from Kansas, Arthur Capper, the Lieutenant-Governor of New York, Herbert H. Lehman, Frank Murphy, Mayor of Detroit, Judge James A. Cobb; such social workers as Jane Addams, Florence Kelley, and Mary White Ovington; publicists, educators, and authors such as Dr. W. E. B. Du Bois, James Weldon Johnson, J. E. Spingarn, and President William Allan Neilson of Smith College.

The Communists sought vigorously to weaken or destroy confidence in this organization and to injure the reputation it had built up over a period of two decades. Its officers were attacked as being "in league with the lyncher-bosses of the South," as plotters to "murder the Scottsboro martyrs," as sycophantic "tools of the capitalists." Determined efforts were made to break up meetings of the N.A.A.C.P., in some instances police officers being necessary to avert serious disorder. Communists were scattered throughout the audiences and, at a prearranged signal, began to shout for the right to be heard. When this was denied, handfuls of Communist literature were flung into the air and such disorder created as to break up some of the meetings. A favorite device would be for a Communist to announce that one of the "mothers" was present and demanded the right to speak. When at first such permission was granted, a Communist would make a lengthy harangue on Communism as an "introduction." When the supply of "mothers" was inadequate to cover such meetings—there are but five living mothers—substitutes were found. All over the country "mothers" were produced; in one instance the "mother" presented had lived in that Northern city for upwards of twenty years. Editors of Negro newspapers were approached with proposals to divide the money raised locally in exchange for boosting of Communist meetings.

In July, Negro share-croppers and tenant-farmers in rural Alabama were organized by Communist agents—two of them white and one a Negro—into a movement to gain relief from poverty "by mass action of white and black workers." Someone—no one seems to know who—telephoned the sheriff the time and place of a meeting of the Negro farmers and informed him that the meeting was called for the purpose of killing him and other officials. As a result the sheriff was wounded, one Negro killed, twenty or more were wounded, and thirty-four arrested and charged with plotting an insurrection. Meanwhile, the two white organizers had vanished, leaving their Negro comrade "to complete the work of organization." When later some of the arrested Negroes were freed, the local officials realizing that they were dupes of the Communists, the *Daily Worker* loudly and jubilantly shouted that "fear of united mass action" had caused the freeing of the men.

In Chicago where unemployment and suffering are most acute among Negroes, Communist agents were very active among the homeless and hungry on the South Side. Whenever word came of the eviction of a Negro family for non-payment of rent, crowds were speedily mobilized to march to the house and replace the furniture. The police for a week or more sought to avoid trouble by paying no attention and doing nothing about such action, whereupon the Communists loudly proclaimed to Negroes on the South Side that "we've got the police on the run—they're scared of us!" When court bailiffs who were dispossessing a Negro widow with several small children sent in a call for the riot squad, *two Negroes* were killed and others wounded. No *white* Communist was hurt. Mayor Cermak of Chicago, however, was stirred to action and ordered evictions stopped. In October a similar episode in Cleveland led to the death of two Negroes.

In New York, Detroit, Akron, Pittsburgh, Baltimore—in fact, in every city, town, and village where there is an appreciable number of Negroes—the same tactics were used in attempted thwarting of evictions, or in other spectacular appeals. Fortunately, to the time of writing, none has resulted fatally as in Chicago, and Cleveland, where the funerals of the Negroes killed were utilized for huge parades sprinkled abundantly with banners and speeches advocating the overthrow of capitalism.

IV

And what was the soil into which the Communist propaganda fell? As I write I sit in a large Middle-western industrial city. Yesterday I was told by a social worker of a case he had encountered a day or so before. A Negro industrial worker employed by a large rubber company was about to be evicted from his tiny, humble home for non-payment of three months' rent amounting to sixty dollars. He owed a balance of forty-eight dollars on a loan, and the loan company had garnisheed his wages. With a wife and five children wholly dependent on his wages, his wife a chronic invalid, two girls in high school, and the entire family suffering from undernutrition, the man's wages are *thirteen dollars a week*. Less than two dollars a day to feed seven mouths, pay rent, buy clothing.

Two weeks ago I visited Alabama, Georgia, and other Southern States. The collapse of cotton prices will hit the Negro farmers—some four million of them—

harder than any other group, inasmuch as they are now and have been for some time on the ragged edge. A recent survey by the National Urban League reveals that in Chicago Negroes form four per cent of the population but four times that percentage of the unemployed; in Pittsburgh Negroes make up eight per cent of the total population but 38 per cent of those out of work; in Baltimore the percentages are 17 and 31.5; in Buffalo 3 and 25.8; in Houston, Texas, 25 and 50; in Little Rock, Arkansas, 20 and 54; in Memphis, 38 and 75; in Philadelphia, 7 and 25.

Usually the last to be hired and first to be fired, kept out of the skilled and semi-skilled trades even when amply qualified by ability and training to perform skilled work at correspondingly higher wages, the Negro unquestionably is suffering during this period of distress more than almost any other group. Lynchings have declined in number during recent years but are still frequent enough to hang ominously over the heads of Negroes, particularly in the Southern and border States, as a not unlikely fate should they stir the mob's hostility, ever near the surface. The benefits of unionization are denied them; the American Federation of Labor has even ceased passing perfunctory resolutions against the color line in union membership, while the majority of its constituent unions bar Negroes from membership by constitutional provision or unwritten law. According to Edwin R. Embree, President of the Julius Rosenwald Fund, in his recent book, *Brown America*, though Negroes are taxed at the same rate as whites, yet the average annual expenditure in eight Southern States for education per colored child is but $12.50 against $44.31 for each white child. In Georgia the average is $35.42 for whites and $6.38 for Negroes; in Mississippi, $45.34 and $5.45.

These are but the immediate pin pricks, sharp as they are. For it is not generally realized that an enormous change has taken place in Negro thinking since the World War. More and more the Negro has realized that the problem he encounters in the United States is only a part of the whole structure of race prejudice which the modern age of imperialism has created. The stirrings of thought and unrest in Africa, Asia, and the Far East of black and brown and yellow races have not been without their counterpart in the United States. The War shattered whatever notions of the white man's infallibility and invulnerability the Negro and other colored races unquestionably held prior to 1914. Thoughtful Negroes see all too clearly that the world order which seemed so impregnable before the shooting at Sarajevo is in a bad way if it isn't on the point of collapse. They realize, as does Paul Hutchinson in his *World Revolution and Religion*, that the white nations of the present world have no intention of changing materially the scheme whereby the colored races of mankind have so small a share of the wealth and power they help create; and the ruling classes among the white nations of the earth seem to them to be as filled as ever with pride and greed and sublime contempt towards every race and color but their own.

It is through such an embittered Negro world that the Communists shrewdly sought to spread their theories and to gain a large following. At first their efforts met with a success which amazed the more conservative leaders of Negro opinion. A man who is starving, homeless, exploited, and oppressed is always a fertile field for those who advocate a change. Many Negroes looked upon the Communist as a new Messiah, a new Moses sent to lead them from the bondage which had become almost unbearable. With jesuitical zeal and cleverness the American Communist agitator sought to fan this flame of discontent which the slave trader, the lyncher, the disfranchiser, the denier of decent jobs and wages and homes had lighted and kept alive through three centuries. He resorted to every possible means to impress upon the Negro that he had no stake in his own land, that a philosophy of complete despair was the only sane and intelligent attitude for him to take. All this was centered about the Scottsboro cases as the basis for a highly emotional appeal. Negroes and whites were urged to give vent to their resentment against the farcical trials accorded the nine Negro boys by sending telegrams to the Governor of Alabama or to other officials of that State, peremptorily demanding immediate release of the defendants. Often the industrious Communists volunteered to write the messages for less literate Negroes. It is reported that Governor Miller of Alabama has received more than seventeen hundred such messages.

When this campaign of threats was denounced by non-Communist organizations like the N.A.A.C.P., the vials of wrath of Communist publications were poured upon them and they were denounced as "traitors" and as conspirators to execute the boys.

For a time some of the Negro editors accepted without question the stories sent to them and the interpretations put into those stories by the Communists. "What does it matter whether God, the devil, or Communists save those helpless black boys down there in Alabama?" declared an Oklahoma paper editorially. "We don't by a long sight endorse the complete program of the Communists; we see that organization just as we see everything else. There is good and bad in everything and everybody. When the Communists talk about the overthrow of government we quit their program, but when they talk of race equality and the protection of constitutional rights of citizens, we are with them one hundred per cent and we are not ashamed to say so."

Another paper in Texas, after pointing out that America with all her boasted wealth and genius is unable to protect her own citizens either from the mob or starvation, declared, "We are hearing much in America during these times about Communism and the efforts of Soviet agitators to make converts in this country, and despite the fact that the press of the nation does not regard this type of propaganda as a menace, yet when men and women are victimized by hunger, want, privation and suffering, almost any kind of radical and revolutionary doctrine, which offers them certain relief and liberation from the system under which they are suffering will make considerable headway among a large element of such a population."

V

Seldom in the history of modern times has a field so fruitful been ready and waiting. That the opportunity to take lasting advantage of this was lost is almost entirely due to the shortsightedness of the leaders of the Communist party in the United States. Had they been more intelligent, honest, and truthful there is no way of estimating how deeply they might have penetrated into Negro life and consciousness. At the beginning of the Scottsboro Case they talked much and often of a "united front," but it was soon to be seen that all who did not submit wholly to Communist dictation were classed and branded as "enemies" and "tools of the capitalists." The suspicion began to grow in the Negro mind—and this suspicion was more than confirmed—that at least some of the Communists did not want the nine boys saved but sought instead to make "martyrs" of them for purposes of spreading Communist propaganda among Negroes. Negroes, too, saw that in the present stage of events the only Southern whites who were trying to get a new trial for the nine boys were capitalists, one of them the son of a former governor of Alabama, while the mob which had surrounded the courthouse at Scottsboro had been made up largely of white "workers." Negroes realized that ill-advised, threatening tactics would serve no other immediate purpose than to make their own lot infinitely harder; that enemies of the Negro would surely utilize Communist agitation as a pretext for refusal to remedy bad conditions, for stifling legitimate protest by Negroes through attributing it to "Communist" propaganda. Disillusionment replaced the hope which the Communist orators had brought.

It is unfortunate that the American leaders of Communism were not blessed with more common sense. Their bungling and dangerous tactics in the Scottsboro cases have even led to sharp criticism from within their own party. The *Revolutionary Age*, for example, says of the methods used:

> Such is the poisonous blight spread in every direction by the new sectarian policies dominating the Communist Party today, that even this glorious page [taking up defense of the nine boys] has been darkened by its ominous shadow. False and suicidal tactics have well nigh undone the achievements of profoundly correct principles! When the I.L.D. initiated its Scottsboro campaign, it outlined a program of great promise. A broad and real united front movement was planned with slogans that would draw in the most backward masses and their organizations, both white and black. An end to the insanity of "social-fascism" and a cessation to the orgies of irresponsible abuse were promised. But the promises turned into ashes. . . .
>
> It did not take very long before it became clear enough that the Communist Party leadership had no conception whatever of what the united front really is. At the beginning, every friendly word in the Negro press, every sympathetic gesture was hailed in the columns of the *Daily Worker* as the "broadening of the united front." Then suddenly everything changed. Only those who accepted the ultimate slogans of the Communists and subordinated themselves to the I.L.D. were regarded as "in the united front"—all others became "staunch allies of the white masters."
>
> . . . Coupled with this altogether false conception of the united front came an equally false estimation of the role of petty bourgeois organizations among the Negroes as an oppressed people. Nor was any sign exhibited of an appreciation of the importance of gaining a labor base among the white workers. The same old story resulted—"conferences" which represented nobody, "united fronts" based on appeals to "follow" the Communist Party, discredit, isolation. . . .

Thus has the Communist Party again gotten itself into the unenviable position that it has been in altogether too frequently in recent months—that of a force for disunity and splitting.

Among Negroes the pendulum swung sharply away from the American Communist program, even among those of intelligence who had looked, if not with sympathy, at least with interest upon the economic and social experiment which is going on in Soviet Russia. Among these is the distinguished Negro sociologist and editor, Dr. W. E. B. Du Bois, who wrote in the September issue of the *Crisis* that if the Communists had been really intelligent they would have joined hands with any and all bodies and individuals who honestly sought to provide the best legal defense possible, and then, the case won, they "could have proceeded to point out that legal defense alone, even if successful, will never solve the larger Negro problem but that further and more radical steps are needed."

"Unfortunately," Doctor Du Bois added, the tactics of the American Communists were "neither wise nor intelligent. . . . If the Communists want these lads murdered, then their tactics of threatening judges and yelling for mass action on the part of white Southern workers is calculated to insure this."

Clarence Darrow's entrance into the cases at Scottsboro effectively silences in the minds of all but the most intransigent the argument that "capitalists" are trying to murder the nine Negro boys of the Scottsboro cases. In the meantime the United States can, if it will, learn a lesson from these cases, tragically so typical of three centuries of oppression of the Negro here. The Negro is not turning red just yet; but that circumstance is due chiefly to the blunders of the Communists.

For three hundred years the Negroes have been unswervingly loyal. Should the burdens they have borne so long not be lightened, they can hardly be blamed if sheer hopelessness descends upon them and they are tempted to turn on their oppressors. They know that they will be in doubled jeopardy if they face both anti-Negro and anti-Communist feeling. Some of them are willing, nevertheless, to face even that and death rather than go on as things now stand.

There is but one effective and intelligent way in which to counteract Communist efforts at proselyting among American Negroes, and that method is drastic revision of the almost chronic American indifference to the Negro's plight. Give him jobs, decent living conditions, and homes. Assure him of justice in the courts and protection of life and property in Mississippi as well as in New York. Put an end to flagrant and unchecked disregard of the Negro's constitutional right to vote. Let labor unions—conservative and liberal *as well as radical*—abolish written or implied barriers against the Negro, doing so in sheer enlightened selfishness, if for no other reason, since it is self-evident that white labor will never be free as long as black labor is enslaved and exploited. Let employers of labor even in this time of acute depression see to it that Negro workingmen are treated no worse than white. In brief, the only antidote to the spread among American Negroes of revolutionary doctrines is even-handed justice.

IV

THE NUMBERS
RUNNER

Of all the hustlers that prey in poorer black communities, none is considered more sympathetically than the numbers runner or the numbers writer. The poor, of course, are more likely to be victimized by lottery games but they often feel that such a gamble is giving them a better chance to get something than anything legitimate that society has to offer. Perhaps the most famous numbers man was Caspar Holstein (1877–1944), who became known as the "King of Policy." Holstein was very interested in his native Virgin Islands as well as in blacks generally. (Some of his essays on the Virgin Islands are included elsewhere in this volume.) He was supportive of the Harlem Renaissance and gave money to support *Opportunity* magazine's annual literary contests. Here are two different views of the numbers game.

THE NUMBERS WRITER

A Portrait

JULIAN MAYFIELD was born on June 6, 1928. He is a novelist, essayist, playwright, teacher, Broadway and Hollywood actor, and adviser to the late Kwame Nkrumah of Ghana and Prime Minister Forbes Burnham of Guyana. His most famous piece of writing is the screenplay for the 1968 film *Uptight*, based on the famous 1930s John Ford classic film of Irish rebellion and betrayal, *The Informer*. Jules Dassin directed *Uptight*. "The Numbers Writer: A Portrait" was published in the *Nation* on May 14, 1960.

The policy racket was in the news again. Adam Clayton Powell (D., NY) had charged that the New York City police were cooperating with white numbers bankers to drive Negro bankers out of Harlem. Police Commissioner Kennedy replied that the charges were irresponsible. Representative Powell, whose district includes most of Harlem, read names and addresses of white "policy barons" into the *Congressional Record*, and there was a wave of arrests in Harlem. The newspapers vied with one another to see which could produce the loudest headlines. It seemed that, after half a century, a real attack was about to be mounted against the numbers game.

I wondered what my friend Jimmy Slick thought about all this furor, and I went up to Harlem to see him. Jimmy is a numbers writer who has spent more than half of his forty years in the racket. In the early afternoon he is always at his favorite barroom on Seventh Avenue, where he writes down the bets of his customers, and it was there I found him going about business-as-usual. When I asked him what he thought of Mr. Powell's declaration of war on the numbers game, he set his glass on the bar and cursed—not violently, but tiredly, as if he were weary of everything, even his own curses.

Jimmy was one of those who had been picked up a few days before during the mass arrests. The young white plainclothesman who took him to the precinct station had been very embarrassed because he himself was on the policy payroll, the same as Jimmy. The detective had been full of apologies, but Jimmy had comforted him, assuring him that everything was cool, that such things were to be expected from time to time. "This cop," Jimmy said, "is one of my regular players. He's been betting 507 with me for two years."

I asked Jimmy if he thought he would receive less "action" (betting) as a result of all of the unfavorable publicity, and he stared at me as if I had suggested he run for President. "Man," he said, "you can't stop people from playing the numbers. And, furthermore, nobody is going to try to stop them. This is a business." He said it with a quiet assurance that is disconcerting to a person who believes in the possibilities of genuine social reform.

Since 1900, there have been countless exposés of the policy racket, and there have been several vigorous spurts of prosecutions. Indeed, it can be argued that one man, Thomas E. Dewey, almost reached the White House on the fame he achieved in his war on the numbers. But today the racket is more highly organized than ever and, as a business, it shows no signs of experiencing even a mild recession during the present municipal soul-searching. In each of the greater urban centers, it is the employer of several thousand people, and in New York City alone its annual take is estimated to be a *quarter of a billion* dollars.

Even the most tolerant among us must by now be convinced that the policy racket can no longer be considered a harmless pastime. It is a cancerous growth on city life. It siphons millions of dollars a year from the sections of the population that can least afford it. A huge share of its revenue is used to bribe the police and public officials who protect it. Worse, the easy atmosphere of corruption in which it flourishes destroys respect for social institutions and encourages juvenile delinquency. Moreover, the well-greased and efficient machinery of the numbers game is used for other criminal activity; many of the policy barons are knee-deep in the dope traffic, using the capital acquired from one to furnish cash needed for the other.

I like to think that Jimmy Slick is unaware of the anti-human ramifications of his trade. He is, after all, only a minor figure in the operation. But perhaps he is aware, for I have heard him say, defensively: "This is a business, man, like any other. Millions of dollars are involved. You can't stop business. Business comes first."

I believe that is the heart of the matter. Jimmy Slick and his world view, his *Weltanschauung*, were not created by the policy racket. Both Jimmy and the racket were spawned out of—and are sustained by—certain generally accepted attitudes which many people fear now dominate our national character. These attitudes might be summed up as follows: The highest motivation of mankind is to look out for Number One; corruption and compromise of principle are as natural to human society as breathing; and, in the end the only thing that matters is success (the getting of money, influence or power).

It is in this framework that we must test Jimmy Slick's cynicism. To him the policy racket is merely a thread in the quilt of national corruption. He did not share the outrage that many people felt when the deep-freeze exposés shook the Truman Administration or when Sherman Adams was driven out of Washington for accepting favors from a person doing business with the government. Jimmy has assumed for many years that nearly everyone in public office is on the make one way or the other, that where there is no actual graft there is the use of influence and the exchange of favors for personal gain. The hullabaloo over the fixed TV quiz shows and payola confuses him, for he cannot believe so many people are genuinely indignant over something that is so perfectly natural. To a barroom pal who was excoriating Charles Van Doren, Jimmy said: "Cut the bull, man. Nobody turns down $123,000, no matter what he has to do for it." Few people, privately, would disagree with him.

Jimmy's attitude is more complex toward prominent Negroes who find themselves in trouble, but it is consistent with his philosophy. He defends Adam Clayton Powell and Hulan Jack, but he does not protest their innocence. He is convinced that politics are behind the prosecutions. Besides, he points out, the amounts of money involved are piddling compared to the sums he has heard changed hands during certain Title I slum-clearance deals. The one thing for which Jimmy will never forgive Mr. Jack is that he received only $5,500. Jimmy says scornfully, "That was a disgrace to Harlem!" Why, he demands (echoing Mr. Powell's outcry against the police and the white policy barons) should the Negro get a smaller share of the spoils?

Jimmy never believed that Congress would pass a strong civil-rights bill this year. He is even a little amused at the circus that was staged in Washington, for he wonders how it appeared to the rest of the world. He expresses no outrage that President Eisenhower, while vacationing at a Jim Crow golf course in Augusta, pontificates about the challenges facing the free world while he refuses to take a forthright stand on human freedom at home. To Jimmy this *is* the American way of life.

It is years since he has been stirred by the promise in the Bill of Rights, and he would be downright embarrassed pledging his allegiance to the flag of the United States. He remembers the Star Spangled Banner nostalgically only because of a verse he and his Harlem schoolmates used to sing to the tune:

Oh, say, can you see
Any bedbugs on me . . .
If you do, take a few
Because they came from you . . .

Obviously, Jimmy is not typical of any large segment of our society. But this should give no one comfort, for his attitudes, while not typical, are symptomatic of a growing cynicism among those who once dreamed of seeing our nation realize its great potential. The cold war, the constant threat of a nuclear holocaust, the era of McCarthyism and a creeping apathy have taken an awesome toll of the most visionary elements in our community.

Idealism has given way not to complacency, but to resignation. How are we to meet the challenge presented by Jimmy Slick? Do we still have the capacity to regenerate his faith in the American promise? Or have we resigned our prerogatives as free citizens to such an extent that there is now a little of Jimmy Slick in all of us?

THE POOR PAY MORE, EVEN FOR THEIR DREAMS

ETHERIDGE KNIGHT was a poet and essayist who achieved considerable notice in the early 1970s for his anthology, *Black Voices From Prison* (1970), which featured most of the work that Knight himself is famous for. Knight served time in Indiana State Prison. *Black Voices From Prison* was one of several works by black male writers in prison—Eldridge Cleaver and George Jackson are two other black writers who come to mind immediately—a sort of sub-genre that enjoyed a vogue in those days. "The Poor Pay More, Even for Their Dreams," a darker, more despairing look at the numbers game, is an essay by Knight from *Black Voices From Prison*.

One of the most familiar replies heard in a black community to the casual greetings, "What'cha know?" and "How're you doing?" is the reply: "Just the same old three-six-nine." The despair and futility, even to the uninitiated, is clearly conveyed in the replier's tone, but to those devotees of the "numbers game" and "dream books," there is still a deeper meaning that sums up in one word, in one symbol, the total attitude of the replier. To such a person, 3-6-9 means shit. According to the "dream books," whenever one dreams of shit he should, immediately upon arising, "play" 3-6-9 with his favorite "numbers writer"—even if it means using the rent money to do so.

In the "numbers game," a player determines (via dream books, license numbers, astrology, hunches, etc.) which numbers he wants to play, and, along with his wager, he gives them to a writer, who usually has a route of steady customers and who usually has established a timetable to be in certain bars, poolrooms, and hangouts. The given numbers, the player's wager and the writer's "mark" are written down, in triplicate, on a small pad called the "slip." The player is given a "slip," the writer keeps one, and the third copy, along with the player's wager, is turned in to a "station."

The winning numbers are determined either by certain digits taken from the *advance, decline,* and *unchanged* columns of the New York Stock Exchange report, or by a "wheel" which is generally a barrel-like device in which, say, a thousand chits, numbered from one to a hundred, are placed. The "wheel" is spun; a given amount of chits are withdrawn from it, and their numbers are recorded on a slip of paper, from which hundreds of mimeographed copies are made and distributed to various "drops" and "stations" throughout the city. Thus, a player, according to the particular organization, can find out if he has "hit" the numbers simply by reading a daily paper, or else by stopping by a "station" and picking up a "drawing."

If a player has chosen the right combination of digits, he wins about $300 for a ten-cent wager. He can also win a lesser amount if three of his four digits have appeared in a predicted sequence. The odds, however, against picking the winning combination from the New York Stock Exchange report is something like one in 15,000. The odds against picking the winning combination from a "policy wheel" is sometimes more, sometimes less; it is left entirely up to the individual "banker" to decide how many chits are to be placed in the "wheel." (Some bankers, in order to establish an honest reputation, sometimes allow a few writers and players to witness a drawing of the chits. And they also contrive "hits" to stimulate business, to make the poor shell out more money for their dreams.)

The numbers operation is highly organized. At the base of the business are the writers, the men and women who roam through the black neighborhoods collecting the dreams of black people in the form of "plays" that generally range from a dime to a dollar. The writers, at designated times, turn the bets and slips in to a station, or drop, which is most often the back room of a tavern or poolroom. Then a "runner" picks up the slips and bets (and the dreams) and takes them to the "clearing house" or "bank."

At the next level is the "baron" or "banker." In the black neighborhoods, he is nowadays usually a Negro; he is in charge of the clearing house and of that particular district. He directly oversees the "counters"—usually a corps of black women—who tally the wagers and slips (and dreams) and set aside the writer's commission, which is perhaps 15 percent of the amount he turns in. The baron is always a man of means and influence. He often controls a large amount of black votes, and he can fix a traffic ticket or minor beef. In some cases he can handle a "nigger-knifing" or "nigger-killing"; most likely, he has two or three "nigger-killings" to his own credit. He is seldom arrested. (But when the real heat is on, it is he or one of his chief lieutenants who goes to prison.)

At the head of the numbers operation is the shadowy "big man," who looms like a specter not only over the numbers game but over the entire neighborhood. He is the representative of an organized criminal syndicate which, according to some law officials, plucks an annual $6 billion out of the pocketbooks and dreams of black people. In return for this enormous sum, the "big man" and his invisible partners, through their political connections and with their hired guns, provide the baron and his subordinates with protection from the police and also from ambitious independent operators or young black men who might be bold enough to stick up a station or clearing house. (The threat of the syndicate's guns also ensures that the banker and his subordinates do not "hold out" any of the take.) The "big man," often in partnership with the baron, has his fingers in other pies: crap games, narcotics, prostitution, loan-sharking—all of which suck the blood out of black neighborhoods.

The numbers operation with its blood-sucking corollaries could not exist without the aid and assistance of a corrupt political system whose bosses also grow fat off the dimes and dreams of black people. According to the *Report by the President's Commission on Law Enforcement and Administration of Justice*: "Today's corruption is less visible, more subtle and therefore more difficult to detect and assess than the corruption of the prohibition era. [But] All available data indicate that organized crime flourishes only where it has corrupted local officials. . . . To secure political power, organized crime tries by bribes or political contributions to corrupt the non-office holding political leaders to whom judges, mayors, prosecuting attorneys and correctional officials may be responsive."

In some neighborhoods there have been times in which the local political system was so corrupt that the "big man" could have policemen, ostensibly patrolling the neighborhood, guard the drops and clearing houses against stickup men. From time to time a writer or runner is arrested (especially before a local election) or a drop or clearing house is raided. The small fish are then fined or given short jail sentences. And there are times when federal officials intervene in the rackets and a baron—or one of his lieutenants—is arrested and sentenced to prison. But neither the "big man," the principals in the crime syndicate, nor the corrupt political officials are ever arrested and convicted of a crime.

When the real heat is on, say after a baron has been busted, a numbers operation may fold. But immediately another springs up, brandishing an exotic name—"Yellow Dog" or "Blue Angel" or "Bright Star." The demand for business is always great. The black people still have their dimes and their dreams, and the syndicate and the politicians still have their connections and their greed.

There is little doubt that the numbers games are an influence in the lives of many ghetto people. It is as common to hear a mother say, "I gotta get my number in today," with the same concern—and sometimes in the same breath—as she says, "I gotta feed the baby." Men, on their way to and from work, play their numbers as regularly as they punch the time clock. Hustlers, whores, deacons, and grandmothers, all play their favorite numbers. In some homes the "dream book" is as familiar and is read with almost the same reverence as the Bible.

And there are others, besides the organized criminals and corrupt politicians, who live off the dreams of black people. Along any main avenue of a black community one can find, crammed in against the poolrooms, pawnshops, and storefront churches, a shop specializing in lucky numbers, herbs, holy water, and "dream books" (*Gypsy Queen, Aunt Mandy, Black Sal,* etc.). Negro weekly newspapers carry advertisements by "prophets" and "preachers," who, for a fee of course, will bless numbers, interpret dreams, and prophesy "hits."

Some people argue the desirability of the numbers game. Saul Alinsky, a nationally known community organizer, has said that playing the numbers has been one of the major ways that black people have sustained their hopes over these many years of oppression. Others argue that a numbers operation provides employment for a group of people, that the "hits" stimulate the flow of money in black neighborhoods, and that "people will just naturally gamble."

Now, while there may be just a little truth to their arguments, how do they measure the truth of the dreams that are crumpled along with each slip or policy drawing that flutters in the gutter while the baron, the "big man," and the greedy politicians glide by in their shiny cars. The benefits to a black community from a numbers operation is a mouse's tit compared to the elephant's udder suckled by the syndicate and politicians. And, perhaps some scholar on the subject of the collective dreams of an oppressed people could explain to those who argue for the numbers operation why it is that three of the constantly played combinations are 6-6-60, 5-10-15, and 2-19-29, which, according to the dream books, are respectively sexual intercourse, clear water, and money. And also why the two most often played combinations of all are: 3-6-9 and 7-11-44. The former is shit; the latter is blood.

V

BOXING

Black writers have written about the sport of boxing more than any other sport. Considering the impact that some black boxing champions have had on American popular culture and American politics, the preoccupation that some black intellectuals have had with boxing is understandable. Few blacks have had a greater presence in America than Jack Johnson, the first heavyweight boxing champion (1908–1915), Joe Louis, heavyweight champion during the late thirties through nearly the entire decade of the forties, and Muhammad Ali, boxing champion from 1964 to 1967 and from 1974 to 1978. Other black boxers such as Sugar Ray Robinson, Sugar Ray Leonard, Archie Moore, Henry Armstrong, Sandy Saddler, Kid Chocolate, and Kid Gavilan were important stylistic innovators—not only in boxing but in black culture generally—who were particularly revered among black fans. The following essays offer various perspectives on the sport.

HIGH TIDE IN HARLEM

Joe Louis as a Symbol of Freedom

RICHARD WRIGHT's *Native Son* (1940) remains one of the monumental novels in American literature. His short fiction in *Uncle Tom's Children* (1937) and his autobiography, *Black Boy* (1945), have become standard texts in college and high school literature courses. If there is a black writer who has become "classic," Wright is probably the closest to it. Born in Mississippi in 1908, Wright became active in the Communist party in both Chicago and New York during the Depression but grew increasingly dissatisfied with some of its policies in relation to the race question. He finally dissociated himself from the communists in the early forties. After the Second World War, he lived abroad, mostly in Paris, dying there in 1960. He wrote several nonfiction works while abroad, including a study of Kwame Nkrumah and Ghana, a travelogue of Spain, and an account of the Bandung Conference. After years of neglect, these books are beginning to generate both academic and popular interest. "High Tide in Harlem" was published on July 5, 1938 for *New Masses*, one of the left-wing magazines that were essential to Wright's early development as a writer. It was the last of three pieces he was to write on Joe Louis and it was his longest and his most intricately argued, examining as it does the cultural symbolism of the second Louis–Schmeling fight, one of the major sporting events in American social history.

The colossal bowl of seventy thousand hazy faces, an oval, an oval-shaped tableau compounded of criss-crossed beams of light and shadow, waited almost in silence for the gong to sound that would start the Louis–Schmeling million-dollar fight. The gaze of the seventy thousand eyes was centered on the "squared circle," a single diadem-like spot of canvas lit to blinding whiteness under the intense glaze of overhead floodlights. So dwarfed was the ring by the mammoth stadium that it seemed that each man and woman was straining forward to peer at a colorful puppet show.

The Louis-Schmeling fight for the heavyweight championship of the word at the Yankee Stadium was one of the greatest dramas of make-believe ever witnessed in America, a drama which manipulated the common symbols and impulses in the minds and bodies of millions of people so effectively as to put to shame our professional playwrights, our O'Neills, our Lawsons, and our Caldwells. Promoter Mike Jacobs, prompted purely by commercial motives, has accidentally won the rare right, whether he wants to claim it or not, of wearing the purple robes customarily reserved for Euripides and Sophocles.

Each of the seventy thousand who had so eagerly jammed his way into the bowl's steel tiers under the open sky had come already emotionally conditioned as to the values that would triumph if *his* puppet won. Attached to each puppet, a white puppet and a black puppet, was a configuration of social images whose intensity and clarity had been heightened through weeks of skillful and constant agitation: social images whose emotional appeal could evoke attitudes tantamount to two distinct ways of life in the world today. Whichever puppet went down the Greek route to defeat that night would leave the path clear for the imperious sway of the balked impulses of one side or the other. The puppet emerging victorious would be the symbol of a fond wish gratified, would feed the starved faith of men caught in the mesh of circumstances.

Joe Louis, the black puppet who wore black trunks, was the betting favorite; but that was no indication as to how much actual sentiment there was for him among the seventy thousand spectators, for men like to bet on winners. And, too, just how much sentiment there was for Max Schmeling, the white puppet who wore purple trunks, no one, perhaps, will ever know; for now that the violent drama is ended the backers of the loser do not want to parade their disappointment for the scorn of others. But the two puppets were dissimilar enough in "race, creed, and previous condition of servitude" as to make their partisans wax militant, hopeful.

But out beyond the walls of the stadium were twelve million Negroes to whom the black puppet symbolized the living refutation of the hatred spewed forth daily over radio, in newspapers, in movies, and in books about their lives. Day by day, since their alleged emancipation, they have watched a picture of themselves being painted as lazy, stupid, and diseased. In helpless horror they have suffered the attacks and exploitation which followed in the wake of their being branded as "inferiors." True, hundreds of thousands of these Negroes would have preferred that the refutation could have been made in some form other than pugilism; but so effectively and completely have they been isolated and restricted in vocation that they rarely have had the opportunity to participate in the meaningful processes of America's national life. Jim Crowed in the army and navy, barred from many trades and professions, excluded from commerce and finance, relegated to menial positions in government, segregated residentially, denied the right of franchise for the most part; in short, forced to live a separate and impoverished life, they were glad for even the meager acceptance of their humanity implied in the championship of Joe Louis.

Visits to Joe Louis's training camp revealed throngs of Negroes standing around in a state of deep awe, waiting for just one glimpse of their champion. They were good, simple-hearted people, longing deeply for something of their own to be loyal to. When Joe appeared, a hush fell upon them and they stared. They took Joe into their hearts because he was a public idol and was respectfully enshrined in the public's imagination in a way they knew they would never be.

But because Joe's a Negro, even though he has to his credit a most enviable list of victories, there have been constant warnings issued by the Bilbos and Ellenders from south of the Mason-Dixon Line as to the wisdom of allowing a Negro to defeat a white man in public. The reactionary argument ran that such spectacles tended to create in Negroes too much pride and made them "intractable."

Naturally, Max Schmeling's victory over Louis two years ago was greeted with elation in reactionary quarters. A close study of Louis's stance, which revealed that he could be hit, together with a foul blow delivered after the bell, enabled the German boxer to win. Louis's defeat came as a shock to the boxing world and provided material for countless conversations and speculations. It was taken for granted that the second-rate Schmeling's defeat of the then reigning champion, the aging Braddock, was but a matter of time. But due to squabbles among promoters, Louis, not Schmeling, fought Braddock for the championship and won the title by a knockout in a thrilling bout in Chicago. Immediately, the Nazi press, in America and in Germany, launched a campaign of slurs against Louis, dubbing him the "so-called champion," and declaring that Schmeling's prior victory over Louis was proof of "Negro inferiority." Schmeling boasted to the press that it would be easy for him to defeat the Negro again because (1) Negroes never forget beatings, (2) his mere "white" presence would be enough to throw fear into Louis's heart, and (3) he would enter the ring with a "psychological edge" over the Negro. An open friend of Hitler and an avowed supporter of the Nazis, Schmeling caught the fancy of many reactionary Americans, plus the leaders of Nazi Germany, fascist Italy, Japan, and even certain circles in England. To bolster the aims of the forces of fascism, Schmeling's victory was interpreted to mean the ability of the "Aryan race to out-think inferior races." The logical implication of such a line of reasoning was that all Negroes, colonial people, and small nations were inherently backward, physically cowardly, a drag upon the rest of civilization, and should be conquered and sub-jected for the benefit of mankind.

But when faced with this specious proposition, the common people instinct-ively revolted. They knew that the majority of all prizefighters came from the so-called "backward people," that is, the working class; their capacity to fight stemming from an early life of toil in steel and iron foundries, coal mines, factories, and fields. Consequently, in his fight against Schmeling, Louis carried the good wishes of even the poor whites of the Deep South, something unparalleled in the history of America.

The appearance of the white puppet sent the crowd into a frenzy. The black puppet's ovation seemed incidental. The ring was cleared and the fight was on. The entire seventy thousand rose as one man. At the beginning of the fight there was a wild shriek which gradually died as the seconds flew. What was happening was so stunning that even cheering was out of place. The black puppet, contrary to all

Nazi racial laws, was punching the white puppet so rapidly that the eye could not follow the blows. It was not really a fight, it was an act of revenge, of dominance, of complete mastery. The black puppet glided from his corner and simply wiped his feet on the white puppet's face. The black puppet was contemptuous, swift; his victory was complete, unquestionable, decisive; his blows must have jarred the marrow not only in the white puppet's but in Hitler's own bones.

In Harlem, that area of a few square blocks in upper Manhattan where a quarter of a million Negroes are forced to live through an elaborate connivance among landlords, merchants, and politicians, a hundred thousand black people surged out of taprooms, flats, restaurants, and filled the streets and sidewalks, like the Mississippi River overflowing in flood-time. With their faces to the night sky, they filled their lungs with air and let out a scream of joy that it seemed would never end, and a scream that seemed to come from untold reserves of strength. They wanted to make a noise comparable to the happiness bubbling in their hearts, but they were poor and had nothing. So they went to the garbage pails and got tin cans; they went to their kitchens and got tin pots, pans, washboards, wooden boxes, and took possession of the streets. They shouted, sang, laughed, yelled, blew paper horns, clasped hands, and formed weaving snake-lines, whistled, sounded sirens, and honked auto horns. From the windows of the tall, dreary tenements torn scraps of newspaper floated down. With the reiteration that evoked a hypnotic atmosphere, they chanted with eyes half-closed, heads lilting in unison, legs and shoulders moving and touching:

"Ain't you glad? Ain't you glad?"

Knowing full well the political effect of Louis's victory on the popular mind the world over, thousands yelled:

"Heil Louis!"

It was Harlem's mocking taunt to fascist Hitler's boast of the superiority of "Aryans" over other races. And they ridiculed the Nazi salute of the outstretched palm by throwing up their own dark ones to show how little they feared and thought of the humbug of fascist ritual.

With no less than a hundred thousand participating, it was the largest and most spontaneous political demonstration ever seen in Harlem and marked the highest tide of popular political enthusiasm ever witnessed among American Negroes.

Negro voices called fraternally to Jewish-looking faces in passing autos:

"I bet all the Jews are happy tonight!"

Men, women, and children gathered in thick knots and did the Big Apple, the Lindy Hop, the Truck—Harlem's gesture of defiance to the high cost of food, high rent, and misery. These ghetto-dwellers, under the stress of the joy of one of their own kind having wiped out the stain of defeat and having thrown the lie of "inferiority" into the teeth of the fascist, threw off restraint and fear. Each time a downtown auto slowed, it became covered with Joe Louis rooters, and the autos looked like clusters of black ripe grapes. A bus stopped and at once became filled with laughing throngs who "forgot" to pay their fares; children clambered up its tall sides and crawled over the hoods and fenders.

It was the celebration of Louis's victory over Carnera, Baer, Pastor, Farr, and Braddock all rolled into one. Ethiopian and American flags fluttered. Effigies of Schmeling chalked with the swastika were dragged through the streets.

Then, nobody knows from where and nobody bothered to ask, there appeared on the surface of the sea of people white placards hurling slogans of defiance at fascist pretensions and calling upon native lovers of democracy to be true to democratic ideals. *Oust Hitler's Spies and Agents; Pass the Anti-Lynching Bill; Down with Hitler and Mussolini; Alabama Produced Joe Louis; Free the Scottsboro Boys; Democracies Must Fight Fascism Everywhere.*

Carry the dream on for yourself; lift it out of the trifling guise of a prizefight celebration and supply the social and economic details and you have the secret dynamics of proletarian aspiration. The eyes of these people were bold that night. Their fear of property, of the armed police fell away. There was in their chant a hunger deeper than that for bread as they marched along. In their joy they were feeling an impulse which only the oppressed can feel to the full. They wanted to fling the heavy burden out of their hearts and embrace the world. They wanted to feel that their expanding feelings were not limited; that the earth was theirs as much as anybody else's; that they did not have to live by proscription in one corner of it; that they could go where they wanted to and do what they wanted to, eat and live where they wanted to, like others. They wanted to own things in common and do things in common. They wanted a holiday.

A STUDY OF THE BLACK FIGHTER

NATHAN HARE is a writer, university professor, psychologist, lecturer, and, as his essay makes clear, a former boxer. A prolific author for many years, he has also served as associate editor of *The Black Scholar*, one of the major intellectual Afrocentric journals currently being published in the United States. "A Study of the Black Fighter" was published in *The Black Scholar* in November 1971.

Fighters occupy a peculiar position within the realm of the professional athlete. They emerge from the most oppressed strata within the major cities and excite widespread attention as the most exploited group within the athletic world. Currently, most (more than 70 per cent) are black, and the "white hope" syndrome is so intense as to enter into fights between two blacks.

When the late Sonny Liston was preparing to fight Floyd Patterson, the NAACP and Ralph Bunche both made public statements that victory for Liston would strike a serious blow for the black struggle for equality.[1] When Muhammad Ali joined the the black muslims, Martin Luther King remarked that he had become "a champion of racial segregation." Ali responded that he was "an example for the youth of the whole world."[2] Today, when Ali fights, blacks and whites of a variety of political persuasions will regard him and his fight as a political force.

Fighters as a group are:

. . . set apart in the public mind by the fact that the object of their sport is to inflict bodily injury. Thus to some people they represent brutality and degradation; to others, virility and courage . . . They are very human individuals, equipped with all the human reactions and emotions. Most fighters know the natural fear of getting hurt. Most of them do not enjoy hurting their opponents and feel a compulsion to rationalize this as a business necessity. Although they are all looking for financial reward, the greatest number are impelled even more by the desire for recognition and prestige. They long for the approval of the fans and for public understanding and acceptance. In their private lives they have a number of special problems, and when they retire they find it difficult to adjust to routine life.[3]

For the black fighter, these and other problems are intensified. I know this to be true for two main reasons. One is that I was a boxer myself.[4] Although I boxed mainly as an avocation and never attained great heights as a fighter, I did have thirty-six fights, both amateur and professional. In my last professional fight on December 5, 1967 in the Washington, D.C. Coliseum, I knocked out my opponent in two minutes and twenty-two seconds of the first round. In all, I won twenty-eight and lost eight and was never knocked down or badly beaten.

In the process, I came to know personally hundreds of fighters and retired fighters, including Muhammad Ali and Bobby Foster, the light heavyweight champion, with whom I frequently sparred in the days when he was still an up and coming fighter.

However, my observations on professional fighters go beyond my daily contacts with them. For my master's thesis at the University of Chicago, I conducted a systematic study of fifty-eight professional fighters, some active, some retired, and nearly all of them black. I sought to discover what forces lured them into the boxing ring and what happened to them after retirement.

During months of canvassing gymnasiums, I witnessed the inter-ethnic conflict, rivalries and other private emotions the fighters expressed. I saw ethnic groups stealing the towels of another group and listened to their hostile racial jokes. I saw that it was a particular comedown for a black fighter to lose to a white fighter. Many black fighters relieve racial hostility in their fights with white fighters. Whenever a black fighter has a fight scheduled with a white fighter, his comrades kid him with the query as to whether he is "afraid of white folks," a fear which has been said to motivate even Muhammad Ali in part.

A Louisville friend, who had known Ali since childhood, once observed:

> Even when he's talking about race—when he says, "I don't want to be bombed, I don't want to be set on fire, I don't want to be lynched or have no dogs chase me"—he's expressing more of a general fright than he is a real racial attitude. I think he finds it safer to be with Negroes, his own kind. It allays his fear of all those things his father used to tell him the whites'd do to him. He keeps this tight little Negro group around him and he's scared to death to venture away from it.[5]

Fighters are products of the racial hostilities and socio-economic conflicts in which they live. Professor Kirson Weinberg, of Chicago's Roosevelt University, has found that professional boxers reflect changes in the ethnic composition of the lower strata of the urban slums. In the early part of the century the Irish predominated. By 1928 Jewish fighters had replaced them; by 1936 the Italians succeeded them.

Since 1948 the blacks have dominated.[6] Currently, seven of the eleven best heavy-weights in the world are black Americans.[7] Except for the four years Rocky Marciano was champion, and the year Ingemar Johannson borrowed the title briefly from Floyd Patterson, blacks have held the heavyweight championship since 1936. In recent years, Tampa, Florida barred professional boxing because, the commission's report read in part, "boxers no longer represent a cross-section of America."[8]

A "natural" to the fight mob connotes any fight which pits a white man against a Negro, although the Madison Avenue boys who have moved into the promotional forefront of the sport would seek a euphemistic definition. By any definition it brings loot . . . It has been traditional that any "white hope" is matched against a colored champion, a natural is in the making. It appeals to all that is primitive and basic in this most primitive and basic of all sports.[9]

Because of this premium placed on white fighters, black fighters feel that they must fight them harder in order to get ahead. Black fighters especially are forced to seek in boxing the financial security and the social esteem denied them outside the ring, not to mention the knawing resentments built up from a lifetime of abuse suffered at the hands of white supremacists. Joe Louis was so enraged by Max Schmeling's pre-bout boasts that Germans are superior to blacks, he attacked the Nordic with a fury that left him hospitalized. In this reaction, Louis was not unique.

Most black persons do not become fighters, however. To find out why some turn to boxing, I went to the origins of the fighters in my sample. From the Illinois State Athletic Commission I obtained the address from which each fighter applied for his first professional license. I visited each dwelling and noted the economic need of their family origins. Only 35 percent had working fathers at home when they turned professional. All the working fathers were laborers, except one who operated a small laundry. Twenty-nine percent said their fathers had deserted the family, and five per cent said their fathers had died.

Since most poor boys do not become fighters either, I sought out the specific reasons why those in my group had entered the ring. Thirty-one said they first became interested in boxing because a relative, friend or neighbor (a role model) was a fighter. Thirteen traced their interest to natural ability discovered in street fights. Fourteen gave other reasons such as childhood membership in an organization sponsoring boxing or a fondness for sports in general and boxing in particular.

One interesting point was that only five per cent of the scientific boxers attributed their initial interest to street fighting, whereas 48 per cent of the sluggers gave this reason. My survey findings are borne out by the cases of various well-known fighters. Sluggers such as Sonny Liston and Henry Hank had much success in street fights. It was different with scientific boxers like Ray Robinson and Ezzard Charles.

Robinson, who used to run from street fights as a child, started to box because he lived in the same Detroit neighborhood as Joe Louis, and often carried Louis's bag to the gym. Charles first became interested when, near his home in Cincinnati one day, he saw Kid Chocolate, the featherweight champion, in an expensive car, and heard Chocolate tell of his sizeable wardrobe.

Boys in the black slums take note of these and other benefits a boxing career can offer, and are moved to use this means of escaping slum deprivation. Joe Louis, after his humiliation of Max Schmeling, became a hero for blacks all over the nation; and nonwhites throughout the world also were able to take him for a model.

Many fighters, far from being "born" fighters, had to learn fighting to get by as boys in their tough slum environments. Professor Weinberg even found fighters who took up fighting because as boys they suffered insults to their manliness.[10] The girlish name of one, for instance, attracted the jeers of playmates. The boy eventually altered his name to make it manly sounding, and set out to learn boxing to back up his new name. He was soon able to convince his jesters that he was at least as manly as they.

This problem also has plagued well-known fighters. At the weighing-in ceremonies before the bout in which champion Benny Kid Paret was fatally injured a few years ago, Paret called Griffith a "woman," apparently because Griffith used to be a choirboy and is now a designer of ladies' hats. Paret's widow, Lucy, blames this insult for the "bad blood" between the fighters and the savage fury of Griffith's punches.[11]

Although almost all fighters start with the idea of making money, 45 percent in my sample told me that after three or more years they liked the recognition and prestige even more than the financial rewards. Joe Law, a lightweight, expressed it this way: "A guy knocks you down. You get up and put up a good fight and the crowd cheers you. Drop into a night club and people recognize you. The emcee says, 'We got a celebrity in the house,' and shines the spotlight on you. I'm telling you, it makes you feel good."

Sonny Liston explained:

I never had a dime to my name before I became a fighter. I never had friends before, or respect. Now when people see me on the street, they turn around and say, "ain't that Sonny Liston, the fighter?"[12]

Muhammad Ali has said: "I started boxing because I thought this was the fastest way for a black person to make it in this country."[13]

Most fighters begin with an exaggerated idea of the prestige and money to be made. They read about the huge purses received by the Alis and Louises and Robinsons and have little understanding of how much must be deducted for taxes, expenses and manager's share. Of the forty-eight retired fighters I questioned, none said they had saved most of the money they earned in fighting. Two out of three had saved little, and 25 percent had saved none at all.

"My manager was like a father to me," said a lightweight who won forty-six of his sixty-three fights, "but you've still got expenses and a lot of friends. Everybody wants to have a good time off your money. Once I made $5,000 in a fight in California, but by the time I got home I only had about $500."

"The higher a fighter goes in the fight game, the higher the class of people he runs around with," another fighter told me. "He's got to spend money to keep up with the crowd. His manager won't let him keep on livin' on State Street, payin' cheap rent, because it won't look right. A boxer comes from the bottom. He ain't been used to nothin' or he wouldn't be fighting in the first place."

In the effort to squeeze the most from the fighter as a commodity, managers must seek to extract a viciousness and disdain for suffering in the fighter. Trainers assist them in conditioning the fighter to taking and giving punishment. "This ain't no baby game. You got to be mean. You got to be tough," trainers repeatedly tell their fighters. "You got to try to kill that guy; he's going to try to knock your head off. Try to kill him. Try to knock his eye out. He's going to knock yours out if he can."

The fighter who succeeds best is thus able to suppress his emotions sufficiently to sustain a "killer instinct" and take advantage of his opponent. Questioned after his fatal injury of then featherweight champion Davey Moore, Sugar Ramos remarked: "As long as a man keeps hitting me back I know I have to hit him back." After fatally injuring Art Doyle, Sugar Ray Robinson said simply that "hurting people is my business."

To force him to fight harder, Jonny Bratton's manager used to bet his fighter's purse on the outcome of his fights, leaving Bratton broke and wanting whenever he lost.[14] In the exploitation of the boxer by his handlers, it is necessary to exercise intensive control and constraint over the fighter's thinking and behavior, to dominate the fighter and his total mood. Manager Cus D'Amato was said to receive a "sadistic delight in keeping Floyd Patterson under his hypnotic spell." He would tell Floyd over and over again: "The entire world is against you, trust no one but me."[15]

At the same time, a fighter cannot always count on his manager's good intentions. While most fighters are black, almost all managers are white. One manager I know bet against his fighter, then secured a woman for the fighter shortly before the fight to weaken him for defeat.

Beyond this, many fighters feel resentful that a fighter's success depends too little on what he knows and too much on whom his manager knows. "You have to be in a clique," a former fighter insisted to me. "You take some guys that are fighting in the preliminaries, and if they had the right backing they could get somewhere. It used to be that when you lost three or four fights you dropped in the ratings. Now some fighters lose three or four and then fight for the title."

Further evidence of the exploitation and racism of promoters is that today, when most fighters are black, most fight clubs still pay their preliminary fighters what they paid them thirty years ago when prices and tickets were cheaper.

The financial exploitation of the fighter compounds the special strain which his career places upon marriage. Forty of the fifty-eight I talked to were, or had been, married. Among the forty-eight retired fighters in the group, twenty five were still married, but the wives of ten others had deserted them.

The glamour of boxing and, in the case of successful fighters, the huge sums of money they make, enables boxers frequently to marry women from higher social classes. Joe Louis, for instance, who did not complete high school, is married to a prominent attorney. Thus, many fighters encounter class conflict in their marriages.

"A fighter starts at the bottom," one told me. "Every notch you move up in boxing, you move up a notch with the big shots. That's how come a lot of fighters marry women too high for them. Or if they don't do that, they get their wives too used to luxury and prestige. Then after you quit, and can't keep it up, she gets where she can't stand you and leaves."

I found this fighter in his room in a third class hotel. He had missed a previous appointment with me because, he explained, he had been drunk. He told me that he had taken to alcohol after his wife had left him. "I'd be the happiest man in the world," he said, "if I could just find her and get her back."

Another fighter, who had become close enough as a friend to invite me to be the best man in his wedding to a Washington, D.C. school teacher, told me that some individuals were telling him that to continue fighting would degrade his wife's profession.

"No wife, I mean no wife, approves," one fighter told me. "All wives like the glory, but they also got to see you come in with your face all beat in—see you nursing your face at night."

Many wives grow impatient with a fighter's financial progress. "I'm like you," I once heard a young fighter confide to another in a Chicago dressing room. "My wife's getting tired of me not being able to keep a job more'n six months at a time. I get money from a fight and I give it to her, but I don't get that too regular, so all the time she's buying the groceries. She just bought nineteen dollars worth of food last Saturday and that's all gone. I made the mistake of asking her for a dollar—I caught hell before I got that dollar. She's tired of it," he said. "You know, living with her peoples and they know whenever we get in an argument, and I ain't fucking her or nothing trying to get in shape for a fight."

A common reason for marriage failure among fighters is the enforced separation that their training rules demand. Managers and trainers caution fighters to limit their sexual relations as much as possible. But many fighters find it hard to "hold out" against their women, wanting to end long sexual vacations before a fight. Some trainers will go so far as to sleep with their fighters before an important bout in order to keep them out of trouble with their wives. Sixty-two per cent of the fighters in my sample told me, however, that they often broke one rule or another in their relationships with women. In general, fighters feel that about two weeks of celibate living before a fight is sufficient—three said only one day—but all who had experienced marriage named this as a major problem.

"You got to keep up your homework," a middleweight told me one night in a Chicago tavern frequented by fighters and ex-fighters. "If you don't, somebody else'll be doing it for you. A fighter fights in so many different cities it's best for him not to have a wife, because she'll cheat on him. It's a mental disturbance to leave, knowing she'll cheat. You can't box if your mind is split on something else."

In spite of all this, only ten of thirty-four who had an opinion on the subject thought marriage was bad for a fighter. Managers and trainers, on the other hand, are almost unanimous in believing that fighters should not burden themselves with marital responsibilities.

"It's better to leave your wife at home," a trainer told me in Washington, D.C. "Of course, if she was rooting for you, she'd come unbeknownst to you. But it's better to leave her home." Later, he told a young fighter not to bring any of his relatives because he might try to "show off" and end up doing worse than ever.

Most of the fighters I studied had launched their careers with the approval of their families. Only about one-sixth of the fathers disapproved, and only two-fifths of the mothers. A fighter's relations with his family generally change, however, during his career and immediately following it. His family's admiration for him fluctuates with his success and usually wanes when his career is ended.

One of the most pathetic examples was a former welterweight—now in his thirties and unemployed—who said he had made enough money during his career to send his sister through college. I found him living with his mother in a third-floor walk-up apartment on Chicago's South Side. He was dressed in a shirt and old slacks. I suggested that we go out for a beer.

"My sister's a schoolteacher. My brother's got a good government job," he told me in the tavern. "I'm the bum in the family. My mother wouldn't allow my youngest brother to become a fighter, and he was a natural. I wasn't—I had to develop my skill. My mother can't stand the sight of a fighter, especially me. I had a birthday last month, and I didn't get one present from my family."

At that point he fell silent, and a friend of his entered the bar and walked over to him. "Your mother wants you to come home and clean out the cellar," he said. "I got to get out of this," the former fighter said to me.

Another put his brother into business, but they soon fell into periodic fights in which he beat his brother. Finally his brother took out a warrant for his arrest and won't speak to him or give him money now that he is broke.

Such factors lead most fighters to long to return to the ring. Almost 70 per cent of the retired fighters at one time or another got the urge to resume, and 40 per cent actually did make one or more comeback attempts. This indicates the difficulty most fighters experience in trying to adjust occupationally and otherwise after their ring careers end. The problems of physically and mentally impaired ex-boxers have been widely publicized, but it seems to me that too little attention has been paid to the more common problem of maladjustment.

Fighters come mostly from urban slum areas where there is a lower standard of living and a higher prevalence of mental and physical disease. Professional boxing fails to equip its graduates for other work. In fact, it tends to prejudice them against it. Managers and trainers are opposed to having their fighters learn other trades or work at other jobs during their careers. They want a fighter to devote himself completely to boxing. They also feel that a fighter who has no other means of support and no other skills will train harder and, when the going in the ring gets rough, fight harder.

There is no way in which a fighter can use his special skills after retirement, unless he becomes a trainer of fighters. He finds it hard to accept the routine, time-clock nature of most jobs, and he has become used to receiving his pay in comparatively large, lump sums, rather than in small, fixed amounts at regular intervals. In the partnership of boxer, manager and trainer, the fighter rightfully is the important party. He loses and misses this sense of importance when he embarks upon another line of work.

"I ain't going to do no hard work," an ex-fighter who had tried nine jobs in six months told me. "Look. Feel my hands. I never had a callus in my life. When I was boxin' I wasn't used to havin' a boss and workin' all day. Oh, before I'd steal I'd work for a while, but I'd do it where nobody could see me. I'd die if somebody saw me."

White boxers typically do better in post career life because of greater benevolence on the part of their managers (c.f. Rocky Marciano and Joe Louis). Also, for small-time fighters (by far the majority) there are better jobs available to whites after retirement.

Thirty-seven of the forty-eight retired fighters I visited did have steady jobs, but 60 per cent of those said they would be happier in different work. Most of them were unskilled or semi-skilled laborers. Four operated small taverns or restaurants, one was a jazz musician and one ran a dry-cleaning establishment.

I found that scientific boxers adjusted to post-career life slightly better than the sluggers. The unsuccessful scientific boxers adjusted best of all, and the successful sluggers experienced the most difficulty. Half of all the retired fighters, however, told me that they would need more than an additional $100 a week to live the way they wanted.

We may conclude, then, that boxing does not leave all its scars on a fighter's face. The tragedy of the fighter's life is that when his career comes to an end in his late twenties or early thirties—an age at which most young men are just approaching their prime—he feels that the best years of his life are already behind him. For too many this is the unfortunate truth.

In the gyms, I watched the active fighters working and waiting for the lucky break which, they believed, would take them to the wealth and glory of a championship. In the taverns and poolrooms, I listened to the former fighters reliving their own fighting careers, boasting to sustain their pride, dissatisfied now with their present lot and trying to call back in conversation the youth and skills that had once been theirs.

Three years after winning the welterweight championship, Johnny Saxton was charged with two burglaries and held in a New Jersey jail. There he tried to take his own life and had to be confined for a while in the New Jersey State Mental Hospital. "I used to be somebody," the ex-champ explained, "but now I'm nobody. I wish the police had shot me."

I have seen ex-fighters trying to borrow carfare with no avail and, in the case of a blind ex-fighter, doing calisthenics and shadowboxing nightly in his hotel room. One night I found a fighter who retired about thirty years ago after sixteen years in the ring, but whose name still evokes memories for fight fans who go back that far. I found him living with his wife in a transient-hotel room in a slum area, reminiscing about the days when he was the National Boxing Association middleweight champion, boxing throughout this country and in Paris, and she was a professional dancer.

Boxing is good for some black men, allowing them to escape the deprivation of the slums, but for most, it merely reflects and aggravates their basic oppression.

NOTES

1. Barry Gottenhrer, "How Great Is Sonny Liston?" *Boxing Yearbook*, 1964, p. 11.

2. Jose Torres, *Sting Like a Bee*, New York: Abelard-Schuman, 1971, pp. 138–139.

3. Nathan Hare, "What Makes a Man a Fighter?" ed. by W. C. Heinz, *Saturday Evening Post*, (March 8, 1958), p. 27.

4. "Dr. Nathan Hare: Black Power Professor with a Punch," *Sepia* (April, 1968), pp. 50–54. Bernard Garrett, "Fired Howard University Teacher Returns to Boxing Career," *Jet* (October 26, 1967), pp. 16–21.

5. Jack Olsen, *Black Is Best: The Riddle of Cassius Clay*, New York: Dell, 1967, p. 93.

6. S. Kirson Weinberg and Henry Arond, "The Occupational Culture of the Boxer," *American Journal of Sociology* (March, 1952), p. 460.

7. "Boxing Illustrated's World Boxing Ratings," *Boxing Illustrated* (August, 1971), p. 16.

8. Nathan Hare, "White Supremacy Backfires in Boxing," *Flamingo* (September, 1962), p. 42.

9. Jack Zanger, "Here Comes Ingo . . . Again," *Boxing Annual*, 1963, p. 10.

10. Aronds and Weinberg, *op. cit.*, p. 461.

11. Hare, *op. cit.*, p. 44.

12. Alexander Berger, "Best Bet for the Big Title," *Boxing Illustrated*, (August, 1959), p. 35.

13. Torres, *op. cit.*, p. 83.

14. George Puscas, "Child of Tragedy," *Negro Digest*, (April, 1962), p. 42.

15. Wendell Smith, "Patterson—The Recluse," *Boxing and Wrestling*, (January, 1962), p. 41.

IN DEFENSE
OF CASSIUS CLAY

Who does he think he is, sounding off like that? A free, white American intellectual?

A monologue with Gay Talese

FLOYD PATTERSON was born in Waco, North
Carolina on January 4, 1935. He grew up in New York as a terribly
introverted and troubled boy who found self-expression and release in
boxing. After winning the 1952 Olympic gold medal as a middleweight,
Patterson, trained and managed by Cus D'Amato, who was also to
mentor Mike Tyson, embarked on a professional boxing career,
eventually winning the heavyweight title by beating Archie Moore in five
rounds on November 30, 1956. He first lost the title to Ingemar
Johansson on September 26, 1959, but regained it by knocking out
Johansson on June 20, 1960, becoming the first heavyweight to
accomplish the feat of regaining the title. He lost the title to Sonny
Liston by knockout in the first round on September 23, 1962. He was
never champion again. In the middle sixties, his chief nemesis was the
young Cassius Clay, who was to change his name to Muhammad Ali
when he announced his membership in the Nation of Islam shortly after
he won the title by beating Sonny Liston in 1964. Ali's antics and his
intensely racial politics disturbed and annoyed Patterson, who wrote
articles about the young champion in *Sports Illustrated*. Patterson and
Ali fought on November 22, 1965 with Ali emerging the easy winner.
After the fight, criticism of Ali by both the boxing power elite and the
general white public became more intense, especially over the issue of
whether Ali should be drafted. "In Defense of Cassius Clay" (Patterson
refused to call Ali by his Muslim name) was published in *Esquire* in
August 1966. Despite the dislike between the two men, Patterson's piece
was a thought-provoking, sensitive, and generally honest examination of
Clay, boxing, and the issue of the politicization of American sports.

I have been called a "coward" and a "rabbit" and an "Uncle Tom" by Cassius Clay, and many people think that I share their contempt for him, but I do not. Cassius Clay, I think, is at heart a modest man. He can listen a long time without saying anything, he can charm you with his politeness. So much of his bragging and stomping, his histrionics and wisecracks are all part of an act. He is a kind of actor—a bad actor, some say, but an actor—and the main purpose behind his behavior is to get people to buy tickets to his fights, hoping to see him put his foot in his mouth.

He never gave them that satisfaction in the ring, he is a fine fighter, but he may have shot off his mouth too much outside the ring this year. Now he is in real trouble. At first people laughed at Clay's outrageous speeches and poetry, but then it got around that he was a member of the Black Muslims, and then he publicly denounced the draft and criticized America's policy in Vietnam. It's not so bad for politicians and Pulitzer Prize poets and certain intellectuals in this country to sign petitions and speak out against the war in Vietnam, but when Cassius Clay did it he paid a heavy price for Freedom of Speech. The draft board moved in on him, his title fight with George Chuvalo was banned from New York and Chicago and several other cities, and many closed-circuit television theaters boycotted it, and Clay earned relatively little money from the fight, which ended up in Toronto.

The prizefighter in America is not supposed to shoot off his mouth about politics, particularly when his views oppose the Government's and might influence many among the working classes who follow boxing. The prizefighter is considered by most people to be merely a tough, insensitive man, a dumb half-naked entertainer wearing a muzzled mouthpiece. He is supposed to stick to his trade—fighting and keeping his mouth shut and pretending that he hates his opponent. There is so much hate among people, so much contempt inside people who'd like you to think they're moral, that they have to hire prizefighters to do their hating for them. And we do. We get into a ring and act out other people's hates. We are happy to do it. How else can Negroes like Clay and myself, born in the South, poor, and with little education, make so much money? I think boxing is a good thing. I do not think that it should be abolished, as do some hypocritical editorial writers on *The New York Times*, because the elimination of boxing will not eliminate the hate that people have, and the wars. If people did not have such things as boxing they'd invent something else, maybe something that would not give poor people a chance at the big money.

So I'm all for boxing, although I admit that the existence of boxing says something about our society and the violence that it needs. When a fighter kills in the ring he does not go to jail; instead he gains a strange new respect from some people, maybe just bloodthirsty people, but this respect is something like that given to a war hero who has killed many men in battle, and when a fighter becomes a killer the boxing promoters know that more people will come out to watch him fight the next time. So violence and hate are part of the prizefighter's world. Clay's world and mine, although we do not hate one another, nor do I hate Liston or Ingemar Johansson or any other opponent, and I am sure the feeling is the same with them. We fight but we do not really hate down deep, although we try to pretend we hate. Sometimes it is all very confusing, we become very mixed up. And we are afraid.

We are not afraid of getting hurt but we are afraid of losing. Losing in the ring is like losing nowhere else. People who lose in business—get fired from their job, or lose a client, or "get kicked upstairs"—can still go down with some dignity and they might also blame their defeat on an ungrateful employer or on the unfair competition. But a prizefighter who gets knocked out or is badly outclassed suffers in a way he will never forget. He is beaten under the bright lights in front of thousands of witnesses who curse him and spit at him, and he knows that he is being watched, too, by many thousands more on television and in the movies, and he knows that the tax agents will soon visit him—they always try to get their share before he winds up flat broke—and the fighter cannot shift the blame for his defeat on his trainers or managers or anybody else, although if he won you can be sure that the trainers and managers would be taking bows.

The losing fighter loses more than just his pride and the fight; he loses part of his future, is one step closer to the slum he came from, and I am sure that before each fight Cassius Clay also goes through the mental torture and doubt. He knows how happy thousands of Americans would be if he got beaten bad, and maybe that is why Clay has to keep saying, "I'm the greatest, I'm the greatest"—day after day, hour after hour, loud and clear, on television and in the newspapers: "I'm the greatest." He wants people to say, "You're not!" and then he is forced to meet the challenge, put himself in a do-or-die frame of mind, go a little crazy maybe, crazy with some ferocious fear. So far it has worked for him. What he will be like if he loses I do not know, but the fear of losing causes strange things to happen to fighters, and it caused me to hate myself so much that I wore a fake moustache and beard and tried to hide. I did not want to face the public that I had let down. This pressure was due partly to my being built up as such a "good guy," and when I lost to Sonny Liston, the "bad guy," it was like a national disaster.

I have gotten over that beard business now, thank God, but the "good-guy" image still drives me to do strange things, to behave in ways that are a little unnatural, just as I imagine the "bad-guy" role that Cassius Clay has inherited from Sonny Liston has influenced many of the crazy things he does in public. Before my fight with Cassius Clay I remember one day he came stomping up to my camp. He was surrounded by Muslims and he came barging in, calling me "rabbit," and he held a bunch of carrots in his arms. All the television cameras and photographers moved in close to get action shots of Clay coming over to me with those carrots. I guess they were expecting a nice bloody scene. But they were disappointed. Clay handed me the carrots and I took them. The photographers took pictures, the pictures got into the papers and on television, and I guess it all helped sell tickets to the fight. But in that split second that Cassius Clay's eyes met with mine, I could sense that he was a little embarrassed by it all. He seemed to be apologizing, saying, "This is what I have to do." And later on, when we had a press conference before the fight, and Clay was screaming and bragging to a bunch of sportswriters, he leaned over and whispered to me once: "You want to make some money, don't you, Floyd? You want to make lots of money, don't you?"

He seemed to feel that he had to explain his public actions to me, maybe because he goes so much further than the rest ever have, or maybe because he is such a convincing bad guy. That has probably been part of his problem. He has been too convincing. Maybe he has overplayed his part, made it bigger than it was supposed to be, and the public is not sure that it likes its fighters, its hired haters, to go beyond the role it expects them to play, which does not include joining the Black Muslims or denouncing the draft or criticizing America's policy in the Vietnamese war.

When I first met Cassius Clay, his public image was so different. It was in 1960. I was the champion then and was traveling through Rome. I'd had an audience with the Pope, then visited the American Olympic team there and met Cassius Clay. He was the star boxer for the American team, and he was very polite and full of enthusiasm, and I remember how, when I arrived at the Olympic camp, he jumped up and grabbed my hand and said, "Com'on, let me show you around." He led me all around the place and the only unusual thing about him was this overenthusiasm, but other than that he was a modest and very likable guy.

In 1965 in Las Vegas I fought against him and was stopped in a technical knockout. Before the fight he'd said that if he lost he would listen to my viewpoint on Catholicism, and if I lost I should hear him out on the Black Muslims, but this was, again, all part of the pre-fight buildup. In the fight itself, I did not have a chance. I boxed him well in the first round, but in the second round my back went out. I took a swing at him and missed, and got a muscle spasm, and after that I could not swing without great pain. In fact I could not even stand up straight, and the pain was unlike anything I've ever felt, and in the later rounds I was hoping that Clay would knock me out. It is not pleasant admitting this, but it is the truth. I had had such high hopes for this fight, so much riding on it, so many people cheering for me. I remember how, on the morning of the fight, Frank Sinatra had asked to see me, and I was escorted over to his suite in the Sands Hotel by Al Silvani, a friend of Sinatra's who was one of my trainers. I really did not know Silvani very well before the fight, but Sinatra had called me up earlier in the year after the death of my trainer, Dan Florio, and said that if I wanted Al Silvani to help me I could have him. I did not say yes at first. I thought it over, and decided to wait. Then Sinatra again called and said I could have Silvani, who was then working in Sinatra's film company, and finally I said okay, and Silvani, two days before the fight, arrived in Las Vegas to help train me for Cassius Clay, and on the morning of the fight Silvani escorted me to Sinatra's suite, and Sinatra was very nice that morning, very encouraging, he told me I could win, how so many people in America were counting on me to win back the championship from Clay.

After I lost the fight, I paid Sinatra another visit in his suite. I told him I was sorry I had let him down, and all the others, but Sinatra was a very different guy after I lost to Clay. I was talking to him in his suite and then he did a strange thing. He got up and walked all the way over to the other side of the room, and he sat down there, so far away that I could hardly talk to him. I got the message. I left.

During the fight itself, Clay, in the clinches, said many things about white people, trying to hit me again with that Uncle Tom thing. But it was all I could do to stand up that night; as I said, I really wanted to be knocked out. I wanted to be knocked out with a good punch, though, or a good combination of punches. I wanted to go down with something that would be worthy of a knockout. But in the tenth and eleventh rounds, Cassius Clay wasn't landing anything good. He was just jabbing. Jab, jab, jab, jab, you know, and he was standing at a distance. It was strange, but Clay was taking no chances, and yet he must have known that I was in pain with my back.

Then in the twelfth round, Clay became a punching maniac. He still took no chances but he came in and began landing punches here, here, here, and here— punches began to land all over my head, and a very, very strange thing began to happen then. A happiness feeling came over me. I knew the end was near. The pain of standing up in the ring, that sharp knife in my back that accompanied every move I made, would soon end. I would soon be out. And as Clay began to land these punches, I was feeling groggy and happy. But then the referee stepped in to break us up, to stop Clay's punches. And you may remember, if you saw the fight in the films, seeing me turn to the referee, shaking my head, "No, *no!*" Many people thought I was protesting his decision to stop the fight. I *really* was protesting his stopping those punches. I wanted to be hit by one really good one. I wanted to go out with a great punch, to go down that way. It never happened, and that is why I was protesting to the referee.

After the fight many sportswriters suggested that Clay was carrying me, but this was not true. And Clay himself said nothing of the kind until, on a television show after the fight, a sportscaster named Howard Cosell, who was a very good friend of mine, watched a rerun of the fight with Clay and kept making the remark over and over that Clay seemed to be carrying me. Cosell began to put the idea into Clay's head as the two of them watched the rerun, and Cosell would say, "Cassius, you're carrying Patterson, you seem to be carrying him," and Clay said no, but by the eleventh round Clay started giving in, saying, yes, he seemed to be carrying me. But I repeat, Clay did not carry me in that fight. I might have been carried out of that fight, but I definitely was not carried during the fight.

Since then I have seen Clay once. We were in a photographer's studio posing for the picture you see on the cover of this magazine. Clay flew into New York from Chicago just to do that, and I believe he was very happy to hear that I was saying some complimentary things about him for publication and was very surprised too, because he's become accustomed to reading only the worst things these days. He gave me a big bear hug when I walked in the door, had a big smile on his face, and there was real warmth there. Then we sat down and he asked if my back is responding to treatment (it is), and then said that he would like to go on a boxing tour with Liston and myself to make some extra money. He didn't make much in Toronto for the Chuvalo fight, he said, not with all that bad publicity, and he added that he needed money these days to pay his alimony and settle other debts. He was very polite and gentle throughout the evening, and when he said good-bye I called him Cassius—I never call him by his Muslim name, Muhammad Ali—and then I added, "It's all right if I call you Cassius, isn't it?" He smiled and said, "Any time, Floyd."

He seemed no different to me then than he did when I first met him in Rome in 1960, and I think that *that* Cassius Clay is the real one, but I believe that he has made some very serious mistakes since then and does not know how to get out of them now. I believe that he joined the Black Muslims without even knowing what it stands for, without checking into it. It just sounded good. He was very young then, twenty-one or twenty-two, and much impressed with Malcom X, who *was* an impressive man, a spellbinding man who could talk faster than anybody, including Cassius.

Then Malcolm X said some very bad things and fell out with the Muslim leaders in Chicago, and then he was shot. I think this really frightened Cassius Clay. He'll not admit it, but I think it really got to him. Now he's trapped. He could not get out of the Black Muslims even if he wanted to, I think, because he'd never know what might happen as a result. I remember my own feeling as I entered the ring in Las Vegas last November for the Clay fight: I wondered if there might not be some shots fired into the ring. Whenever I tried to dismiss the idea as ridiculous, I kept remembering that Malcolm X was murdered before a large crowd of people and so was President Kennedy, and if people want to get you, they'll get you anywhere. I thought about this until the bell rang, and then I forgot about it and concentrated on the fight, but I have since thought about it again, and even now as I say these things I wonder if I might not be endangering my own life.

Joining the Muslims was one reason for Clay's decline in popularity, and his views on Vietnam and the draft are others, and I happen to disagree with everything he is saying on these three subjects, and I think the Cassius Clay viewpoint is working against the civil-rights movement and the best interests of the nation. I certainly would fight willingly in Vietnam for my country, and have no soft feelings toward the Black Muslims. But what bothers me about Cassius Clay's situation is that he is being made to pay too stiff a penalty for saying and doing what he thinks is right. I happen not to agree with him, but he certainly has a right to express his opinion on Vietnam and the draft and the Muslims without having half the nation jumping on his back. Why? Because Clay was exercising his right of free speech. He did not, as far as I know, break any law. I read in the newspapers recently that he was charged with defying a police officer who stopped a car in which he was riding, and for passing a stop sign, but he has not been found guilty of any major crime, and so I think he should be getting a bigger break than he has gotten this year.

It isn't enough that he is a fine fighter, unfortunately. The public demands that its champions also be popular, and sometimes popularity is achieved by keeping your mouth shut, but Clay isn't this way. I'm more this way, and Clay isn't like me in the least, but in our democracy people have a right to be different. But I know this may just be wishful thinking on my part, and I do not see how Clay can get out of the mess he got himself into unless he quits the Muslims, and that might be dangerous, as I said. If he joined the United States Army he might be helping his cause, although he'd probably have to do something pretty dramatic—he'd have to go to Vietnam and be photographed running through the woods with a knife in his back and carrying a wounded white G.I. on his shoulders. Or he might retire from boxing for a while, and if he did not have the heavyweight title the Muslims might not find him so useful, and maybe he could then stay out of the spotlight until the public forgot about him a little and found a new "bad guy."

But if he does none of these things I still feel that he deserves better treatment than he is getting, and I think the public is partly to blame. The public fails to understand what he is—a twenty-four-year-old fighter, an entertainer, a very individualistic young man whose life is far from easy, and they should make allowances for him. I do not think these should be anything special, but maybe once in a while they should stop booing him, maybe even cheer him for a change, make him feel more liked, more reputable within himself, more responsible. Right now the only people in America who are not booing him are the Black Muslims, and maybe that is one reason he prefers being with them. Maybe if there were a few cheers from the other side of fence, and a little more tolerance too, people would realize that Cassius Clay is not as bad as he seems, and maybe then he would also return the favor once in a while and keep his mouth shut.

BLACK HEAVIES

JERVIS ANDERSON is a native of Jamaica and a graduate of New York University. Among his works are A. *Philip Randolph* (1972), a fine biography of the great black labor leader, and *This Was Harlem* (1981). He has been on the staff of the *New Yorker* for many years. "Black Heavies" first appeared in the *American Scholar* in the Summer, 1978 issue.

The name Jack Johnson sounds exactly right for the man who made it famous, for the sort of man we hear and read that he was: tall, black, powerfully built, controversial, saucy, irreverent, and a brilliantly gifted boxer of former days. His grin, which was frequent—and sometimes defiant—revealed a tooth of gold; and he loved to hear it described as his "golden smile." Only he knew the many things he was smiling at or smiling with. But to the ordinary onlooker his smile suggested at least two things: that he was oblivious to any unfavorable opinion the world might hold about him, and that he was enjoying some genius in himself—of which he was quite the best judge, and which others were welcome to share, if they so desired. Some observers shared the pleasure he took in his golden smile, and others wanted nothing so badly as to see it knocked off his face. From the look of him, he might have made a great stage entertainer: one sees him, a cane in one hand and a top hat in the other, doing a most elegant soft-shoe. Altogether a character of extravagant outlines. If his name had been Amos Greene, the imagination would have had to change it to Jack Johnson. Almost no other name would do.

But it is as one of the great heavyweight boxers of history that he made his entry into America's consciousness, and it is from this position that we should try to make a reacquaintance with him. Johnson fought seriously from the late 1890s to the mid-1920s; and what glimpses we now get of him are provided by still photographs or by those ancient filmstrips that television sometimes digs up and uses in one documentary or another about how boxing or America used to be. But these strips, made in the days when the camera was just learning how to capture action, do not give us the picture of Johnson we would like to have. With their furious and stilted Chaplinesque motion, they do not show the true pace and flow of Johnson's movements—do not enable us to form an accurate impression of his style, or to compare his technique with those of boxers from whom we have, in more recent times, developed our sense of what is excellent in the ring.

Thus when we hear from people who saw Jack Johnson that he was probably the greatest heavyweight boxer who has ever lived, we are not sure what to make of it. Perhaps these people are right. Perhaps, again, they are only saying what folks of former days are inclined to say—that the stars of their time were superior to any who have come along since. In any case, we hesitate to concur. It is a little hard to believe that Johnson, who fought during what, we now know, was a primitive era of the sport, could have been superior to the modern masters—men who have refined and extended the art of pugilism beyond what it was in Johnson's time. There is, however, one distinction of Johnson's that we are not permitted to question. He was the first black man to become heavyweight champion of the world. Here is a distinction that must not only impress us but must also detain us.

That he was the first of his race to win the championship—in 1908, at an age, thirty, when most boxers have passed their prime (unless it was Jersey Joe Walcott, who, many years later, won the championship at the age of thirty-six or thirty-seven)—signifies something of the spirit and ability that Johnson had, and something as well of a circumstance in American boxing, or American life, that had prevented any other black heavyweight from fighting for the title. If ability had been all that counted in the early days, then Johnson might not have been the first of his race to fight for the championship; nor, in all probability, would he have been the first to win it.

The early and partly buried annals of prizefighting are crowded with the names of exceptional black heavyweights, one or two of whom may have been just as talented as Johnson was. Among these are the names of Peter Jackson, Joe Jeannette, Sam Langford, and Sam McVey. All these men fought around the turn of the century, when the heavyweight champions were John L. Sullivan, James J. Corbett, Bob Fitzsimmons, and James J. Jefferies. Their gifts, however, were left to flourish mostly in the dark—which, of course, was mostly among fighters of their own color. It was Sullivan, the first of what are termed the modern heavyweight champions, who drew the line against boxers of color. He would not, he said, risk his championship against "niggers." A good many white Americans applauded Sullivan's policy; and his white successors in the championship saw no reason to break with Sullivan's precedent. Only by an unusual combination of ability, unforeseen circumstance, and chutzpah was Jack Johnson able to outflank this policy, shatter the color line, and capture the heavyweight championship.

To those white Americans who took an interest in these matters—those, certainly, who understood the racial significance of the heavyweight championship of the world—Johnson's seizing of the title was a profoundly unsettling event. To put it less mildly, the event was seen as a catastrophic development in American race relations. Not only had the championship—one of the most prized possessions in the trophy room of white supremacy—passed into the hands of the Negro race but the agent of its passing was a man who seemed to have no sense whatever of his place in American life. White Americans were surely not going to stand for it.

In 1915, after a number of attempts had been made to restore the *status quo ante*, a way was found to separate both Jack Johnson and his race from the heavyweight championship. This done, and the title, now back in the possession of its original and "rightful" owners, the color line was redrawn, and remained drawn for more than twenty years. Not until 1937 was another black heavyweight, Joe Louis, allowed to cross this line; and, probably to the great surprise of his hosts, Louis won the championship. The color line went out of existence after that. The only two white heavyweight champions since 1937—Rocky Marciano and Ingemar Johansson—showed no interest in restoring it.

Leaping over a few years and a few champions, we land in the age of Muhammad Ali. He is not the third black heavyweight to have won the championship, but, along with Jack Johnson and Joe Louis, he stands as one of the three truly great black heavyweight champions the sport has seen. As this is written, Ali no longer holds the title. His loss of the championship (to Leon Spinks) is disappointing to his millions of admirers. But it cannot have been too surprising. Since Ali's magnificent struggle against Joe Frazier in Manila, he had not been looking like the heavyweight champion he was supposed to be. The late accomplishments of his reign, those that were beyond dispute, had consisted mainly in the growing size of his purses. No matter what the size of his savings account, inside the ring very little seemed to remain of the marvelous nest egg of talent he once possessed. He appeared to have been clinging to the title partly by dint of savvy and partly by the apparent reluctance of scorekeepers—the Pilates of the ringside—to return a final judgment against him. The latter was a striking factor indeed. It was a sign—especially when one recalls what happened to Jack Johnson—of how far American heavyweight boxing had come, or of how much it had overcome, since the early days of the century, when no blacks were wanted as heavyweight champions. For here was Ali—who, in his own way, has been as abrasive to conventional American sensitivities as Johnson was—being helped to hold on to his championship by a boxing establishment that remains largely white.

The reasons are not difficult to uncover. For one, the racial passions that once surrounded the heavyweight championship have abated. But another reason is less easily grasped. It springs—or so many people have felt—from a claim that Ali had upon the conscience of organized boxing. This claim dates back to 1968, when Ali refused induction during the war in Vietnam, and when the rulers of boxing, exceeding the terms of their mandate, punished him in behalf of patriotic sentiment. They stripped him of his title, revoked his license, and, as a result, deprived him not only of his livelihood but also of the four years of his professional life during which his gifts might have reached the height of their flowering. Hence the desire of the boxing powers to mark the scorecards in his favor, no matter how shakily he has performed. The reason this act of atonement has not been so easily understandable is that it comes from the inner life of an institution, organized boxing, whose capacity for remorse or humane feeling had not, for a very long time, been publicly known.

Still, it was the view of a steadily increasing number of people—some who had never disliked Ali and some who had never done anything else—that the time had come for him to be left to stand or fall on his own. He may have been left to his own resources last February, when he lost the championship to Leon Spinks. All the same, there was a certain historical inconvenience in Ali's downfall at that time. Thinking about it now, one finds oneself wishing that his dethronement had not come before March 31 of this year. Jack Johnson's autobiography, *Jack Johnson: In the Ring and Out* (first issued in 1927, and now out in a new edition) carries the reminder that he would have been 100 years old at the end of last March. It would have been fitting if the centennial of Johnson's birth had found Ali still in possession of the title, for, both in personal and in boxing style, no two heavyweight champions have borne so close a resemblance.

In temperament and technique—to say nothing of the dissimilar influence he had upon the public attitudes of his period—Joe Louis stands between Ali and Johnson like an immensely powerful but mute effigy, although one in which a good deal of eloquence seems to be trapped. Louis was as splendidly gifted a fighter as either of these two men. For that reason he too must have had his share of enemies, however small, among white Americans who still had not made peace with the idea of a black heavyweight champion. But because his personal style was more winning, or at any rate less troubling, than Ali's or Johnson's, he enjoyed a greater affection and wider acceptance among his fellow citizens. His opinions on public matters—on the rare occasions when he revealed himself to be in possession of any—were of the soothing and reassuring kind. He is not known to have rocked the boat on any vexed social question, or to have dissented publicly from any national attitude that was strongly held.

The country first took Joe Louis to its heart in 1938, when he destroyed the Aryan pretender to the championship, the German heavyweight Max Schmeling. This occurred at an hour when, under Hitler's broadening shadow, the lights were once more going out all over Europe, and at just the time when the morale of the Western democracies stood in need of a boost. At that moment, Joe Louis also became a more inspiring symbol within the black communities of America than Jack Johnson had been or Muhammad Ali was to become. In the war that followed, Louis enlisted willingly on his country's side—which, in one of his infrequent disclosures of opinion, he announced to be God's side as well. In the course of the acclaim he received, almost everyone said he was an asset to his country and—a term that now sounds quaint and faintly condescending—a credit to his race. Of course, not every black person in the United States shared those sentiments about Louis. Many members of his race would have liked a more assertive and irreverent public style in their heavyweight champion. To them, the championship was not just a pedestal but a platform which, especially when occupied by a black American, was to be used as much for purposes of advocacy as of ornament.

But one forms the impression that Louis was not as seriously taken with himself as the public was. While people were praising him for one thing or upbraiding him for another, he was satisfied to remain the simple, laconic, and retiring man he felt himself to be. From some of the photographs that were taken of him at the height of his fame, one senses that he was not always present in the spirit of whatever fuss was being made over him. He seems to have understood that he was required to surrender himself from time to time into the hands of those who—more impressed with his position than he was—felt he was worthy of tribute. But during all these rites there was on his face either the slightest of smiles or a look that suggested he would just as soon be back in his room taking a nap or enjoying a bowl of his favorite ice cream.

By comparison, Jack Johnson looks to have been the sort of man who never sat still long enough to take a nap, and whose taste did not run to anything quite so bland as ice cream. By no means the taciturn and self-effacing man that Louis is, and just barely short of being as garrulous and boastful a one as Ali, Johnson took a very serious view of his position as champion; and he did not allow modesty, since he had none, to discourage him from celebrating himself or anyone else from acclaiming him. The ways in which he was different from Louis were almost as many as the ways in which he resembled Ali. Yet there were at least two important characteristics that all three men shared: each was superbly gifted as a boxer, and each desired very much to be himself. In Johnson, the latter trait is said to have expressed itself in the form of arrogance. That at least was the view taken by some of his contemporaries. But this is not the impression one gains from his own account of his life. Rather one gets the impression of confidence (perhaps overconfidence), high self-esteem, a strong belief in his legal rights as a citizen, and a joyous obedience to what was dramatic and colorful in his character. This is worth pointing out, although, as we know only too well, self-portraits do not customarily accommodate themselves to the unflattering or inconvenient detail.

Here, at all events, are some of the forms of conduct for which Johnson was considered arrogant. For a long time he simply had no equal in the ring; he knew this, and he left no one in any doubt that he enjoyed the knowledge immensely. During some of his fights, even when he appeared to be taking a licking, he was to be seen flashing his golden smile in the face of his adversary or in the faces of people at ringside who were cheering hoarsely for his defeat—which, in most instances, was chiefly what they had come out to witness. Like Ali, he sometimes taunted his opponents; left his chin or his chest wide open and invited them to throw their best punches; and did not take as much pleasure in knocking out opponents as he did in out-boxing them, embarrassing them, prolonging their suffering. One observer has said that Johnson "avoided scoring knockouts, as a rule, not out of kindliness but because he simply liked to 'keep order' in the ring and demonstrate his defensive speed of hand and eye." He himself was once quoted as saying: "If I were a bullfighter, I would make the public think I was within inches of death, but I'd keep my margin of safety. I did in the ring . . . against the men I beat when I was at my best. I was padding backwards round the ring for three rounds out of four. Defense always wins in the end, if it is good enough."

Outside the ring, Johnson dined and dressed splendidly. He sometimes drank the best wines through a straw. He made and maintained friendships among white women, at least two of whom he married. He owned the fastest and most expensive automobiles of his day, and was known among his friends as a speed fiend. He once opened a place in Chicago, his Cabaret de Champion, that was more richly furnished than any similar establishment in town, right down to its silver cuspidors, decorated in gold. And, overall, he carried himself as unapologetically as any white champion or citizen was entitled to do.

But there seems to have been another side to Johnson that only his acquaintances knew or cared to know. One of them has written:

> While he makes no claim for scholarly attainments, [he] is nevertheless no stranger in the world of books and writers. . . . He browsed through books on all subjects—fiction, science, art, history; he has read them in three languages—English, French, and Spanish. He is conversant with works of Shakespeare, and can discuss and quote the plays of this greatest of English writers with an ease which reveals that he has delved deeply into his volumes. With the modern writers he also has close acquaintanceship through their books, but when discussing books and the names of Alexander Dumas and Victor Hugo are mentioned, Johnson becomes more alert than ever, for these are two of his favorite writers and he has read them thoroughly. While his schooling was interrupted before he reached high school, he has nevertheless attained an education of thoroughgoing character. . . . The classics are quite to his liking, and he not only joys in hearing the finest compositions of the masters, but he plays their compositions himself, for he is a musician of no mean ability, his favorite instrument being the bass viol, which he plays in a talented manner.

I am not qualified to state whether all of this is true or not. Johnson does allude to some of it in his book, but that may be no guarantee of its accuracy. Damon Runyon once said of Johnson's life story that it is an enthralling tale "if he tells the truth." At any rate, all the high-culture stuff about Johnson makes for a complex and arresting addition to the stereotyped picture of him that exists in the public mind. Whether the public of Johnson's day would have behaved any differently toward him, had the intellectual dimensions of his personality been widely known, is a question that cannot be answered now. It is for his "arrogance" that he was known; and on that account he paid a higher price in public hostility than anyone in the history of American prizefighting.

Writing in *The New Yorker* nearly thirty years ago, the late John Lardner referred to the conditions that prevailed in heavyweight boxing until the time that Johnson won the championship. Lardner wrote:

> It is indicative of the character of Johnson that he defied white-black conventions in the ring and managed, by sheer stubbornness, to circumvent a phenomenon called "the color line" in winning the heavyweight championship. The color line was introduced in America by the first American heavyweight champion of the world, John L. Sullivan, who refused to meet Peter Jackson, an outstanding boxer from the West Indies. For years, it was invoked by each succeeding champion, including Jefferies. Jefferies did box with one Negro, Hank Griffin, not long after he won the championship, but that was a four-

round match, merely a sort of exhibition. As Jefferies's reputation and dignity increased, he drew the line firmly. When he retired, unbeaten, he named a pair of relatively harmless Nordics—Marvin Hart and Jack Root—as leading contenders for the title. Hart beat Root. Hart was then beaten, in 1906, by Noah Brusso, a Canadian, who boxed under the name of Tommy Burns. . . . He whipped a number of Americans, after which he went abroad.

In Tommy Burns's departure with the title, Johnson saw an opportunity he could never hope to gain here at home. By then, he had beaten most of the best heavyweights in America, except, of course, the reigning champions. Wherever Tommy Burns went—through England, Ireland, and France—Johnson followed, challenging the champion at every stop. Burns treated the matter with the contempt that was then customary, and proceeded to Australia. Arriving in Sydney in 1908, and finding that Johnson had followed him there too, Burns relented and accepted the challenge. Johnson was not so elated with that turn of events as to overlook the problem of refereeing. While he did not doubt his ability to wrest the championship from Burns, he was not sure he would be able to do so in the presence of a referee who was pledged to protect Burns's interest—Australia being an even whiter country than the United States. Allowed, then, to have a referee of his choice, Johnson turned to a man who he felt would be no more than moderately unfair to him. "For every point I'm given," Johnson said to the referee of his choice, "I'll have earned two, because I'm a Negro. But I want to be sure I get my one point, anyway. There's only one man I know I can trust to give it to me, and that's you."

The ensuing battle was, from all accounts, a mismatch. Johnson, in characteristic fashion, toyed lengthily with Burns. Hot words were exchanged. One such word was "yellow." Burns had called him yellow before the fight began. "Who's yellow now, Tommy?" he said. This was a surprising word to use to a man of Johnson's fighting record and obvious determination, and an even more surprising one to use to a man of his color. Burns, it is said, was alluding to the story that when Johnson was a boy, growing up in Galveston, Texas, a member of his family had accused him of having a yellow streak. Burns was not the first of Johnson's opponents who had made use of the story. Certainly the streak was nowhere in evidence against the champion, unless it was to be seen in Johnson's reluctance to throw a knockout punch. After he had outboxed Burns for fourteen rounds, a detachment of the Sydney police called an end to the proceedings—not wishing any further embarrassment either to themselves or to the man who had clearly lost the championship.

Under ordinary circumstances, the new champion, on his return to America, would have received a hero's welcome. He had, after all, reclaimed a title that had come to be regarded as American property. But the circumstances were not, of course, ordinary. Johnson was black; and, although he was also American, the property he had brought back home belonged to the portion of his country that was white. The manner of his returning was far more painful to white Americans than had been the manner of Tommy Burns's leaving—for Johnson was received much as though he were the bearer of goods that he himself had stolen. According to John Lardner, "The fundamental tenet of a good many anti-Johnsonites was that rule of the heavyweights by any Negro was a threat to civilization. The idea was developed mostly in saloon and street-corner talk, but it had sporadic support in newspapers, too—in large Northern cities as well as in the South." Since a man like Johnson could not be permitted to keep the championship, it became necessary to unearth some pearl of a white challenger to take it away from him. The search for such a redeemer went on from 1909 to 1915, and it was during these years that the term "white hope" entered the American language.

After Johnson defeated the first couple of white hopes that came to the surface, a call went out to James J. Jefferies. The view was suddenly taken that if there *was* a heavyweight champion in America, then, by God, that man was Jefferies. After all, he had retired undefeated. Although he was now, in 1910, thirty-five years old, he had retired only six years earlier, and could not, it was felt, already have lost his great powers. It was therefore his duty to come out of retirement and, as one writer put it, "redeem his race's honor in person."

Jefferies answered the summons, and met Johnson in Reno, Nevada. According to Johnson, the fight was "attended by more famous sporting men, boxers and promoters than any other. . . . Prominent men from all walks of life had come from England, France, Spain, Mexico, Australia, Canada and every corner of the world to see what they hoped would be the return of the heavyweight crown to the head of a Caucasian." Jefferies must also have been aware of the international character of the assembly. He was surely aware of its hopes. He gave of his best, but he was knocked out in the fifteenth round. Whatever might have been the outcome six years earlier, Jefferies was in no shape to beat Johnson in 1910. Here are parts of Johnson's report:

> The crowd gave me a hearty reception, but that given Jeff was twenty times greater than mine. . . . Hardly a blow had been struck when I knew that I was Jeff's master. From the start the fight was mine. . . . He fought his best. . . . His brain was working keenly, but he found it impossible to get through my defense. . . . He landed on me frequently but with no effect. . . . I took part in the palaver that went on, addressing myself particularly to Jim Corbett, a member of Jeff's training staff, who took occasion to send a few jeering remarks in my direction. I told Corbett to come in the ring, that I would take him on too. . . . I hit Jeff at will. There was no place that was beyond my reach. . . . I really did not have any desire to punish him unnecessarily. The cheering for Jeff never ceased. The spectators . . . gave him every possible encouragement, but their cheering turned to moans and groans when they saw that he was suffering as he was. . . . I heard them shout: "Stop it! Stop it!" The great crowd cheered Jefferies for his grit. . . . The crowd was by no means pleased. The "white hope" had failed, and as far as the championship was concerned it was just where it was before . . . except that I had established my rightful claim to it beyond all possible dispute.

At least, in Johnson's own eyes. In the eyes of most others, his victory meant only that the search for a white hope had to be intensified.

In July 1912, Johnson was brought up on a charge of violating the Mann Act—transporting a woman across state lines for immoral purposes. Johnson said that he was innocent; that the woman, who happened to be white, was his secretary; and that the charge was clearly part of the campaign to drive him from the championship. His plea was not accepted. Although he married his traveling companion before the trial began, he was found guilty and sentenced to a year and a day in jail. Rather than serve, he escaped to Europe, where he spent the next nine years.

In Europe he seems to have been something of a celebrity. An American who visited Europe at the time said later, "I saw his limousine blocking traffic in the Paris boulevards while the white people struggled to shake hands with the burly black man." In his book, Johnson alleges that he "rubbed shoulders" with European royalty and aristocrats; "disported on the French and Italian Rivieras"; was a bull-fighter in Spain; gained entry to "some of the finest homes in Mayfair"; in Moscow associated with Russian field marshals and aides to Czar Nicholas; mixed with artists, scientists, and writers; and, on one or two visits to Mexico, became friendly with President Carranza.

During the first three years of Johnson's exile, the search for a white hope went on in America. Whenever one was found he was dispatched to Europe to find Johnson and retrieve the championship. But none of these missions bore fruit. The campaign to replace him as champion finally paid off in April 1915, when Johnson was induced to come to Havana, Cuba, and risk his title against Jess Willard, the latest of the white hopes. As the records show, Johnson was knocked out in the twenty-sixth round, thereby relinquishing the title to the original line of succession.

One has to say "the records show" because the circumstances leading up to the fight in Havana, and whether or not Johnson was indeed knocked out, are not clear. There are at least three versions of what happened. One is that Johnson was then dissipating himself in Europe, that he was in a weakened condition, and that the boxing promoters in America had seized that opportunity to put him in the ring against Willard, their greatest white hope yet. Another is that Johnson was broke, and had agreed to come to Havana and exchange his championship for the right amount of cash. A third is that he had been promised that if he surrendered the championship to Willard all would be forgiven, and he would be allowed to return to America as a free man. The last explanation is the one Johnson himself gave in his book:

> Preceding the Willard fight it was hinted to me in terms which I could not mistake that if I permitted Willard to win, which would give him the title, much of the prejudice against me would be wiped out. Those who chafed under the disappointment of having a man of my race hold the championship, I was told, would be mollified, and it would be easier to have the charges against me dropped . . . that there would be no further prosecution of me, and that I might settle down quietly and live in peace with my fellowmen.

The promise, if indeed it was made, was either not meant or not kept. Johnson went on:

> I had cause to regret my action, for after I had allowed the title to pass to Willard, I found that such offers or hints of leniency as had been tendered

were without substantial foundation, and that immediate prospects for my return to my own country without going to prison were so slight that I could not give them serious thought.

So Johnson returned to Europe and resumed his wanderings.

Six years later, at the age of forty-three, he crossed the Mexican border into the United States, having, in his words, been "haunted by the constant wish to see my own country and to live amid the scenes that were dearest to me." He was taken into custody and later sent to Leavenworth, where he served the major portion of the sentence he had received in 1912. When Johnson was released, Jack Dempsey, who had won the heavyweight title from Jess Willard in 1919, was still the champion. But Dempsey was not risking his title with black heavyweights. The color line had been reinstated. Harry Wills, the best black heavyweight to emerge in Johnson's absence, was studiously avoided by Dempsey—although it is still believed that it was not the color line Dempsey was obeying so much as it was his fear of losing to Wills. Jack Johnson, however, was never allowed near the heavyweight championship again. His challenges were refused with the explanation that he was now too old to fight for the title. Still, he is said to have remained in remarkably good physical shape. And it was his feeling that even approaching his middle forties he would have extended Dempsey, with a good chance of beating him. But former champions are like that: they seldom know when their great powers are gone. Johnson went on fighting, off and on, for a number of years, mostly in exhibitions. His last fight is said to have taken place in 1945, when he was sixty-seven. He died a year later, in an automobile accident near Raleigh, North Carolina.

A question that is commonly debated among boxing fans concerns the following: Who was the superior champion—Ali, Louis, or Johnson? Each faction, like schoolboys on a playground, welcomes the opportunity to display its arguments but remains quite inaccessible—except in rare instances—to persuasion. At least two of the champions in question have displayed a similar fidelity to their own opinions. The more voluble example of the two is Muhammad Ali, who never fails to maintain that he is the greatest heavyweight champion that there ever has been or ever will be. Although he needs absolutely no help in advertising his claim or himself, millions of his admirers have joined him in the effort. Here, though, is a testimony from Harry Carpenter, a British sports journalist, who had this to say, after watching Ali's victory over George Foreman, in Zaire: "How many years had I been hearing Ali say: 'I'm the Greatest'? Always I had listened, laughed, enjoyed, and yet kept a doubt aflame in my mind. The Greatest? With Johnson, Dempsey, Louis, Marciano there before him? As the sun came up in Zaire . . . I reflected upon what I had just seen, and admitted to myself: yes, very likely he is the Greatest."

Harry Carpenter belongs to that faction which, on the rare occasion, changes its mind. He had once held an opinion about Joe Louis similar to the one he later came to hold about Ali. A pity he ended up being converted, because no heavyweight champion has stood in greater need of spokesmen than Joe Louis—so little, during his career, and even now, has he bothered to say for himself. He has neither made nor encouraged comparisons of himself and other champions, whatever his private views may be. One cannot remember an athlete of similar status who has been more reticent on the subject of his own merits, or has seemed less concerned with what ranking he is assigned in the history of his profession. Perhaps Louis feels secure enough in his private judgments. Perhaps he is genuinely indifferent to what others may have to say. Perhaps he considers this whole business of historical handicapping to be more than slightly risible. But one suspects that it may also be some strain of civility in him, or a certain dignity he associates with the position of champion, which forbids his engaging in the cheap exercise of promoting himself, of earning self-regard at the cost of belittling the importance or accomplishments of others. It has been said that one great work of art does not displace another. Perhaps Louis carries this piece of knowledge in him, along with his trapped eloquence. Such claims as have been made on his behalf have come from his supporters, especially those who remember the magnificent fighter he was in the late 1930s and early 1940s. To some, like Bob Considine, a columnist for the Hearst press, Louis was too good to be believed. "Joe Louis," Considine wrote in 1940, "may be the greatest heavyweight we've ever had, or just the best of a bad lot." And this is what Harry Carpenter had once thought, before he changed his mind about Ali: "Louis had the look of the finest fighting machine yet produced. . . . No man's perfect. But Louis came as close as anyone."

Jack Johnson did not claim, in his autobiography, that he was the greatest of the heavyweights, although he may have had quite a lot to say outside its pages. Of course, he did not have Ali or Louis to think about. When he wrote, in 1927, Ali was not yet born, and Louis was a boy in his teens. Those with whom he contested for historical supremacy were the white champions (from Gene Tunney all the way back to John L. Sullivan) and all the great black heavyweights who had never been allowed to fight for the championship. There is, however, enough evidence in Johnson's book to show that he considered himself second to none. Before sending the book off to the publishers, Johnson solicited a few prefatory comments from his contemporaries "in regard to my boxing ability." From what is known about Johnson, it may be safely said that he was not the sort of man to request testimonials from sources that were likely to dissent from the opinion he held about himself. Ed W. Smith, a referee and sportswriter, who had witnessed a number of Johnson's fights, replied that "Jack presents ability that is impossible to rate too highly and next to impossible to match, then, now, and possibly ever." One J. B. Lewis stated that Johnson was "credited by all as being the greatest defensive fighter of all time." A sports columnist for the New York *Evening World*, who wrote under the name of TAD, gave the opinion that "Johnson was the greatest heavyweight of all time." Damon Runyon said that "no greater defensive fighter than Johnson ever lived." And in the main text of his book Johnson cited the result of a poll conducted by *Ring* magazine, in June 1927, which "shows that those competent to judge overwhelmingly nominate me as the greatest heavyweight boxer of all time."

Clearly, it is not only the fans of former days who are chauvinistic about their own heroes and their own times. Latter-day fans concede nothing to earlier heroes and earlier times, either. In the realm of sports, people do not very much esteem the achievements that they themselves did not see, and find it hard to imagine that future ones can be better. Imagining these three great fighters as finalists in a championship, one wonders what the outcome would be. Each contained strengths and weaknesses that make it difficult to predict, now, how well one would do against the other. In some ways, the issue is better left unresolved, for we retain three discrete gems whose facets sparkle and fascinate in various ways.

Toward the end of his life, Jack Johnson did have the opportunity to witness Joe Louis's ascent to the heavyweight championship of the world. It could not have been a pleasant experience for Johnson. Ever since he had become the first black man to win the championship, he had been somewhat reserved in his praise of other black heavyweights; indeed, he had not had much that was good to say about any of them. During his reign as champion, he had made a point of avoiding the better black contenders. It is possible he did not wish to endanger his position as the only black champion in history. In watching Joe Louis acquire the championship, then, he was seeing a man who had robbed him of one of his great distinctions—and, in view of the public acclaim and affection Louis was enjoying, a man who seemed to be surpassing whatever measure of popularity he once enjoyed.

Johnson does not appear to have liked or to have been impressed by what he was seeing of Louis. In July 1939, a columnist for the New York *Age*, now defunct but once the leading newspaper in Harlem, reported upon an interview he had recently had with Johnson. "I asked him," the writer said, "what he thought of Louis. He said he was not interested. But he told me of his trip to Norwalk, Connecticut, to visit an old friend, Mayor Stack. The Mayor closed down business to entertain Jack and took a ride in Jack's Lincoln Zephyr, with Jack at the wheel; they had a motorcycle escort all over town and into the colored section, where they had a grand ball. The Mayor showed Jack some of the new projects that are in construction in behalf of race people. Everybody went for the ex-champ."

Jack Johnson may not have liked what he saw of Joe Louis, but perhaps he *was* impressed: impressed enough to profess a lack of interest in Louis, and to seek reassurance from one of the recent pages of his own yellowing scrapbook. Old champions being, of course, what they are.

UNCLE RUFUS RAPS
ON THE SQUARED CIRCLE

L ARRY N EAL (1937–1981) was a poet, critic, playwright,
and filmmaker. His most famous collection of poetry is *Hoodoo Hollerin
Bebop Ghosts* (1971). He was also co-editor (along with Amiri Baraka) of
the noted black literature compilation, *Black Fire: An Anthology of Afro-
American Writing* (1968). He was also among the few black male literary
critics during the late sixties who had a deep and abiding appreciation for
the work of Zora Neale Hurston. (He wrote the introduction for
Hurston's *Dust Tracks on a Road* when it was reissued by the Arno Press
in 1971.) His untimely death from a heart attack in 1981 was a great loss
to black letters. "Uncle Rufus Raps on the Squared Circle" appeared in
the *Partisan Review* in the Spring 1972 issue.

Once I saw a prize fighter boxing a yokel. The fighter was swift and
amazingly scientific. His body was one violent flow of rapid rhythmic
action. He hit the yokel a hundred times while the yokel held up his arms
in stunned surprise. But suddenly the yokel, rolling about in the gale of
boxing gloves, struck one blow and knocked science, speed and footwork
as cold as a well-digger's posterior. The smart money hit the canvas. The
long shot got the nod. The yokel had simply stepped inside of his oppo-
nent's sense of time. . . .

—R ALPH E LLISON , *Invisible Man*

S porting events, like beauty contests, horse shows, public assassinations—
all forms of spectacle—have implicit within them a distinct metaphysical
character, said Uncle Rufus while lighting his cigar. We had been talking
about the Ali–Frazier fight. He had once been a boxer. Then later he became a
singer and dancer in a minstrel show. Needless to say, Uncle Rufus is a most
fascinating gentleman. Following our discussion, I discovered that he was one of
the prime sources for Melvin B. Tolson's extremely muscular masterpiece entitled

The Harlem Gallery. Further, Uncle Rufus staunchly maintains that he knew the real John Henry who, by the way, was an excellent bare-knuckle fighter.

The day after the Ali–Frazier fight, I met him uptown at a little spot in Harlem called My Bar. The bar is a very hip joint. It's run by a tall yellow guy named Julian May. It's a good place to talk all kinds of sports. Julian's got himself a brand new color TV in the back room. And there's a bartender there, Ray, who is a statistical and historical expert on all sports, especially the ones in which we dominate, or the ones in which we have determined the stylistic mode and strategy. But Ray would never speak in these terms, he absorbs his data on sports because he loves them and sees them as a significant encounter with the unknowable nature of the world. Ray's attitude towards sports like boxing, football and basketball is a healthy blend of the mysterious and scientific.

I am sitting at the bar, discussing with Ray the function of energy in athletics when Uncle Rufus bops into the door. He peacocks in a pearl gray Homburg. The coat is blue cashmere. He sports a golden-headed serpent cane; the shoes, French, Shriner and Urner, contrast exquisitely with his spats which are the same pearl gray color as the Homburg.

I order him a Jack Daniels, and introduce him to Ray. A discussion ensues concerning the geometry of basketball. I feel shut out of the conversation; and besides, I didn't invite my Uncle here to talk about basketball. I was really getting irritated with the whole thing when some customers finally worked into the bar.

So now that I had Uncle Rufus to myself, I asked him his opinion of the Ali–Frazier fight. He began the discussion with some commentary on a few of the events that transpired in the aftermath of Jack Johnson's victory over Jim Jefferies back in Reno on July 4th, 1910.

"It was during the days of the steamboat, and after that famous bout," he said, "there was fighting going on between the blacks and the whites. This happened because the whites were so infuriated by Jack's victory that they began beating up on the colored. A man got lynched in Cape Girardeau when he tried to collect a bet he had made with a white farmer by the name of Cyrus Compton.

"I was working on a show called Stall's Minstrels. Now this show was out of Cairo, Illinois, which is smack on the Mississippi River. But we was working in a dance hall in Henderson, Kentucky. I think they called that hall The Stomp. All the great troupes had worked it. *The Creole Show* and *Black Patti's Troubadours* had also been through there. And while I was in Henderson, I heard a splendid concert of operatic selections by Sissieretta Jones."

"Well what about the fight?" I asked.

"Oh . . . the fight? Which fight?"

"It's hard to tell now; I asked you about the Ali–Frazier fight, and you started talking about Jack Johnson which, it seems to me, doesn't have much to do with this conversation."

"Let's put it this way son: You order me another one of these Jack Daniels, and sit back patiently so you can learn something for once in your life."

If you wasn't my Uncle Rufus, I would tell you to go and eat shit, talking to me that way.

"Never mind that . . . I want it on the rocks with water on the side."

I ordered the drink. Ray came over, poured his drink then mine. I think I saw them exchange winks.

"Well as I was trying to say, I was in Henderson, and I heard that they was fighting and all."

"*Who* was fighting and all?"

"The colored and white.

"They say, no sooner did Jack win the match than the fighting broke out. Well, I was in Henderson, and I heard that they was fighting in Evansville, Indiana. Evansville is right across the Ohio River from Henderson, so I went up there. Man, even with the fighting and all going on, them colored people was celebrating. But not like they was doing in '35 when Joe Louis won his match against Carnera. No it was nothing compared to that. But it was still some celebration.

"The next day, after the all-night-long parties, some smart-ass little colored boy by the name of Open Mouth Rainey got shot to death in the Silver Dollar Bar and Grill. It seems this guy, Open Mouth, strolled into the restaurant and asked the owner for a cup of coffee as strong as Jack Johnson, and a steak beat up like Jim Jefferies. When he said that, the owner slapped him, reaching quickly for his six-shooter which was right under the counter. Open Mouth Rainey pulled his forty-four, but it was too late. The man had gotten the drop on Open Mouth. He burned him five times. Open Mouth barely had a chance. Let me tell you: some of them crackers was sure mad that a nigger was now the heavyweight champion of the world.

"But the colored knew that it was quite natural for there to be a black champion. Since we was the first boxers in this country anyway. You see, Larry, boxing started out in Virginia. There it was the custom for the sons of aristocratic families to go to England where they received a first-rate education in the humanities. Also, while there, they were supposed to acquire the finer virtues by circulating among and socializing with the English gentry. Now along with education of the mind went the education of the body. Therefore, they were trained in the manly art of boxing. Now these scions of Southern aristocracy returned home from England with a good education and a knowledge of the rudiments of boxing. Back home, they started training some of the young slaves to be boxers. So they held contests among the slaves from different plantations.

"Pugilism, as it relates to us, son, got its formal start, however, with the career of one Tom Molyneaux. Mr. Molyneaux was the first colored champion. He was born in Virginia, a slave; and when he was, through some mysterious process, granted his freedom, he traveled to New York. By then, he had beaten everybody around, both Negroes and whites. Then he went to England to fight Tom Cribb who was then the world champion. This fight took place in December of 1810; I forget the exact date. But it was at Capthall Common in Sussex. These were the days before the Queensberry rules. As I recall, it was a dreary day, the fight lasted forty rounds. Tom Cribb won, but a lots of folks, particularly a guy they called West Indian Charlie, protested that there was tricknology involved in Cribb's victory. But be that as it may, that's how the colored got into boxing.

"All of the plantation owners, from all points, used to gather at their respective plantations to place wagers on one slave or the other. These men were all gentlemen, fine education, breeding, and plenty of money. So in many ways, they didn't care who really won the fight. It was all just considered good sport. They liked the way them niggers circled each other and doing them fancy steps, and dropping them bombs and so. Naturally, they got specially excited when one of them fellers drew blood. I once saw two slaves beat each other to death."

It is late in the afternoon, sun swarming all over us. I am inside of a bull of a man named Silas. Amos swings a wild right at me. I block it easily, but he catches me with a left hook. It seems like all day we have been fighting like this. My arms and his arms are heavy, but we smash at each other and at the white blurry faces surrounding us. We go on like this until the sun begins going down. . . . The shouting and the rooting has died down now; now we lean on each other breathing hard and tied up in sweat like wrestlers. The contest has boiled down to grunts and awkward swings. . . . As darkness comes, we are both still standing. Judge Tate calls it a tie. They throw me in the buckboard, and carry me back to the plantation.

"You got the right idea son. That's almost exactly how it was in those days. Yeah, that's just the way it went down. Them folks really liked the sports. And since they had lots of money, and not much to do, they just gambles all the time.

"Yes siree, them folks liked the sports and the sporting houses too. And I'm sure you know that they had betting tables in them houses too. An ex-boxer by the name of Bill Richmond ran one of the biggest whore houses in the city of New Orleans; but even though he himself was colored, he didn't allow no colored in there—'cept them girls he had working for him.

"I told you I used to be a boxer before I went to Stall's Minstrels. Woody Johnson was manager (may he rest in peace). I was swift and dancy, in the bantamweight class, like Eligio Sardinas who was otherwise known as "Kid Chocolate." I had me a pretty snappy jab, and my left hook was a monster. I got tired of the fight game though. And then I decided to go into show business. Why? 'Cause there was some very nice people in the business in those days, real educated and refined people like J. Rosamund Johnson. And I wanted to be one of them. So I gave up the fight game, even though I was good. In my time, I was on good terms with boxers like Battling Siki, Tiger Flowers, Joe Gans, Sammy The Smasher and Sam Langford. Me and Sam used to party a lot together. I'm not just name-dropping son; I'm simply giving you my credentials so you will fully appreciate the facts I'm about to give you concerning the squared circle.

"A lots of black guys started hanging round the sporting events. In those days, we referred to these guys as the 'Sporting Crowd'; or we called them 'Sports' for short. Now all these sportsmens was fast livers. They dressed in the latest fashions, and wore finely tailored suits. Jelly Roll Morton used to hang around with that bunch quite often. Jelly Roll was the real sporting type. He played a wicked piano, was a ladies' man, spoke French and had him a diamond ring on every finger. He even had a diamond in his middle tooth. You was liable to see old Jelly Roll anywhere and with anybody. He was around boxers and jockeys as much as he was round musicians.

"Well now that we're talking about Jelly Roll, this brings me to the part of my discussion about boxing in general, and the Ali–Frazier fight in particular. Did you know that there is a distinct connection between boxing and music? You say you didn't know that? Well there is. You see it's like this: boxing is just another kind of rhythm activity. Like all sports is based on rhythm. Dig: if you ain't got no rhythm, you can't play no sports. Like jumping rope ain't nothing but dancing. Beating on the punching-bag is the same as beating on drums. Everything connected with sports is connected with rhythm. You just think about it for a while. Every fighter has his own particular rhythmic style just the way musicians do. You ever notice that some fighters dance around a lot, doing fast rhythms; while some other guy is slower, likes to do the slow-drag instead of the Lindy Hop or the jitterbug. Yes, Larry, this is so with all of its possible variations.

"All sports are just expressions of a particular attitude toward rhythm. But boxing unlike many other sports confines the players to a very small area of confrontation. Boxers are contained within a square. And this makes for particular difficulties. But it also makes for the particular attraction to the sport. Most men can identify with the sport because most men, at one time or the other, have had to hold their hands up. But what about the square? What has it to do with the sport? Well the square symbolizes a discrete universe. That is to say, it brings to bear upon the material universe a particular sense of order. All geometrical constructs do. For example, the triangle, the Trinity and other ternary clusters seem to represent spiritual dynamism. The circle, on the other hand, represents some aspect of infinity. Perhaps oneness in God. The square, in its quaternary aspect, appears to symbolize the material realm, or the rational intellect. There is a negative aspect to the square though. In some ways the square implies stasis, and even decadence. But regardless of all of these factors, the square is the context in which one fighter confronts another one.

"Here we are dealing with the underlying premises behind the sport. We could say something about ritual here, but that side of the street has already been covered in great detail by Mr. Jack Johnson in his autobiography. Instead here, we are discussing the metaphysics of geometrical and dynamic modality.

"Now there are several things that determine the winner of a fight, or any sporting contest for that matter. But all of these things are essentially tied up with rhythm. Because even though there is an implied circle within the square (and naturally without the square), one rhythmically described by the fighters themselves, the square, in this connection, is the creation of a particular historical sensibility. This sensibility manifests itself in all spheres of life and art. We see it asserting itself in architecture, technology and sociopolitical theories. The circle, on the other hand, exists as an ever evolving metaconstruct. The fighter's duty is to rhythmically discern the essential unity between the circle and the square.

"Take this Muhammed Ali, for example; he knows all about squares and circles cause he is a Muslim. And all of them folks knows all about things like that. Like $360° =$ Allah. That kind of thing. He even know about rhythm. I hear he's a poet. Rhythm concerns the modality of space, sound, motion and existence. Both space and motion can be manipulated rhythmically. Existence can also be manipulated in like manner; but we'll deal with that some other time when we are discussing contests that involve more than four persons. If we went into that now, we would have to discuss history, and that bitch is not the subject of my discussion.

"All fighters must understand the principles of rhythmic modality. The fighter who best understands these principles will most likely win the contest. Again, young man, rhythm here refers to the duration and the structure of the contest, its interlocking spatial and dynamic relationships, the manner in which one proceeds to handle the space dominated by his own body, and the body of his opponent. It also refers to the artistic or technical manipulation of the space encompassed by the square which these fools erroneously call the "ring." By the use of a calculus, therefore, we arrive at the conclusion that the Ali–Frazier fight was, in fact, a contest of essentially different attitudes toward music.

"This was the secret wisdom that Jelly Roll Morton passed on to boxers of the twenties. This principle was orally transmitted through a long line of boxers until it was momentarily obscured by Floyd Patterson who was the first Hamlet of the boxing profession.

"Now Ali understands these principles of rhythm and music. Theoretically, that's what's so sweet about him. You see, he believes in riffing. He certainly has got the body, the legs and the mouth for it. But Frazier is somewhere else in the musical universe. Frazier is stomp-down blues, bacon, grits and Sunday church. Course them Muslims is different. They don't be eating none of that hog. They say it ruin your brains. It didn't seem to do Frazier no harm though, 'cept he do seem a little slow with the rap sometimes. But Joe Louis, an Alabama boy, raised on black strap molasses, was slow with the rap too. And you know how mean he could be upon entering the squared circle. But Ali is body bebop. While Frazier is slow brooding blues with a gospel bearing. Ali understands the mysteries of the circles and the squares, the same as Sufi poets do. That is to say Larry, the essential metaphysics of these forms are, for him, a constant source of religious and intellectual meditation. Ali prays (does his salats) in quiet meditation. But most likely, Frazier wants to shout in church. However, Ali, as a Muslim intellectual, has been forced to suppress his gospel impulse. But he can't suppress it totally. You can still hear it in his voice when he speaks, or when he tries to sing. But blues and gospel ain't his thing. Frazier can't sing, but he sings better than Ali. And that's why Frazier won the fight.

"I don't mean that he outsung Ali during the fight. I mean, instead, that he sang his particular song better than Ali sang his. Old slow-blues, pork-eating Frazier is moody and relentless. He got plenty killer in him. But bebop-body, your man, is the urbanized philosopher of the would-be righteous, the future shaper in many respects. However, he is a blasé singer, having a tendency to sound down mammy-loving country boys who lack causes, and who are grateful for any desperate break they can get. Boys like Frazier envision purple suits, full length Russian sable, beige El Dorados, the perfumed cluster of female flesh and triumphant kisses from the Sepia Queen.

"Ali envisions a Nation full of intricate order, like an interlocking network of squares and rectangles. He dreams of kissing the black stone of Mecca. No loose perfumed ladies there. Perhaps there, mosques fly as zones of ultimate righteousness. The Muslim women wear long dresses; they pursue long periods of silence as they side-step sin, murmuring polite Koranic knowledge.

"Your problem, my boy, primarily concerns making both of them understand the implicit unity between the circle and the square. Using a variant of the calculus that we set up earlier, I would say, therefore, that Frazier needs Ali's squares, and Ali needs Frazier's circles. I can't see it no other way.

"The essential dynamics of the squared circle demand that each contestant really understand how he sings best. That he choreograph and orchestrate his game in terms of what he does best. Theoretically, everyone in the sporting game knows this. But the pragmatics or translation of this abstract knowledge often eludes us. In the case of the particular spectacle under discussion, the fighters were very much evenly matched. They just simply manifested different choreographic styles. But given the pressure of the evening, its particular psychological atmosphere, its *forced* political overtone, the winner would be the one who most acutely understood the principles of spatial and psyche rhythm. Ali's science was winning until the first stunning blow caught him somewhere around the eighth round. (Note the quaternity of the number eight [8].) But Ali also had not paced himself properly from the beginning of the match. He allowed himself to enter Frazier's system of deceptive choreography; a system full of treacherous memories that lay in the cut ready to pummel that bebopping body of his. The way to fight slow grinding powerhouses like Frazier is to not let them touch you at all—if it's humanly possible. Because, beneath that dull rap, there is a mad churning engine. And you have got to respect that kind of power."

He looked at his watch. "How about one for the road?" I said.

"That's all right with me, but it has got to be a quickie. I'm supposed to meet this chippy in a little while."

When the next round of drinks came, I toasted him and thanked him for his time. "Wow! Uncle Rufus, all the time you was talking you never told me who you were pulling for."

He looked at me long and hard. Then his black face broke into a sarcastic smile. He reached down beneath the bar stool, and pulled his cane out. He held it up so that the golden-headed serpent would glitter as it caught the low amber light of the My Bar. He looked at the cane, and then at me. I could see now, looking at him full in the face, that he was really much older than he seemed. I saw the cane swiftly fly back. Before I had time to react, Uncle Rufus had whacked me hard across my arm.

"What was that about?" I whined, rubbing my aching arm.

"It's about you not learning to ask the right questions, especially after I done took all this time explaining things to you. Sheeet! I really shouldn't give you no answer. But since you once told me you wanted to be a boxer, here it is: I was pulling for *both* of them. But this time, your old uncle put his money on slow blues. . . ."

THE BLACK INTELLECTUAL AND THE SPORT OF PRIZEFIGHTING

GERALD EARLY is professor of English and Afro-American Studies at Washington University in St. Louis. He is the author of a collection of essays entitled, *Tuxedo Junction: Essays on American Culture* (1989). "The Black Intellectual and the Sport of Prizefighting" originally appeared *The Kenyon Review* in the Summer of 1988.

Once I saw a prize fighter boxing a yokel. The fighter was swift and amazingly scientific. His body was one violent flow of rapid rhythmic action. He hit the yokel a hundred times while the yokel held up his arms in stunned surprise. But suddenly the yokel, rolling about in the gale of boxing gloves, struck one blow and knocked science, speed, and footwork as cold as a well-digger's posterior. The smart money hit the canvas. The long shot got the nod. The yokel had simply stepped inside of his opponent's sense of time . . .

I

A THEORETICAL PRELUDE

This quotation is from Ralph Ellison's *Invisible Man*,[1] a novel that makes a number of allusions and references to prizefighting. This quotation resonates in a number of very crucial ways. It is, of course, the classic dialectic of boxing: the speedy, scientific boxer versus the artless puncher. But it is also the story of the tortoise and the hare, the con man and the homeboy, the country mouse and the city mouse, Brer Fox and Brer Rabbit. Yet all those classical metaphors of innocence and experience collapse into the image of the prizefighter's confrontation with his opposite, his nemesis, the very antithesis of himself. It was Mark Twain who wrote in his 1889 novel, *A Connecticut Yankee in King Arthur's Court,* that the world's best swordsman needn't fear the second best swordsman in the world; he needs to fear the man who has never held a sword. In this light, the world's best boxer needn't fear the man who is almost his equal but rather the man who could not possibly match his skill. In other words, the Trickster, inasmuch as he is represented by the slick accomplished boxer, does not need to fear another formidable Trickster; rather he needs to fear that which is the negation of the Trickster, for in the brutal pantomime of the prize ring the Trickster's technique masks the fact that he is the personification of anarchy. Thus, his technique is not a virtue but utter decadence, his paradoxical expression of the contempt of both virtue and technique. And his negation is he who through the complete absence of technique wishes to rescue technique from the Trickster's laughing and lurid display of it as a stunt.

Technique—and boxing since its inception in the bare-knuckle days of Broughton and Slack in England has been, in part, nothing more than the history of its own rationalization through the obsessive quest for more reified technique and rules—must always fear, not other techniques but the utter void of technique. It is no accident to speak of confidence games in connection with the metaphor raised by the Ellison quotation. Professional prizefighting, from its early brawling days in eighteenth-century England, has been the sport of the gambler, and the gambler's romance—his dream—has always been to have the long shot come through as a sure thing. Variations on the theme of the victory of the yokel as a fixed fight can be found in such sources as David W. Maurer's accounts of various fight store cons in *The American Confidence Man* and the short stories of Charles Emmet Van Loan in *Inside the Ropes* (1913) and *Taking the Count* (1915). In these stories, in that maddening fluidity of identity that has come to characterize the American, long shots disguise themselves as sure things and sure things masquerade as long shots. Other sources include the actual history of American prizefighting itself: the halcyon days of New York's Horton Law, 1896–1900 (a nice historical chunk detailing sordid wheelings and dealings designed to rip off the unsuspecting public), or a fight such as the Billy Fox–Jake LaMotta middleweight bout on November 14, 1947. LaMotta admitted, several years later before a Senate investigating committee, that he threw this fight on orders of members of organized crime so that the long shot—Fox—would win (which he did by a fourth round knockout). This is only one of many such examples that riddle a sport that has problems with honesty.

The two most powerful, most staying, images of the yokel and the prizefighter can be drawn from two entirely different realms of American culture, and both involve white fighters. The first is Francis Wallace's 1936 novel, *Kid Galahad*, which was made into a film twice: the first, "The Battling Bellhop," in 1937 (original theater title was "Kid Galahad") featured Bette Davis; the latter, "Kid Galahad," in the early sixties was a star vehicle for Elvis Presley. It has been made into two films nearly thirty years apart and its basic theme—the good, incorruptible middlewestern country boy goes to the city, becomes a crude but effective boxer in order to save the family farm—has been used in a number of other films. This shows how deeply the Galahad myth of male American innocence (for example, Billy Budd, the American Adam) and inadvertent Horatio-Alger-like success (humility and determination as forms of grace from Ben Franklin to Sylvester Stallone's Rocky) is ingrained in our national consciousness. Dubbed in the novel "Galahad" because of his purity of heart, the former bellhop, fresh from the Navy, is always the long shot in his fights and always knocks out his opponents with one punch. His opponents are always better boxers, better stylists in the ring than he is. The films tend to stress Galahad's ineptitude more than the novel does. Wallace, in the end, is ambiguous. The Kid over the course of the book becomes a pretty good boxer/stylist and in his last fight—a grudge match, as these confrontations usually are in novels and films— is actually beaten severely for the first several rounds. His manager, Nick, pressured by the gangsters and affected by his own jealousy of Galahad, gives him the wrong advice and has him slugging instead of boxing. Eventually, Nick changes his mind and the Kid, through sly boxing, wins the fight. Of course, at novel's end, the Kid quits boxing. He is, after all, not a pug and his mastery of boxing is not a sign of commitment but an indication of disdain. He does not wish to be tainted by boxing; it is simply the avenue by which he can seize the main chance to remain stolidly agrarian, implacably at peace with a series of values that can scarcely be considered conventional. They are gestures of folksy platitudes: he likes to eat, does not drink, likes to work in the open air, is polite to and shy around women, believes in his country, and yearns for the family hearth. The fact that he has become a decent boxer in the end suggests that he might be corrupted by all this and adopt another series of values—dress fancy, go to nightclubs, chase women, and drink liquor. In the Presley film, the necessity of this reactionary male purity is made clearer by, first, never having Galahad achieve any sort of prowess as a fighter and, second, by having his ultimate opponent be a slick, accomplished Hispanic boxer. The element of race is never very distant in the novel, although none of Galahad's opponents is black or Hispanic. The book is the sort of generally racist fare that one might expect from a bad novel written in the early thirties by a white writer. This was, after all, when the radio serialization of "Amos and Andy" began and books such as *Bigger and Blacker* and *Dark Days and Black Knights* by Octavus Roy Cohen and other such comic denigrations of blacks (published just a few years earlier) were still quite popular. And the country was still segregated. The issue is always Galahad's whiteness as inextricably bound to his maleness and to his pious set of provincial American moral bromides. In this sense, Wallace's novel and the films that resulted from it are nothing more than measured refinements of certain boxing novels by white male writers, both British and American, written during that fifty years preceding the publication of *Galahad*: George Bernard Shaw's *Cashel Byron's Profession* (1886), Arthur Conan Doyle's *Rodney Stone* (1896), Jack London's *The Game* (1905), W. R. H. Trowbridge's *The White Hope* (1913), and Robert E. Howard's *The Iron Man* (1930), the last indicative of the type of pulp material serialized in *Fight Stories* magazine. These books, by and large, being metaphorical discourses on the philosophical issue of the universe-of-force, on the sociopolitical issue of social Darwinism, and on the popular romance of American capitalism simply highlights their preoccupation with race. As Ronald E. Martin has argued in his literary study of the social Darwinism era: "The theme of evolutionary racism is an important one in late-nineteenth century . . ."; or "the universe-of-force viewpoint was of a piece with some of the Western world's most pernicious social practices and theories at the turn of the century. Force-thinking generally rationalized racism, class superiority, imperialism, the acquisition of wealth, and the veneration of the 'fittest.' "[2] (Other scholars of this era, notably George M. Fredrickson, Rayford Logan, and Richard Hofstader have made this point as well.) The good white fighter in these novels, who is not always inept in the technical sense, in the end symbolizes the essence of the "white civilization" that seemed to be standing at the brink of either an endless dawn of imperialistic dominance or the eternal night of nonwhite domination. It is the central myth of the key novel of Victorian America: Edgar Rice Burroughs's *Tarzan of the Apes* (1913), the quintessential blending of athleticism and racism. The power and popularity of this conjunction is revealed ironically in F. Scott Fitzgerald's 1925 novel, *The Great Gatsby*, where Tom Buchanan, the powerful football player, talks about reading Goddard's *The Rise of the Colored Empires*, and it is also suggested by Gatsby's reading of *Hopalong Cassidy*, a dime novel adventure from the same tradition of racist adventure westerns as those of Johnston McCulley, the creator of Zorro. These facts help explain my belief that *Gatsby* is a reworking of a western; in part, at least, a reworking of Owen Wister's *The Virginian*, leading to the great masked avenger, Ben Cameron, in Thomas Dixon's *The Clansman* (1905). This novel is essentially a little boy's adventure-romance about how white civilization must be rescued in much the same manner that a princess is rescued from a dragon. It is indeed quite striking how both vigilantism and terrorism, from Zorro to Batman to G.I. Joe, is the theme of male adolescent literature. Sanitized as a reactionary political literature, it simply becomes a little-boy genre for little-boy minds.

An important historical conjunction was taking place between approximately 1870 and 1930: boxing was changing from a bare-knuckle, irrational sport of indeterminate length to a rationalized sport of gloves governed by time; these changes helped to make it more popular. In addition, social Darwinism in particular and popular science in general were now a part of mass culture; ordinary people thought about science in a positive way, and blacks began to achieve notice in boxing and in American popular culture itself, through the image of bruisers. More so than baseball, pedestrianism (race walking), or jockeying, the other three professional sports that had a significant black presence in the late nineteenth century, boxing was the one sport that could produce an intense if vulgar fame, enough so that Corbett, Sullivan, Fitzsimmons, and Jefferies, the important champions before Jack Johnson, had to draw a color line against black challengers during their reigns. In other words, conditions were such that professional boxing was metamorphosed into an American sport, serving a particular and powerful set of collective psychic needs. With the completion of its final stages of development, the recodification of the rules, and the entry of the black, boxing was now ready to become the most metaphorical drama of male neurosis ever imagined in the modern world.

This leads me to discuss the second example or image of the yokel and the boxer, this taken from an actual prizefight. In April, 1915, black heavyweight champion Jack Johnson defended his title for the last time against Jess Willard of Kansas in Havana. Johnson, who had won the title on Christmas Eve, 1908, when he defeated Tommy Burns in Australia, had not had an easy time of it during his reign. A conviction for the violation of the Mann Act in 1912 led to his flight from America; in 1915, after he had been abroad for a few years, he was no longer lionized, and was in fact broke and possessor of a title that didn't mean much. It was a strange fight. Johnson has always maintained that he threw the fight—he lost by a knockout in the twenty-sixth round—in a deal to return to the United States and beat the Mann Act rap; yet right before the fight he was confident in his utterances published in black and white newspapers and was telling all his black fans including his mother to bet on him. (Of course, black fighters had betrayed black sports in fixed fights before: fifteen years earlier, in December, 1900, in Chicago, black lightweight Joe Gans threw a fight to featherweight Terry McGovern and blacks on the South Side took a bath.) Despite his age—37—and lack of conditioning caused by an extensive period of inactivity and lack of strenuous competition, Johnson was favored to win because he was such an outstanding boxer. Willard was not even the most distinguished of a mediocre lot of white hopes, though he was probably the biggest. Johnson had been involved in a fixed championship fight with a white challenger before: on October 16, 1909, in Colma, California, Johnson fought middleweight champion Stanley Ketchel on the condition that he carry him for the distance and not try to knock him out. When Ketchel tried a doublecross and knocked Johnson down in the twelfth round of the battle, Johnson arose and knocked Ketchel unconscious with an uppercut that broke off Ketchel's front teeth at the gum line. Being a black fighter, Johnson knew all about faking fights with white fighters. It was a common practice at this time. Such notable black fighters as Sam Langford, Sam McVey, Denver Ed Martin, Joe Jeanette, and others carried their share of incompetent white fighters.

But the fact of the matter is that Johnson, despite the claim in his autobiography and in the "Confessions" he sold to *Ring* magazine editor Nat Fleischer, did not throw the fight to Jess Willard. He lost in much the same manner that the slick boxer always loses to the yokel. He could not knock out Willard despite administering substantial punishment. Johnson tired because of his age and lack of condition, and eventually, with the hot sun beating down on him, Willard was able to land the one punch that put him on the floor.

Willard's victory was the beginning of the glorification of the white yokel in boxing (although, admittedly, Willard himself was never very well liked by the white public). Johnson's claim for a fix made the white yokel's claim essentially ambiguous and made the fight between the white yokel and the black boxer a comic encounter. Excepting Jack Dempsey and Gene Tunney, virtually every white champion (despite his style) has been a yokel: Sharkey, Braddock, Schmeling, Baer, Carnera, Marciano, Johansson, Coetzee.

The most notable contests for all of these fighters were against their significant black opponent. Louis fought and defeated the first five mentioned; Walcott, Charles, Louis, and Moore fought Marciano; Patterson became Johansson's alter ego, and Leon Spinks and Greg Page did the same for Coetzee. (One might throw in Jerry Cooney and Jerry Quarry who fit this mold, although they never became champions.) In their fights against black opponents, these fighters were not expected to win by guile or by ability. They were expected to win as Willard had against Johnson: take punishment, then land the ultimate blow.

To be sure, there have been black fighters who have been known as punchers; Sonny Liston comes to mind, as does current heavyweight champion Mike Tyson, though neither of them, to borrow a phrase from A. J. Liebling, would be considered nearly as "gauche and inaccurate" as Rocky Marciano who, along with Dempsey, is the most mythical of the great white fighters. But the greatest black fighters in the twentieth century, those most famous and highly regarded by experts, were tricksters of style: Jack Johnson, Muhammad Ali, Sugar Ray Robinson, and Sugar Ray Leonard: indeed the title "sugar," given to a fighter in recognition of the refulgences of his style, has never been given to a white fighter. Even Joe Louis, despite his reputation as a heavy hitter, was really a stylist, "as elegant as the finest of ballet dancers," Ralph Ellison said in an interview.

Against black opponents the white yokels were not even really fighters; they were more like preservers of the white public's need to see Tricksters pay a price for their disorder. Liebling was right in the end: if the black fighter as Trickster sees the white yokel as nemesis, then the white yokel becomes Ahab and the black Trickster the ultimate blackness of the black whale; the ring itself becomes the place where ideas of order are contested.

II

BLACK WRITERS AND THE SPORT OF PRIZEFIGHTING

There has never been a full-length nonfiction treatise on the sport of boxing by a black writer on the order of those by white authors such as A. J. Liebling's *The Sweet Science* (1982), George Plimpton's *Shadow-Box* (1977), Joyce Carol Oates's *On Boxing* (1987), Thomas Hauser's *The Black Lights* (1986), or Norman Mailer's *The Fight* (1975). Exceptions are the autobiographies of black fighters, the books by blacks such as Art Rust, Harry Edwards, Oceania Chalk and A. S. (Doc) Young that may contain a section on boxing (while discussing blacks in sports generally), former light heavyweight champion José Torres's fine biography of Muhammad Ali, the sociological articles by Nathan Hare, a former boxer, and a book such as Al-Tony Gilmore's *Bad Nigger* (1975) on the trials and tribulations of Jack Johnson. Indeed, the most complete, though not necessarily the most accurate, history of blacks in the sport was written by the previously mentioned Jewish editor of *Ring* magazine, Nat Fleischer; he composed five volumes published between 1938 and 1947 dealing with that subject called *Black Dynamite* that extends from Molineaux to Joe Louis (*Black Dynamite: The Story of the Negro in the Prize Ring from 1782 to 1938*). James Weldon Johnson provided a capsule history of blacks in the sport in his 1930 study *Black Manhattan*; this made him the first black intellectual to consider at any length the cultural importance of prizefighting for Afro-America.[3]

No black mainstream fiction writer has written a novel using a boxing theme in the same manner as Leonard Gardner in *Fat City* (1969), Nelson Algren in *Never Come Morning* (1963), W. C. Heinz in *The Professional* (1958), or Budd Schulberg in *The Harder They Fall* (1947). Boxing has been mentioned in some black novels and has, in fact, figured as an important image in a few, but there has been no black novel on boxing by a major black writer. There is a genre of black novels published by Holloway House in California called "novels of the black experience" generally characterized by potboiler plots and a type of effective, if occasionally pornographic, naturalism. The leading writers of these types of books are Iceberg Slim and the late Donald Goines. One of these may deal with boxing, a likely subject for these books.

It is odd that major works on the sport of prizefighting, either fiction or nonfiction, have not been produced by black writers. Boxing figures prominently in the social and cultural history of blacks in America; indeed, one could argue that the three most important black figures in twentieth-century American culture were prizefighters: Jack Johnson, Joe Louis, and Muhammad Ali. Certainly, there have been no other blacks in the history of this country who have been written about as much and whose actions were scrutinized so closely or reverberated so profoundly. We know from such books as Lawrence Levine's brilliant study, *Black Culture and Black Consciousness* (1977), that black prizefighters were important and celebrated personages in Afro-American folklore; indeed, these fighters were more celebrated in Afro-American folklore and life generally than other important black pioneers in sports such as Jackie Robinson, Jesse Owens, or Wilma Rudolph. Furthermore, prizefighting appears in important instances in other facets of Afro-American culture ranging from Adam Clayton Powell, Sr.'s, funeral oration for African boxer Battling Siki, to jazz trumpeter Miles Davis's fascination with presenting himself, in alter ego guise, as a prizefighter; this obsession culminated artistically with the release in 1971 of his soundtrack album entitled, "Jack Johnson." The subject receives mention in such significant black autobiographies as Maya Angelou's *I Know Why the Caged Bird Sings* (1969) and *The Autobiography of Malcolm X* (1973). It also surfaces in Richard Pryor's routine about Muhammad Ali and Leon Spinks, and rap star L. L. Cool J appears on the back of his latest album punching a heavy bag.

Among the more important works by Afro-American intellectuals and creative writers on the subject of prizefighting are the following: Larry Neal's essay, "Uncle Rufus Raps on the Squared Circle," which originally appeared in the *Partisan Review* (Spring, 1972); Jervis Anderson's "Black Heavies," which appeared in *American Scholar* (Summer, 1978); Eldridge Cleaver's "Lazarus, Come Forth" from his book, *Soul on Ice* (1981); Amiri Baraka's "The Dempsey-Liston Fight" from his book, *Home: Social Essays* (1966); Richard Wright's three journalistic pieces: "Joe Louis Uncovers Dynamite" (October 8, 1935) and "High Tide in Harlem: Joe Louis as a Symbol of Freedom" (July 5, 1938), both published in *New Masses*, and "And Oh—Where Were Hitler's Pagan Gods?" which appeared in the *Daily Worker* (June 24, 1938); and John A. Williams's "Jack Johnson and the Great White Hope" from his book, *Flashbacks* (1973). They are not, taken as a body, the *most* important or impressive interpretative work by a black writer on the sport; the best, aside from Torres's biography of Muhammad Ali, are Ralph Ellison's *Invisible Man* and three essays by former heavyweight champion Floyd Patterson: two 1965 *Sports Illustrated* pieces, "I Want to Destroy Clay" and "Cassius Clay Must Be Beaten," and a later *Esquire* piece entitled "In Defense of Cassius Clay" (August, 1966).

The Baraka essay, written in 1964, and the Cleaver essay which was published in 1968, deal basically with the same thing: the meaning of the phenomenon of Sonny Liston, Floyd Patterson, and Muhammad Ali as the most powerful black presences in American popular culture of the sixties. Their discussion of the racial obsessions that underlie the design of American masculinity is essentially accurate although they both tend to sound like Baldwin, finally; as one unidentified critic put it, Baldwin seems to think that the secret notion behind the pathology of racism is that all whites madly desire to sleep with any Negro they can find.[4] The discussion about boxing and American sport, on the other hand, is quite weak; Cleaver's ultimate summation of American sports as bloodlust and competition is essentially the simplistic polemic of "leftist humanism" that was to characterize later radical writers such as Paul Hoch. It is a criticism that blames the current craze for sports on the commercialization of athletics in bourgeois culture, an assumption that overlooks the popularity of competitive sports in communist countries. There is not a shred of evidence to indicate that sports are any less competitive in communist countries or that having sports run by the State results in a more "humane" or "holistic" concept of sport and play. Allen Guttmann has provided a thorough-going critique of both the Marxist and neo-Marxist analyses of sports in bourgeois culture. Moreover, the political deconstruction of the symbolism of Liston, Patterson, and Ali by Cleaver and Baraka actually seems to be working with the same set of assumptions about the critical reading of fights used by the whites they condemn. Liston, Patterson, and Ali represent the good, the bad, and the ugly in everyone's morality play; it is simply a matter of musical chairs when the time comes to personify the abstraction. In this sense, I assume that Neal's piece, published in 1972, was meant to be a correction, an attempt to escape the previous politically motivated way the black intellectuals read prizefights after the coming of Liston and Ali in the sixties. Neal's article is a strategic plea for reconciliation. Uncle Rap, despite his scientific-mythical jargon which sounds like nothing so much as Sun Ra in one of his more lucid moments, returns the reading of fights and of blacks in American popular culture to the framework of black folklore; this, for Neal, is the only trustworthy critical measure of black aesthetic conceptualization. In this way, the fight between Frazier and Ali is not simply dialectical war—the affirming self and the blank twin of its own negation—but rather the confrontation between two classic aspects of Afro-American style and being, a Ruth Benedict–like assertion of the Apollonian and the Dionysian, a dialectical moralism that implies its own peaceful synthesis through the respectful admission of each for the other's existence as a necessary antithesis.

Williams's essay, originally written in 1968 as a preface for Howard Sackler's hit play, *The Great White Hope*, but which Sackler eventually rejected, is simply a sloppy piece of writing. A paragraph such as the following is really an inexcusable distortion:

> Having failed to dethrone Johnson in the ring, white forces, public and private, launched an attack on his personal life that drove his first wife to suicide and sent Johnson to Europe to avoid going to jail on trumped-up charges. He spent about two years in Europe. He went into show business, fought sparingly,

avoiding other Negro boxers as often as he could. Tutored by Belmonte and Joselito, he also fought a bull in the Barcelona ring. On the whole his life abroad was bitter.[5]

The death of Johnson's wife was not really the result of any public campaign to get him. Williams fails to note the salient point that Johnson's wife was white and committed suicide primarily because of the difficulty white women faced socially at the "degradation" of being married to a black man. Johnson was also notoriously unfaithful. He was convicted for violating the Mann Act, a trumped-up charge only in the sense that the law might be argued to have been trumped-up. The conviction was valid enough. Largely, Johnson ran into trouble because of his public association with several white women, a fact that Williams neglects to mention. Undoubtedly, it was shortsighted, cruel, and utterly reprehensible for Johnson's society to have condemned him because he desired white women, but it is the height of historical disservice not to state the facts of the case because of a disdain of or distaste for them. "Bitter" is surely an odd word to use in connection with Johnson's life. Johnson probably felt a certain amount of bitterness about his exile, but he seems to have made the best of it. Desperation might be a better word to describe Johnson in some stages of his life, for he was always the hustler looking eagerly for the main chance.

Anderson's 1978 essay on Louis, Ali, and Johnson, largely a historical descriptive piece in the same mode, is much better than the Williams piece. When Anderson speaks of Johnson as full of "confidence (perhaps overconfidence), high self-esteem, a strong belief in his legal rights as a citizen, and a joyous obedience to what was dramatic and colorful in his character,"[6] he is much closer to the truth than Williams ever was. Admittedly, of course, the passage of ten years made writing a piece on Johnson a great deal easier because it was not necessary for it to be so politically charged or self-conscious. But it is Anderson who reaches the more politically meaningful conclusion when he writes: "Yet there were at least two important characteristics that all three men [Ali, Louis, and Johnson] shared; each was superbly gifted as a boxer, and each desired very much to be himself." Obviously, there isn't really very much a gifted person could want to be but himself, if he wants to be able to exploit his gifts at all; yet the statement compellingly reveals the true political importance of Ali, Louis, and Johnson; for a black public person to be both gifted and true to himself is not automatic or, one should say, axiomatic, and it is bound to be subversive by extending the scope and expressive range of black humanity in mainstream culture.

The Wright essays are an early indication of his preoccupation with the tyrannical blandishments of American popular culture. In his August, 1938, piece in *New Masses*, "High Tide in Harlem," he calls both Joe Louis and Max Schmeling "puppets," which implies that not only are they manipulated but also their contrived gyrations are manipulating the public that watches them. He calls the second fight between Schmeling and Louis, probably one of the most famous events in the history of sports, "a colorful puppet show," "one of the greatest dramas of make-believe ever witnessed in America," and "a configuration of social images whose intensity and clarity had been heightened through weeks of skillful and constant agitation." Wright's fascination with popular culture would make itself apparent in such later works as *Native Son* (1966) where Bigger Thomas would live in a world of newspapers, cheap magazines, and movies; he would be literally entrapped by the images of popular culture in the room of the Daltons' former chauffeur, Green, whose walls were covered by pictures of "Jack Johnson, Joe Louis, Jack Dempsey, and Henry Armstrong . . . Ginger Rogers, Jean Harlow, and Janet Gaynor."[7] Prizefighters and Hollywood actresses, the kings and queens of American popular culture. (One is reminded of the scene in James Weldon Johnson's 1912 novel, *The Autobiography of an Ex-Colored Man*, where the hero enters the room of his "club" to discover pictures "of Peter Jackson, of all the lesser lights of the prize-fighting ring, of all the famous jockeys and the stage celebrities. . . .")[8] Bigger, who is not very articulate, never smiles, and seems sullen, brings to mind the young Joe Louis who was described by white sportswriters of the period as being sullen and who was featured in a *New Republic* article entitled, "Joe Louis Never Smiles" (October 9, 1935). And the Louis career of the poor southern boy—living with a stepfather since his real father had been placed in an insane asylum—being brought north to the big city by his family in search of employment and fresh opportunities, was the Bigger Thomas career and the Richard Wright career as well. It was also the career of two of Louis's biggest fans in pugilistic circles: Floyd Patterson and Sonny Liston. Incidentally, Thomas was the last name of Joe Louis's character in the 1937 film, "Spirit of Youth," which starred Louis. Wright, a frequent movie goer and admirer of Louis during the 1930s, may have seen this film. He wrote the lyrics to "King Joe," a song honoring Joe Louis. Count Basie wrote the music and Paul Robeson supplied the voice. It may have been, as Ralph Ellison pointed out, an unfortunate collaboration in an aesthetic sense, but it reveals the power of Louis's attraction for Wright. In his autobiography, *Black Boy* (1945), Wright's critique of popular culture continues in the depiction of his growth from reading material like Zane Grey's *Riders of the Purple Sage* (1912) to essays by H. L. Menchen. His conversation with the African boy who wishes to be a detective in *Black Power* (1954), the depiction of the black woman desperately straightening her hair in *The Color Curtain* (1956), the inescapable radio in *Lawd Today* (1963), and the maga-zines read by the white women cafeteria workers in *American Hunger* (1944) all show how the machinations of popular culture are emotionally crippling, self-destructive escapism. The three Wright boxing pieces taken together reveal an essential ambivalence: Joe Louis is a product of American popular culture, a creation of it, in effect, and therefore is nothing more than the convenient bread-and-circus invention of white American capitalists; Joe Louis, however, is a hero of the black masses, a potential source of political mobilization because he can so deeply excite so many blacks. Wright's pieces are absorbed by this idea: how Louis affects large numbers of blacks. Each of his pieces is, in fact, more about how blacks in Harlem respond after a Louis victory than about Louis himself. Wright's ambivalence is not so much that of the Marxist trying to find an ideological way to tap an unrecon-structed political resource as it is that of the black trying to find a psycho-historical way to tap the complexity of his own injured consciousness.

But it is Ellison in *Invisible Man* who fully elaborates upon the ambiguity of the black in boxing that Wright only suggests in his Joe Louis pieces. The battle royal scene at the beginning of Ellison's novel, one of the most famous fictional boxing depictions in American literature, is meant to conjure up images of turn-of-the-century black fighters who received their training in the sport as youths in just this way. Nat Fleischer in his multi-volume history of blacks in the prizefights describes black battle royals as commonplace. But the black fighter that Ellison particularly wants to suggest is Jack Johnson who, as biographers Finis Farr, Al-Tony Gilmore, and Randy Roberts have made clear, was a frequent participant in the battle royal in his youth. In this way, Ellison alludes to the three most important black figures of early twentieth century America: Booker T. Washington—the Invisible Man's graduation speech is in fact Washington's Atlanta Cotton Exposition Speech of 1895; W. E. B. DuBois—the Invisible Man is the tenth boy in the battle royal, a reference to DuBois's concept of the Talented Tenth to which the Invisible Man would naturally feel he belongs (according to Fleischer, normally nine youths participated in a battle royal but, of course, any number could participate); and Jack Johnson—by the battle royal itself. One might imagine that Johnson was much like Tatlock, the tough winner of the encounter. There has been much discussion about the scene showing how white men used both sex—the white woman dancer with the flag tattooed near her genitals—and money—which is what, finally, the boys are fighting for—to manipulate blacks and to keep them divided. Therefore, the scene works, in part, in much the same way as Wright's fight scene with another black boy near the end of *Black Boy*; this fight was instigated, created by white men who wanted to be entertained by seeing two black youths fight. The scene in Wright's book operates as an ironical comment on the event which foreshadows the conclusion of Frederick Douglass's 1845 *Narrative*, his classic confrontation as a teenaged boy with the white slavebreaker, Covey. Like Douglass, Wright is the troubled black boy who cannot live under the system and who ultimately flees. Unlike Douglass, though, Wright, through his fight scene, asserts the utter impossibility of finding his manhood through any sort of direct confrontation with white men. That impossibility is symbolized by Wright's being forced to leave the optical company after being trapped between two benches by a white man at either end. This probably explains why Wright, like many other blacks, was so deeply affected by Louis: Louis had the devoutly-wished-for opportunity that Douglas had—to confront a white man squarely with his fist.

But the most telling part of the Ellison scene occurs when the Invisible Man suggests to Tatlock: "Fake like I knocked you out, you can have the prize." "I'll break your behind," he whispered hoarsely. "For *them?*" "For *me*, sonofabitch!"[9] Louis was heroic, in part, through the accident that he was permitted to fight white men in fights that resonated with meaning for both blacks and whites. But it was not Louis who determined his opponents or defined the meaning of his fights. Presumably, since Louis wanted to be a fighter, he would have fought anyone, black or white. In the days when the color line was drawn in boxing, black fighters did get a chance to fight white fighters on occasion, but very often these fights were fixed so that the white fighter would win. In most instances, great black fighters at the turn of the century spent much of their careers fighting each other; these tended to be their most vicious fights as there was little reason for one black fighter to throw a fight to another black. When the Invisible Man suggests that *he* should win the fake fight, he is putting himself in the position of the white fighter in the integrated fight. Naturally, Tatlock rejects this. Moreover, Tatlock wants to win because, freed from the fakery of the racially integrated fight, he can display completely his abilities as an athlete; he asserts that he does this not for the *audience*, but for *himself.* The ambiguity here which I think is a crucial issue for the black intellectual and prevents him from celebrating boxing in the way the white intellectual can is that boxing, finally, for the black fighter is an apolitical, amoral experience of individualistic esteem which the black fighter purchases at both the expense of his rival's health (and often his own) and his own dignity. For the black intellectual, boxing becomes both a dreaded spectacle and a spectacle of dread. The black fighter is truly heroic for the black masses and the black intellectual only when he is fighting a white fighter, or someone who has been defined as representing white interests; the battle then becomes the classic struggle between the black and the white over the nature of reality. When the black fighter fights another black, how does he differ from Stagolee, the legendary black badman who preyed on his own, or Brer Rabbit, the Trickster, whose victories are limited and short term and whose motives are often selfish and shallow? Moreover, the black fighter's heroic moment is never one in which he is in control but simply his own desperate effort not to be swallowed in a sea of black anonymity. In this regard, it is interesting to note that virtually every heavyweight champion before Louis drew the color line and would not fight black fighters for the championship. This included Jack Johnson, who fought only one black fighter during his eight-year reign as champion. Louis was the first true democratic champion of boxing who fought all comers. In a sense he had to, but nonetheless he established a tradition in the very breadth of his daring and excellence that has produced a certain anxiety-of-influence in the black champions who have come after him.

And this brings us to Patterson's essays on boxing; it was Patterson, oddly enough, who continued the democratic impulse of Louis, not by the example of his career, which was pretty selective, but by the example of one fight. He fought Sonny Liston, giving the ex-con a crack at the title when neither blacks nor whites wanted him to have it. Patterson thought such an opportunity would change Liston, make him respectable and anxiety-ridden. It didn't. But it probably changed Patterson forever. That is, it made him even more insufferably insane about respectability and more anxiety-ridden than anyone has a right to be. Patterson must rank along with José Torres as one of the most thoughtful men ever to enter the boxing ring. Perhaps his constant reflection impaired his ability as a fighter, but it is difficult to say. He was small for a heavyweight and this meant, all other factors being equal, that he stood little chance against either Sonny Liston or Muhammad Ali, his two archrivals, who, through the sheer grandeur of their size, ushered in a new era in boxing. Patterson was fascinated with the man he called Cassius Clay, or rather the man he refused to call Muhammad Ali. Perhaps he saw Ali as an alter ego. Perhaps Ali was the fighter that he, Patterson, always aspired to be. He expresses in the two *Sports Illustrated* articles previously mentioned the belief that if he had fought

Liston the way Ali did, boxing and moving, he would have won. He probably wouldn't have, but isn't it pretty, for Patterson, to think so? These articles were probably condemned by most black intellectuals of the time as the ravings of a particularly pathetic Uncle Tom. To be sure, Patterson did show a certain insipid naïveté and even wrongheadedness in his condemnation of Ali and the black Muslims, expressing feelings akin to the outraged middle-class black who finds that his lower-class cousin has gone balmy over some sort of storefront charlatanism. But his basic instincts about the inadequacy of the Muslim response to American racism proved to be generally correct. The importance of these essays is not, however, what Patterson has to say about Ali, a man he hardly knows and is even less capable of understanding, but what they say about Patterson himself. And it is the subject of Patterson that most concerns Patterson. Despite his claims of loving the sport of boxing, Patterson complains that the sport has alienated him from his wife and children, has made him vicious against his opponents (a viciousness he finds he must have if he is to win and to counter the complaint expressed by Ingemar Johansson that Patterson "is too nice"), and has forced him to act out other people's hatred vicariously and publicly for money. Despite this, Patterson feels deeply that being heavyweight champion of the world means a great deal. As he eloquently puts it:

> You've got to go on. You owe it to yourself, to the tradition of the title, to the public that sees the champion as somebody special, to everything that must become sacred to you the first time you put gloves on your hands. You've got to believe in what you're doing or else nobody can believe that anything is worthwhile. [10]

Or in another passage he reveals his own sense of peculiar burden by virtue of having been champion:

> . . . I do feel partially responsible for the title having fallen into the wrong hands because of my own mistakes. I want to redeem myself in my own eyes and in the mind of the public. I owe so much to boxing—everything I have, the security of my family, my ability to express myself, the places I've been, the people I've met. A man has got to pay his debts or he can't live with himself comfortably. [11]

In the end, he condemns Ali for not recognizing that any black champion must fight out of the Joe Louis tradition: he must be responsible, and he must acknowledge the larger white society whom he is forced to represent by virtue of his position. Patterson virtually admits that boxing is ugly but that it is the duty of the champion, the black champion, to transcend the ugliness of the sport for his society; in this sense he reminds one of Gene Tunney, the last American heavyweight champion who seemed unsuited temperamentally to be a boxer and obsessed with elevating the status of the sport. It is the black champion's burden and his honor. In this instance, of course, he reminds us of Louis. It is no coincidence, then, that he was champion during the late fifties, the era of the Negro proving himself worthy of integration, the era of Sidney Poitier, who was the personification of black honor on the screen: the sort of honor that received, at one time, the dubious recognition from whites that here (in their opinion) was a black who was white inside. Whether Patterson was neurotically fishing for a compliment of that sort, the kind which dogged the great black heavyweight contender of the 1880s, Peter Jackson, is not nearly as important as the fact that honor so painfully bedeviled him, probably because being black and living in the modern world makes it so difficult to find frameworks for the display of it. If Patterson was so disliked by the black intellectuals of the day, it is most likely because his position, as he defined it in the sport of prizefighting, is so similar to their own: part of a tradition which they are unable to denounce but unable to embrace completely, torn by doubts not only about the nature of their ability but also about the meaning of what they do in a society where their position is so precarious; shackled by a seemingly ignoble past that can only be lived down by the pretensions of an inhuman nobility. What Patterson hated about both Ali and Liston was that they both thought they could, through flights of escapism, avoid a dilemma that Patterson thought was ineluctable and, unfortunately, character-building; it was not simply a quest for moral order but for redemptive piety. Liston, through his defeats at the hands of Ali, simply acquiesced in being what whites said he was. In essence and in fact, Liston quit. Liston accepted the blackness of blackness. Ali, by becoming a black Muslim, decided he wished to change the terms to escape the blackness of blackness by redefining the terms in his own way. Liston accepted defeat as his lot; Ali denied its possibility. Patterson felt that the black champion, like the black intellectual, could do neither. For Patterson one could neither accept the terms nor redefine them; one must heroically struggle *with* them, constantly defending one's rights to participate in the discourse. Although there may be several books about prizefighting in the future written by black intellectuals, it is easy to understand why there have been so few thus far. The ambiguities of boxing, so accurately defined and symbolized by Patterson, seem, in some respects, impossible to overcome or to feel comfortable with, as black people, in the final analysis, were never comfortable with Patterson. After all, Patterson lost twice to Liston (1962, 1963) and twice to Ali as well (1965, 1972). Patterson was never able to convince his children that his training headquarters was not his home. It is doubtful he ever convinced himself (and certain he convinced no one else) that his edifice of Negro rectitude is, at last, the house black people wish to live in.

NOTES

1. Ralph Ellison, *Invisible Man* (New York: Modern Library, 1952), p. 7.

2. Ronald E. Martin, *American Literature and the Universe of Force* (Durham: Duke University Press, 1981), p. 71, p. xv.

3. Black intellectuals such as Roi Ottley and J. Saunders Reddings have devoted chapters in certain of their nonfiction work to black prizefighters, notably Joe Louis. Indeed, West Indian scholar C. L. R. James mentions both Louis and boxing in his book on cricket, *Beyond a Boundary* (London: Hutchinson and Co., 1969). Space does not permit me to comment on them, and as the books are unclassifiable, I have not placed them in the list above. Two other notable essays on this subject by Ishmael Reed are "The Greatest; My Own Story," in *Shrovetide in Old New Orleans* (New York:

Doubleday, 1978) and "The Fourth Ali," in *God Made Alaska for the Indians* (New York: Garland Publishing, 1982).

4. Quoted in Fern Marja Eckman, *The Furious Passage of James Baldwin* (New York: M. Evans & Co., 1966), p. 165.

5. John A. Williams, *Flashbacks: A Twenty-Year Diary of Article Writing* (New York: Doubleday, 1973), p. 279.

6. Jervis Anderson, "Black Heavies," *American Scholar* (Summer, 1978), p. 390.

7. Richard Wright, *Native Son* (New York: Harper & Row, 1966), p. 60 (original date of publication, 1940).

8. James Weldon Johnson, *The Autobiography of an Ex-Colored Man* in *Three Negro Classics*, ed. John Hope Franklin (New York: Avon Books, 1965), p. 450.

9. Ellison, *Invisible Man*, p. 20.

10. Floyd Patterson, "I Want to Destroy Cassius Clay," *Sports Illustrated* (October 19, 1964), 61.

11. Patterson, "I Want to Destroy Cassius Clay," p. 44.

BITTER SWEET TWILIGHT
FOR SUGAR

RALPH WILEY is a former staff writer and editor for *Sports Illustrated* and author of *Serenity: A Boxing Memoir, A Search for the Boxer's Peace of Mind, from Joe Louis to Mike Tyson* (1989). He was also a featured commentator on NBC's Sunday football telecasts. "Bitter Sweet Twilight for Sugar" appeared in *Sports Illustrated* on July 13, 1987.

"To be a great champion, you must believe you are the best. If you're not, pretend you are."

—MUHAMMAD ALI

In the fall of 1986, Sugar Ray Leonard signed to fight Marvelous Marvin Hagler. Soon after, a question arose about Leonard. People are civilized now, for the most part, and asked, "Why is he doing it?" Not "Can he win?" but "Why would he risk it?" Was it the money, a guaranteed $11 million? Was it an irrepressible urge that goes with having been a champion? Was it merely ego, a grab for a higher place in boxing history?

No one thought to ask the uncivilized people. Men have lived warmed by the fire of civilization for so long that they have forgotten what it takes to survive with nothing but their wits and bare hands to fend off the jackals that stalk them. So the men who had forgotten this, or had convinced themselves they had, continued to ask, "Why?"

I went to see a man who knows why. He wasn't too hard to find.

"Ray."

No answer.

"Ray."

"Nnnnn."

"Ray."

"Nnn?"

"Can Sugar Ray Leonard beat Marvelous Marvin Hagler?"

Sugar Ray Robinson didn't answer. It might have been that he couldn't answer. That would seem most likely. There is the advancing Alzheimer's disease to consider, and the medication he is regularly given. He also has diabetes and hypertension. Beyond all this, there are the terrible lessons that 201 fights over 25 years have etched on his mind. Finally, there is Millie, his wife of 22 years. Any or all of these could be reasons why Robinson didn't answer. But it also could have been that he chose not to answer. The one incontrovertible truth is that Sugar Ray Robinson earned his silence the hard way. He didn't have to say anything. He left all the answers in the ring.

The 65-year-old former nonpareil welterweight and five-time middleweight champion smiled, then looked toward his lap. He was watched by Millie Robinson, who sat nearby in the modest offices of the Sugar Ray Robinson Youth Foundation, on Crenshaw Boulevard in the mid-Wilshire section of Los Angeles. It was November 1986. The board of directors of the foundation was meeting. Ray sat at the head of the table, his paper plate laden with meat and exotic fruit. He had not taken a bite. He had no appetite. Business was discussed by six other board members, the officers of his legacy. Robinson was oblivious. He was in his own world.

"Ray will still talk, sometimes, a little bit," Sid Lockitch had said earlier at his office in Century City. Lockitch, an accountant, has been Robinson's business manager for more than 20 years and is the treasurer of the foundation. "When Millie's not around, he'll say a word or two. But even years ago, Ray was always a gentleman. He would never have said that Marvin Hagler is going to beat the crap out of Sugar Ray Leonard. He would have said luck to them both."

The telephone rang at the foundation office. For Millie.

"Ray, can Leonard beat Hagler?"

Robinson's smile became even broader, even more vacant. Then he leaned close. "Is he sweeter than me?" he asked, cloaking that once satiny voice in a whisper. I conspired with him.

"No, Ray."

In the spring of 1987, on Monday, April 6, Ray Leonard (33–1), the former welterweight and junior middleweight champion, fought middleweight champion Marvelous Marvin Hagler (62–2–2) in Las Vegas. Leonard, 31, came into the ring after a layoff of more than 1,000 days and with a surgically repaired left eye. The question still hung in the air. Why? Leonard was already known as the greatest welterweight since Robinson. Leonard could never be considered greater than Robinson. Not unless he fought, say, a hundred more times. Certainly not unless he somehow beat Hagler. "I care nothing for history," Leonard said on the Friday before the fight. So saying, he did the improbable—he beat the bigger, stronger man, just as Muhammad Ali had done, more impressively, against Sonny Liston and George Foreman.

"Ali absolutely worshiped Ray," Sid Lockitch says. "Still does. Usually, the greatest fall from grace is by fighters. People tend to avoid ex-fighters. They feel they took one too many. Randy Turpin once asked Ray, 'What's worse, being a has-been or a never-was?' Then Randy committed suicide. But the people never forgot Ray. He felt God had made him a boxer for that reason. So he would not be forgotten. So he could help."

It is eerie, the similarity in technique between the three of them—first Robinson, then Ali, now Leonard. It was Robinson who was the original, the handsome master boxer with matchless hand speed, charisma and the fine legs of a figure skater. It was Robinson who went 123–1–2 to *begin* his career and become the welterweight champion, and it was Robinson who then went on to win the middleweight title those incredible five times. Yet, it was also Robinson who *lost* six times while fighting for the middleweight title. He won the national Golden Gloves featherweight title in 1939 at age 17, when Joe Louis was heavyweight champion of the world. He lost his final fight at 44, to the No. 1 middleweight contender, Joey Archer, in 1965, when Ali was champ. In the years from 1945 to the middle of 1951 Robinson, at 147 pounds, was unbeatable and irresistible. To the men of that era, and to some of their many sons and daughters, Leonard can only be a Sugar substitute.

"I like Ray Leonard," says Irving Rudd, 69, a veteran boxing publicist with Bob Arum's Top Rank, Inc., promoters of the Leonard–Hagler fight. "I think a lot of him as a fighter. That's why I say that, at his very fittest, he might have gone five rounds before Ray Robinson knocked him out. Five rounds, I say. Tops."

"He was the greatest. A distance fighter. A half-distance fighter. An in-fighter. Scientific. He was wonderful to see." Max Schmeling once said that of Robinson.

"The greatest fighter ever to step into the ring." Joe Louis once said that.

"The greatest . . . pound-for-pound," wrote the late columnist Jimmy Cannon, who, it is said, was impressed by hardly anyone—except Sugar Ray. When Ali was champ, the acerbic Cannon told him to enjoy it while he could, because the jackals would come for him one day.

In February 1964, when he was still known as Cassius Clay, a long shot who was about to fight Liston for the heavyweight title, Ali had invoked the name of Robinson, who was in Miami for the bout. "You tell Sonny Liston I'm here with Sugar Ray!" In a weigh-in performance that almost assuredly convinced Liston that he would be defending his title against a madman, Ali screamed to the press at the top of his lungs. "Sugar Ray and I are two pretty dancers. We can't be beat."

"Ray was the pro's pro," says Rudd. "When they told him he had a fight, Ray never asked who the opponent was or where the fight was going to be. Ray only asked, 'How much?' "

The general reaction of the middle-aged and older American public to Sugar Ray Robinson could best be summed up by a reminiscence of the late Red Smith. Smith was reminded of Robinson while visiting the zoo one day. When the columnist stood transfixed at the cage where a jaguar paced back and forth, he gazed at the superbly muscled predator and said, "Good morning, Ray. You're looking good, Ray."

Ray isn't looking so good anymore. "It's very painful to see him like this. The situation is not going to get any better," Lockitch says. Lockitch is referring to Robinson's deteriorating health, but another officer of the youth foundation adds,

"It's like Ray is in prison. Millie treats him like a child. She lets him go nowhere with no one. Not even his own son."

Robinson's 37-year-old son, Ray Jr., says, "My father is virtually being held captive."

I had only wanted to go with Sugar Ray to the barbershop and ask him if Leonard could beat Hagler, and how. That's all. I knew Robinson still went to the barbershop at least once a week, sometimes more often. So I asked Millie about it and she said, "I take care of Uncle Wright. He's 87. I take care of Ray. He's my husband. I love him. I've been what I've been to him for all these years. I could hire help, but I don't mind doing it. I don't need help. I have tears in my eyes, I'm trying so hard. Ray's going to get better. He's not better now. He's not going to the barbershop with you because I'm by his side every minute. He goes to five different barbershops. Only I know which ones. My husband is not a yo-yo for people to jerk around as they please. I'm in charge now. I take care of Ray. I'm the one in control."

"Now. . . ." Millie fixes me with a defiant gaze. There's only one thing she wants to know. She asks, "How much?"

It might seem odd, wanting to watch Sugar Ray Robinson get his hair cut. But, being one of the younger baby-boomers, I am not old enough to remember what it was like to see the Sugar fight in his prime, much less to anticipate his fights, to go through the sweet agony of not knowing . . . and then to be so utterly convinced by his skill. I had missed the pleasure of that tension. I had only seen the old films. The fights had long been decided, the participants' places in history secured.

I first learned of the emotion stirred by Sugar Ray when, as a boy, I went to the barbershop, that sanctuary of masculinity and tonic with the striped pole outside. Inside, hair fell to the floor and the smell of talc hung in the air. Cokes cost a dime. Razor straps were used for their intended purpose. It was a place that buzzed. Great lies and great truths were tossed about like glances.

When I was a boy in the barbershop, one name would come up louder than the rest. The name was Cassius Clay. There would be a great deal of murmuring assent—and an occasional derisive sneer—that a *real* tough guy would eventually show the kid what for. Probably Liston. Then someone would reply: "Liston won't see what hit him. And neither will you." But there was at least one barber—he almost always seemed to be the one holding a pair of scissors perilously close to my ear—who would become agitated and say, "Hold on. Let's get it straight in here. That boy is good. He's *good*. But he ain't no Ray Robinson. There ain't but one Sugar—and Sugar give you diabetes *quick*."

After Ali had gone through the best part of his career and had endured a three-year layoff because of his refusal to be drafted, he signed to fight Oscar Bonavena on Dec. 7, 1970. That was to be a warmup before his real comeback fight—his epic loss to Joe Frazier in Madison Square Garden in March 1971. At the weigh-in with Bonavena, the Argentine attempted to get Ali's goat. He succeeded, to his later sorrow. "Clay? Clay?" Bonavena mocked. He spoke little English. "Clay. . . . Why you no go in ahrrmy? You cheeken? Peep-peep-peep . . . peep-peep-peep."

A look came over Ali's face that I had not seen before—true anger. Usually,

Ali was like Robinson, and Ray usually held his temper. "Don't get mad," Robinson liked to say. "Get even."

Ali grimly asked Bonavena what seemed to be a curious question: "Did you cut your hair?"

"Whaat?" replied Bonavena.

"*Did you cut your hair?*"

"Whaat?"

"I'll cut your hair," said a deadpan Ali, who would knock out Bonavena in the 15th round.

Robinson, for his part, had a nickname for his youngest son. From the time Ray Jr. was a child his father has called him "Trimmer."

"Oh sure, Ray loves to get his hair cut. Loves it," Lockitch says. "He's still vain that way. He wouldn't dream of going anywhere without going to the barbershop. Whenever he'd go to New York, that was the first thing he'd do."

Before he became the fighter's business manager, before he became involved with the foundation, Lockitch was one of the men for whom Robinson was the Sugar. Lockitch became Ray's friend when Ray and Millie moved to Los Angeles, back in '65, right after they were married in Vegas. Lockitch was there when the foundation idea was first proposed in 1969, in Millie Robinson's kitchen in the lime green duplex on the corner of West Adams Boulevard and 10th Avenue. The house is owned by 87-year-old Wright Fillmore.

Millie and Ray still live on the second floor; "Uncle" Wright lives on the first. Fillmore, who was a close friend of Millie's parents, is president of the foundation and has been a benefactor of Ray's since '65. Over the years, he has been the owner of a lot of property on West Adams.

"Ray used to say he knew every man," says Lockitch. "Ask him if he knew the chairman of the board for Standard Oil and Ray would say, 'Sure.' What Ray meant was that the guy knew *him*. All he had to do was call and say 'This is Sugar Ray Robinson,' and the guy would know who he was and do whatever he could to help Ray out."

Ray Robinson's world was a man's world. Women were different, except for his mother, Leila Smith. Women were to be won. They were part of the spoils of war. Even Ray's mother could not completely displace Ray from his male constituency. After young Walker Smith, fighting under the assumed named of Ray Robinson, emerged from anonymity in 1939—by boxing like a dream and being nicknamed Sugar because he fought so sweetly—he was visited by his father, Walker Smith Sr., whom the newly minted Sugar Ray Robinson had not seen in eight years. Robinson happily shelled out some bucks to his pop. When Ray later told his mother what had happened, she was indignant. Walker Smith had walked out on her. On them. Said Robinson to his mother, "That's *your* business."

Still, she was his mother and his biggest fan. "It didn't matter what weight they were. He was the best," says Leila Smith. It is a cold day in January 1987, and she is sitting in the apartment she shares with her daughter, Evelyn Nelson, on University Avenue in the South Bronx. For a woman of 89 years, Leila Smith is full of wit and vitality. Her memory is sharp.

"That Maxim fight. That's the one that Ray shouldn't have had," she says. "The only one."

During his career, Robinson had 20 or more bouts like the one Leonard undertook with Hagler. After overwhelming the welterweights of his day, Robinson moved up to middleweight in 1950 and was involved in stirring battles with the likes of Jake LaMotta, Randy Turpin, Carmen Basilio, Gene Fullmer, Bobo Olson and Paul Pender. He was not the same fighter at the heavier weight, 160 pounds. He was still a great fighter, but he was not the unbeatable Sugar. Then, on June 25, 1952, when he was 31, Robinson climbed into a ring that had been set up in Yankee Stadium to fight Maxim for the light heavyweight title.

"It was 104 degrees that night. It was 130 degrees ringside, that's what they said. I was there. It felt like it," says Leila Smith. "Whatever you call 'great' nowadays, I guess Ray was that then. I went to his fights. I wasn't superstitious. When Ray sat between rounds that night, I dropped my head. People said, 'Why do you drop your head? You crying?' I was praying."

Robinson wore black that night. His mother wore white. Ray had already won the middleweight title from LaMotta, lost it to Turpin, then regained it from Turpin; then he defended it by decisioning Olson and again by knocking out Rocky Graziano with one perfect right in the third round in Chicago. The right was so devastating that Graziano lay stretched out on the canvas with his right leg twitching.

The whole world seemed to be Sugar Ray's oyster, and the Maxim fight would showcase him in his backyard. Robinson was the pride of Harlem, but admiration of his abilities was not restricted to people of his race. Black heavyweight champions like Jack Johnson and Louis had to bear heavy sociological burdens whether they liked it or not. Ray straightened his hair and he was the Sugar to everybody. "Color means nothing to him," Lockitch says.

It seemed that Ray had many friends when he stepped into the ring to fight Maxim in the sweltering early summer heat and under a battery of hot lights. "I had won welter and middle, beaten most of the people in my class," Ray said once. "People wanted to see me fight Maxim."

Maxim's given name was Giuseppe Antonio Berardinelli. He was born in Cleveland. He was strong even for a 6' 1", 175-pounder and he was an earnest campaigner. He had fought 99 times before he met Robinson. He had won 78 times, drawn four. He had been knocked out only once and was better than any light heavyweight in the world except Ezzard Charles, to whom he had lost five times, and Jersey Joe Walcott, who had beaten him twice. As a boxer, Maxim was not in Robinson's class, but he was still an excellent fighter—and *two* classes above Ray in natural weight. Maxim was 30 years old and the light-heavy champ almost by default, since Charles and Walcott had moved up to heavyweight to meet their fates at the hands of each other and Rocky Marciano. Maxim himself had fought once for the heavyweight title, losing to Charles in 1951.

At the end of the 10th round, the referee, on the verge of collapse, had to quit and a substitute took over. "The world swam before my eyes," says Leila Smith. And it swam before Robinson's. He had used his brilliant moves and blinding hand speed to hit Maxim with every punch in his repertoire. In the seventh, he nailed

Maxim with the perfect right—similar to the one that had left Graziano twitching. Maxim was turned sideways by the force of the punch but he did not go down. The light-heavy was too big. Robinson couldn't hurt him. At the end of the 13th, Robinson, well ahead on all cards, was done in by the heat. He staggered across the ring into the arms of his cornermen. He could not answer the bell for the 14th round. If the fight had gone 12 rounds, he would have won. Robinson announced his retirement that December.

"Ray had promised me back in 1940 that I would never have to work again," says Leila Smith. "And I never had to. My son always took care of me."

Upon retirement, Robinson set out for Europe, ostensibly to begin a second career as a tap-dancing troubador and to enjoy the spoils of war. He had been married on May 29, 1944, to Edna-Mae Holly, a beautiful show girl who, in 1949, had borne him Ray Jr. Edna-Mae would later have four miscarriages. Robinson was a man of extravagant tastes, appetites and generosity. He could eat a dozen doughnuts and wash them down with a pitcher of sweet tea. He ordered fuchsia Cadillacs, first-class staterooms and the finest of champagnes for his valets, golf pros, chauffeurs, secretaries and, of course, his barbers. "He wanted to buy me a Cadillac," says Leila Smith. "But I only saw hard men and rough women in those cars. So he bought me a Buick."

Robinson was back in the ring within two years. "Sure, I could use a buck as well as the next guy," he said. "But this was not the reason. I just had the feeling. I got the urge. People wanted to see me fight."

Robinson's ring career would continue for another 11 years and twice more he would hold the middleweight title, but he was never again a god. In 1960, he separated from Edna-Mae, and in the twilight of his boxing days he married Millie Bruce and moved to L.A.

"Now, for four or five years, I don't get nothing, I don't hear nothing," says Leila Smith. "And I don't ask why. Ray had been sick only one day in his life. Pneumonia. Maybe food poisoning. It was before a fight. I had to go to Philadelphia because he wouldn't go to the hospital. He called the hospital a good place to die. He didn't ride elevators, either. Ray is not a man to be trapped."

Five years ago, Robinson fell ill but wouldn't allow Millie to hospitalize him. So Millie sent for Leila Smith. Millie had suffered at Ray's hand physically and she had temporarily moved out. Frank Sinatra, an old friend, called Robinson and told him that Millie would come back to the house if Ray agreed to be hospitalized. But it took Ray's mother to finally convince him to put himself in the doctors' hands.

"The doctor who examined him at the house said his blood sugar was very high. So I went out there," recalls Mrs. Smith. "He wouldn't go to the hospital for nobody but me. He seemed to be delirious. He got upset whenever she [Millie] came near. It was her. Just her. I could go and talk to him. But her—she had gone away, and Ray was waiting for her on the porch. She said Ray had knocked her down before. I told her, 'You better do something or Ray will hurt you.' Sugar is dangerous, you know. She didn't seem to know what was wrong with him.

"That was the last time I saw him. I used to talk to him on the phone. Sometimes, he would repeat himself. Sometimes he'd say, 'Ma, I didn't mean it.' "

Leila Smith took "it" to mean Jimmy Doyle. On June 23, 1947, the night before Robinson fought Doyle in Cleveland, Ray dreamed he killed Doyle with a single left hook. The next morning, a shaken Sugar told his manager, George Gainford, and the fight promoters that he couldn't go into the ring against Doyle, but the promoters brought in a Catholic priest who assured Robinson his fears were unfounded. The fight must go on, that night. In the eighth round Sugar hit Doyle with a textbook left hook. Doyle was taken out of the ring on a stretcher. He died the next day without ever regaining consciousness.

"He meant Doyle. I know my son. But . . . I can't be sure," says Leila Smith. "Ray used to take care of me. I used to know him. To me, Millie is a Johnny-come-lately. I don't know much about this last marriage."

Mildred Bruce, several years Ray's senior, had two sons and a daughter by a previous marriage. Her younger son died at an early age. The other son, Herman, 50, is now called Butch Robinson. He helps run the activities program for the foundation. "She got her son named Robinson," says Leila Smith. "But when little Ray [Ray Jr.] went out there, he was pushed to the back. Just like Leonard. Just took Ray's glory. Millie doesn't care who doesn't like what. She keeps Ray shut away because somebody would see how bad off he is. Evelyn says it's bad. My chances of ever seeing Ray again are poor. If I didn't have Jesus, I wouldn't survive. I would lose my mind. It would hurt me not to be able to even talk to Ray. It brings tears to my eyes just to think about him. I want to do what's right, but what is right these days?"

Later, I talk to Millie. She is upset, which is not good because she suffers from hypertension. "So, you went and talked to Ray's mother behind my back," she says.

"No, Mrs. Robinson. Not behind your back. Mrs. Smith is Ray's mother. She was very kind."

"Well, I'm his wife."

Leila Smith mentioned when I visited that she was a little bit tired. On Monday morning, Feb. 9, 1987, just after midnight, she suffered gastric distress. She was quickly hospitalized and underwent emergency surgery for an intestinal blockage. She was not strong enough to survive the trauma. Before morning light, the mother of the greatest boxer pound-for-pound that ever lived, died in a small room at Montefiore Medical Center in the Bronx.

"Ray."

"*Nnn?*"

"Do you miss New York?"

". . . Well, sure."

A chill wind whips over the burial grounds of Ferncliff Cemetery in Hartsdale, New York, causing the small gathering of mourners to huddle closer together and pull their winter coats tight. It is Valentine's Day. Edna-Mae Robinson holds her hand over her mouth and leans toward her son, Ray Jr., as the minister says simple words over the casket bearing the remains of Leila Smith.

A large wreath of white carnations stands at the head of the open grave. The banner bears the script: YOUR SON, SUGAR RAY. Blood-red boxing gloves are pinned to the center of the arrangement. Once the minister has finished and the mourners have moved reluctantly away, the gloves are removed by the boldest of the male relatives. Some carnations are plucked as melancholy souvenirs. A letter from Ray to his mother was read at the funeral service. Ray was not present. Millie has to help him when he goes to the bathroom, so a transcontinental trip seemed out of the question.

"Oh, I'm real clear on what kind of person Millie is," says Ray Jr. "I guess she doesn't want him in these surroundings anymore. Or out from under the influence of medication. My father is virtually in prison, yes, but it's a strange kind of prison. He can be pumped up to go to a party at Frank Sinatra's house, but he can't come to his own mother's funeral." Actually, Ray Robinson had been hospitalized the day before his mother's funeral. He had become agitated and his blood sugar had risen.

Seven years ago, Ray Jr. moved to Venice, California, to work for the foundation and spend some time with his father. He never got that time—and he never got the job. "My dad had written me an amazing letter. I was thrilled at the chance to get to know him. My father had always been a . . . businessman. His business kept him away. But he wrote and said he wanted me to work with him. When I got there, I was shocked. He weighed 215 pounds. For 6½ years, I've lived not 20 minutes from them. I been in their house no more than 10 times—most times uninvited."

"I don't want any problems with Millie," says Edna-Mae. "I don't want anything. I used to be the first lady. But she is now. When I found out Ray was sick, I sent out literature on high blood pressure and diabetes and Alzheimer's, and she became very upset. Why? My son was in for a rude awakening when he went out there."

Sugar Ray remained fit for 10 years after he retired in '65. He worked out nearly every day, either on the road or with the bags. Lockitch tried to introduce him to health clubs, but Robinson went into one, looked around and said, "This ain't a gym. It's got to look like a gym. It's got to smell like a gym." And so he went off to find a real gym, and he continued working out until 1975, when he finally let it go. But he couldn't really let it go. After all, he was still the Sugar. That would never change.

"It hurt me when they started calling this new young man Sugar Ray," says Edna-Mae. "It must have hurt Ray." If it did, he didn't show it. Robinson posed for a few photographs with Leonard and never said an unkind word about his fistic namesake and heir.

For a time, Robinson was fanatical about the Dodgers. He became a friend of manager Tommy Lasorda. All it took was an introduction. One day at Dodger Stadium when Sylvester Stallone, the cinematic heavyweight champion, was there, a fan asked to shake the actor's hand. Stallone's bodyguard said, "Mr. Stallone doesn't like to be touched." Then Stallone spotted Sugar Ray. His bodyguard asked Robinson if they could meet. Ray sent a message over. "Mr. Robinson doesn't like to be touched." Ray had enjoyed that.

But baseball and one-upmanship could not satisfy Robinson's soul. Robinson remained a womanizer until the diabetes, hypertension and Alzheimer's began to take their toll. Millie was no fool. Neither was Edna-Mae. When Gainford died in 1981, Ray made a trip to New York unaccompanied by Millie, but with a bodyguard. After the funeral service, Ray met Edna-Mae and suggested they go to his hotel together. "I told him I couldn't do that; we weren't married anymore," says Edna-Mae. "He got very upset. I had to tell his bodyguard to please take him away, because I didn't want to get hurt." Robinson returned to California and Millie.

"I could never understand Millie's attitude," says Edna-Mae. "At first I thought it was just because she was afraid she might not get power of attorney. But she has that. She's his wife. But Ray is his son. Leila was his mother. They should have been allowed in his life. That letter they read at the funeral—Ray didn't write that. It was signed, but he didn't sign it, either. In my 17 years with him, when I think of all the thousands of pictures that I signed, 'Good luck, Sugar Ray' . . . so I know. That letter wasn't from him. I don't know what Millie is doing. I suppose she's trying to keep alive the myth of Ray's competence."

"Ray."

"N*nnn*."

Katy Riney is the program administrator of the Sugar Ray Robinson Youth Foundation. It was Riney who drafted the letter and sent the floral arrangement to Leila Smith's funeral. These were merely two of her many duties as the foundation's most indispensable employee. And if the foundation were Robinson's only legacy, it would be a good legacy, the very best. Since the organization became active in 1969, thousands of inner-city children have had constructive activities to fill their idle weekends—from volleyball and flag football to pageants and talent shows. The foundation sponsors no boxing programs.

On one Saturday morning 100 girls are playing volleyball in the gymnasium at Bethune Junior High in south-central Los Angeles. It is some weeks before the Leonard–Hagler fight. Riney referees and takes the girls through their paces, team by team. Outside 150 boys under the supervision of Butch Robinson play flag football. There are six community directors present at Bethune. Most have been with the foundation for 10 years or more. One of them is 40-year-old Reniell Beard.

"I've got all Ray's fights on tape," says Beard. "I had four older brothers. Ray was like a god to them. They stopped me from watching *The Amos and Andy Show* and made me watch Sugar Ray's fights. I guess that's why I do this. It's like repaying a debt. It's nice to do something for the kids, although most of them have no idea who Sugar Ray Robinson is."

One look at these kids at play, keeping amused and interested amid some of the most depressing urban blight to be found in America—in south-central Los Angeles some apartment houses have their street numbers painted on the roofs, the better for police helicopter pilots to identify the buildings—is enough to create genuine admiration for this tangible part of Robinson's legacy.

Michael Dear, 13, has been involved with various foundation programs for one year. I ask him if he knows about Sugar Ray Robinson. "Yeah," he says. "He's fightin' in April." No, that's Sugar Ray *Leonard*. Sugar Ray Robinson.

"They are not the same?"

Jattea Johnson, 16, has been in the program for four years and is now in high school. She still comes by on weekends. It is a good habit she doesn't want to break. "I know Sugar Ray Robinson is an ex-boxer," she says. "All I know is that one Sugar Ray is older than the other one."

"That's O.K.," says Beard. "And as far as the fight goes, the referee will call it before nine. Leonard is in there with a warmonger."

The Sugar Ray Robinson Youth Foundation must pass the scrutiny of the California state legislature every year, and satisfy the state auditors. It won its funding in the first place because former governor Edmund (Pat) Brown was a great fan of Robinson's. "Dollar for dollar, we're the best bargain they have," Lockitch says.

The foundation receives approximately $488,000 a year from the state and $50,000 from Los Angeles County, and this year it got $71,000 from the Olympic Games surplus funds. Some of the money goes for the buses that transport the children to the activities and pageants. Robinson, as the titular head of the foundation, receives a salary of $37,000. "Millie needs that stipend," says Riney.

And so that is why Millie asked, "How much?" Not that she is to be blamed— no more than Robinson was to be blamed for being paid to fight. You use what you have. Butch received money from a gossip tabloid for "revealing" that Ray had Alzheimer's. Evelyn Nelson's son, Kenneth, asked Millie for permission to use Sugar Ray's name for an Urban Coalition fund-raiser, in conjunction with a showing of the Leonard–Hagler fight at the Apollo Theater in Harlem. (Millie said yes, then at the last minute changed her mind and informed the Urban Coalition that she was withdrawing her permission. It was decided that the event would have to be canceled.)

When Robinson became ill after his mother's death, he was admitted to the Cedars-Sinai Medical Center in Los Angeles. He remained hospitalized for a week. A few days after he was released, Robinson sat in their yellow Cadillac while Millie went into the foundation offices. Ray no longer wore the vacant smile. I came over and spoke to him. "Ray. *How* can Ray beat Marvin Hagler?" He didn't respond.

"I don't expect the fight to last long," Ray Jr. had said when he was asked for a prediction. "My father did it, but he always had tune-up fights. And he's my father. There was no one else like him. He was Sugar Ray."

But Leonard did win. He defeated Hagler, in 12 rounds. He is the Sugar now.

Leonard is not to be asked why he fought Hagler. "Why?" is a nervy question to ask a prizefighter. As Robinson often said, "Because it's what people want to see." Leonard fights for us as much as he fights for himself. Like Robinson, like a lot of other people, he can't separate who he is from what he does best.

Sugar Ray Robinson is no different from Sugar Ray Leonard. What he did best was fight. Like Leonard, he's not to be asked why he fought, and these days he can't be asked much of anything. He did indeed leave all the answers in the ring. But Ray Jr. had one thing exactly right about him. While his father may no longer be *the* Sugar, there was—and is—no one else like him.

VI
PORTRAITS,
VOLUME 1

The following four sections of portraits are various essays that are bio-graphical or personal portraits of some noteworthy black figure. These pieces were culled from essentially two places: popular magazines both black and white, and high-brow literary or intellectual magazines and journals both black and white. The intention here is for the reader to see the broad range of styles that constitutes the portrait essay—polemical, journalistic, impressionistic, academic, factual, narrative—and how important this type of essay has been in African-American letters.

PAUL LAURENCE DUNBAR

MARY CHURCH TERRELL (1863–1954) was among the first black women to receive a college degree. She graduated from Oberlin College in 1884. She served on the Board of Education for the District of Columbia; was the first president of the NAACP; was active in the Women's Suffrage Movement, delivering a key speech at the convention in 1900; was elected the first president of the National Association of Colored Women in 1896. She was active in the international conferences such as the International Congress of Women held in Berlin in 1904 in which she gave her address in three languages—French, German, and English. She wrote A *Colored Woman in a White World* (1940), an autobiography. "Paul Laurence Dunbar" and "Susan B. Anthony, The Abolitionist" were published in *The Voice of the Negro*, an important, if relatively short-lived, black publication of the turn of the century. The essay on Dunbar appeared in April 1906; the one on Anthony appeared in June of the same year.

I n the death of Paul Laurence Dunbar the nation as a whole as well as the race to which he belonged have sustained an irreparable loss. He was undoubtedly the greatest poet his own race has ever produced and it is certain Nature has bestowed the gift of poetry upon few, if any, Americans, with more lavish hand than she did upon Paul Dunbar. "Conquerors are a race with whom the world could well dispense," said a great writer, "but a true poet, a man in whose heart resides some effluence of wisdom, some tone of the eternal melodies, is the most precious gift that can be bestowed upon a generation."

The story of Paul Dunbar's life is familiar to all. He was born in poverty in 1872 and spent his youth in Dayton, Ohio in unceasing, grinding toil. Both his parents were slaves, his father having escaped from Kentucky into Canada. Fortunately for the son, however, his parents determined that he should enjoy the educational advantages of which they themselves had been deprived, as he was sent to the public schools of Dayton, Ohio, and from which he graduated, when still in his teens. As soon as he knew how to write, his mother says, he began to scribble rhymes and gave evidence of his genius, when he was only seven years old. Obliged to support himself and mother he secured employment as an elevator boy, after he graduated from the public schools, and it was while engaged in this most prosaic occupation that many of his first poems were written. At that time his life must have been a constant insurrection between the spirit that would soar and the wretched circumstances in which he was placed and which bound him fast to the earth. But while he was chained like a galley slave to the ropes of the elevator earning only $4 a week, the wings of his aspiration refused to be clipped and bore him ever higher and higher.

Paul Dunbar's first appearance as a poet occurred in Dayton Ohio in 1891, when he was 19 years old, when he was presented to the members of the Western Association of Writers and read a poem. This scene was described by Dr. James Newton of Mason, Illinois, as follows: "About half way down the programme the presiding officer announced the reading of a poem by Paul Dunbar. Just the name for a poet, I thought. Great was the surprise of the audience to see stepping lightly down the aisle, between the rows of fluttering fans and assembled beauty and wit of Dayton, a slender Negro lad, as black as the core of Cheops's pyramid. He ascended the rostrum with the coolness and dignity of a cultured entertainer, and delivered a poem in a tone as musical as Apollo's lute. He was applauded to the echo between the stanzas and heartily encored at the conclusion. He then disappeared from the hall as suddenly as had entered it, and many were the whispered conjectures as to the personality of the man and the originality of his verses, *none believing it possible that one of his age and color could produce a thing of such evident merit.* Show me a white boy of nineteen who can excel or even equal this black boy's "Drowsy Day."

After repeated inquiries this man of the dominant race who had been so surprised at the ability Paul Dunbar possessed and so transported by his reading succeeded in finding the rising laureate of the Colored race in the store in which he worked. He was seated in a chair in the lower landing of the elevator, Dr. Newton says, hastily glancing at the July Century and jotting down notes on a handy pencil tablet. Not having time to converse with Dr. Newton, Paul invited him into the elevator and during a few excursions from floor to floor the black poet told his newly found friend the story of his life. In writing to Dr. Newton soon after their first meeting, Mr. Dunbar, whose spirit at that time seemed almost broken, expressed himself as follows: "My hopes are no brighter than when you saw me. I am getting on no better, and what would be impossible, no worse. I am nearer discouraged than I have ever been."

Shortly after this, however, the clouds which had hung so heavy and menacing in the young poet's sky began to clear away and a brighter day dawned. When the illustrious Frederick Douglass, who had become deeply interested in the young poet, was Haitian Commissioner to the World's Fair in 1893, he made Mr. Dunbar his secretary. From that time forth it was no longer necessary for the poet to engage in menial labor to support himself and mother. His first volume of poems Oak and Ivy which was published by his Dayton employer in 1893 brought him instant recognition and his second volume entitled Majors and Minors, published two years later greatly increased his fame. Mr. Howell, the dean of American literature, paid the young poet a glowing tribute which undoubtedly enabled him to secure recognition in certain quarters which would otherwise have been withheld perhaps. James Whitcomb Riley, the Hoosier poet, compared Dunbar's Drowsy Day with Longfellow's Rainy Day and did not hesitate to declare that the black man's poem was superior to his white brother's both in lyrical power and in harmony of expression. So far back as in 1892, when the name of Paul Dunbar had just begun to be heard James Whitcomb Riley sent him the following characteristic letter:

Denver, Col., Nov. 27, 1892.

Paul Dunbar, Esq.—See how your name is traveling, my chirping friend. And it's a good, sound name, too, that seems to imply the brave fine spirit of a singer who should command wide and serious attention. Certainly your gifts as evidenced by this "Drowsy Day" poem alone, is a superior one, and therefore, its fortunate possessor should bear it with a becoming sense of gratitude and meekness, always feeling that for any resultant good, God's is the glory, the singer but His very humble instrument. Already you have many friends and can have thousands more by being simply honest, unaffected and just to yourself and the high source of your endowment. Very earnestly I wish you every good thing.

Your friend,
JAMES WHITCOMB RILEY.

In the best magazines of the country like Scribner's, the Century and others there appeared a series of Negro songs and ballads which impressed themselves upon the reader as being among the best of the kind yet produced.

The name of Paul Dunbar was signed to them, but probably not one of every hundred who read and enjoyed these characteristic little verses, so finished in form and instinct with the true race spirit dreamed that their author was really a Negro. The versification was that of an accomplished writer, whose excellent method was noticeable in spite of the rude dialect used. It was evident to the student that he had mastered more fully than most writers of Negro verse the real genius of the race whose characteristics his verses portrayed. For a long time the editors of the magazine, themselves did not know he was a Negro. They accepted his productions on their merits, which in itself was a high compliment, since only the best of lighter verse appears in the magazines to which Mr. Dunbar contributed. When Mr. Dunbar tried to sell his serious verses in the classic style of English composition, they were refused, although a high estimate was placed upon them by some of the best literary critics of the day, because his characteristic Negro poems were considered so superior and were in such demand.

Mr. Dunbar's reputation as a writer was not enhanced by his prose, although he wrote many short stories and several novels. Among the latter his first "The

Uncalled," which was published in Lippincott's magazine, was probably the best. Altogether Mr. Dunbar published 17 volumes, the last of which Howdy, Honey, Howdy came from the press just a short time before he died, February 9th. The list of his works is as follows:

Oak and Ivy, published in 1893.
Majors and Minors, published in 1895.
Lyrics of Lowly Life, containing an introduction by Wm. Dean Howells.
Folks from Dixie, 1898.
The Uncalled, 1898.
Strength of Gideon and Other Stories. 1900.
Love of Landry, 1900.
Candle Lightin' Time, 1901.
Fanatics, 1901.
Sport of the Gods, 1902.
The Heart of Happy Hollow.
Lyrics of Love and Laughter, 1903.
In Old Plantation Days, 1903.
Lil Gal, 1904.
When Malindy Sings, 1904.
Lyrics of Sunshine and Shadow, 1905.
Howdy, Honey, Howdy, 1906.

After Mr. Dunbar's marriage to Miss Alice Ruth Moore in 1898, he came to Washington to live and was employed for a time in the Congressional Library. Like James Whitcomb Riley no one could read Mr. Dunbar's productions so well as he could himself, so that he was in great demand as a reciter and gave entertainments all over the country, until he was physically unable to stand the strain.

In a short sketch like this it is impossible to give either a satisfactory review of Mr. Dunbar's poems or a comprehensive sketch of his life.

Only a cursory glance at each must suffice.

In Paul Dunbar's poems there is neither affectation nor fustian. He is always true to himself and to his subject. His ideals were not in foreign climes and distant lands, but in the scenes he himself beheld every day and in the people with whom he himself had walked and talked. He had an eye to see, an intellect to understand, a heart to feel and the heart to portray what had passed before him. His hope and despair, the joys and sorrows of his own heart as well as those of his own race he gives articulate voice and every word rings true. Is his muse a bit disheartened and sad? Every line the poet pens is steeped pathos and every cadence a sigh. His own sensibilities are so tremblingly alive that one can feel them pulsate and throb under their mask of words.

Nature appeals to him strongly. The rising of the storm, the woods in summer and winter, the patter of the rain are his delight and charm him into song. The thoughts of love which inflame his heart kindle him to melody. His love of children was genuine and great, and inspired some of his tenderest lines. The sight of a little brown baby and the tragic death of Ella May move him to pity and eloquence. His songs are born of genuine emotion and are the very pulse beats of his heart. Now buoyant, now pathetic, sometimes satirical and then ingenuous, now stern and then tender, Paul Dunbar has words for every mood of man's heart. His own heart was indeed "an ÆOLIAN harp swept by an ever varying breeze." His convictions were invariably expressed with undiluted earnestness and unflinching honesty, no matter what he discussed. It seemed possible for him to transcribe feelings diametrically opposite to each other with equal skill. The desire to cite poems which would best illustrate his versatility is a temptation which I must resist. Everybody who has read Mr. Dunbar's poems will bear testimony to this fact.

His deep and ardent loyalty to his race bursts forth occasionally into white heat. His Ode to Ethiopia quickens the pulse and stirs to its depths the heart of the strongest and most phlegmatic member of the race. With what a fine outburst of enthusiasm he recounts the reasons for his pride in his race whose

"Name is writ on Glory's scroll
In characters of fire."

What a magnificent tribute he has paid his people for the long suffering, uncomplaining manner in which they bore the trials and tribulations heaped upon them during slavery and the Christ-like manner in which after emancipation they forgave those who had despitefully used them, in the following lines:

No other race, or white or black,
When bound as thou wert to the rack,
So seldom stooped to grieving.
No other race, when free again,
Forgot the past and proved them men
So noble in forgiving.

Again when Frederick Douglass dies:

And Ethiopia with bosom torn
Laments the passing of her noblest son,

Paul Dunbar, inspired by reverence and affection for his illustrious benefactor and friend pays him one of the rarest and finest tributes ever offered by poet to mortal man.

Oh Douglass, thou hast passed beyond the shore,
But still thy voice is ringing o'er the gale.
Thou's taught thy race how high her hopes may soar
And bade her seek the heights, nor faint nor fail
She will not fail, she heeds thy stirring cry,
She knows thy guardian spirit will be nigh,
And rising from beneath the chastening rod,
She stretches out her bleeding hand to God.

It is difficult to speak of his ode to "The Colored Soldiers" in terms of quiet moderation and use language which may not smack of exaggeration to some. How Paul Dunbar glories in their dauntless courage and delights to recount the great service they rendered their country during the Civil War:

So when war in savage triumph,
Spread abroad his funeral pall—
Then you called the colored soldiers,
And they answered to your call.

And like hounds unleashed and eager
For the life blood of the prey,
Sprung they forth and bore them bravely
In the thickest of the fray.

And where'er the fight was hottest—
Where the bullets fastest fell,
There they pressed unblanched and fearless
At the very mouth of hell.

He takes a pardonably fierce delight in reminding this country that his race is not indebted entirely to others for its emancipation from the awful bondage it endured.

Yes the blacks enjoy their freedom
And they won it dearly too;
For the life blood of their thousands
Did the southern fields bedew:

In the darkness of their bondage,
In their depths of slavery's night:
Their muskets flashed the dawning
And they fought their way to light.

They were comrades then and brothers,
Are they more or less to-day?
They were good to stop a bullet,
And to front the fearful fray.

They were citizens and soldiers,
When rebellion raised its head;
And the traits that made them worthy—
Ah! these virtues are not dead.

And their deeds shall find a record
In the registry of Fame;
For their blood has cleansed completely
Every blot of slavery's shame.

So all honor and all the glory
To those noble sons of Ham—
To those gallant colored soldiers,
Who fought for Uncle Sam.

So long as there remains in this country a man even remotely connected with the race, whose soldiers have been so immortalized by the eloquence and the music of the verses just quoted, and so long as the blood courses warm in the heart of such a man, so long will it thrill under this heroic ode, one of the best that was ever written and which can be compared only with Burns's "Scots, who hae wi' Wallace bled."

It can be asserted without fear of successful contradiction that in range of genius as well as in power and aptness of expression Mr. Dunbar has not been excelled by any poet born in the United States. If he infrequently rose into the region of great ideas, the peculiar conditions surrounding him and not his mental limitations are responsible for this failure to soar aloft. To some of his more serious poems reference has already been made. In the same class his "Life," "Comparison," "A Creed and Not a Creed," together with others equally as good, are as elevated in sentiment, as profound in philosophy, as musical in tone, as perfect in form and as complete in treatment as some of the best poems written by the most inspired singers of the past.

Attention has already been directed to the attitude of the editors who published Mr. Dunbar's poems and who insisted upon his confining himself to dialect. So far as I know, with but a single exception, this advice was given him by all his literary advisers and friends.

In two little stanzas entitled "The Poet," which Mr. Dunbar wrote to explain his position with reference to the more serious efforts which he wished to make but from which he was withheld by the public one cannot help feeling the bitter regret which disturbed his peace of mind and the resentment which rankled in his heart.

THE POET.

He sang of life serenely sweet,
With now and then a deeper note,
On some high peak, nigh yet remote,
He voiced the world's absorbing beat.

He sang of love, when earth was young,
And love itself was in his lays,
But ah! the world, it turned to praise,
A jingle in a broken tongue.

It is always pleasant for me to recall that the first time I ever heard of Paul Dunbar was when the illustrious Frederick Douglass told me about him, while we were in his library at Cedar Hill one afternoon and read me one of the young poet's early productions entitled the Drowsy Day. Previous to the reading, however, Mr. Douglass had spoken with deep feeling about the young man's poverty and had expressed regret that he had been so seriously handicapped in his career. And so as he afterward read the poem, the great man was so deeply affected by it, that he could not restrain his tears. When Mr. Dunbar first took up his residence in Washington, he lived in a house at 1934 4th street N.W., next door to the one in which we were living at that time. Near neighbors as we were, it was quite natural that we should see a great deal of each other and we did. Being a hero worshiper by nature, and inclination as well as by cultivation, particularly where members of my own race are concerned, I did not try to conceal from Mr. Dunbar how great and genuine was my admiration of his gifts and how brilliant were the hopes I entertained of his future success. It happened, therefore, that many a time he honored me by coming to my home to read me his poems or his short stories, telling me in what magazine they had appeared or would appear. He would also tell me how much he had received for his articles, when I was impertinent enough to inquire, which I frequently did, just for the pleasure of hearing how well he was compensated for the product of his genius and his brain. On one occasion he invited me to his home, so that he might read a play which he had just written and which I hope may someday be produced.

Mr. Dunbar was a man of charming personality with a bold, warm, buoyant humor of character which manifested itself delightfully to his friends. Mingled with his affability of manner were a dignity and poise of bearing which prevented the overbold from coming too near. While there was nothing intrusive or forward about Paul Dunbar, when he found himself among eminent scholars or distinguished people in the highest social circles, he showed both by his manner and his conversation that he felt he was just exactly where he was entitled to be. There was nothing that smacked of truckling, and nobody in the wildest flight of his imagination could dream that Paul Dunbar felt particularly flattered at the attention he received. The maturity of intellectual power was manifested in his conversation as well as in his writing and his fund of information was remarkable, considering both his youth and his meagre opportunities for culture.

His wit was decidedly pungent at times and then nobody in his presence was immune therefrom. His sense of the ludicrous was highly developed and nothing ridiculous or funny escaped him. I can never hear certain styles of music rendered without being convulsed, when I remember the comments made by Dunbar at a musical we attended once.

Last July Mr. Dunbar extended me a cordial invitation to be the guest of himself and his mother, while I was attending the convention of the Ohio Federation of Colored Women's clubs which was held at Dayton, Ohio, and which I had been asked to address. I accepted and spent several days at his home. I am glad I did, for I am sure I learned more about the character of the man and the genius of the poet during the short visit with him in Dayton than it would have been possible for me to ascertain in any other way. I account it a privilege to have had such an excellent opportunity of becoming thoroughly acquainted with the greatest poet the race has ever produced. During the few days spent with Mr. Dunbar last summer I discovered there were depths in his character that I had never sounded and qualities of heart of which I had never dreamed, although I saw him frequently while he lived in Washington.

Owen Meredith says that

The heart of a man is like that delicate weed
Which requires to be trampled on, boldly indeed
Ere it gives forth the fragrance you wish to extract.
Tis a simile, trust me, if not new, exact.

Whether affliction and sorrow always bring out the best there is in a man, I cannot say. I do know however, that the physical and mental pain which Paul

Dunbar endured for at least a year before he passed away, developed the highest and noblest qualities in him. When I saw Paul Dunbar last summer, he was shut in, wasted and worn by disease, coughing his young and precious life away, yet full of cheer, when not actually racked with pain, and perfectly resigned to his fate. I shall always think of his patience under his severe affliction as a veritable miracle of modern times. In the flush of early manhood, full of promise of still greater literary achievement in the future than he had been able to attain in the past, fond of life as the young should be and usually are, there he sat, rapidly losing his physical strength every hour, and yet, miracle of miracles, no bitter complaint of his cruel fate did I hear escape his lips a single time. The weakness and inertia of his worn and wasted body contrasted sadly and strangely with the strength and activity of his vigorous mind. As I looked at him, pity for the afflicted man himself and pity for the race to which he belonged and which I knew would soon sustain such an irreparable loss in his death almost overcame me more than once. As incredible as it may appear, his moods were often sunny and then it was delightful to hear the flood of merriment roll cheerily from his lips.

It was gratifying to see the homage paid Mr. Dunbar by some of the most cultured and some of the wealthiest people of the dominant race in Dayton. As soon as I reached his house, I saw a chair most elaborately decorated in royal purple and was informed that a company of distinguished people of the dominant race had improvised a birth day party for the young poet a few days before I arrived and had thus festooned this chair in his honor. One of Mr. Dunbar's white friends did all his stenography for him for nothing, refusing to take a cent of pay. What an invaluable service was thus rendered is easily seen and appreciated, when it is known that Mr. Dunbar's last two volumes of poems, Lyrics of Sunshine and Shadow, and Howdy, Honey, Howdy, were prepared for publication by this same generous and unselfish friend. Mr. Dunbar's mother told me that the white people of Dayton had helped her care for her son in every conceivable way.

On one occasion after some beautiful girls who had called to pay their respects to Mr. Dunbar had gone, in a nervous effort to relieve the tension of my own feelings, I turned to him and said, "Sometimes I am tempted to believe you are not half so ill as you pretend to be. I believe you are just playing the roll of interesting invalid, so as to receive the sympathy and the homage of these beautiful girls." "Sometimes I think I am just loafing myself," he laughingly replied. How well he remembered this was shown a short while after I returned home. He sent me a copy of his Lyrics of Sunshine and Shadow which at that time was his latest book. On the fly leaf he had written with his own hand, a feat which during the first year of his illness he was often unable to perform, the following lines.

Look hyeah, Molly
Aint it jolly
Jes a loafin 'roun'?

Tell the Jedge
Not to hedge
For I am still in town.

Whether Paul Dunbar will be rated a great poet or not, no human being can tell. It is impossible for his contemporaries either to get a proper perspective of his achievement or to accurately gauge his genius. Personally I believe he will occupy as high a place in American literature as Burns does in the British, if not higher.

But whether Paul Dunbar will be rated great or not, it is certain that he has rendered an invaluable service to his race. Because he has lived and wrought, the race to which he belonged has been lifted to a higher plane. Each and every person in the United States remotely identified with his race is held in higher esteem because of the ability which Paul Dunbar possessed and the success he undoubtedly attained.

Indeed the whole civilized world has greater respect for that race which some have the ignorance to underestimate and others the hardihood to despise, because this black man, through whose veins not a drop of Caucasian blood was known to flow, has given such a splendid and striking proof of its capacity for high intellectual achievement.

The more one thinks of the obstacles Paul Dunbar was obliged to surmount, the more remarkable appear both the quality and quantity of the literary labor which he performed. Other poets have been born poor before and were cruelly handicapped for years by hard and grinding toil. In the history of men who have enlightened the world through the medium of their pens or lightened its sorrows by their wit and mirth, poverty is no new thing. Milton was poor and so was Burns, between whom and Paul Dunbar there is a striking similarity in several respects. But Milton and Burns were forced to fight poverty alone. Prejudice against their race did not rear its huge and hideous proportions athwart their path to literary achievement and success. Heine's position, so far as concerns prejudice against his race, more closely resembles Paul Dunbar's than that of any poet with whom he may be compared perhaps. But Heine's burden was far lighter than the one which the black American poet was forced to carry.

Heine was a Jew to be sure, and he was born and reared in Germany where Jews are hated and ostracized. But in the very beginning of Heine's career he was blessed with a comfort and an inspiration which Paul Dunbar was denied. Heine's race from time immemorial had produced authors and poets and great men galore. Therefore, no taunt of racial inferiority flaunted itself in Heine's face and filled his soul with tormenting doubts concerning his ability to succeed in a literary career. More than a hundred years before Paul Dunbar was born Phyllis Wheatley, a little African girl who had been brought to this country packed like a sardine in a slave ship had poured forth her soul in song, to be sure. But in spite of the fact that she was a slave, she was loved and encouraged and protected by her devoted master and mistress so that the atmosphere which she herself breathed was more conducive to the development of her talent than that in which Paul Dunbar lived. And so to a certain extent, at least Paul Dunbar had to blaze his path.

Though the empyrean soul of Paul Laurence Dunbar has winged its way to another world, the light of its celestial nature, which often groaned under the weight of a weary life, will never be dimmed. In the flower and fruit of his genius he has bestowed upon his country and his race an imperishable gift. In grateful appreciation of his services and in genuine affection Paul Dunbar lies to-day enshrined in our hearts, a far nobler mausoleum, after all, than one built of marble could possibly be.

SUSAN B. ANTHONY, THE ABOLITIONIST

MARY CHURCH TERRELL

A mong the men and women who have paid tributes to Susan B. Anthony since she closed her eyes in death March 13th, not one owes her such a debt of gratitude as I myself. My obligation to her is two-fold, for I am a woman as well as a representative of that race of whose freedom Miss Anthony worked so indefatigably, so conscientiously and so well. The debt of gratitude which women, not only in this country, but all over the civilized world owe Miss Anthony is great enough to be sure. But the representatives of that race which but fifty years ago bowed under a yoke of cruel bondage in this country in addition to bearing the burdens of a handicapped sex, owe her a debt of gratitude which cannot be expressed in words.

Though Miss Anthony rendered signal and conspicuous service during those dark days, when there was neither light nor shadow of turning for the slave, the work she subsequently performed for the amelioration of the condition of women was so prodigious that her anti-slavery record during the last decade or two has become partially obscured. Nevertheless, among the abolitionists who strove so earnestly to break the fetters of the slave, not one worked with such sublime heroism and more ardent zeal than did that noble woman, whose loss is so sincerely mourned all over the civilized world. It is difficult to speak of such valiant and valuable service as that rendered by Miss Anthony to my race in language which some may not consider extravagant and fulsome. There are so many recorded, indisputable facts, however, which show the incredible amount of work she performed in behalf of my oppressed race as well as her own handicapped sex, so many facts which prove her clear title to our gratitude and love that it is unnecessary for me or anybody else to resort to fiction to add one jot or one tittle to her fame.

From the moment Susan B. Anthony accepted the invitation of the American

Anti-Slavery Society to assist it in breaking the fetters of the oppressed, till the shackles had fallen from the last slave, she consecrated herself to this cause with all her heart and soul and labored for it with unflagging zeal. Routes for herself and others were planned and meetings arranged with the greatest skill and care. Into towns great and small, some of them off the railroad and reached only by stage, Miss Anthony went, preaching the gospel of freedom, portraying the horrors of slavery and imploring the people to extirpate it root and branch. With the mercury many degrees below zero, we see her emerging from one snow drift, only to plunge into another, or shivering with cold in a sleigh nearly buried in a snow bank, while the bewildered driver goes to the nearest farm house, only to discover that he has missed the road and driven over a fence into a field, but urged, nevertheless by the dauntless, determined Miss Anthony to do his level best to reach the town for which they are bound, so that she may touch the hearts and arouse the conscience of the people in behalf of the imbruted, wretched slave.

During a winter of unusual severity, when the men who were her co-laborers in the cause of abolition broke down physically, one after another, cancelled their engagements and converted their letters to their family and friends into veritable Jeremiads, full of the most pathetic complaints about their heads, their backs, their throats, their lungs and their eyes, Miss Anthony trudged bravely, heroically on. Though she herself doubtless ached many a time from her head to her feet, was sick for the comforts to which she had been accustomed in her comfortable home but which she often lacked on the road, and was sad and heavy of heart because of the awful persecution which as a woman supporting two unpopular causes she was forced to endure, so literally did she crucify the flesh in behalf of that cause for whose triumph she worked with such desperate, effective earnestness, she neither missed a single engagement nor lost a day from her work. In every fibre of her being she loathed an institution which robbed an unfortunate race of every right that men hold dear, tore mother from child and separated husband from wife. Having devoted this unnatural, brutal system to destruction, so far as in her lay, she allowed neither height nor depth nor any other creature to turn her aside from this work.

So great was the confidence reposed in Miss Anthony's ability by the men who represented the brain and the conscience of the abolition movement that the whole State of New York was at one time placed under her control. "We want your name to all letters and your hand in all arrangements," Mr. May, the secretary of the Anti-Slavery Society wrote her once. "I think," said he, "that the efficiency and the success of our operations in New York this winter will depend more upon your personal attendance and direction than upon that of any other worker. We need your earnestness, your practical talent, your energy and your perseverance to make the conventions a success. We want your cheerfulness and your spirit, in short, we want yourself."

Considering how many giants there were in those days among the dominant sex, this was high praise indeed for a representative of that half of humanity, whose menial inferiority and dearth of intellectual prospects were accepted as foregone conclusions both by wise men in the new and progressive West and by their brothers in the ancient and stagnant East.

In addition to being violently hated by the advocates of slavery in the North as well as in the South, Miss Anthony had no sooner proclaimed the Garrisonian doctrine "No Union With Slaveholders," than she incurred the bitter hostility of that party destined to crush the rebellion and break the fetters of the slave, but which at one time did not stand for the abolition of slavery and simply opposed its extension. It happened, therefore, in a series of meetings planned one season for the Anti-Slavery Society by Miss Anthony, she was mobbed in every city and town she entered from Albany to Buffalo. But neither the winter's cold nor the white heat of wicked men's wrath could force or frighten her from the work in behalf of freedom and justice to which she had devoted her life and consecrated her powers. When at Syracuse, New York, eggs were promiscuously thrown around and about her and benches were broken, when pistols and knives gleamed in every direction, Susan B. Anthony, the only woman in the midst of that hissing, howling, murderous mob stood determined, fearless and serene. Hideous effigies of herself were dragged through the streets and burned, but such exhibitions of hatred only nerved her all the more for the holy warfare in which she was engaged.

But Miss Anthony's service to the anti-slavery movement did not consist entirely either in the speeches which she herself delivered or in the meetings she arranged for others. The emancipation proclamation had no sooner been issued by Abraham Lincoln than this far-sighted woman and close student of human nature saw clearly that the resourceful, infuriated masters who had lost their human chattels would do everything in their power to render this document null and void. The fact that the jails of loyal Kentucky were filled with slaves from Alabama, Georgia and Mississippi who were advertised to be sold for their jail fees according to law, just as they were before their emancipation was proclaimed, filled Miss Anthony with the gravest apprehension and inspired her to work in their behalf with renewed energy and redoubled zeal. Firmly convinced that the only way of securing freedom for the slave was by and through an act of Congress, Miss Anthony and Mrs. Elizabeth Cady Stanton called upon the women of the free States to do their duty to their government as well as to the slave by signing petitions urging Congress to pass a law forever abolishing slavery in the United States. As a result of this call the Woman's National Loyal League was formed. With her headquarters in Cooper Union in New York City and without the guarantee of a single cent for expenses Miss Anthony worked throughout the long hot summer of 1863 with might and main, scattering letters far and wide, arousing men and women to a sense of their duty and directing the affairs of this organization with the sagacity and the skill of a general. Not until the Senate had passed a bill prohibiting slavery and there was no doubt about the intention of the House to concur did Miss Anthony cease to secure and send petitions to Congress and close her headquarters in Cooper Union. The untiring, persistent, consecrated chief of this Woman's National Loyal League, the head, the heart, the feet and the hands of that magnificent movement was the noble, justice-loving woman whose memory is so dear to us today.

Not only in her public work and by her platform utterances did Miss Anthony help to create sentiment in behalf of an oppressed and persecuted race, but by her daily example and by her private conversation as well. Shortly after she had left home for the first time to teach, she wrote her family that she had had the pleasure of visiting four colored people and taking tea with them. With great emphasis she asserted that "it affords me unspeakable satisfaction to show this kind of people respect in this heathen land." Again she writes a scathing denunciation of some "meek followers of Christ" as she sarcastically calls them, who refused to allow a colored man to sit in their Church in Tarrytown, New York, and who could not worship the God who is no respecter of persons with their sable companion sitting by their side.

If at any time Miss Anthony's zeal in behalf of the race for whose freedom she had labored so faithfully and so hard seemed to abate, it was not because she desired justice for them less, but because she yearned for justice toward all God's creatures more. Having worked with such genuine, devoted loyalty and such unflagging zeal to help free an oppressed race, it is no wonder that Miss Anthony was wounded to the heart's core, when the men whom she had rendered such invaluable assistance in this cause, coolly advised her to wait for a more convenient season or refused absolutely to assist her, when she implored them to help her secure justice and equality before the law for her own disfranchised sex. Although Miss Anthony was accustomed to the hisses of the mob and the persecution of her enemies, this attitude of her former co-laborers and friends, which literally seemed ingratitude more strong than traitors arms, almost vanquished her.

Though Susan B. Anthony was an ardent advocate and an eloquent champion of an oppressed race, she will be known to future generations principally for the prodigious amount of work she accomplished for the amelioration of the condition of her sex. When she was born near Adams, Massachusetts, in 1820, not a single college or university in the United States admitted women. Miss Anthony was 13 years old, before the initiative was taken by Oberlin, which was the first college in this country, just, broad and benevolent enough to extend a cordial invitation to the Colored-American and to open its doors to women on an equal footing with men. When Susan B. Anthony was young, if a woman by some fortunate chance had acquired a thorough education, it was considered extremely indelicate and decidedly impolitic for her to let the public know she possessed such intellectual attainments. If she did, her chances of getting a husband were exceedingly slim.

Sixty years ago, when the agitation for equal rights began, only one occupation, not menial, was open to women, and the pay received by the woman teacher was very small as compared with the salary paid men. The woman who was strong physically, who enjoyed excellent health, who did not faint at the sight of a mouse or some man who precipitated himself unexpectedly in her presence was considered coarse and unrefined.

Even in so enlightened a state as Massachusetts before 1855 a woman could not hold her own property, either earned or acquired by inheritance. If unmarried, she was obliged to place it in the hands of a trustee, to whose will she was subject. If she contemplated marriage, and desired to call her property her own, she was forced by law to make a contract with her intended husband, by which she gave up all title or claim to it. The common law of Massachusetts held man and wife to be one person, but that person was the husband. By will he could not only deprive her of all his property, but even of the property she herself had owned before her marriage. The husband had the income of his wife's real estate till she died, and if they had a living child, his ownership of the real estate continued to his death. A husband could forbid a wife in Massachusetts to buy a loaf of bread or a pound of sugar or contract for a load of wood to keep the family warm. A wife did not own a rag of her own clothing. Her husband could steal her children, rob her of her clothing and her earnings, neglect to support the family, while she had no legal redress. Not until 1879 was an act passed in Massachusetts which provided that a married woman might own her own clothing to the value of $2,000.

Today much of this injustice to women is recalled only as any other relic of the dark ages is mentioned. Not only in Massachusetts, but in nearly all our states, a married woman can hold her own property, if it is held or bought in her own name and can make a will disposing of it. A married woman can make contracts, carry on business, invest her own earnings for her own use—and she is also responsible for her debts.

Today, thanks to the herculean labor and the heroic sacrifices of Susan B. Anthony and the other noble women who aided her, the best schools, colleges and universities in the country open their doors to women, while in a goodly number of countries across the sea a similar opportunity of cultivating their minds is afforded them. In four States of the Union the elective franchise has been granted to women. In Wyoming, Utah, Colorado and Idaho women go to the polls with their husbands and sons. In addition to the profession of teaching women to preach, practice medicine, plead before the courts as lawyers and engage in nearly as many vocations as do men. In many states the presence of women as members of School Boards, Boards of Visitors to the Penal and Correctional Institutions and other organizations of a similar nature attracts no attention at all and is considered a matter of course. In certain States women still have no legal authority over their children, but there has been a great gain on this point during the last twenty years.

That such a revolution in sentiment concerning the sphere and capacity of women has been wrought, that such golden opportunities for self-culture and usefulness in the world are offered women today is due in large measure to Susan B. Anthony, who for nearly sixty years devoted her life to this work.

It has always been gratifying to me to know that Frederick Douglass was among the first men in this country to advocate equal rights and equal opportunities for women. It was Frederick Douglass who saved from defeat the resolution urging women to secure for themselves the elective franchise which was offered in Seneca Falls, July 1848, where the first woman's rights convention ever called in the United States or in the world, for that matter, was held. Eleven resolutions were presented and all had been unanimously carried except this one to which reference had been made. Frederick Douglass and Mrs. Elizabeth Cady Stanton, realizing that the power to choose rulers and make laws was the right by which all others could be secured, advocated this resolution with such eloquence and logic that it was finally carried by a small majority. When Frederick Douglass himself was disfranchised on account of his race, it is gratifying to reflect that he was not so inconsistent and selfish as to wish to deny to woman the rights and privileges withheld from her simply on account of her sex. For the same arguments advanced against the right of women to participate in the affairs of their government and their respective States are used by those enemies of the Colored American who have robbed him of his right of citizenship in 11 States.

It was my privilege and pleasure to be entertained by Miss Anthony and her sister Mary in their comfortable and interesting home in Rochester, New York, a year ago last December. The time spent under the roof of those great-souled, progressive, hospitable women will always be recalled as red letter days in my life. The two volumes of her own life written by Ida Husted Harper which Miss Anthony presented to my little daughter as a Christmas gift in 1904, and the four volumes of the History of Woman Suffrage which she gave me, each and every one of which contains an inscription written by her own dear hand, together with numerous pamphlets which she sent me from time to time are and will ever remain among the most cherished treasure which I possess.

From the moment Susan B. Anthony was capable of thinking for herself till she entered upon her well-earned rest, her life was one long protest against injustice in all its forms toward any of God's creatures, whether man or woman, black or white. So permeated was she herself with a glowing, all-consuming desire for justice that it is no wonder she was able to kindle the sacred flame in the breast of so many with whom she walked and talked. So long as there lives in the United States a single human being through whose veins flows one drop of African blood, so long will Susan B. Anthony be held in grateful remembrance, so long will her name be loved and revered. Although Miss Anthony worked continually and faithfully to secure justice for every American and actually accomplished much to compass this end, a vast amount of work along this line yet remains to be done. May Miss Anthony's prayer for justice, for which she hungered and thirsted 86 years, but for which, to a certain extent at least, she hungered and thirsted in vain soon be answered all over the world. May Justice, absolute, impartial Justice, without regard to race, color, sex or class soon extend her dominions to the uttermost part of the earth. May the spirit of Susan B. Anthony, who was the incarnation of justice, enter the breast of a mighty host of American women and impel them to battle against injustice as fearlessly and valiantly as did our peerless leader who did not know the meaning of compromise or surrender and scorned the suggestion of defeat. But Susan B. Anthony is gone, that friend of the oppressed that champion of right. To the thorny, tear-wet path her weary feet have trod I would not call her back. To her memory has been erected a monument more precious than marble, more enduring than brass or stone. In the heart of a grateful race, in the heart of the manhood of the world she lives and Susan B. Anthony will never die.

HENRY OSSAWA TANNER

JESSIE REDMON FAUSET was probably born in
1895 into an old-line, middle-class black Philadelphia family. (Although
what it means to be "middle-class" by white standards is quite different
from what "middle-class" status actually is among blacks. According to
recent studies, Fauset grew up with her share of economic hardship.) She
died in New York in 1961. She studied at Cornell University (where she
earned a Phi Beta Kappa key), the University of Pennsylvania, and the
Sorbonne. She became the literary editor of *The Crisis* magazine in
1919, resigning a position as a public school teacher in Washington,
D.C. She was an influential figure in the Renaissance, giving guidance
and encouragement to many of the younger writers. For instance,
Langston Hughes points out that it was she, not W. E. B. Du Bois, who
accepted his early submissions to *The Crisis* and who was supportive in
his early career. Between 1924 and 1933 Fauset wrote four novels. Her
first, *There Is Confusion*, a novel about middle-class educated urban
blacks was lauded by the Renaissance leaders as the sort of novel that best
represented black America. The essay included here on Henry O.
Tanner, a black expatriate painter, was published in *The Crisis* in April
1924.

The presence of the great Artist brought to my mind immediately certain
felicitous phrases. He is tall and slender with grizzled hair and beard and
he is rather given to wearing grey. Wherefore I thought of "the good grey
poet" for the connection was obvious to triteness. But later as I sat there listening
to his gentle, courteous voice and noting his fine unaffected gestures, something
within me kept saying: "The bravest are the tenderest." I was unable to "get" that
at first and then it came to me that a question of superlatives was involved and that

what my sub-conscious was really driving at was some such expression as "The greatest are the simplest."

For Henry Ossawa Tanner is of all the great men who have achieved, undoubtedly the least affected and the least conscious of personal glory. I liked that lack of affectation and understood it. It has always seemed to me to be of the essence of the greatness which is so real that it seeks no extra trappings, no blare of trumpets. It is content to be.

Mr. Tanner did not see his life biographic-wise so I had to prompt with questions—an easy thing for me to do for I am ever eager to know what makes the clock go. He had always wanted to paint, he said, frowning a little with the effort perhaps to remember if anything else ever had meant a great deal to him. And so in the 'eighties after his father had moved from Pittsburgh, Pennsylvania, where the artist was born, he found himself in the Academy of Fine Arts in Philadelphia studying under Thomas Eakins with whom he stayed for four or five years. Here he studied drawing, modelling and painting. I was surprised to learn of the modelling but the making of portrait busts he assured me, has long since been with him a favorite method of artistic expression. In those early days he had done a bust of Bishop Daniel Payne and this field of art still intrigues and engrosses him.

Painting was naturally his forte. He is known internationally now as a painter of religious subjects. But he used to paint landscapes and many marine sketches and of these he had an exhibit at the Academy of Fine Arts even before 1892. The significance of that "even" will be apparent later. He told me drolly that in those years it was difficult to dispose of a picture and that about this time he had sold one to a dealer for fifteen dollars. Two and a half years later the dealer sold the picture to one of his patrons for two hundred and fifty dollars! Instead of lamenting his luck the young artist took this as indicative of his real worth. Five or six years ago Mr. Tanner met the fortunate possessor of that fifteen dollar picture. The man not only had never bought another "Tanner," but he considered that particular one the best of the Artist's works!

It is pleasant to know that a picture painted in Atlantic City—"A Windy Day on the Meadows"—now in the Academy of Fine Arts brought him not long after this one hundred dollars. This startled the Artist's friends and gave him necessary encouragement.

"There is a tide in the affairs of men"—that tide came for Mr. Tanner in 1891. "I had saved a little money," he told me, "and I sailed for Europe the end of December and arrived there in January, 1892." He became a pupil of two masters, Benjamin Constant and Jean-Paul Laurens, who conducted a studio together. This gave the student the advantage of a contrast in temperament and technic, in mood and method, from which he doubtless evolved a third, an individual mode, for himself. M. Constant remained a faithful and devoted friend of Mr. Tanner and indeed played the part of the Mentor of his studio for many years. His was one of the most important and distinguished figures in the Paris artist world, yet, many a morning, Mr. Tanner, gratefully reminiscent, assured me, the great master left his *atelier* to visit with his former pupil.

Paris, toward which the artist had set his face instinctively in 1891, was destined, it turned out, to be his real home. From that time on although for a period of years he made frequent pilgrimages back to the United States, he never was long from his chosen city. And Paris repaid his fealty. He had by now been exhibiting at the *Salon* and in 1897 he received the gold medal for his picture, "The Raising of Lazarus" which was subsequently bought by the French Government. This gave him the final lacking fillip of self-confidence. He began turning out with a surer hand and a truer eye those masterpieces which brought him last year the ultimate distinction of being made by France a member of the Legion of Honor.

In 1898 the "Annunciation" which now hangs in Memorial Hall in Fairmout Park in Philadelphia was added to the Wilstack Collection. Two years later "Nicodemus Coming to Christ" was purchased by the Pennsylvania Academy of Fine Arts and hung there. And Mr. Tanner was awarded the Lippincott Prize. The dawn of a new century was at hand—it seemed to the young artist to presage the dawn of a new era. He married that year in London, Miss Jessie Macaulay, and the couple started their life in Paris. Today their son Jesse Ossawa Tanner is a student in Cambridge University in England.

Recognition of Mr. Tanner's work was now definite and widely spread. He is not a rapid worker; three pictures a year mark his top speed, but when was genius ever prodigal? Because his work has been leisured, its disposition has been certain. His paintings have found homes in this country in the collection of Andrew Carnegie, in the museums of Pittsburgh and in the Art Institute of Chicago. For one of these last the "Two Disciples at the Tomb," Mr. Tanner received the Harris Prize. In 1907 the French Government honored him again and bought his "Disciples at Emmaus" for the Luxembourg.

With all his honors and his interest in his art Mr. Tanner had time to help in the Great War. He worked with the Red Cross in Paris and even as far toward the front as Neufchateau. From the time America entered the war up to the time of the Armistice he was in charge of convalescent camps.

His life holds but three great interests: his wife, his boy and his Art. He and his family live simply in Paris where he has the same studio which was his twenty-five years ago. Their summers are spent at Etaples or rather a brief space away from that "dirty but picturesque town," in a house which the artist has had put up in the forest. It was here that he received word of his greatest honor that of election to the Legion of Honor. Avidly, my eyes fixed on the bit of ribbon in his buttonhole. I asked for details of this.

He was not sure; he could not quite remember! As he recalled it some French friends had strolled over to the house in the forest to tell Mrs. Tanner that they had seen a notice in the *Journal Officiel* to the effect that one "Ash O. Tannaire" (H. O. Tanner) had been awarded the Legion of Honor for his work in art. "It said, 'artiste américain'; we thought it must be your husband." A belated letter in the post-office at Etaples revealed the fact that it was indeed her husband. Vainly I asked how the letter read. But this he could not recall!

On this visit he has spent about twelve weeks in America. Most of his time has been passed in conducting a successful exhibit of his paintings in the Grand Central Palace in New York. America amazes and confuses him. There is too much noise;

too much bustle; too much driving to save time and too little sensible expenditure of the time which has been saved. American colored people—his own people— interest and astound him—"they have made great progress and they are becoming a very attractive-looking folk." But "not for all his faith could see" would he exchange Paris, whither he returns March 22, for New York.

He has a nice chuckling sense of humor, this good, grey, courteous, kindly genius. His father was the eminent Bishop Benjamin Tucker Tanner who died recently, an octogenarian. A man came to the Artist not long ago and said: "I want you to tell me the truth of this story. I understand that years ago your father wanted you to be a minister, but that you replied: 'No, father, you preach from the pulpit and I will preach with my brush.' Now is that true?"

"My answer," said the Artist, "was: 'That's a pretty story—I won't destroy it.' "

It's my business to be curious and when I add my prerogative to my natural endowment! "But did your father want you to be a minister and did you answer him in that way?" I asked him. So he told me the facts of the case.

For the first time in my life I resemble a great artist. I won't destroy a pretty story.

MADAM C. J. WALKER

Pioneer Big Business Woman of America

GEORGE S. SCHUYLER (1895–1977) was a writer very much in the vein of H. L. Mencken. Perhaps that is why Mencken was predisposed to publish him often in the *American Mercury* during the 1920s. Schuyler was noted for his satirical and conservative politics. His books include the novel *Black No More* (1931) and *Black and Conservative: The Autobiography of George S. Schuyler* (1966). This extremely complimentary piece on Madam C. J. Walker appeared in the August 1924 issue of *The Messenger*, a magazine that Schuyler wrote for regularly.

We had been discussing the effect of the unprecedented development of the technological arts on politics, customs, jurisprudence and ethics. It was a strange conversation for the top of a Fifth avenue bus. For a few moments neither spoke as we watched the mass of pedestrians strolling along, window-shopping and chatting, through the brilliantly lighted thoroughfare. The bus crawled slowly and intermittently between the great pinnacles of stone and steel whose countless windows looked down upon the ant-like beings who had erected them. As we approached the lower business section and the crowds thinned out, we returned to the conversation.

"Undoubtedly," Porter began, "the development of the machine industry has worked marvelous changes in society, especially in the attitude toward women and their place in the scheme of things."

"It is very interesting to note how people's attitudes on many things undergo marked changes with a change in environment. What was frowned upon a few years ago is approved of today."

"Yes, you're right, there," I replied. "The old idea about women's place being in the home has gone by the board, and the change in society wrought by the industrial revolution has done the trick. For instance, a large number of women of intelligence are no longer willing to remain in economic servitude to a man when they can take up a trade or profession and be independent. That's one thing we must thank capitalism for. Its frantic search for a larger and cheaper labor supply has made it possible for us to see in the not-too-distant future the complete abolition of probably the oldest form of servitude and property.

"And, like all forms of servitude that the human race has experienced, the slaves acquiesce in their slavery and fight against its abolition. But despite the indifference and hostility of the majority of women to their new economic freedom, the inexorable laws of economic evolution majestically move on, and the old order passeth, whether we wish it or not."

"And I think we should hail its passing," said Porter. "Along with it will gradually pass the 'eternal feminine' of the past. Man and woman will be more nearly equal than ever before in history, with the possible exception of the communistic societies of Neolithic times. With woman on the same economic footing as man, thanks to the spread and intense development of machine production, we can expect to see a complete change of opinion on many things now considered 'human nature.' "

"For many things that folks ascribe to human nature are merely habits; individual habits or tribal customs, to which the environment has given birth. While it is true that man, like the other animals, is born with certain primal urges, i.e., the hunger urge, the sex urge and the urge for safety, nearly all his other activities, his feelings, fears, hatreds, etc., are built in by parents and society. As industrial evolution continues, it brings about changes in social life which in turn affect the family and the child. Hence, much of what we call 'human nature' will undergo a profound change. There are always developed in every society a group capable of seeing the necessity for a broader attitude on things in general."

"Quite true," I agreed, "and a great deal of credit is due that small group of women and men who years ago saw the way things were going and fought for the means by which woman might be able to protect the new economic status we now see her achieving. I refer, of course, to the pioneers of woman suffrage. You doubtless recall that it was Sojourner Truth, a Negro woman, who got up in the second National Woman's Suffrage Convention, in Akron, Ohio, in 1852, and in an eloquent address saved the day for the great idea now embodied in the 19th Amendment."

"Historians relate how the second day of the convention was characterized by very hot discussion indulged in mainly by Baptist, Methodist, Episcopalian, Presbyterian and Universalist ministers. They rose one after another and vehemently argued against the principle of woman suffrage. Some of them claimed that man's intellect was very much superior to woman's; others resurrected the mythical 'sin' of Eve as evidence of woman's unfitness for the ballot. They say that things looked very dark for the cause. The pale, drawn faces of the little battalion of women registered blank dismay. Most of them, due to their earlier training, were too timid to 'speak out in meetings.' The tide seemed to be against them that day and only an oratorical miracle would save their cause. It seemed that there was no woman there who was capable or courageous enough to turn the tide of opinion into favorable channels.

"Then it was that the 'Libyan Sibyl,' the gaunt black Sojourner Truth, who had sat silently in a corner, crouched against the wall listening intently to the vociferous discourses of the learned clergymen, arose slowly from her seat, moved to the front of the building and laid her bonnet at her feet. Mrs. Gage, the presiding officer, eager to grasp at any straw that might turn the tide, announced 'Sojourner Truth,' and pleaded to the house for silence. Every eye was turned upon the giant Negro woman. Her clear and deep tones rang through the great auditorium. To one man who had referred to woman's weakness and helplessness, she said, 'Nobody eber helped me into carriages, or ober mud puddles, or gibs me any best place,' and then she asked in a voice like thunder, 'And a'nt I a woman? Look at me. Look at my arm.' And she bared her powerful arm to the shoulder. 'I have plowed and planted, and gathered into barns, and no man could head me—and a'nt I a woman? I could work as much and eat as much as a man, when I could get it, and bear de lash as well—and a'nt I a woman? I have borne five children and seen 'em mos' all sold off into slavery, and when I cried out with a mother's grief, none but Jesus heard—and a'nt I a woman? Dey talks about dis ting in de head—what dis dey call it?' 'Intellect,' cried some one. 'Dat's it, honey. What's dat got to do wid women's rights or niggers' rights? If my cup wont hold but a pint and yourn holds a quart wouldn't ye be mean not to let me have my little half-measure full?' And she pointed a significant finger at the minister who had made the argument. There was a storm of applause. 'Den dat little man in black dar, he say women can't have as much rights as man 'cause Christ wa'nt a woman. But whar did Christ come from?' The house was as silent as a graveyard. With rising tones she repeated, 'Whar did Christ come from? From God and Woman. Man had nothing to do with Him.' It is written that the applause was deafening. Then she took another objector to task on the question of the 'sin' of Eve. Her 'logic and wit carried the vast assemblage by storm; and she ended by asserting, 'If de fust woman God made was strong enough to turn the world upside down, all alone, dese togedder ought to be able to turn it back and git it right-side up again, and now dey is askin' to do it, de men better let 'em.'

"She returned to her corner amid tremendous roars of applause, leaving the women's eyes filled with tears and their hearts bursting with gratitude. In this way Sojourner Truth went up and down the land turning seeming defeats into victories, and making eloquent pleas for the enslaved Negro and disfranchised woman. It is a thrilling story and, somehow, I can never forego the pleasure of telling it when the occasion presents itself."

"When you stop to think of it," my companion mused, "Negroes have taken a part, and a big part, in beginning everything that ever took place in this country, from its so-called discovery by Columbus, one of whose captains was a Negro, to the great World War. Even more important than the propaganda of feminism was the actual participation of women in modern business, because people are more influenced by example than by precept. Due to the fact that emancipation left most of the Negroes with nothing beside the clothes on their backs, Negro women have always taken a prominent place in business and industry. The difficulties under which the men folk labored left no alternative.

"And, we should remember right at this point," I added, "that probably the pioneer big business woman in the United States was Mme. C. J. Walker. I am speaking of her now as a woman and not as a Negro woman. I know of no other woman, white or black, who, previous to her time, had built up such a large and successful business. There was a woman who starting with absolutely nothing left a great factory, a thriving business in all parts of the world, a beautiful home in Indianapolis, a mansion on 136th street in New York City, and a residence fit for a king at Irvington-on-the-Hudson."

"Surely this is a record to be proud of. I imagine there are any number of women who have been left fortunes by their husbands or other male relatives, and have gone into business, but I doubt if any have started with as little as Madam Walker started with and done so much for her race, her family and herself."

"Of course," said Porter, "I have heard of Mme. Walker and the big business she built up. One couldn't help but know of it. I understand that the company has nearly 20,000 agents, and certainly I have seen some representative of the company everywhere I have ever traveled. I confess, though, that I know little about the woman herself or how she built up her business. I am sure it must be a very interesting story. Tell me something about her, will you?"

"Certainly," I replied. We had reached Washington Square and were passing under the great arch. As this is the end of the line, we decided not to return to Harlem immediately, but to sit in the park and talk for a little while. When we had left the bus and found a bench in a quiet corner of the park, we took up again the thread of our conversation.

"Madam Walker," I began, "was born in the midst of great poverty in the little village of Delta, Louisiana. Her parents, I believe, were Owen and Minerva Breedlove. At the age of seven years she was left an orphan by the death of her parents, under the care of a sister. At the age of fourteen, alone and hopeless, she married in order that she might have a home. This was in Vicksburg, Mississippi. When she was twenty years of age and had one child, a little girl, her husband died and left her on her own resources. She moved from Vicksburg, Mississippi, to St. Louis, Missouri, where she lived for eighteen years. Enduring many hardships, toiling day and night, she reared and educated her daughter.

"In 1905 she discovered her renowned treatment for the hair. She soon decided to make a business of it, after having tried it with excellent results on herself and family. In July, 1905, she left St. Louis for Denver, Colorado, where she began the business of hair treatment. Though beset by many obstacles and difficulties which would have discouraged one of less stamina, she finally succeeded in building up quite a good business in that city, where she remained about a year."

"Where did she go then?" my friend asked.

"Well, she felt that in order to make her business really successful by banishing the scepticism of the public, it would be necessary to travel," I replied. "Many of her friends tried to dissuade her, claiming that she would be unable to make her expenses from one town to another. But she turned a deaf ear to them and with real American determination and grit set out to seek her fortune. It was September 15, 1906, when she started out on this work that was destined to bear so much fruit. For over eighteen months she traveled all over the country, placing her goods on the market. At the end of that time her mail order business had grown to such proportions that she was forced to settle somewhere at least temporarily, in order to take care of it. After devoting some thought to the subject, she selected the city of Pittsburgh, Pennsylvania, for that purpose. After thoroughly establishing the business there, she began traveling again. She left her daughter in charge of the Pittsburgh office. After considerable traveling about, she arrived in Indianapolis, Indiana, on February 10, 1910. She was greatly impressed with the city, its business possibilities and the very cordial welcome extended to her. She decided to make Indianapolis her home."

"How did she make out there?" my companion inquired.

"With her usual keen insight into business possibilities," I proceeded, "she seems to have chosen the ideal place, for she was very successful after locating in Indianapolis. Almost immediately she purchased a home and next door equipped the factory and laboratory of The Madam C. J. Walker Manufacturing Company. This edifice is said to be the most complete of its kind in the United States, which probably means, the world."

"Indeed, she was a most remarkable and accomplished woman," Porter exclaimed.

"Have you ever been to the residence of Mrs. Wilson, her daughter, on 136th street?" I asked.

"Oh! Yes," he replied. "I shall always remember how I was dazzled by the elegance and refinement of the place, interior and exterior. You know there are well equipped parlors in the building also."

"But Madam Walker's home at Irvington-on-the-Hudson," I continued, "is an architectural poem. Do you remember how the great white newspapers all over the country ran feature articles about it when it was completed?"

"Certainly," he assented. "I read many of them myself with great interest. It was interesting to note the editorial comment in the leading papers, such as the *Times*, the *Tribune* and the *World*. But tell me something more about the company. I am rather interested in the development of great businesses, Negro and otherwise." After passing cigars and lighting up, I began again.

"Well, it's a rather long story—a story that will keep one continuously harping on success, for that one word practically tells the history of the company. The very pulse of her enterprise in Indianapolis seemed to be growth, development and expansion. At first the factory, as I neglected to state before, was located in the rear of her beautiful residence at 640 North West street. In less than two years, however, the tremendous growth of trade compelled her to purchase the adjoining space at 644 North West Street for extensions. Now I understand that the company is in search of further accommodations for its rapidly increasing business. In a very short time a very modern mechanically up-to-date factory will be constructed. The business was incorporated in 1911, with Madam C. J. Walker as sole owner, and today the company ranks among the largest business concerns in the United States."

*   *   *

"I suppose there are Walker agents all over the country," my companion stated.

"All over the country!" I exclaimed. "Why man, her goods and representatives are found in every state and every city of any size in the Union. However, I believe the bulk of her business is in the Central, Southern and Southwestern states. But she wasn't content to have the rest of the world in ignorance of her goods. Early in 1913 she visited Panama, Cuba and other places in the West Indies. She soon had such a large foreign trade that it became necessary to maintain a Foreign Department. I have heard on very good authority that the advertising and correspondence is now carried on in four languages—English, French, Spanish and Portuguese."

"The products this company manufactures have meant much to the women of our race. It is fast becoming a rare thing to see a woman who has not a beautiful and well kept head of hair, and much of this new self-pride and personal ambition is born of the proven merit and unquestioned effectiveness of Madam C. J. Walker's preparations.

"In the United States the Negro is in a very peculiar position, as you are well aware. Ostracized, segregated and discriminated against on every hand; taught that he is inferior, and treated that way, it is little wonder that many came to believe it. The feeling that one is the mudsill of humanity is hardly conducive to the growth of pride and personal esteem. What a boon it was, then, for one of their own race to stand upon the pinnacle and exhort the womanhood of her race to come forth, lift up their heads and beautify and improve their looks, even as Woman has done all through the ages. The psychological effect of Madam Walker's great activity has been of great importance and can hardly be over-estimated. Besides giving dignified employment to thousands of women who would otherwise have had to make their living in domestic service, she stimulated a great deal of interest generally in the care of the hair.

"As you know, nearly every part of the body has received more consideration from the medical profession than the human scalp. This is probably due to the fact that the disease of the scalp seldom prove fatal and have been considered to an extent unavoidable, therefore, to be borne with patience and resignation.

"The most important part of the hair is the follicle, from which the hair grows. Into this follicle are emptied the secretions of the sebaceous glands, which give the hair its oily nourishment and lustre. Each follicle has its blood and nerve supply for the growth of hair, and, of course, where the follicle has been destroyed no hair can be made to grow, but where the follicle exists, though it may be diseased, it is possible to get it in a healthy condition and not only make the hair grow, but restore it.

"The scaly condition of the scalp interferes with the nourishment of the hair follicles through the sebaceous glands and the result is that the hair is poorly nourished, becomes dry and brittle and the inevitable result is that the hair falls out or breaks off.

"You cannot expect hair to grow and be healthy on a scalp that is unclean—a scalp covered with a parasite growth like dandruff. You wouldn't expect the flowers in your garden to grow fast and bloom profusely if choked by weeds, which also would sap the soil's nutrition to the detriment of the flowers. Thick, healthy hair can grow only on a scalp that is free from dandruff and scalp diseases.

"Flakes of scurf, or outer skin of the body refuse from the oil glands of the scalp; and the accumulation of dirt and waste matter thrown off by the skin—these constitute dandruff, the greatest enemy of thick, healthy hair.

"Dandruff is simply sebaceous matter, which dries into flakes, each flake full of microbic growth, and carrying with it the deadly, hair-destroying principle. Dandruff is therefore contagious. When once introduced into the hair, it is followed by itching of the scalp, falling hair and baldness.

"In treating dandruff and scalp diseases, liquids many times are failures, because they do not possess the deep penetrating powers, nor do they contain sufficient of the necessary ingredients to successfully combat this disease. Scientists admit that dandruff is a germ disease. Isn't it plain, then, that to effect a cure, one must destroy the cause?

"Madam Walker was an expert in all matters dealing with the scalp and the hair. Her wonderful hair preparations and scientific scalp treatment are directly opposed to harmful germ life—they attack only diseased tissues and tend to keep a scalp free from dandruff, scales and other waste matter—clean and sweet—a condition that is an absolute necessity to a beautiful head of hair.

"The System developed by Madam C. J. Walker for the treatment of hair and the culture of beauty is based wholly on scientific rules of hygiene, and if practiced as outlined and as the agents of the Walker company are taught, it will prove beneficial and in no wise harmful.

"Many people have referred to Madam Walker's representatives as 'hair straighteners.' This, however, is a grave error. They are not 'hair straighteners,' but hair culturists and scalp specialists. Madam Walker's system of growing hair is conducive to a natural growth and consists of dressing the hair to bring out its fine natural texture. A strand of hair, as you may know, is round like a cylinder. To straighten this round strand of hair by the use of tongs, hot pullers, etc., is like placing your finger in a hot blacksmith's vise and screwing it up tightly. It is lengthened, true enough, and will lie flat, but it is lifeless and its pores are stopped, and instead of growing, it breaks off and is left short, brittle and discolored. Madam C. J. Walker's treatment promotes the growth and softens the most short and stubborn kinds of hair and restores to health the most badly diseased scalps. To have given the world this great discovery is by no means a small achievement."

"Such a large business should surely open up great opportunities for young colored men and women." Porter exclaimed. "One thing that makes the development of Negro business very important from the viewpoint of racial advancement is the opportunity afforded the young men and women of the race, who possess the training and qualifications, to hold important positions that they would otherwise have great difficulty in obtaining in large firms owned and operated by white people. In this respect the Negro business man and woman have been a decided asset to the race. For after all, we must admit that economic advancement is the foundation upon which all other advancement is erected. Unless the foundation is sound, it cannot be expected that the structure will be sound. In the early flush of emancipation, and even at the present time, there is a large group within our group who have laid more emphasis on acquiring the evidences of wealth and leisure than on acquiring the solid economic basis that the possession of these things presupposes.

Too many of us are yet satisfied to have 'a five dollar hat on a fifty cent head,' as Booker T. Washington put it."

"Too many of us are striving to get an automobile before we get a home; to spend in one night what it takes us a week or more to earn; too many of us fail to heed the old adage that, 'a bird in the hand is worth two in the bush.' "

"That's true," I assented. "Undoubtedly Madam Walker did much, and her company is doing much, to give employment to many who would otherwise be in domestic service. In the offices of the company in Indianapolis, scores of Negroes are working with the most modern office equipment as bookkeepers, stenographers and shipping clerks. They have a forelady in the factory, and they have an attorney regularly employed to look after the legal side of their affairs. Then, of course, they have several representatives on the road at all times, and a large advertising department. Mrs. Leila Walker-Wilson, her daughter, has succeeded Madam Walker as president of the company, as you doubtless are aware. You remember my saying that her daughter took over the business in Pittsburgh, Pennsylvania when Madam Walker undertook the Indianapolis establishment? Well, Mrs. Wilson proved her true worth in business tact and skill by carrying out the plans of her resourceful mother. Hence, she was prepared to handle the business when the call came for her to do so. So Madam Walker's policies have been continued as she wished.

"When Mrs. Wilson succeeded her mother as President of the Madam C. J. Walker Manufacturing Company, and assumed the duties of her office, she immediately stated that she had no new policies to outline, but would simply carry out her mother's wishes in connection with the operation of the business."

"In more ways than one was she a remarkable woman, for I suppose you know that in her youth she lacked all the opportunities for mental training other than the hard school of experience. She was a self-educated woman. She not only created, developed and perfected one of the largest enterprises of its kind in the United States, but she determined to educate herself. She read everything in sight, including the Bible, which she called her main guide. But she was not contented with this alone. She employed a tutor and after business was over she could be found until the small hours of the morning studiously perusing her books. As she advanced she provided herself with the masterpieces of literature. As her business grew she made up her mind to develop with it. To that end she took commercial and business courses until she was well informed on all phases of business procedure. Those who knew Madam Walker intimately watched her unfolding with great interest. They saw the pupil outstrip the teacher and in Madam Walker they found a character who laughed at obstacles. Though often discouraged, she persevered. Apparently baffled time and time again, by sheer will power she forced herself back into the fight. Undoubtedly history will record her as one of the great women of her time without regard to race or color. For it cannot be denied that she was the pioneer big business woman in the United States. There may have been others who were left with fortunes on their hands by husbands or relatives, but I doubt if there is an earlier case of a woman building up such a big business from absolutely nothing at all."

"What do you think of the esthetic value of her work?" Porter asked as he blew ringlets of smoke into the air.

"That was something I was just going to touch upon," I replied. "Considering the previous position of the Negro in American life and the psychology that he had developed, it was a great service to the race to be able to show them how they—the despised black people—could make themselves more comely and more attractive. It can hardly be gainsaid that the improvement in the appearance of Negro women has been very marked. And the more attractive the women, the higher the men's opinion of them, or at least it seems that way to me. For, after all is said and done, it must be admitted that people bow to beauty first and then to brains."

"I have heard a great deal of Madam Walker's benevolence, too," my friend stated. "I suppose she has given away large sums to various charities?"

"Yes," I continued, "Madam Walker, while best known by her wonderful hair preparations, is also widely and equally well known because of her sterling Christian character. There is no greater evidence of this than her many donations and contributions to charity and to many charitable institutions. Much has been said about Madam Walker being the first to donate so largely to the Colored Y.M.C.A. of Indianapolis, Indiana. In this connection, I think her well-meaning friends did her an injustice in over-emphasizing the gift as a mere gift. The real greatness of the act rested in the fact that Madam Walker was the first of her race to give so largely, and the further fact that such an unselfish act on her part had a most wholesome and wonderful effect on others. It induced many to give who otherwise would not have given at all, certainly not as generously as they subsequently did. It served not only to encourage others, but aroused them to a high and true sense of duty. In this respect Madam Walker blazed the trail, and has no peer among the members of her race. She set an example not only to be praised and commended, but should and evidently will, be emulated by others who are in a position to help the race and racial enterprises.

"Madam Walker's donations to charity were many and varied, and of the many, none perhaps show the real heart of the woman as her annual donation of fifty Christmas baskets to the poor families of Indianapolis. These people Madam Walker did not know; many of them she never met and never expected to meet, but she arranged that this be made an annual affair. I can imagine that many earnest prayers went up for her from the homes that she made bright by providing them with well-filled baskets on Christmas morning. Aside from the annual donations to Old Folks' Home and Orphans' Home of Indianapolis, St. Louis and other cities, Madam Walker donates largely, through her will, to the temperance cause, and gives fifty dollars annually for the current expenses of the Young Women's Christian Association and the Young Men's Christian Association of Indianapolis, as well as contributes one hundred dollars a year to the International Y.M.C.A. work. By her will she proved her great interest in and love for her people in the most striking way. Under her will one-third of the net proceeds of her business goes to her daughter, Lelia Walker-Wilson, and two-thirds to worthy race charities, 'such as I have always been interested in.' That means the Y.M.C.A., the Y.W.C.A., Orphans' Home, Old Folks' Home, missionary societies and scholarships. Such provisions do not apply to any one state, but to any of such organizations that are deemed worthy wherever located."

"Why," exclaimed my companion, "that means that the business is practically conducted for philanthropic purposes!"

"Exactly," I agreed. "It means that for all time to come two-thirds of the net proceeds of this vast business enterprise will go to help individuals and worthy race institutions. To carry this out the will provided that five trustees have charge of this fund, three of whom are named in the will and two are appointed by the Judge of the Probate Court, the will specifying that all must be members of the Negro race. These trustees are under bond to carry out the terms of the will. All the charities I have enumerated are to be kept up by the terms of the will. Thus, Madam Walker, though dead, still lives, lives through her will, and for all time to come extends a helping hand to struggling Negro students and worthy race institutions. She was thoroughly a race woman and her every thought seemed to be as to how best she could advance her race. This is evidenced by the setting aside of a certain percentage of her annual income for the establishment and maintenance of an Industrial Missionary School on the continent of Africa, and the many scholarships that she now maintains at Tuskegee and other institutions.

"Two or three years ago, Mrs. Lelia Walker-Wilson made an extended tour of Europe, Africa and the Holy Lands. While there, she thought of what a boon it would be if some of the Negro clergymen from the United States could have an opportunity to see the things she was seeing: Jerusalem, Bethlehem, the Dead Sea, and all the landmarks of Biblical history. No sooner had she returned to the United States than the company announced a great contest which would enable the most popular ministers to enjoy a trip to that far country at the expense of the company. The idea caught like wildfire and all over the land loyal congregations are working very hard to win the trip for their respective clergymen."

"I think that very commendable," my friend enthusiastically exclaimed.

"Yes, it shows a great breadth of vision," I replied. "So far as I have been able to ascertain, no other firm, white or black, ever thought up a project of more educational and inspirational value. In addition to this, the Walker Company is offering each year a grand total of nearly $2,000 to its army of agents throughout the country. These agents have clubs in all of the cities and towns and carry on the spirit of Madam C. J. Walker by engaging in all sorts of charitable work. To the club reporting the largest amount of benevolent work done during the year, a prize of $100 is given. There are second and third prizes of $75 and $50 respectively. As a matter of fact, this firm is doing so much for the betterment of the race that it has really become an American institution."

For some time we sat in silence, watching the speeding lights of automobiles and the passing throngs. After a while we boarded a Harlem bus and were soon rolling up the avenue toward the great colored settlement. Finally my friend began speaking again.

"Yes, women are undoubtedly taking a more and more prominent place in the economic life of the nation. As we were saying before, the development of industry is forcing them to do so. That small minority of men who are still wont to claim superiority over the female, should know more about such pioneers as Madam

C. J. Walker, the great business she built up, and the excellent philanthropic work she did, and now carries on through her will."

"It is an inspiration," I added, "not only to Negro youth, but to all youth. Anyone who can in a few short years amass a fortune, build a great business, benefit the needy and afford great opportunities to the struggling of an oppressed race, has indeed achieved greatness."

Soon we had reached our destination. Bidding Porter adieu, I ran up the steps, admitted myself, and in a few moments was sitting in my favorite arm chair, preparing for an hour's communion with my pipe and books. Reaching under the reading table among a mass of magazines and periodicals, I picked out the "1924 Year Book and Almanac, published by The Madam C. J. Walker Mfg., Co. (Incorporated)." Glancing through this booklet I was amazed at the amount of information contained therein.

This "Year Book" is excellently printed on fine coated paper, is profusely illustrated and contains much worth while matter of interest to those interested in hair culture, and also information of racial interest. Those who are curious to know the reasons for the unprecedented success of the Madam C. J. Walker Mfg. Co., may find them on page 6:

WHY THIS COMPANY SUCCEEDED

Because this Company was founded and is operated on the principle of an unselfish service to humanity and a full measure of both quality and quantity, it has succeeded. With faith in its products and because:

We actually believe that our goods are the best on the market for hair growing—

First—They bring results.

Second—They have given satisfaction to every one who has used them properly.

Third—They cured scalps when they were in a most frightful condition.

Fourth—They are continually doing the same for others without a single complaint.

Fifth—Many persons had hair less than a finger's length when they began using it.

Sixth—Their hair grew sixteen inches in less than three years that they used it.

Seventh—They have improved the condition of scalps of persons who have used it and whose hair was short and stubby all their lives.

Eighth—They are positively the only remedies on the market that do not record a single failure to do all that they are recommended to do."

I was more impressed by Madam Walker's motto:

THE SECRET OF A HAPPY LIFE

Lord help me live from day to day
In such a self-forgetful way

That when I kneel to pray
My prayer shall be for—OTHERS.

Help me in all the work I do
To ever be sincere and true
And know that all I'd do for You.
Must needs be done for—OTHERS.

Embodied in these two verses is a philosophy which might well be learned by all.

It was several days before I saw Porter again. We were both dining in one of the popular restaurants of the Negro metropolis. Charming brown waitresses were hurrying to and fro serving the crowd of diners. Even before one entered the delicious odor of well-prepared food was borne through the doors and windows by the gusts from the whirring electric fans.

"Well, how's everything today?" I asked as I sank into the chair opposite my friend and gave a nod of recognition to the approaching waitress.

"Fine and dandy," he replied. "By the way, I understand that the Walker agents of the entire country are to hold a convention here in New York in August. It seems that it is an annual affair."

"Last year," I informed him, "the convention was held in Detroit and was a great success. Agents were present representing the Walker Clubs of the entire country. It lasted for three days. I suppose you know that one of Madam Walker's greatest hobbies was the assistance, education and development of her numerous agents throughout the United States, the West Indies, Central and South America. She managed this by having the agents in every community where there were five or more band themselves together into a Madam Walker Club. In a short time, a sort of women's business league was formed in that way. In each community these women would come together and talk over ways and means of transacting, increasing and generally developing their business. But of course their activities are not solely confined to distinctly business matters. They engage in all sorts of charitable and social welfare work in every city and town—Christmas baskets, summer outings for poor children, assistance of needy families and persons, and in many other ways too numerous to mention. Through these clubs Madam Walker has perpetuated her great spirit of benevolence in every section of the world."

"I suppose there must be a large number of them by this time," Porter ventured as he adjusted his napkin.

"Yes, a very large number," I replied. "Over a hundred, I have heard. Each year every club sends a representative to the National Convention of Madam C. J. Walker Agents. In reality this is the first big economic conference of people in the same profession ever founded by a Negro woman. Here earnest, intelligent women from all parts of the world meet annually and thoroughly discuss plans of how best to continue the Madam C. J. Walker business and to best serve the increasing patronage. As an added incentive to their agents, the company awards many annual prizes to individual agents and to clubs. For instance, the agent making the largest number of agents over '15' above the Mason-Dixon Line is awarded a prize of $50, the second prize being $25; the successful agents below the Mason-Dixon Line are awarded similar prizes.

The clubs selling the largest amount of goods above the Mason-Dixon Line and below it as well, are awarded first prizes of $100; second prizes of $50; and third prizes of $25. Then there are prizes for the agents in the North and South selling the largest amount of goods; the club reporting the largest amount of benevolent work; the agents above and below the Mason-Dixon Line selling the largest amount of toilet preparations over $50; the club selling the largest amount of toilet preparations over $50. These prizes are awarded on the last day of the big annual convention."

"There must be a great deal of good-natured rivalry for these generous awards," my friend stated as the waitress placed the steaming soup before us.

"You bet there is," I assented, "and it just shows what a business genius Madam Walker proved herself to be. It is generally recognized in all organizations— commercial, religious, military and political, that their success or failure depends upon the amount of interest manifested by the rank and file. Some call it *morale*, others call it *esprit de corps*. At any rate, Madam Walker was well enough versed in organization and its secrets to know how to obtain and retain that interest from her agents that is absolutely essential to the success of any great business enterprise, or any other enterprise for that matter. That her policy of developing and organizing local organizations of her agents in every community was sound, is evidenced by the increasing business of the Madam C. J. Walker Company and the great interest shown by all Negroes in the big annual conventions of the Walker agents."

"I suppose you have read a great deal in the Negro press about the ten greatest Negroes America has produced?" my friend queried. "Well," he continued, as I nodded in assent, "you undoubtedly noticed that Madam Walker was one of the first mentioned."

"She certainly was," I answered, "and rightly so, for there are few men or women in America who stand as high on the ladder of achievement and service to her group. She will always be an inspiration to the ambitious, striving and energetic youth of the race in their struggle toward the pinnacle of success." For some time we ate in silence, glancing around at the smartly dressed people who shared the room with us. Finally, as we were stirring our coffee, Porter spoke again.

"Undoubtedly you have noticed," he began, "that pioneers are always conspicuous by their absence. Most people are followers. About one person in every million or so is a great pioneer, a great inventor, a great leader. It seems to me that Madam Walker was all of these. I have traveled all over the United States and wherever I have gone I have heard both white and colored people speak enthusiastically of Madam Walker and her work; her great value to the race economically, socially and culturally."

"Yes," I added, as we strolled out to the avenue, "and why shouldn't they? Was she not one of the greatest figures of her time? Is she not one of the great examples of those American qualities of thrift, perseverance, business acumen, and benevolence?"

"Quite true," he agreed. "And, as I was saying the other night Madam Walker was one of the first American women to demonstrate what women can accomplish in the economic field. She was the herald of a new social order in which women will be independent and the oldest form of property will vanish forever."

VII

PORTRAITS,
VOLUME 2

BOY MEETS KING
(LOUIS ARMSTRONG)

REX STEWART (1907–1967) was a jazz trumpeter who played with both Duke Ellington and Fletcher Henderson. He was also one of the few musicians who could write well about music. His *Jazz Masters of the 30s* (originally published in 1972) was a collection of vivid and well-crafted essays about Stewart's meetings with remarkable jazz men. "Boy Meets King (Louis Armstrong)" is a mid-1960s essay taken from the *Jazz Masters* book.

Satchmo's time and place in the history of music is firmly etched, chronicled, and, thanks to the phonograph recordings, entirely documented. Future students and researchers will certainly benefit from this fortunate circumstance. Consider how much of the other early jazzmen's influences have been lost, because of the sublime unawareness of the sociological impact of this music and its early creators. But happily, Joe Oliver recorded the first true ragtime ensembles for Gennett—at least, he was the first one I ever heard.

In those early days of jazz, the real shape and substance of what was to be in music came from people such as Ford Dabney and William Grant Still in New York (they wrote the first ragtime arrangements back in 1910), from Doc Cook in Chicago, and from Joe (King) Oliver. These men, plus Dave Peyton and Erskine Tate in Chicago, helped comprise an atmosphere and proving ground for Louis Armstrong. There in Chicago, away from the catch-as-catch-can climate of New Orleans, putting himself past the rough-and-ready musical chaos of the river, Louis came to maturity. He added his magic to the pastel of progress in music with his horn when he left New Orleans in 1922 to join Oliver's Creole Jazz Band.

During the period when Joe Oliver was around New York, which was after his Chicago days, I got to know him through his nephew, Dave Nelson. Joe's best playing days were over, but he recounted many tales of how he and "Dipper" (Louis) upset everybody when they played together. But Papa Joe's days of glory were fading while Louis's star was ascending.

Every record Louis made was a winner. On his personal appearances, he'd cream the crowd by hitting 100 high Cs as the band counted them one by one. Then, the new King would top this effort with a high F. Often King Oliver would be in the audience, rooting for his pupil, along with everybody else. There was no jealousy despite the ironic turn of events. Fate had denied Oliver's sharing in the great acclaim.

I remember Joe's telling me how sorry he was that New York did not hear them together. I asked him why they had preferred Chicago, and he told me there had been two good reasons, both of them spelled "syndicate." No booker wanted to incur the ill will of the Chicago syndicate that operated the club (Lincoln Gardens) where they played. Even if a booker dared attempt a New York deal, there was no place in New York where they could play. Later, Louis got so good that more and more offers came his way. Joe reluctantly bade Satchmo Godspeed, and the greatest team the world of jazz was ever to know was no longer.

When Satchmo left Chicago in 1924 to join Fletcher Henderson's band in New York, there was quite a bit of old New Orleans still clinging to him. His was not the fictional, courtly, genteel New Orleans of moonlit nights tinged with romance and honeysuckle. What he carried with him was the aroma of red beans and rice, with more than a hint of voodoo and "gris-gris." He conveyed this to the world by the insouciant challenge of his loping walk, the cap on his head tilted at an angle, which back home meant: "Look out! I'm a bad cat—don't mess with me!" These, plus the box-back coat and the high-top shoes, all added to young Louis's facade in those days.

However, when Louis returned to his Chicago south-side stomping grounds in 1925, the youngster had changed into a worldly man, a sophisticated creator of music that people looked up to. He had arrived, and a world was waiting for the king of the trumpet. The climate for his homecoming couldn't have been better, owing to the south-side theaters' emulating Paul Ash's successful band shows in the Loop.

Louis started drawing huge crowds that came just to be sent by his horn, whether he was playing with the theater bands of Dave Peyton or Erskine Tate, both of whom vied for his talent. They competed so vigorously that sometimes he would appear with both of them on the same night. The movie or the stage show took second place to Satch's specialty act in the overture.

Louis was quite an eater in those days, and for many years he carried a lot of weight, but he burned up a lot of that food in his musical exertions. Louis really had, and still has, great physical stamina, doubtless because of his love of sports during his formative years. Buster Bailey, the elegant delineator of the clarinet, used to tell about the fun around Chicago in the early twenties. Summers were spent at the beach with Darnell Howard, Guy Kelly, Johnny Dodds, and others cavorting like porpoises in Lake Michigan. Louis outswam almost everybody, doing at least a mile a day. This sort of training paid off later, as endurance and breath control enhanced his imaginative talents in scaling the ultimate heights of his instrument.

Our mutual friend, Luis Russell, told this one on Satchmo, which happened during those Chicago days. He and Louis were invited to dinner, and the hostess went all out preparing a sumptuous banquet for her distinguished guests. Russell said they sat down to a huge table loaded with roast beef, fried chicken, mixed greens, mashed potatoes, red beans, and corn on the cob—this feast was topped off with peach cobbler and ice cream. The guys paid proper tribute and ate and ate, while the hostess glanced from one to the other in pride at their appreciation. Finally, there was nothing left but the chicken bones. The woman said, "My, it sure is nice to have somebody enjoy my cooking like you boys did." Then Louis said, "I know what you mean, but if you *only* had some rice to go with those red beans, I could start all over again!"

Although it has been forty years since I first met Ol' Dipper, as he was nicknamed then, I don't feel that I really know Daniel L. Armstrong. Somehow, I suspect that most of his disciples are no closer than I am to knowing this solid cornerstone of American jazz who is largely responsible for the shape and structure of this art form. Nevertheless, Louis remains an enigma even to his close friends, presenting an ever-changing kaleidoscope-montage of moods.

Sometimes he is gregarious, extroverted, loyal, and considerate. He is the sort of person who buys a youngster a trumpet, or pays the rent for some unfortunate. These things he never speaks of. Then again, he sometimes behaves as if there were some compulsion to prove he is the same as the rest of us, excepting for his great talent. Then there are the times that he presents a withdrawn, glum attitude like a smoldering volcano primed to erupt at any moment; however, this phase is always temporary, and the sunshine inevitably beams in Satch's smile.

Before his audiences, he is always the lovable, mugging, blowing-up-a-storm Louis the Great. His feet may be killing him or that famed Swiss Kriss acting up, but all that he shows to his public is a handkerchief-waving, eye-poping *Hello, Dolly* type of communication—to the delight of most. Many a time I have sat in an audience, transfixed by the imagination, stamina, and, above all, the innate sense of timing Louis possesses in such superlative abundance. He can take one note and swing you into bad health on that same note. His rhythmic concept is *that* profound.

Despite these obvious attributes, there are those who do not understand or appreciate the master. These, of course, are far outnumbered by the legions who feel that Satch may well be the present-day personification of Moses whom they would gladly follow to the promised land of jazz.

How regrettable it is that, despite the current recognition and acclaim, simultaneously his name and great efforts are anathema to many. Some of the musicians who have succumbed to the siren song of contemporary commercialism project the belief that anything old is of no value. Others consciously resent Louis's antebellum Uncle Tomism. The youngsters object to his ever-present grin, which they interpret as Tomming. This I feel is a misunderstanding. No matter where Louis had been brought up, his natural ebullience and warmth would have emerged just as creative and strong. This is not to say that even today, in an unguarded moment, a trace of the old environment, a fleeting lapse into the jargon of his youth will make some people cringe with embarrassment.

There is justification for both sides of opinion on Louis today. I would not presume to pass judgment. However, I will say that I do feel grateful to have existed in the same musical environment as the King.

This exposure started at the old Savoy Ballroom in New York City. I was playing with a now long-forgotten band, Leon Abby's Savoy Bluesicians. Louis was then with Henderson's outfit, and it was making one of its rare Harlem appearances.

Our trumpet section consisted of Demas Dean on first trumpet, myself, and another man whose name I've forgotten. We decided that the only proper way to enjoy Armstrong was to help the mood along with liquid refreshments. So we all filled Coca-Cola bottles with our favorite beverage. I chose gin, which was a mistake, because the combination of Louis's artistry and that gin caused me to be put out of the ballroom in the middle of the dance. This was a most humiliating climax to an eventful evening. For some reason, I was bounced out of the joint merely for showing my appreciation of Louis's high notes! Every time he'd end on a soaring F, I tossed a Coke bottle, and you couldn't even hear the crash over the applause. But the bouncers didn't understand.

While most of the musicians drank a good deal, Armstrong never was a fellow for hanging out in the bars much. In New York, on any given night, you could run into almost anybody who considered himself a real blower in Big John's or the Mimo Club when Bojangles ran it. But not Louis.

So I was pleasantly surprised one night when I fell into the Brittwood Bar, which was near the Savoy Ballroom, and I saw Satch sitting there. By this time, we knew each other on sight. I called him Pops and he called me Boy. He still calls me Boy, and I don't remember his ever calling me by name. But that night at the Brittwood, I had had enough whiskey to make me sleepy. I went to a rear table, sat down, and promptly fell asleep. The next thing I knew, I heard a gravel voice saying, "Boy, get up and get you some Pluto water. Yeah, Pluto water, that's what you need. You should be 'shamed of yourself, young as you are drinking all of that whiskey. I'm gonna tell you something. If you don't quit acting the fool with that juice, they gonna be giving you flowers, and you won't even smell 'em." Then Louis laughed and left. There was a hint of a sequel, though, because for the next few years, whenever our paths crossed, he'd say "hi, Pluto" as he passed.

From the time Louis catapulted onto the New York scene, everybody and his brother tried to play like him, with the possible exception of Johnny Dunn and Bubber Miley. Now, with the passing years, Satch's impact has diminished to the point where no one consciously tries to sound like him, but at the same time, almost every player in the throes of improvisation plays something that can be traced to Louis Armstrong.

Louis was the musician's musician. I was only one of his ardent admirers. I tried to walk like him, talk like him. I bought shoes and a suit like the Great One wore. I remember a time that a few of us—Ward Pinkett, Gus Akins, and a couple of others—thought it would be a good idea to stand under Louis's window and serenade him. This occurred to us in the wee hours after we had emerged from a bar. We had just got started when the cop on the beat discouraged us by saying, "Get the hell off the streets before I run ya in."

There were so many fellows showering Satchmo with unblushing adulation that I didn't think he knew me from the rest of the young trumpet players. One night, when I was playing with Elmer Snowden at the Nest Club, I was startled to spot Louis, Buster Bailey, and Big Green in the crowd. (Bailey and trombonist Green also were in Henderson's band.) Snowden had spotted them first and called a tune on which I was supposed to solo as long as I wanted to, set my own tempo, and show off. I must have played pretty well, because Louis and other fellows in Henderson's band took to dropping in from time to time. Since I was partly responsible for their attendance, I was really set up.

But the really big moment of my life came a month or so later. One evening at the Nest Club, an attendant came to the stand and said there was a phone call for me. I wondered who could be calling me on the job. I couldn't believe it when a voice said, "I've got a job for you, Boy." I thought I recognized the gravel voice but wasn't sure if maybe it wasn't a gag, so I played along. I think I answered, "Yeah? Where is this job?" The guy laughed and said, "This is Louis, and I want you to take my place with Smack. I'm going back to Chicago." It really was Louis, and the offer was for real! I took the job with Fletcher, but my heart wasn't in it. The horn wasn't born that could follow the King—and I still feel that way.

A few years after the Coke-bottle episode, Louis played the Savoy again. I wanted to hear him but had been barred from the premises because of my misbehavior. So I pulled my coat collar up to cover my face, bought a ticket, and slunk past Big George the doorman, determined to conduct myself like a gentleman this time.

Besides Louis with one band, Benny Carter was also leading a group, his first big band. I stood off to the side of the stand, trying not to be noticed by the floorwalker. All went well, and I was thoroughly enjoying Louis. Unfortunately, when his set ended, Benny spied me and beckoned me to come up on the stand. I shook my head no, meaning: "No, I'm not here." Benny would not take no for an answer, however, and before I knew it, I was on the stand playing *Tiger Rag*. To this day, I don't know why, but I received a very good hand from the crowd. Instead of being elated, I tried to get off the stand and become part of the woodwork again, but Benny struck up *Tiger Rag* again, and this time the crowd gave me a big hand. I wasn't put out, but I couldn't enjoy the rest of the evening; I expected every moment to be given the bum's rush.

A few days later, I ran into Louis on the street and went over to say hello, but he only grunted and walked away. We weren't tight like that anymore for several years, and I found out subsequently from Zutty Singleton that Louis thought that I had tried to cut him! Honestly, Louis, I have never tried to. As far as I am concerned, you are the Boss and always will be.

Jabbo Smith obviously didn't share my feelings, and as a matter of fact, Jabbo tried on several occasions to prove he was better on trumpet than King Louis. He was never able to convince any of the other musicians, but he certainly tried hard.

One such occasion comes to mind. It was an Easter Monday morning breakfast dance at Rockland Palace, Harlem's biggest dancehall. Jabbo was starring in Charlie Johnson's band from Small's Paradise, but Don Redman's band, featuring Satch, from Connie's Inn was the top attraction. It was a beautiful sight—no flower garden could compete with the beauty of the gals' bonnets. There was also intense factionalism in the air, because no one from Charleston, South Carolina, would concede Armstrong's superiority over their hometown boy, Jabbo. We musicians tried to tell the Charlestonians that while Jabbo was great, Louis was King. We needn't have bothered. For weeks before the dance, arguments raged, bets were made, and, finally, the great moment came.

I rushed up from Roseland, as soon as the last note was played, intending to get a front-row view of the battle. But when I entered the hall, I found that more than a hundred musicians had beaten me to any choice spot, so I pulled out my horn and got on the stand with Charlie's band. Nobody said anything, which figured, because I always sat in with anybody around town in those days.

Jabbo was standing out in front, and I'll say this, he was *blowing*—really coming on like the angel Gabriel himself. Every time he'd fan that brass derby on a high F or G, Altis, his buddy from Small's, would yell, "Play it, Jabbo! Go ahead, Rice!" (Everybody from Charleston called each other Rice. It was the hometown nickname.) "Who needs Louis?" he yelled, "You can blow him down anytime." Although there were only about a hundred or so of the South Carolina contingent in the crowd of some 2,000, these people created a real uproar for their idol. When Johnson's set ended with Jabbo soaring above the rhythm and the crowd noise, everybody gave them a big hand. I could tell from the broad grin on Jabbo's face that he felt that once and for all he'd shown Satch who was king.

Then, all of a sudden, the shouts and applause died down as Louis bounced onto the opposite stage, immaculate in a white suit. Somehow, the way the lights reflected off his trumpet made the instrument look like anything but a horn. It looked as if he were holding a wand of rainbows or a cluster of sunlight, something from out of this world. I found out later that I was not the only one who had the strong impression of something verging on the mystical in Louis's entrance. I can still see the scene in my mind's eye. I've forgotten the tune, but I'll never forget his first note. He blew a searing, soaring, altissimo, fantastic high note and held it long enough for every one of us musicians to gasp. Benny Carter, who has perfect pitch, said, "Damn! That's high F!" Just about that time, Louis went into a series of cadenzas and continued into his first number.

Since everyone is not a trumpet player and cannot know how the range of the instrument has grown over the years, I should explain how significant a high F was. Back in the twenties, the acceptable high-note range for the trumpet was high C and to hit or play over C made the player exceptional. That is until Louis came along with his strong chops, ending choruses on F. We guys strained might and main to emulate him but missed most of the time. That is why we were so flabbergasted at Satchmo's first note. Lots of guys ruined their lips and their career trying to play like Satchmo.

Louis never let up that night, and it seemed that each climax topped its predecessor. Every time he'd take a break, the applause was thunderous, and swarms of women kept rushing the stand for his autograph. They handed him everything from programs to whiskey bottles to put his signature on. One woman even took off her pants and pleaded with him to sign them!

Years ago, Erskine Tate told me this story about the time Louis was doing a satire on something called *The Preaching Blues*. He was wearing a frock coat and battered top hat, singing a kind of ring-chant tune with Louis making calls like a Baptist preacher, while the audience made the responses. Eventually one sister became confused as the mood grew more and more frantic, and her voice could be heard above the crowd. She was easily spotted because when the number ended, she rushed down the aisle shouting, "Don't stop, Brother Louis, don't stop." The audience in the theater broke up.

Louis has retained over the years his direct, uncluttered approach to his music, preferring to surround himself with competent people rather than easing the burden by choosing dynamic personalities or instrumentalists who would be able to give him the relief he has earned. The King still carries the ball.

This, of course, is a recent development, as the original Louis Armstrong All-Stars were just what the name implied. That was the group that at one time boasted Jack Teagarden, Barney Bigard, Earl Hines, Big Sid Catlett, and a phenomenal young star on bass, Arvell Shaw. It turned out to be a wise move on the part of whoever made the decision when Satch shed the overwhelmingly ponderous big band of the thirties and early forties and returned in 1947 to the Hot Five concept with which he began. He regained the winning element of spontaneous freewheeling, a proper framework for his talents. Armstrong's big-band efforts were, as a whole, constricting him, reminding some observers of a champion race horse pulling a heavy junk wagon. This was the effect, whether the background was a fully manned Hollywood type of creation or the more sympathetic Harlem-trained big-band crew that had the verve and also the right feeling but, unfortunately, usually played quite out of tune.

The question crops up invariably: why does Satch drive himself so hard on those interminable one-nighters? He still maintains a schedule that would wreck the health of a weaker musician, but lately there have been indications that the passing years are mellowing Armstrong. For example, I was surprised to read a recent statement credited to him in which he publicly came out strongly for civil rights.

My thoughts immediately went back to the period when a bunch of us, including Roy Eldridge, Erskine Hawkins, Cootie Williams, Dizzy Gillespie, and myself, tried to form what we tentatively labeled Trumpet Council of America. The purpose was to help gifted youngsters whom we would meet during our tours, recommending them to bandleaders, giving them encouragement, and also buying them instruments if necessary. This idea germinated in Los Angeles, where we had one meeting, but we planned to organize in New York. We felt that we needed Armstrong's name to assure success. We wanted him to be at least our honorary president. I was nominated to get in touch with Louis about it.

When I went backstage at the Apollo to sound him out, Pops was in good humor, asking about mutual chums, but when I brought up the idea about the association, his good spirits faded. He said gruffly, "You'll have to see Joe about that." As I vainly tried to explain that Joe Glaser, his manager, would not be interested and that all we wanted was the use of his name, his reply never changed. He still said, "See Joe."

There's no doubt that Glaser has exercised a tremendous influence on Louis, and perhaps this is fitting and proper. However, it is refreshing to note that at long last Louis has arrived at a point when he occasionally speaks his own piece.

Louis has bestowed so many gifts upon the world that it is almost impossible to assess in which area his definitive impact has been most felt. My vote would be for his tremendous talent of communication. As profoundly creative as his trumpet ability is, I would place this in a secondary position. He was revered mostly by other professionals, whereas his gravel-voiced singing has carried the message far and wide, to regions and places where not only was the music little known and the language foreign, but where there also was the further barrier of a political system having labeled jazz as decadent. But when Satchmo sang, the entire picture changed. People saw the truth.

Another, perhaps curious, phenomenon is the reaction of some Americans abroad who, back home, never cared about jazz, Louis, or the Negro people. But when you meet them overseas, they say with pride, "That's *our* Satchmo." Sometimes, this inadvertent awakening leads to a permanent change of attitude—at least, the thinking Negro musician likes to believe so.

To some people, Louis projects the "ambassador" by acclamation, the creator by virtue of his God-given gifts. To me, it remains more than ample just to have existed in the same musical atmosphere as the King. The great debt I owe him for setting the stage, worldwide, for American jazz music, I can never repay. The New Orleans waif who in some ways never left home, who gave music more than he'll ever take from it, deserves further recognition from the American people.

Baseball has its Hall of Fame, other nations have places where statues of the noteworthy are exhibited, and I propose that we erect a suitable monument to Ambassador Louis. We really should pay homage to one of the immortals of this original American art form.

"JELLY ROLL" MORTON
(1885?–1941)

Portrait of a Jazz Giant

STERLING A. BROWN (1901–1989), like Langston
Hughes, was one of the folk poets of the Harlem Renaissance, although
the bulk of Brown's work was written in the 1930s and later, after the
accepted dates for the Renaissance. Brown graduated from Williams
College in 1923 and earned an M.A. from Harvard. He was also an
important literary critic and anthologist. This essay on Jelly Roll Morton
grew out of his love for black music, particularly jazz and blues. It
appeared in *Black World* in February 1974.

On his calling card were the engraved words "Originator of Jazz." This
title was, of course, that of a pretender. He was a big talker, a big boaster,
a big liar. But amid all the bluster, the false front, one big truth stands
out: Jelly Roll Morton is rightfully one of the biggest names in the develop-
ment and excellence of Jazz.

The last time I saw "Jelly Roll" Morton was in the late Thirties at Nick's
in the Village, New York City. Charles Edward Smith, the jazz historian,
and I approached Jelly at the bar after his small group had just finished
a rousing set of tunes. We had both met and listened to Jelly when he was playing
at the Jungle Inn, a joint on Washington's "You" Street, in the heart of the ghetto.
We congratulated Jelly, and reminded him that we had talked with him there. Jelly
was gruff. To Charlie Smith, known to be a writer on jazz, he bent a little, but to
me, green and effusive, he turned a cold shoulder. When I mentioned that I was
from Washington and taught at Howard, he grimly stated his dislike for Washington,
and turned away to his fellow jazzmen.

My effusiveness was a mistake, but it was honestly derived. I had known of
Jelly Roll Morton on records since 1927, when Victor issued "Doctor Jazz," and
my students at Lincoln University, Missouri, and I were knocked for a loop by
clarinetist Omer Simeon's fantastic holding of a single note while the choruses
drove behind him.

Jelly's coldness to Washington I could well understand. When I heard Jelly play at the Jungle Inn, he seemed disdainful and bored. He spent the greater time in bragging to the scanty few customers, most of whom only wanted a little musical background while drinking their beer. The Jungle Inn *was* a dump, and Jelly, who had played in much fancier surroundings, naturally resented it. He wanted no reminders of Washington.

Still, I mused, as I took my seat at our table, Washington had done him some good. It had led to the productive sessions at the Library of Congress, whose assistant curator of Folklore Archives, Alan Lomax, wished to record him. Jelly gladly assented. Daily for over eight weeks, Jelly drove his long Lincoln to the imposing Library Entrance. Alan Lomax, who knows it best, tells this story:

> Jelly Roll, unimpressed by the austere setting of the most exclusive chamber-music recitals in the world, tossed his expensive summer straw on the bench of the Steinway grand, raised the lid to stash away the bourbon bottle, and then fell to larruping away [on the piano]. . . . The plaster busts of Bach, Beethoven, and Brahms looked sternly down, but if Jelly noticed them, he probably figured they were learning a thing or two. . . . That hot May afternoon in the Library of Congress a new way of writing history began—history with music cues, the music evoking recollection and poignant feeling—history intoned out of the heart of one man, sparkling with dialogue and purple with ego. . . .

While playing "soft, strange chords at the lazy tempo," Jelly reflected aloud, his

> gravel voice melting at the edges, not talking, but spinning out a life in something close to song. . . . He came to the Library of Congress to put himself forever on record, to carve his proper niche in the hall of history and incidentally to lay the groundwork for his fight to climb back into bigtime. . . .[1]

Jelly had only three years left for this long climb. Meanwhile, he had bequeathed us a unique masterpiece of musical history, invaluable to jazz lover, historian, psychologist, sociologist, and student of Americana. This vast collection, however, went unknown for nearly a decade. In the Folk Archives, the records were inaccessible. Hostile with good reason to commercial recording companies, Jelly left instructions that they and certain individuals were never to have access to the records.

Rudi Blesh, jazz historian and president of Circle Records, a company devoted to "the righteous jazz," saw the urgency, since the records, poorly cut at the best, were deteriorating and the material was vital for the understanding of jazz history. This brings me to my second reminiscence relating to Jelly Roll Morton.

Circle Record's field director, Kenneth "Fats" Bright, an ex-student and close friend of mine, was sent to California to confer with Attorney Hugh Macbeth, a friend of Jelly's and the executor of his estate. Macbeth knew the scabrous vocabulary of his friend Jelly, and the bawdy, low-down surroundings of both his early and later years. As a staunch friend of the family and a good race-man (put your best foot forward), he was opposed to issuing the records. Kenneth argued and argued. Then he telephoned me. I sent letters to Macbeth or to Kenneth (I don't remember which, it was so long ago) stressing my long connection with Howard University (you can't get much more respectable than that); my respect for Jelly Roll, the man and his music; and my certainty that posterity stood in need of these records. (I firmly believed and believe this, but for Attorney Macbeth, I laid it on with highfalu-tin' prose.) Macbeth at last consented; Circle Records brought out a selection of the records, in 12 volumes, 24 long-playing sides, entitled *The Saga of Mr. Jelly Lord*. *The Saga* was slightly laundered (some bawdiness still lurked, since, for Rudi Blesh, Jelly's lingo was often a second language). So I had a little something to do with resurrecting Jelly's reputation, and I am naturally proud of that.

(Way down yonder in New Orleans)

The best source for Jelly Roll's biography is obviously *Mr. Jelly Lord*, a book written by Alan Lomax, leaning on the Library of Congress records, supplemented by diligent research and interviews with relatives of Jelly Roll Morton and fellow jazzmen.[2] I have also used reminiscences of such historians as Rudi Blesh, Marshall Stearns, Charles Edward Smith, and Frederic Ramsey Jr., and autobiographies by such jazzmen as Perry Bradford, Jelly Roll Morton, Willie-the-Lion Smith and Duke Ellington.

The record of Jelly Roll's life is shrouded. Whether from Creole secretiveness, a confidence man's cunning, a cynic's dislike for prying questioners, a raconteur's overdramatization, or a mere lapse of memory, many of Jelly Roll's "facts" trip over each other in errant contradiction; dates go haywire, memories warmly narrated come up against the cold reality of documentation from unimpeachable sources.

We do not know the date of Jelly Roll's birth; he gave us the choice of three (1885, 1886, 1890). We do not know the place of his birth; some say Gulfport, some New Orleans; I choose New Orleans. His father soon drifts away from the family. Jelly says little of him, but expatiates on ancestors who were among the earliest settlers of Louisiana: "As I can understand, my folks were in the city of New Orleans long before the Louisiana Purchase."

Ferdinand Le Menthe was born to a genteel but poor Creole[3] family. He says that he changed the name Le Menthe to Morton for business reasons; his sister says it was because his stepfather, the only father Ferdinand knew, was named Morton. Ferdinand's mother died when he was quite young; his upbringing was the charge of Mimi, a strong-willed Creole matriarch; and his godmother, Enlalie Echo, a dark-skinned Creole learned in herbs and spells.

Ferdinand tells us little about his schooling, though his fantastic grammar that at times punctuates his grandiloquent declamation in the Coolidge Auditorium— he split verbs with a flair—indicates that he did not take school too seriously. He did take music seriously, starting with a tub and strings upon which he emulated the music he and his family heard in their segregated tier at the French Opera House. He graduated to the jew's harp and the guitar. His womenfolk (two sisters and the grandmother) urged him to try the piano. At first he balked, considering piano-playing to be sissy. But the performance of a master pianist enthralled him.

One of his piano teachers was named Miss Moment. She gets a momentary place in history when Ferdinand writes of her, "She was no doubt the biggest ham of a teacher I've ever heard or seen since or before." She rattled off every number the same way. Rid of her, he studied under Professor Nickerson[4] at St. Joseph's, a Catholic College. There he learned piano and theory. They stood him in good stead.

Ferdinand's family was poor, so he worked at odd jobs. When about 14, he got his best paying job in a cooperage, lining barrels. His heart, however, was in music. While his family was interested only in the light classics found in the French Opera House, Ferdinand's ears were being besieged by the abundant music of New Orleans: the brass-band street marches, the funeral processions mournful on the way to the graveyard and uproarious on the way back. In the forbidden but neighboring tenderloin district of Storyville, he heard honky-tonk, barrel-house piano coming out of the cribs and saloons; through the elegant windows of the high-class brothels, old stately mansions, he could hear the tantalizing chords of a Tony Jackson or a Albert Cahill. Ferdinand had a pleasing baritone-bass voice and he sang with a quartette at wakes and funerals.

He rapidly advanced in piano technique until he was considered one of "the best junior pianists in the whole city." Soon he was sneaking away at night to play piano in some sporting house and to make some real money. "I began to make more money than I had ever heard of in my life. I bought a new suit and a hat with the emblem Stetson in it and a pair of St. Louis flats. . . ." The popularity went to his head; he became careless. Early one Sunday morning, returning from a long night's work, he met his great grandmother coming from early mass. She soon ferreted the truth out of him. She was cold and firm. "A musician is nothing but a bum and a scalawag. I don't want you round your sisters. I reckon you better move."

> **I'm just the wining boy**
> **Don't deny my name**

With the home door shut in his face, Ferdinand headed for Biloxi, where his godmother had a summer place. For a couple of years he bummed around, playing piano here and there. His last job was playing for a white sporting house woman named Mattie Bailey.

> Nobody but white came there, and, as it was a dangerous place, I always carried a .38 Special. Mattie Bailey would keep me behind to close up the place for her, and, because I was always the last man out, talk began to get around that something was going on between the two of us. By her being a white woman, they didn't approve of my being intimate with her, as they thought. One day she told me they were talking about lynching me and right then I decided it was time for me to roll on back to my good old home town, New Orleans. [Alan Lomax, p. 42]

He headed back to New Orleans and inevitably Storyville, the red-light district. There he won immediate success; he was a handsome, impudent rascal, definitely on the make, a wisecracker, a hustler, an artist. He soon won the name Wining Boy (the boy serving the wine) and/or Winding Ball, both names having sexual connotations. He was also dubbed Jelly Roll,[5] the name that stuck with him for nearly 40 years.

Jelly played piano in some of the most glamorous houses. The girls were white, octoroon, quadroon, brown or black. Jelly Roll was popular with all. When Jelly Roll or one of the Negro pianists—and most of the "professors" were Negro—played the "Naked Dance" to which the girls danced naked, a screen separated the "professor at the piano" from the dancers and the white clientele, lest, in the words of one madame, "there should be contamination."

> Piano keys opened doors . . . gave him money and fine clothes and raised him above his brother musicians. He played the music the whores liked. Tony was dicty. But Jelly would sit there and play that barrelhouse music all night—blues and such as that. He'd play and sing the blues till way up in the day and all them gals would holler, "Listen at Winding Boy!" [Lomax, p. 104–105]

Jelly Roll played music with the Spanish Tinge; he played compositions by his friend and tutor and superior Tony Jackson, who composed "Pretty Baby" and "I've Got Elgin Movements in My Hips, With Twenty Years Guarantee"; he played "Maple Leaf Rag" and Original Rags by Scott Joplin. But he was learning another kind of music too. Often, according to Bunk Johnson, Jelly would meet him in the dawn after work and they would jam together on blues for hours on end. Jelly Roll knew Buddy Bolden, for whom he wrote a blues; he swore that Bolden's horn was so powerful that it could call his children home from places miles away. Jelly also knew and admired King Oliver, Kid Ory, Sidney Bechet, Johnny Dodds; Louis Armstrong was just a shaver.

Oh, didn't he ramble
He rambled till the butcher cut him down

Success in Storyville could not slake Jelly's restlessness. A hustler, pool shark and gambler, he wandered where he thought the money was. His itinerary is vague: Memphis, Helena, Arkansas, St. Louis, Chicago, New York, Houston, Los Angeles. Sometimes he would be with a band, more often he organized from local talent.

In Chicago in 1913, Jelly Roll Morton met Perry Bradford, the blues pianist. Becoming fast friends, they put together a big act and tried it out in South Chicago. According to Bradford, "the act laid an omelette, it was so terrible." Bradford wisecracked on Morton's ham acting, but acknowledged he "could really play a mean piano."[6] But Jelly's mean piano could not make his pick-up bands popular in Chicago. His friend and fellow New Orleansian Freddy Keppard was the rage with his Original Creole Band. Jelly left for greener pastures in California.

For a time he found them. He married a girl, Anita Gonzales, the sister of a fellow New Orleans jazzman. She brought him some money and was believed to have paid for the diamond set in his gold front tooth. Jelly owned a gambling palace, a dance hall and managed a cabaret. Anita, who was the first of the two women whom Jelly called "the only woman I ever loved," bought a small hotel, a kind of rooming house that did not make much money. Jelly was living high with his many enterprises; he sported many shirts, clothes, cars and diamonds (he even wore diamonds pinned to his underwear). Anita had three or four fur coats. But music was never far from his interest. Believing in the superiority of New Orleans musicians, he sent home for three musicians to improve his band. They arrived in box-back coats and trousers "so tight you couldn't button the top button." On the job they brought their own victuals—a bucket of red beans and rice which they would cook right on the job. When Jelly, in his sophistication and care for appearances kidded them, they (as sensitive as Jelly) left for New Orleans without any notice.

Jelly Roll barnstormed the Pacific Coast, taking Anita with him. In San Diego, Jelly learned that the hotel paid white musicians $75 a week, much more than his men were being paid. Without warning, Jelly pulled out his band. His bands were not great ones; Jelly split his interests; the affair with Anita was growing tense; and Jelly Roll unfortunately teamed up in a music and publishing business with Reb and Johnny Spikes, two white vaudevillians. Jelly considered them "cornfed," but they succeeded in stealing some of his best works, such as "Someday Sweetheart" and "Wolverine Blues."

By this time, 1923, Chicago (not New York) had become the jazz capital of the world. With Anita's consent, since he promised to send her the second thousand he made, Jelly left for the Windy City. Here he struck the attention of the Melrose brothers, who exploited his talents, but also got him the difficult recording opportunities. Jelly at first considered the Melroses "polite Southern boys who needed a break." They were much more. Lester, who could not read or sing a note, said, "I reckon I own about three thousand tunes, most of them blues." He described Jelly as "a superior folk-artist with a low level of musical literacy." Walter Melrose, who preferred King Oliver because he was "more the old Southern-type nigger," felt that Jelly Roll, while prolific, was ungrateful. He admitted that Jelly's songs "did pretty well" (the 26 Morton tunes he published sold phenomenally). "We published his tunes. We got him a Victory contract. And he lived off his royalties." Jelly also made the Melroses millionaires.

Though Jelly Roll's orchestras were eclipsed by Joe Oliver as far as the bigger jobs went, his Red Hot Peppers became one of the great small bands. Jelly Roll selected almost all-star bands, with George Mitchell or Ward Pinkett on trumpet; Kid Ory on trombone; Omer Simeon, Johnny Dodds or Albert Nicholas on clarinet, Johnny St. Cyr on banjo or guitar; Bill Benford or John Lindsay on tuba or bass; Tom Benford or Baby Dodds on drums. The records of the Red Hot Peppers became jazz classics.

Jelly was also one of the first Negroes to play with a mixed band. The New Orleans Rhythm Kings needed a first-rate pianist, and this need probably overcame Louisiana tradition, because they sought out Jelly as their pianist.

In Chicago, the affair with Anita having long ago dissolved, Jelly courted and won another New Orleans beauty, second instance of the "only woman he ever loved." Mabel had been a dancer in *Shuffle Along*, a singer and dancer on the Keith Circuit.[7]

On "You" Street in Washington, across the alley from the Lincoln Theatre
was a hamburger joint with a nightclub upstairs. Jelly bought a share in
this dubious venture, entering partnership with Cordelia. It never promised
Jelly much; it paid him even less.

In 1938, stimulated by the enthusiastic praise by Marshall Stearns, a young critic, Jelly Roll stepped out of his obscurity. Irritated by a broadcast of Robert Ripley's *Believe It or Not* acclaiming W. C. Handy as the originator of jazz and the blues, Jelly Roll wrote an open letter to the Afro-American. It started, "W. C. Handy is a Liar. . . ." It continued with such attacks as, "Who ever heard of anyone wearing the name of a professor advocate Ragtime, Jazz, Stomps, Blues, *etc.* . . . Of course Handy could not play any of these types and I can assure you has not learned them yet. Mr. Handy cannot prove anything in music that he has created." Jelly then wrote:

> Mr. Ripley, these untruthful statements Mr. Handy has made, or caused you
> to make, will maybe cause him to be branded the most dastardly imposter in
> the history of music. [Lomax, p. 236]

His unfavorable impressions of W. C. Handy dated from his meeting him in Memphis, while on a vaudeville tour:

> I know his musical abilities because I used to play in his band from time to
> time. In 1908 Handy didn't know anything about the blues and he doesn't
> know anything about jazz and stomps to this day.[8]

Jelly Roll insisted that Handy had lifted his blues; of the "Memphis Blues" he said, "The first strain is a Black Butts [boogie-woogie] strain all dressed up," the second strain was Jelly Roll's own, and the last strain was Tony Jackson's. Disputing the claim that "The Memphis Blues" was the first blues to be published, Jelly proved that his "New Orleans Blues" was written and published earlier. Jelly Roll laid claim to "Alabama Blues," written by him and pirated from him in 1907.

Handy answered the Downbeat tirade briefly and calmly, and did not mention Jelly Roll in his autobiography, *Father of the Blues*. There is no question that the title of the autobiography is a misnomer; as Handy's own comments establish, the blues go back much, much further than 1912. And much of his product is 80-proof folk stuff, slightly diluted (*e.g.*, "Make Me A Pallet on the Floor," "Hesitation Blues" and "Long Gone, Last John"). There is also no question that Handy did not feel the blues as deeply, or play them as convincingly as Jelly Roll Morton. Handy admits that he "took up with low folk forms hesitantly. I approached them with fear and trembling."[9] In the 1940s, to honor the old man, a group of top-notch jazzmen backed the old man's cornet for eight sides of blues. Handy's cornet was correct; he played every note exactly, his tempo was metronomically correct; his tone was pure. It was a timid exercise but it was not jazz. The blues came out not as *baaaad* music, but simply as bad.

Jelly's carping, part jealousy and part veracity, has helped to fix Handy's place in history. Handy is not the father of the blues and he is not a jazz musician. He recognized the first clause; he would have been gratified by the second. But his niche is sure. The author of many fine blues; the striker of a rich lode of Negro folk music, as Joel Chandler Harris had been of the Negro folk-tale and Thomas Wentworth Higginson of the spiritual; the interpreter and poetic re-creator; the composer of "St. Louis Blues," "Beale Street Blues," "Yellow Dog Blues," and "Atlanta Blues"; probably the best known composer of jazz classics over the wide world, Handy can be assured of his honored place in the history of jazz.

Having overthrown Handy's exaggerated claims, Jelly Roll started exaggerating for himself: "I happened to be the creator in the year 1901." Some of his comments follow: Paul Whiteman had "no actual knowledge of jazz"; Duke's "Jungle Music was no more than a flutter tongue on trumpet or trombone." For years, Jelly Roll said he was "Number One Man with the Victor Recording Company" (they dropped him for "Fats" Waller). Musicians hate to give credit but they will say, "I heard Jelly Roll play it first."

> My figurations . . . were impossible at that time, and arguments would arise, stating no one could put this idea on a sheet. . . . I myself figured out the peculiar form of mathematics and harmonies that was strange to all the world but me.
>
> My contributions were many: First clown director, with witty sayings and flashily dressed, now called master of ceremonies; first glee club in orchestra; the first washboard was recorded by me; bass fiddle, drums—which was supposed to be impossible to record. [Ralph Toledano, p. 107]

Soon after the confrontation with Handy, Jelly had the opportunity to set the record straight with his sessions at the Library of Congress. Jelly was now riding high. Back in the sleazy dining room at the Jungle Inn, over champagne cocktails, Jelly introduced Alan Lomax to the staring hangers-on and curiosity seekers with a grandiose sweep: "I have the honor to present the Librarian of Congress." (Alan was only the assistant to the Folklore Archivist, his father.)

The breaks seemed to be coming his way. The end of the Thirties signaled the New Orleans Revival of Bunk Johnson, Kid Ory, the refurbished Dixieland of Turk Murphy. Jelly Roll did not need "reviving"; he merely had to be found. Charles E. Smith managed a recording date of piano solos for Commodore, and an everlasting record, doing new things with the blues, resulted. Then, after other small-company pressings, Victor called him back from exile.

With such famous side-men as fellow New Orleansians Sidney Bechet on soprano saxophone, Albert Nicholas on clarinet, Zutty Singleton on drums, and such seasoned troupers as Happy Cauldwell on tenor saxophone, Claude Jones on trombone, Sidney De Paris on trumpet, and Wellman Braud on bass, Jelly could not help returning with smash hits. He played songs reminiscent of old New Orleans: a swift, rollicking parody of a street funeral in "Oh Didn't He Ramble," the ribald "I Thought I Heard Buddy Bolden Say" and the plangent, nostalgic "Wining Boy." But it was in that New Orleans standby "High Society," made famous by clarinetist Alphonse Picou, that Jelly Roll and his "New Orleans Jazzmen" hit their peak. The two peers, Jelly and Sidney Bechet, inspired each other; Sidney De Paris and Claude Jones laid down a spirited background, and Bechet took chorus after soaring chorus; then in the finale, with the mood being "get the hell off of my note," Albert

Nicholas suddenly broke loose, and his piercing clarinet showed both Picou and Bechet, the *nonpareil*, how the obbligato should be played.

This session of recordings was the apex for Jelly Roll. From here on in, it was downhill. The records were smash hits with the critics, but Jelly returned to Washington, exhilarated for a while by his revival, but doubting its validity. He did not want to be a museum piece. He had more to give than memories.

His health was failing. His partner in the Jungle Inn was a grasping, aggressive woman, and as business declined, her nagging grew. Hearing that his beloved godmother was ill in California, he drove his Lincoln the long miles across the country, though ill himself with asthma and a heart condition. He tried to organize a band desultorily, but spent most of his time in bed. He could send Mabel no money and this embittered him.

He died in July, 1941. Kid Ory and his bandsmen were the pallbearers at the Catholic high-requiem mass. For all of the looseness of his living, he had remained a Catholic. Few people attended his funeral.

Within a few years, Bunk Johnson would be brought from New Iberian rice fields to New York and be lionized: Kid Ory had already captured the Pacific Coast. Within a score of years the bands of Benny Goodman, Duke Ellington, Louis Armstrong, and Dizzy Gillespie and others would tour the world under State Department auspices. Even the Preservation Band of New Orleans oldsters would be sent to Japan. Jazz was celebrated in festivals, in concert halls, in Kennedy Center, and in museums, especially in his native New Orleans.

Jelly Roll Morton died too soon for the furor. Even had he lived, it is likely that his rasping personality would have prevented his becoming an ambassador. Still, he is known the world over. In Ireland, Thomas Cusack, a professor of Tudor Drama at Queens University, has prepared the authoritative discography after many absorbed years. From England to Australia, the Netherlands to Thailand, in Africa and Asia enthusiasts collect his records. In America, in colleges, clubs and museums, Jelly Roll Morton is sedulously studied. In Washington, Bob Greene, a devotee, has assimilated the Jelly Roll style, and has devoted his professional life to the interpretation of his music. He has played Morton at Jazz Festivals and seeks to spread the Jelly Roll Gospel over the nation. Neglected during his lifetime, Jelly Roll Morton has become the object of a cult, in which fine company I am proud to be enrolled.

Jazz Criticism

The earliest histories of jazz, such as Gilbert Seldes' *Seven Lively Arts* and Osgood's *So This Is Jazz*, of course do not mention Morton (nor for that matter any Negro jazz bands), preserving their accolades for such as Art Hickman and Paul Whiteman and that apex of achievement, Gershwin's "Rhapsody in Blue." Negro music was too dissonant, crude, and ear-shattering for their delicate sensibilities. More surprisingly, Jelly's name is not mentioned in Locke's *The Negro in Music* or in Margaret Butcher's *The Negro in American Culture* (derived from Locke's materials), although Whiteman, Bix Beiderbecke, and Gene Krupa are.[10] Even such a chronicler of the real Jazz as Hugues Panassie (the discoverer of jazz from phonograph records in

Paris) gives Jelly Roll Morton scant attention. In *Jazz* (*From the Congo to the Metropolitan*), Robert Goffin (the discoverer of jazz from phonograph records in Belgium) praises Jelly's album of New Orleans Memories for "a sweet naïvete [will the real Jelly Roll please stand up?] marked with the imprint of sensibility and beauty in its purest state," but otherwise underestimates him.

Panassie later wrote that Jelly Roll's importance cannot be overrated, that he was a "very original composer, probably the most creative jazz music has known, outside of Duke Ellington" and that Jelly's piano in the Trio records has an "indescribable charm." Martin Williams says that, "Morton was the first great master of form in jazz. In this respect, he belongs perhaps with the Fletcher Henderson of the mid-1930s, and certainly with Duke Ellington, John Lewis and Thelonious Monk" (Nat Hentoff and Albert McCarthy, *Jazz*, p. 62). Fred Ramsey Jr., folklorist and jazz historian, writes, "No one knew better than Jelly Roll the freshness, melodic lilt and classic structure of New Orleans jazz; no one played it to greater effect" (*A Guide to Longplay Records*, p. 143). Orin Keepnews praised him as an original, saying that, other musicians whose life stories have been "legendized, embellished and refurbished," unlike those who have praised themselves brashly and "whose careers have taken them from obscurity to the top and back again," there was only one Jelly Morton (Nat Shapiro and Nat Hentoff, *The Jazz Makers*, p. 4). The height of praise was probably stated by two devotees of New Orleans and Dixieland Jazz, William L. Grossman and Jack W. Farrell, who echo Alan Lomax's phrase "a Creole Benvenuto Cellini," and prophesy that as great as were Louis Armstrong's gifts, "it is not unlikely that, in the years ahead, the stature of Morton will maintain a higher level than that of Armstrong" (Grossman and Farrell, *The Heart of Jazz*, p. 171). Leonard Feather noncommittally tries to steer a middle course between the cultists—between Avakian's "Many will assure you that no greater jazzman ever sat down at the keyboard" and John Hammond's "His limited technique got in the way of his producing any real music as a pianist" (*The Encyclopedia of Jazz*, p. 233).

Younger jazz pianists like Duke Ellington and Mary Lou Williams were unimpressed by Jelly Roll's style. The Harlem stride pianist James P. Johnson respected his playing and admired his composing. Willie-the-Lion liked his personal "style" rather than his playing the rags, stomps, and blues, but esteemed him highly. The flamboyant called out to the flamboyant. Willie remembers:

> When Morton entered a place he would come in smiling so everyone would get a glance at his diamond-studded tooth. As he arrived at the piano, he would take off his coat with a fancy flourish and lay it on top of the piano with the expensive lining turned outward for all to see. Then he would carefully wipe off the piano bench or stool with a large silk handkerchief. Out of the corner or his eye he would look to see whether or not he was getting the proper attention. If so, he would sit down, and like all pianists of the day hit his signature chord.[11]

Willie defended Jelly: "It used to make me mad to hear those New York cats who hadn't been out of Harlem making fun of Morton." Still, he had to cut Jelly's pretentions down. One day he found Jelly standing on a corner. "Look, Mr. One Hand," he said, "let's go inside and let me give you your lesson on cutting." Willie brags that he was the only one that Jelly would listen to without opening his mouth. "I must have played nearly everything you could name and when I got through, I said, 'Well Jelly, you'll be quiet now.' And true as I'm sitting here, Jelly would be quiet." (Smith, p. 212). Jelly was quiet about this encounter in his autobiography, too.

Many of Jelly's fellow musicians praise his piano style. Mezz Mezzrow, a white clarinetist who tried to pass for colored, wrote:

> Somebody was playing the piano . . . in a way that made me know he was colored, and when I busted in, I came face to face with Jelly Roll Morton, the composer of many a jazz classic. Nobody ever played just like him—he was lyrical and didn't have as much of a beat as some guys, but his delicate and flowery touch was Jelly's trademark. We got to be pals fast. [Mezz Mezzrow and Bernard Wolfe, *Really The Blues*, p. 59]

Jelly's piano style had even more fervent admirers. Rudi Blesh and Harriet Janis wrote: "Today's generation of pianists, with a few notable exceptions, laugh Jelly Roll off as corny and old-fashioned. His recorded playing remains a challenge, however, that not many care to meet as they dazzle a gullible public with wiggling scale work and a few cheap easy tricks" (Blesh and Janis, *They All Played Ragtime*, pp. 182–183).

Rudi Blesh isolates the elements of Jelly Roll's individual piano style, a style of classic precision and incredible technique:

> the impeccable, varied and forceful left hand laying the beat firmly and furnishing transitional passages of downward octaves which hesitate then accelerate dizzily in harmonic, melodic, or thematic transitions: the right hand chording solidly off and on the beat. Then there are the runs, like swift coruscations through the sky, never mere ornamental display but integral thermal variations. [Blesh and Janis, *Shining Trumpets*, p. 193]

Four jazzmen bear witness: Russell Procope, alto saxophone and clarinet with John Kirby and Duke Ellington: "Jelly Roll had a tremendous influence on me. . . . I liked what he was doing. It was strictly jazz. . . . He really knew about the blues, too."

John St. Cyr, famed banjoist and guitarist: "Jelly was a very, very agreeable man to cut a record with, largely because he would let his men take breaks and choruses as and where they felt they best could . . . he'd leave it to your own judgement and he was always open for suggestion."

Omer Simeon (famed clarinetist): "One thing about Jelly, he would back up everything he said by what he could *do*."

Baby Dodds, famous New Orleans drummer and brother of Johnny Dodds, clarinetist:

> You did what Jelly Roll wanted you to do, no more and no less. And his own playing was remarkable and kept us in good spirits. He wasn't fussy, but

he was positive. He knew what he wanted and he would get the men he knew could produce it. . . . But Jelly wasn't a man to get angry. I never saw him upset and he didn't raise his voice at any time. . . .[12]

The jazz critic for the *New York Times*, John S. Wilson writes:

> Morton believed in a strong, steady beat for the left hand and no holds barred with the right. . . . Morton advocated three types of plenty—plenty pretty, plenty swing, plenty breaks. Things keep happening in a Morton solo, much as they do in more involved form in Hines' solos.[13]

His small-group jazz performances are gems, thoroughly individualistic, with a spare, oddly accented style, and the stamp of his robust personality on almost every group of musicians that he collected for a recording date.

Jelly Roll Morton was a legend even in his own time. He was a lady's man, a pimp, a pool shark, a hustler, a vaudeville ham. His character was paradoxical: now arrogant, now insecure, now gregarious, now solitary; now euphoric, now melancholy; now shrewd, now superstitious; now tyrannical, now considerate; now gentle, now acerbic; now profane, now religious. The paradox is intriguing. But Jelly Roll Morton remains legend today not because of his flash, his personality, his escapades. He remains one of our treasures because of his music.

The highest praise and truest appreciation probably come from Charles Edward Smith, the pioneer in jazz history and criticism. Having studied Jelly Roll's career and character with genuine loving care, Smith calls him the Mozart of jazz.

The comparison seems to have some of Morton's effrontery, but the pith of the matter is that both Mozart and Morton were paid entertainers. Mozart was supported by crowned heads and nobles; Jelly at the start played piano in brothels for plutocrats and whoever else (white) came with the price. The morality of the Viennese ducal circles and the Storyville clientele, however, in all likelihood did not greatly vary. But Smith meant more than this: he saw in Jelly Roll Morton's achievement in the jazz idiom what musicologists have found in Mozart's achievement in the classical: inventiveness, absorption in music, venturesome experimentation, and the final stamp of excellence. Both had enduring love affairs with music. W. J. Turner, Mozart's biographer, says of his early death from nephritis: "It only took six months to exterminate a man who throughout his life had been obliged to fight . . . in order to have bread to eat." So Jelly Roll Morton.

But Jelly Roll Morton would consider this comparison too tall and essentially jive talk. Jelly Roll Morton did not wish to be anybody's Mozart. Why should he? He was Ferdinand Morton, born Le Menthe, the Wining Boy, the Winding Ball, Jelly Roll, Mr. Jelly Lord, and ultimately the uncrowned King of Jazz, a title bestowed in amazing ignorance upon one Paul Whiteman, a mediocre fiddler, a purveyor of ersatz jass, (jazz), while Jelly Roll, though playing the authentic jazz, was scuffling in Kansas City.

Jelly Roll Morton *was* frustrated and neglected in his lifetime. But before he died, too young in his mid-fifties, after years of frenzied living and stirring creations, he left us the legacy in a stack of records. He was a fine solo pianist, a pioneer in jazz-band orchestration and leadership (big band and small), a moving interpreter of the blues; a valuable historian (for all of his big lies) of jazz and its ambient world; a spell-binding raconteur (for all of his bluster and egotism); a good ensemble leader. We have the records. We owe him the respect and admiration that this legacy deserves. He was one of the foremost contributors to a great American music.

Hello, Central
Give me Doctor Jazz. . . .

ANTHOLOGY OF 12 FAVORITE RECORDS[14]

Blues	1. Winin' Boy Blues	Commodore FL 23 A
	2. Mamie's Blues	Commodore FL 23 A
	3. I Thought I Heard Buddy Bolden Say	Commodore FL 23 A
Solo	4. The Naked Dance	Commodore FL 24 A
	5. King Porter Stomp	Commodore FL 24 A
Trio	6. Turtle Twist (with Barney Bigard)	B 10194
	7. Mr. Jelly Lord (with Johnny Dodds)	B 10258
	Shreve Port (Omer Simeon)	B 7710
	8. Doctor Jazz (Omer Simeon, Jelly Roll vocal)	B 10255
	9. Cannon Ball Blues	B 10254
	10. Kansas City Stomps	B 7757
	11. Oh Didn't He Ramble	B 10429A
	12. High Society	B 10429B

Recent Issues by RCA Victor in the Vintage Series

Vol. I	The King of New Orleans Jazz (No. 1) With his Red Hot Peppers
Vol. II	Jelly Roll Morton's Orchestra and the Morton Trio
Vol. III	Hot Jazz, Top Jazz, Hokum and Hilarity (with the Red Hot Peppers, Jelly Roll's Orchestra and Wilton Crawley with the Washboard Rhythm Kings)
Vol. IV	Jelly Roll Morton (No. 2) with his New Orleans Jazz Band

NOTES

1. Alan Lomax, *Mister Jelly Lord*.

2. There is no gainsaying the friendliness, thoroughness and eloquence of Alan Lomax's book. It is indispensable for the study of Jelly Roll and of jazz history. It must be said, however, that Alan Lomax accented the nostalgic and the raffish. Most of the questions are those of a skillful interviewer. At times, however, Lomax is obtrusive. Once, while Jelly was narrating the customs of a New Orleans funeral, he was singing "Nearer (Nero) my God to thee" in a deep, moving voice. Alan seemed uneasy at the depth of feeling, and wisecracked to Jelly about his mind really being on ham in the kitchen. Jelly complaisantly agreed, but went on back to bassing the hymn. It is in cocksure generalizations about "the Negro" that Alan Lomax's prejudices are showing: *e.g.* "Jelly did not feel the blues, because he always refused to admit he was a Negro and that he was lonely." I would demur: I think he feels the blues as deeply as any blues singer: Blind Lemon, Lonnie Johnson, Josh White, B.B. King, any of them. He says he feels them deeply; he shows he feels them deeply; he makes his hearers feel them deeply. The blues often spring from loneliness; why should the lonely Jelly Roll refuse their solace? Alan Lomax praises Jelly Roll for his lack of protest, because "within himself he accepted Jim Crow, economic inequality, frustration and his own eternal insecurity as part of the natural order of things." (How you do talk, Reverend Lomack! You'd better say you

reckon!) *The Saga of Mr. Jelly Lord,* heard with any sensitivity, gives the lie to this canard. That Jelly Roll, like many clannish Creoles, disliked the word Negro is probably true. That he did not identify himself with his fellow jazzmen, that he was oblivious of race, seems ridiculous. That he didn't express protest openly to Alan Lomax is likely, and according to his lights was smart. As white interviewers have demonstrated from Joel Chandler Harris to the Lomaxes (cf. their book on Leadbelly) they are most often naively unaware of Negro irony, of what Zora Neale Hurston calls "hitting a straight lick with a crooked stick." Why Alan Lomax thinks that a Negro, born and raised in the Deep South, would reveal bitterness and protest to a white man who has just plied him with "good" bourbon, who is promising him immortality, and has sat him down in front of a grand piano in one of the hallowed halls of white territory, is more than I comprehend. A final whopper: Jelly Roll's whole life was constructed around his denial of his Negro status. I would say that Jelly Roll's life was chiefly centered around music. Jelly Roll condemned rowdiness, lethargy, stupidity, ignorance—certainly faults of many Negroes Jelly Roll knew. But how Alan Lomax, well acquainted with white people, both poor white and wealthy, how he could equate rowdiness and ignorance and the rest with what he called "Negro status" is again past my understanding. Jelly Roll resented his status as poor, underpaid, overworked, unappreciated, neglected and abused. And the special disabilities of race poured salt upon the wound.

3. White aristocrats insist that the word Creole applies only to "pure white" descendants of the Spanish and French colonists. Louisiana parlance, however, has long been different. *The American Heritage Dictionary* gives the meaning generally accepted in Louisiana. Creole means "a person descended from the original French settlers of Louisiana." Since these settlers sired children of Indian and Negro women indiscriminately, their descendants would be Creoles. Creoles range in color from Aryan white to black. Ferdinand Le Menthe was descended from a long line of Creoles *de couleur,* but most of these call themselves Creole, feeling the phrase *"de couleur"* to be needless. Just look in the mirror; you will find the *couleur.*

4. Professor Nickerson was the father of Camille Nickerson, retired professor in the Music School of Howard University, and collector of Creole folk songs.

5. "Jelly Roll." The Belgian Goffin considers the word "grotesque." The French critic Andre Francis calls it *"le sobriquet violemment obscène qu'on traduit par 'gateauroulé a la confiture.'"* The expression "Jelly Roll" has such wide currency in jazz songs:

> *I ain't gonna give you none of my jelly roll*
> *Wouldn't give you none of this cake to save your soul*

as sung by Lizzie Miles or in "Jelly, Jelly," the best seller by Billy Eckstine, that it no longer strikes consternation in the righteous. "Jelly Roll's" first meaning refers to women's sexual equipment; when applied to Ferdinand Morton, it refers to his proficiency in the use of his equipment. At least so Ferdinand said.

6. Perry Bradford, *Born With The Blues,* p. 95.

7. A leading vaudeville theatrical circuit that played in key theater chains. Though many Blacks were equipped to perform on the circuit, few ever made it.

8. Ralph Toledano, ed., *Frontiers of Jazz.* "I Discovered Jazz in 1902," from *Downbeat* Magazine, p. 105.

9. W. C. Handy, *Father of the Blues,* ed. by Arna Bontemps, p. 76.

10. Incidentally, the foremost ragtime composer, Scott Joplin, a Black from Sedalia, Mo., is identified as a white pianist in both books.

11. Willie-the-Lion Smith, *Music on My Mind,* p. 53.

12. Martin Williams, *Jelly Roll Morton,* p. 25.

13. John S. Wilson, *The Collector's Jazz,* p. 202ff.

14. There are over 50 labels featuring Jelly Roll Morton over the world. Frederic Ramsey Jr. kindly supplied information for the above listing.

THE CHARLIE CHRISTIAN
STORY

RALPH ELLISON is probably best known for his 1952
novel, *Invisible Man*, considered by many critics and readers to be the
finest novel by a black American. Ellison, born in Oklahoma, was
especially fascinated with musicians from the Southwest as this essay on
Texas jazz guitarist Charlie Christian, who was to make a name for
himself with the Benny Goodman band, attests. Ellison himself was a
musician, and had intended to pursue the trumpet and musical
composition, and not literature, as a career. This essay appeared in the
1964 collection *Shadow and Act* and was originally published in
Saturday Review in 1958.

azz, like the country which gave it birth, is fecund in its inventiveness, swift
and traumatic in its developments and terribly wasteful of its resources. It is
an orgiastic art which demands great physical stamina of its practitioners, and
many of its most talented creators die young. More often than not (and this is
especially true of its Negro exponents) its heroes remain local figures known only
to small-town dance halls, and whose reputations are limited to the radius of a few
hundred miles.

A case in point, and a compelling argument for closer study of roots and causes,
is a recording devoted to the art of Charlie Christian, probably the greatest of jazz
guitarists. He died in 1942 after a brief, spectacular career with the Benny Goodman
Sextet. Had he not come from Oklahoma City in 1939, at the instigation of John
Hammond, he might have shared the fate of many we knew in the period when
Christian was growing up (and I doubt that it has changed very much today).

Some of the most brilliant of jazzmen made no records; their names appeared
in print only in announcements of some local dance or remote "battles of music"
against equally uncelebrated bands. Being devoted to an art which traditionally

thrives on improvisation, these unrecorded artists very often have their most original ideas enter the public domain almost as rapidly as they are conceived to be quickly absorbed into the thought and technique of their fellows. Thus the riffs which swung the dancers and the band on some transcendent evening, and which inspired others to competitive flights of invention, become all too swiftly a part of the general style, leaving the originator as anonymous as the creators of the architecture called Gothic.

There is in this a cruel contradiction implicit in the art form itself. For true jazz is an art of individual assertion within and against the group. Each true jazz moment (as distinct from the uninspired commercial performance) springs from a contest in which each artist challenges all the rest; each solo flight, or improvisation, represents (like the successive canvases of a painter) a definition of his identity: as individual, as member of the collectivity and as a link in the chain of tradition. Thus, because jazz finds its very life in an endless improvisation upon traditional materials, the jazzman must lose his identity even as he finds it—how often do we see even the most famous of jazz artists being devoured alive by their imitators, and, shamelessly, in the public spotlight?

So at best the musical contributions of these local, unrecorded heroes of jazz are enjoyed by a few fellow musicians and by a few dancers who admire them and afford them the meager economic return which allows them to keep playing but very often they live beyond the period of youthful dedication, hoping in vain that some visiting big-band leader will provide the opportunity to break through to the wider spheres of jazz. Indeed, to escape these fates the artists must be very talented, very individual, as restlessly inventive as Picasso, and very lucky.

Charles Christian, when Hammond brought him to the attention of Goodman, was for most of his life such a local jazz hero. Nor do I use the term loosely, for having known him since 1923, when he and my younger brother were members of the same first-grade class, I can recall no time when he was not admired for his skillful playing of stringed instruments. Indeed, a great part of his time in the manual-training department of Douglass School was spent constructing guitars from cigar boxes, instruments upon which both he and his older brother, Clarence, were dazzlingly adept. Incidentally, in their excellent notes to the album Al Avakian and Bob Prince are mistaken when they assume that Christian was innocent of contact with musical forms more sophisticated than the blues, and it would be well that here I offer a correction. Before Charlie was big enough to handle a guitar himself he served as a guide for his father, a blind guitarist and singer. Later he joined with his father, his brothers Clarence and Edward (an arranger, pianist, violinist and performer on the string bass and tuba), and made his contribution to the family income by strolling with them through the white middle-class sections of Oklahoma City, where they played serenades on request. Their repertory included the light classics as well as the blues, and there was no doubt in the minds of those who heard them that the musical value they gave was worth far more than the money they received. Later on Edward, who took leading roles in the standard operettas performed by members of the high-school chorus, led his own band and played gigs from time to time with such musicians as "Hot Lips" Paige, Walter Page, Sammy

Price, Lem C. Johnson (to mention a few), all members at some point of the Blue Devils Orchestra, which later merged with the Benny Moten group to become the famous Count Basie Band. I need only mention that Oklahoma City was a regular stopping point for Kansas City-based orchestras, or that a number of the local musicians were conservatory-trained and were capable of sight-reading the hodge-podge scores which during the "million-dollar production" stage of the silent movies were furnished in the stands of pit orchestras.

The facts in these matters are always more intriguing than the legends. In the school which we attended harmony was taught from the ninth through the twelfth grades; there was an extensive and compulsory music-appreciation program, and, though Charles was never a member, a concert band and orchestra and several vocal organizations. In brief, both in his home and in the community Charles Christian was subjected to many diverse musical influences. It was the era of radio, and for a while a local newspaper gave away cheap plastic recordings of such orchestras as Jean Goldkette's along with subscriptions. The big media of communication were active for better or worse, even then, and the Negro community was never completely isolated from their influence.

However, perhaps the most stimulating influence upon Christian, and one with whom he was later to be identified, was that of a tall, intense young musician who arrived in Oklahoma City sometime in 1929 and who, with his heavy white sweater, blue stocking cap and up-and-out-thrust silver saxophone, left absolutely no reed player and few young players of any instrument unstirred by the wild, excitingly original flights of his imagination. Who else but Lester Young, who with his battered horn upset the entire Negro section of the town. One of our friends gave up his valved instrument for the tenor saxophone and soon ran away from home to carry the new message to Baltimore, while a good part of the efforts of the rest was spent trying to absorb and transform the Youngian style. Indeed, only one other young musician created anything like the excitement attending Young's stay in the town. This was Carlton George, who had played with Earl Hines and whose trumpet style was shaped after the excursions of Hines's right hand. He, however, was a minor influence, having arrived during the national ascendancy of Louis Armstrong and during the local reign of Oran ("Hot Lips") Paige.

When we consider the stylistic development of Charles Christian we are reminded how little we actually know of the origins of even the most recent of jazz styles, or of when and where they actually started; or of the tensions, personal, sociological, or technical, out of which such an original artist achieves his stylistic identity. For while there is now a rather extensive history of discography and recording sessions there is but the bare beginnings of a historiography of jazz. We know much of jazz as entertainment, but a mere handful of clichés constitutes our knowledge of jazz as experience. Worse, it is this which is frequently taken for all there is, and we get the impression that jazz styles are created in some club on some particular occasion and there and then codified according to the preconceptions of the jazz publicists in an atmosphere as grave and traditional, say, as that attending the deliberations of the Academie Française. It is this which leads to the notion that jazz was invented in a particular house of ill fame by "Jelly Roll" Morton, who admitted the crime himself; that swing was invented by Goodman about 1935; that T. Monk, K. Clark, and J. B. "D" Gillespie invented "progressive" jazz at Minton's Playhouse in Harlem about 1941.

This is, of course, convenient but only relatively true, and the effort to let the history of jazz as entertainment stand for the whole of jazz ignores the most fundamental knowledge of the dynamics of stylistic growth which has been acquired from studies in other branches of music and from our knowledge of the growth of other art forms. The jazz artist who becomes nationally known is written about as though he came into existence only upon his arrival in New York. His career in the big cities, where jazz is more of a commercial entertainment than part of a total way of life, is stressed at the expense of his life in the South, the Southwest and the Midwest, where most Negro musicians at least found their early development. Thus we are left with an impression of mysterious rootlessness, and the true and often annoying complexity of American cultural experience is oversimplified.

With jazz this has made for the phenomenon of an art form existing in a curious state of history and pre-history simultaneously. Not that it isn't recognized that it is an art with deep roots in the past, but that the nature of its deep connection with social conditions here and now is slighted. Charlie Christian is a case in point. He flowered from a background with roots not only in a tradition of music, but in a deep division in the Negro community as well. He spent much of his life in a slum in which all the forms of disintegration attending the urbanization of rural Negroes ran riot. Although he himself was from a respectable family, the wooden tenement in which he grew up was full of poverty, crime and sickness. It was also alive and exciting, and I enjoyed visiting there, for the people both lived and sang the blues. Nonetheless, it was doubtless here that he developed the tuberculosis from which he died.

More important, jazz was regarded by most of the respectable Negroes of the town as a backward, low-class form of expression, and there was a marked difference between those who accepted and lived close to their folk experience and those whose status strivings led them to reject and deny it. Charlie rejected this attitude in turn, along with those who held it—even to the point of not participating in the musical activities of the school. Like Jimmy Rushing, whose father was a businessman and whose mother was active in church affairs, he had heard the voice of jazz and would hear no other. Ironically, what was perhaps his greatest social triumph came in death, when the respectable Negro middle-class not only joined in the public mourning, but acclaimed him hero and took credit for his development. The attention which the sheer quality of his music should have secured him was won only by his big-town success.

Fortunately for us, Charles concentrated on the guitar and left the school band to his brother Edward, and his decision was a major part of his luck. For although it is seldom recognized, there is a conflict between what the Negro American musician feels in the community around him and the given (or classical) techniques of his instrument. He feels a tension between his desire to master the classical style of playing and his compulsion to express those sounds which form a musical definition of Negro American experience. In early jazz these sounds found their fullest expression in the timbre of the blues voice, and the use of mutes, water glasses and derbies on the bells of their horns arose out of an attempt to imitate this sound. Among the younger musicians of the thirties, especially those who contributed to the growth of bop, this desire to master the classical technique was linked with the struggle for recognition in the larger society, and with a desire to throw off those non-musical features which came into jazz from the minstrel tradition. Actually, it was for this reason that Louis Armstrong (who is not only a great performing artist but a clown in the Elizabethan sense of the word) became their scapegoat. What was not always understood was that there were actually two separate bodies of instrumental techniques: the one classic and widely recognized and "correct"; and the other eclectic, partly unconscious, and "jazzy." And it was the tension between these two bodies of technique which led to many of the technical discoveries of jazz. Further, we are now aware of the existence of a fully developed and endlessly flexible technique of jazz expression, which has become quite independent of the social environment in which it developed if not of its spirit.

Interestingly enough, the guitar (long regarded as a traditional instrument of Southern Negroes) was subjected to little of this conflict between techniques and ways of experiencing the world. Its role in the jazz orchestra was important but unobtrusive, and before Christian little had been done to explore its full potentialities for jazz. Thus Christian was able to experiment with the least influence from either traditional or contemporary sources. Starting long before he was aware of his mission—as would seem to be the way with important innovators in the arts—he taught himself to voice the guitar as a solo instrument, a development made possible through the perfecting of the electronically amplified instrument—and the rest is history.

With Christian the guitar found its jazz voice. With his entry into the jazz circles his musical intelligence was able to exert its influence upon his peers and to affect the course of the future development of jazz. This album of his work—so irresistible and danceable in its swing, so intellectually stimulating in its ideas—is important not only for its contribution to our knowledge of the evolution of contemporary jazz style; it also offers one of the best arguments for bringing more serious critical intelligence to this branch of our national culture.

RESTORING THE PERSPECTIVE

Robert Hayden's
"The Dream"

GAYL JONES is a novelist, short story writer, and critic whose books have had a tremendous impact, particularly in feminist circles both black and white. Most of her fiction was published in the 1970s and, after being out of print for several years, is now beginning to be reprinted. Her major novels are *Corregidora* (1975) and *Eva's Man* (1976). "Restoring the Perspective: Robert Hayden's 'The Dream' " is a rare essay by Jones that was featured in a special memorial issue of *Obsidian* (Spring 1981) dedicated to black poet Robert Hayden.

I n Ralph Ellison's *Invisible Man*, the narrator asks the question, "What had an old slave have to do with humanity?"[1] Then in his search for his identity (humanity?), he encounters an "old slave" symbolically realized in Brother Tarp, and acknowledges, "he had restored my perspective."[2] Robert Hayden's historical poem "The Dream" does this same restoring of perspective. In an interview novelist and poet Alice Walker has expressed the texture, motives and aesthetics of this restoration in her description of the writing—the Afro-American literary model—that "exposes the *subconscious* of a people, because the people's dreams, imaginings, rituals, legends, etc. are known to be important, are known to contain the accumulated collective reality of the people themselves."[3] Hayden's "The Dream" restores perspective in this sense; from the beginning our attention is given to Sinda, her dream, her imaginings.

> That evening Sinda thought she heard the drums
> and hobbled from her cabin to the yard.
> The quarters now were lonely-still in the willow dusk

after the morning's ragged jubilo,
   when laughing crying singing the folks went off
with Marse Lincum's soldier boys.
   But Sinda hiding would not follow them: those
Buckras with their ornery
   funning, cussed commands, oh they were not
the hosts the dream had promised her.[4]

The narrative that introduces her is aural-literary. In his article "Covenant of Timelessness and Time: Symbolism and History in Robert Hayden's *Angle of Ascent*," Wilburn Williams, Jr. notes the inclusion of the slave's voice, and song, in the narrative structure:

> The poem is obviously a third-person narrative, but the space separating narrator and actor is frequently violated. The speaker's voice modulates effortlessly into the cadences of the slaves. "Marse Lincum," "Buckra," and "ornery" are words heard in the accents of the slaves. The pathos of the cry "oh they were not were not" is so extraordinary because, syntax notwithstanding, it is Sinda's own voice we hear, and not the poet's.[5]

The voice is Sinda's, the "command" is hers, and the contradictory landscape of consciousness between the dream (the promise) and the reality.
   The human portrait, the restoring of perspective and "authority" is continued and assured through the letter, the written document.

> and hope when these few lines reaches your hand they will fine you well. I am tired some but it is war you know and ole jeff Davis muss be ketch an hung to a sour apple tree like it says in the song I seen some akshun but that is what i listed for not to see the sights ha ha More of our peeples coming every day. The Kernul calls them contrybans and has them work aroun the Camp and learning to be soljurs. How is the wether home. Its warm this evening but theres been lots of rain

In this literate context, there is also the dramatic impact of voice, of statement. We acknowledge the diction and metaphors from folk speech and fragments of song, the spelling changes. It is important to note here that rather than giving a sense of linguistic distortion or aberration which occurs with many other applications of orthographical changes to denote the "semi-literate" folk, this letter seems to rivet our attention; it seems to make us *see* the words as if we'd never seen them before or to see them in a new way; it makes us pay a new attention to them. Though an historical poem, this lends it a dramatic immediacy. And certainly in addition to the renewed sense of language and human voice, there is the restored perspective, restoring the slave as a "human face" in history; it provides an historical remembrance to counter the "historical forgetfulness."[6]
   The next "movement" of the poem clarifies the vision of Sinda's dream; again there is a kind of restoration: of "the hosts the dream had promised her."

How many times that dream had come to her—
more vision than a dream—
    the great big soldiers marching out of gunburst,
their faces those of Cal and Joe
    and Charlie sold to the ricefields oh sold away
a-many and a-many a long year ago.
    Fevered, gasping, Sinda listened, knew this was
the ending of her dream and prayed
    that death, grown fretful and impatient, nagging her,
would wait a little longer, would let her see.

There is also the inclusion of the spiritual in the narrative, as an assertion of Sinda's voice.

As we encountered the letter "in progress" we return to it. The second excerpt again acts on memory and imagination, provides the poetic tension in the juxtaposition of Sinda's "fevered gasping" and the resourceful, assuring voice of the letter.

and we been marching sleeping too in cold rain and mirey mud a heap a times. Tell Mama Thanks for The Bible an not worry so. Did brother fix the roof yet like he promised? this mus of been a real nice place befor the fighting uglied it all up the judas trees is blossommed out so pretty same as if the hurt and truble wasn't going on. Almos like somthing you mite dream about i take it for a sign The Lord remembers Us Theres talk we will be moving into Battle very soon agin

This second excerpt also contains the historical references and sense of place of the first. Here there is personal contact. The relationship between the slaves themselves, often excluded from the slaves' own histories,[7] is brought to the forefront here. The statements are therefore not trivial or perfunctory merely, but have profound thematic significance, restoring the sense and sensibility of human contact. Also, the pain and beauty of the South comes with the same insistence of Jean Toomer's *Cane*. The dream and nightmare co-exist in the same space and time.

In the third movement, again there is the resolution of Sinda's voice into the narrative: "Hep me, Jesus." The "wavering yard," the "tenuous moonlight" mirror character and consciousness.

    Trembling tottering Hep me, Jesus Sinda crossed
the wavering yard, reached
    a rebud tree in bloom, could go no farther, clung
to the bole and clinging fell
    to her knees. She tried to stand, could not so much
as lift her head, tried to hold
    the bannering sounds, heard only the whipoorwills
in tenuous moonlight; struggled to rise
    and make her way to the road to welcome Joe and Cal
and Charlie, fought with brittle strength to rise.

As Sinda struggles to rise and make the dream real, we are aware of the tension between the dream and the possible reality, the tension between her belief (or dream) and the possibilities in the world.

The third excerpt of the letter seems to function as prophecy at the same time that it continues to restore perspective and the slave's humanity.[8]

> So pray for me that if the Bullit with my name rote on it get me it will not get me in retreet i do not think them kine of thots so much no need in Dying till you die I all ways figger, course if the hardtack and the bullybeef do not kill me nuthing can i guess. Tell Joe I hav shure seen me some ficety gals down here in Dixieland & i mite jus go ahead and jump over the broomstick with one and bring her home, well I muss close with Love to all & hope to see you soon Yrs Cal

This not only restores the human dimension but the heroic dimension to the slaves' portrait and historical authority. In an interview, Robert Hayden stated of his historical poems, "I also hoped to correct the false impression of our past, to reveal something of its heroic and human aspects."[9] Restoring of perspective here becomes the restoring of the heroic image; the slave-narrator is participant in this image-making.

In addition, the lines of humor,[10] the statement of love (and the acknowledgment of love in its various forms) are also important here; in the face of difficult times and uncertainty, there are the reserves (reservoirs) of humor, of tenderness. Love and humor are also restoratives.

NOTES

1. Ralph Ellison, *Invisible Man*, (New York, 1952), p. 307.

2. Ibid, p. 338.

3. John O'Brien, *Interviews With Black Writers*, (New York, 1973), p. 202.

4. Robert Hayden, "The Dream," *New Black Voices*, ed. Abraham Chapman, (New York, 1972), pp. 206–207. All quotations from the poem are taken from this book.

5. Wilburn Williams, Jr., "Covenant of Timelessness and Time: Symbolism and History in Robert Hayden's *Angle of Ascent*," *Chant of Saints*, eds., Michael S. Harper and Robert B. Steptoe, (Illinois, 1979), pp. 75–76.

6. Ralph Ellison, *Shadow and Act*, (New York, 1972), p. 124.

7. Note that in Frederick Douglass's *Narrative* personal relationships between slaves is excluded and not dramatized. The concentration is on scenes of black-white conflict.

8. Note in Hayden's "Middle Passage" poem the slaves are described as "sweltering cattle" by the masters, then Lewwonder, "But, oh, the living look at you with human eyes."

9. O'Brien, p. 118.

10. Contrast with the "ornery funny" of the beginning stanza.

VIII

PORTRAITS, VOLUME 3

ETHEL WATERS

WILLIAM GARDNER SMITH (1927–1974)

attended Central High School in Philadelphia where he was inspired and mentored by English teacher Gerald Hamm. He also studied at Temple University. He was a novelist, editor, and reporter. His books include *Last of the Conquerors* (1948), *Anger at Innocence* (1950), *South Street* (1954), this last being named for a noted black Philadelphia thoroughfare. Ethel Waters (1896–1977) also grew up in Philadelphia and after an unsuccessful marriage at 13 went on stage and eventually became "Sweet Mama Stringbean," a successful singer and dancer. She was also a Broadway and Hollywood actress, appearing in, among other productions, *As Thousands Cheer, Cabin in the Sky,* and *Member of the Wedding.* Always a faithful Catholic, in later life Waters joined the Billy Graham Crusades. She wrote two autobiographies, *His Eye Is on the Sparrow* (1951) and *To Me It's Wonderful* (1972). This profile on Ethel Waters appeared in *Phylon,* Second Quarter, 1950.

"A rose is a rose is a rose," said Gertrude Stein, which seems to us a rather prosaic way of putting it. A rose is sunlight, wind, rain, the good earth, the symbol of love, and the symbol of innocence. It is spring and summer, happy children, picnics, a girl attending her first prom, a young man trying to make an impression. It is illness, sadness, death—all and any of the things which come to mind when the word "rose" is mentioned.

Ethel Waters is an age. She is part of the legend of a time gone by—a time which was never quite what we like to think it was, but whose embroidered memory persists in our national consciousness, symbol of a spirit which may never return.

What do you think of when you hear the name Ethel Waters? I think of bookstore windows filled with copies of Carl Van Vechten's *Nigger Heaven.* I see

Prohibition and the hip flask, short, tight skirts, bobbed hair, horrendous hats, eyes made grotesque by the eyebrow pencil, and ears heavy laden with earrings. There, this night, coming down the street, is Peggy Hopkins Joyce, the jewel queen, and her entourage, headed for some Harlem cellar cafe. Coupled in the air are the excitement of sin and belief in eternal prosperity.

The bull market. The Palmer raids. Gang warfare. The heart of a nation throbs. "Fledgling nation," the world called us. "The international youth." The youngest nation in the world was experiencing the first thrills following adolescence. It was exciting, it was unending. A time for laughter and song.

The wildness of youth is akin to savagery, marked by the absence of many inhibitions, the absence of many taboos. And what segment of the American population was believed to be closer to this "natural state" than the Negroes? If it was a time for singing, a time for dancing, a time for sin and sex, then it was a time for kinship with the American Negroes—particularly that wild and charming breed spawned in the tenements of Harlem.

What did it matter that Negroes were not, really, any closer to savagery than the white American? What did it matter if the vision of the Negro as native existed only in the chauvinistic white mind? The *belief* was enough. The symbol sufficed. Back to nature (said the misinterpreters of Freud) was the order of the day; and back to the Negroes was its concrete manifestation.

The flowering of Negro "culture" some have called it. Do you recall the combinations Miller and Lyles, or Sissle and Blake? Do you remember Florence Mills in *Shuffle Along*, with her striped pants, satin shoes and knapsack on a pole— her every movement a pleasure to behold? Or Paul Robeson, not then so serious as now (the world was not as serious), singing "Old Man River" in *Showboat*? There was an endless procession of Negro shows—*Blackbirds*, *The Chocolate Dandies*, *All God's Chillun Got Wings*, *Deep River*, *Porgy*, *The Green Pastures*, *Stevedore*, *Four Saints in Three Acts*, *Porgy and Bess*, and countless others.

Bert Williams rolled 'em in the aisles in the Ziegfeld Follies. (And W. C. Fields said of him: "He is the funniest man I ever saw, and the saddest man I ever knew.") The nation throbbed to the original rhythms of Louis Armstrong (ah, hear that trumpet!), Cab Calloway (hair flying, then as now) and Duke Ellington (the classical swingster). Bill Robinson tapped up and down the stairs. And what could be more delightfully typical of the spirit of the times than Orson Welles' fantastic production of the Harlem *Macbeth*?—called by one critic "the Emperor Jones gone beautifully mad!" Nor was the Negro artist performing solely within our national borders. Charles Gilpin was carrying *The Emperor Jones* to the royalty of Europe, and in Paris, the eternal Josephine Baker was drawing from critics comments like that of Audre Levinson: "She is an idol that enslaves and incites mankind."

Into this world place Ethel Waters. What rank did she occupy? "The greatest artist of her race and generation," said Ashton Stevens of the Chicago *American*. "America's number one Negro actress," *Life* magazine was later to say. "The greatest artist of her generation regardless of race," was the recent judgment of Earl Dancer (once her manager) in the Amsterdam *News*.

Was she the greatest? It is hard to say, in a world filled with greats. But this much, surely, is certain: if she did not stand head and shoulders above everyone else, at least no one stood even an inch above *her*. She occupied the heights held by Calloway and Ellington and Robinson—so that a latter day biographer of the Duke was led to remark that the downtown Cotton Club folded solely because it could not obtain enough acts of their caliber to keep the place going between engagements of these "titans."

What was the secret of her success? Perhaps it was her warmth, her visible humanity. Audiences felt drawn to her, caught up by her, held by the personality which came through words and dance. Physically, she was not beautiful; yet, where before or since has one seen such eyes as she possessed: soft, inviting, and yet—somehow—shy. Her smile, also, contained this mixture of coquetry and shyness. She did the hottest shake dance of her, or any other, day. She used to hold her arms far out from her body, to give the freest movement to all parts of her anatomy; she wore tassles on her hips sometimes, and a large buckle on her belt, to accentuate the movements of her body. She could squirm, twist, shake and vibrate in a way which was absolutely uncanny. And yet—who ever felt the slightest sense of vulgarity? One had the impression that she could bathe in mud and still remain clean. She raised her full, clear voice in songs with triple-meanings without making the most sensitive souls among her audience withdraw. For whatever the song, whatever the act, she added a special cleansing substance. That was—herself. It was Ethel Waters, the personality, the warmth, the human being. It was this vital addition to the bare material which the crowds swarmed out to see.

She romped through the roaring twenties, touring the vaudeville circuits, bringing down the houses. The Theater Owners Booking Association, Keith's Western Vaudeville, Keith-Orpheum—these and other circuits sponsored her hit tours. This was the beginning of her rise; previously, she had played, chiefly, the cellar cafes. She was slender, with smooth skin and nice legs; her voice and her dancing carried her name to many lips. When she made several recordings, she became known to many more.

Even when teamed with other acts, Ethel Waters invariably stole the shows. There was never any sense of strain in her performances; she was forever herself, Ethel Waters, in complete control of herself and her audience. A keen judge of people (by intuition), she could divine the mood of her audience, seize it, twist it, squeeze it dry, and manipulate it in any way that suited her fancy. As though through hypnotism she dominated the crowds who came to see her; she ruled the theater while on stage. Playing the big spots later in the years, she brought down the houses with her renditions of such songs as "Dinah" and "St. Louis Blues." She was the first Negro woman ever to star alone on Broadway; this was at the Palace, where she was compelled by the crowd to do a forty-five minute show—a record topped only by Al Jolson. Milwaukee, St. Louis, Chicago, Detroit, Philadelphia—all these became familiar with her dancing, singing, and name.

In the thirties, the mood of the people had changed. The money which had seemed so endless the decade previous was now much harder to come by. Where there had been the most delirious optimism, there was now a sense of despair, of imminent danger. The world was embroiled in the greatest crisis it had ever known—the crisis of Depression and international bankruptcy. Now, in Germany, Hitler's ranting could be heard; now, in Italy, Mussolini's dream of empire was shouted more loudly to the world. Herbert Hoover, trapped by and made the butt of a joke of fate, cried weakly to a starving nation that prosperity was "just around the corner." There were soup lines, labor unrest, lockouts, the flight of capital. The decade was to witness the nightmare of Hitler, the thwarted Spanish revolution, and the beginning of the Second World War. And yet—the shows went on.

Ethel Waters, said *Life* magazine, made her songs sound "like humanity in general." This, certainly, was true. It is part of the warmth I spoke of previously. The nation—and particularly the Negro people—saw only blackness in the future. Disorganized, demoralized, they longed for a voice to utter their feelings and, at the same time, still some of their doubts.

If Ethel Waters was popular in the twenties, when the nation was wild and prosperous, she was the voice of America in the decade of the thirties. The long sad notes of "Stormy Weather," "St. Louis Blues," and "Am I Blue"—sung as only Ethel Waters could sing them—sounded, indeed, like "humanity in general." And, when a change of pace—escape—was needed, she could switch over to "Heat Wave," "They Say" or even "I'm Comin', Virginia." The nation drew close to her, as to a mother.

In rapid succession came her greatest shows: *Blackbirds, Rhapsody in Black, As Thousands Cheer, At Home Abroad* (with Bea Lillie), *Mamba's Daughters*, and *Cabin in the Sky*. For awhile, she had a radio program. In 1938, she held a recital at Carnegie Hall.

There were people in those days who could not think of certain songs without thinking immediately of Ethel Waters. There were Negro women who could not wash the clothes or clean the homes of their white employers without thinking of the woman who sang "St. Louis Blues." There are people today who believe that the nation would not have been able to weather the economic storm of the Depression without the constant uplift and sympathy of stars of stage, screen, vaudeville, and radio—among whom loomed high the figure of Ethel Waters. She sang of their sorrows; she sang of their hopes; she gave them relief by singing of love, or faith, or God. She personified the needs of the people of her day. And, incidentally, she made a million dollars.

There is something of sadness and of loneliness in Ethel Waters. You hear it in her songs, you see it in her eyes. She is trapped, even today, by the memory of her childhood, I believe. Suffering in youth imprints itself irradicably upon the soul, regardless of the change in outward circumstances. A peace in God and economic security have been found by Ethel Waters; but the essential alienation, the loneliness, remains.

Born October 31, 1900, in Chester, Pennsylvania, the daughter of John Wesley and Louisa Waters, the woman who was to become an American legend was a member of a large and poverty-stricken family. While she was still a child the family moved to Philadelphia, where, on the North and South sides, she knew only the continuation of poverty and the sad, painful, violent worlds of South Street, Ridge Avenue, and Columbia Avenue.

"I've stolen food to live on when I was a child," she has said. "I was a tough child. I was too large and too poor to fit, and I fought back."

It seemed a losing fight, in those days of unemployment and low Negro morale. The NAACP was just being born; there were few Negro newspapers; the Negro nation was just emerging from the degrading era of Booker T. Washington and the other compromisers. It was a time when men were ashamed to be Negroes, when members of the race believed the stereotypes white Americans painted of them. There was no collective Negro consciousness, no collective Negro struggle. And jobs, for Negroes, were hard to come by.

She attended a nuns' school. The kindly women who had renounced the world of the flesh recognized, none the less, the needs of the flesh, and they could see that Ethel was being deprived of these needs. They wanted to help her; but the young Ethel was proud, and the nuns had to use subterfuges. They invented work for Ethel to do, devised needless errands for her to run. Then, in return, they could invite her to lunch or dinner. The little girl knew what was happening. She was grateful because they let her retain her pride.

When she was sixteen years old, Ethel Waters went to work in a second-class Philadelphia hotel, as chambermaid and laundress. Her wages were $4.75 per week, which seemed fairly reasonable to a poor girl in those days. Then came a night off—which happened to fall on her birthday, Hallowe'en—and to celebrate she went to a night club on Juniper Street, wearing a mask for protection. It was a gay party, in which everyone in the audience participated. Someone recognized her, and persuaded her to sing two songs. Two neighborhood boys, who were present, recognized the talent which lay here untapped. They had a proposition: how about turning professional?

That was how it began. The quiet, shy girl, who had to be begged to sing, went on the stage. The money, compared to what she had received in the past, seemed good. When, at the age of seventeen, she appeared on the stage of the Lincoln Theater in Baltimore, singing "St. Louis Blues," she was pulling down a "salary" of nine dollars per week, which excited her greatly—until she learned that her two "managers" were pocketing twenty-five dollars of her money. Thus ended their tenure as her managers. (Who could have believed, during those years, that one day she would receive seventy-five thousand dollars for co-starring with Clifton Webb and Helen Broderick in *As Thousands Cheer*?)

There followed other engagements, chiefly in the South. She was a shake dancer and a singer of shady songs. Gradually, people began to hear about her. Still in her 'teens, she moved into the New York cellar cafes, where the socialites came to hear her. The word spread around: "this Waters gal has got something." She was making more money than she had ever made before. Still, she was not happy. The work was hard, and she did not particularly care for the type of songs she was compelled to sing.

"When I was a honky-tonk entertainer," she told Earl Wilson, "I used to work from nine until unconscious. I was just a young girl, and when I tried to sing anything but the double-meaning songs, they'd say: 'Oh, my God, Ethel, get hot!' "

And later she told a New York *Post* writer: "Every time they'd write a serious or sweet song, they'd give it to Florence Mills, Minto Cato, or somebody else."

At home, she sang Negro spirituals.

Around 1923 she got a break, moving downtown to the Plantation Club to substitute for Florence Mills. It was all she needed. She created a sensation, particularly with her rendition of "Dinah." Earl Dancer, who was then her manager, reports that "it was in this show that Ethel Waters developed into the greatest comedienne of her day on Broadway's after-theater spots."

Miss Waters tells an interesting story about the Plantation Club. Were it not for a decision of hers, it seems, the fabulous tradition of Josephine Baker might have never been established—or would, at the very least, have been considerably delayed. For while Ethel Waters was at the Plantation, she was invited to sing in Paris. Not really wanting to travel, she demanded $500 per week—a tremendous sum in those days. This demand was, of course, refused; they took an end girl instead, and her name was Josephine Baker.

"But she was great with my stuff," Miss Waters comments.

The rise was now complete; Ethel Waters was "made." Show followed show, night club engagement followed night club engagement, and money poured in. Her name spread like wildfire. She made a picture, *On With the Show*. Beneath it all, she remained essentially the Ethel Waters of the poor districts of Philadelphia— and she remains so even today, as she adds to her achievements in Broadway's *The Member of the Wedding*.

She is a deeply religious person. When fame and fortune first were hers, she purchased two apartment houses in New York and took a ten-room suite as her own. One of these rooms was devoted exclusively to religion and religious objects. Here she went to pray to God who was her great strength and her great friend, filling the void which must have existed inside her because of the human companionship she seemed to shy away from. She asked God for many things—chiefly spiritual qualities.

"I ask the Lord for so much," she said, "that I guess I keep him scufflin'."

Ethel Waters dislikes "phonies"—people who pretend to be more than they are, or who feel themselves superior to other people. She believes in being natural, in saying what she thinks. Asked once if she weighed "around 160 pounds," she laughed and said, "Honey, if you say 185, we'll call it a deal."

She likes children, and has about a dozen godchildren. At the conclusion of her shows, she used to come home in her chauffeur-driven Lincoln-Zephyr and entertain a couple of these children. She had a marvelous collection of bracelets, assembled from all over the world; she loved horseback riding, wedgies (shoes) and black dresses. She had, and still has, a terrific temper, loves to fight. "It got so bad," she said, "I had to start controlling myself."

Yet, peace, quiet, and the everlasting shyness are her essential moods. The lights of her dressing rooms are invariably kept low; visitors must knock, speak quietly, and leave as soon as possible. She does not seek publicity, does not like interviews. She shies away from the limelight.

It has been like this always. When she was a member of the cast of *As Thousands Cheer*, Irving Berlin and Moss Hart used to give weekly parties for the cast. Ethel would never come. Pressed hard one evening, she told the two producers that she would come to one party and sing a song if they liked—but only on condition that she be allowed to leave immediately afterwards.

Peace, quiet, tranquillity. A Negro, she is, of course, subject to the indignities visited upon members of the race. But she feels no bitterness.

"I don't lament the prejudice," she once said. "You can read *Native Son* and there is one statement of the Negro's cause, and you can then read *Grapes of Wrath* and realize that white holds down white. It's all a struggle for supremacy."

Ethel Waters. The legend and the woman: both are fabulous. This woman, nearing fifty, who is famous for hot songs, shake dances and comedy, found her fullest satisfaction in the role of Hagar, in *Mamba's Daughters*, in which she played the part of Fredi Washington's mother. She said of this play:

"When it was over, I just wanted to put myself away and retire. I didn't want nothing to spoil it. Don't mention anything I've ever done on the musical stage in the same breath with Hagar."

Her favorite role. And small wonder. The contradictions of Hagar—her softness and great strength, her gentleness and violent temper, her religion and her endurance and self-reliance—add up to Ethel Waters herself.

RICHARD WRIGHT'S COMPLEXES AND BLACK WRITING TODAY

CECIL BROWN is an essayist, novelist, screenwriter, and lecturer. He attended North Carolina A and T, Columbia University, and the University of Chicago. His novels include *The Life and Loves of Mr. Jiveass Nigger* (1969) and *Days Without Weather* (1982). "Richard Wright's Complexes and Black Writing Today," an important piece in reassessing Richard Wright in the light of the then-emerging and still inchoate theory of the Black Aesthetic (black value system) or the overt politicization of literary analysis, appeared in *Negro Digest* in December 1968.

I

So notoriously void of honesty is White Society in this country that any writer made famous by it is an immediate suspect, and if he is a Negro writer, double suspect. Black writers, who are of extreme value to the Black Community, for example, cannot, by definition, be of much value to White Society (I am thinking of such writers as LeRoi Jones and Eldridge Cleaver); and conversely, white writers of national popularity are the Black Community's enemy. One might say that a writer of Richard Wright's status is an exception, but let me hasten to add that, as a chronic, black reader of literature, I have felt, in reading Wright's books, a strange uneasiness, not about the sub-human puppets dangled before me, but about the man controlling these puppets—who is, really, the Booker T. Washington of American letters. (And is it not the messianic urge for another B. T. Washington that haunts the white critic like Irving Howe, who can so swiftly conclude that Wright is Ralph Ellison's and James Baldwin's "spiritual father"?)

Because I had barely survived the dirt farms of North Carolina myself, I stayed away from Wright as long as I could; and even after I broke down and read *Native*

Son and enjoyed it and was surprised, even then I felt I was patronizing "Negro Literature." When I read Baldwin, Ellison, Jones, or Cleaver, however, I read for myself; I feel I understand something about myself as a black man and a writer; I feel involved with these writers' lives because they, themselves, are involved in explaining to themselves and to all who listen to their weird position in White America; Wright, in contrast, spent his life explaining someone *else* (*i.e.* the Bigger Thomases) to white people who were anxious to believe that, indeed, Bigger existed, but not Wright himself.

It is not that the social reality portrayed by Wright is false, but that, in so far as it represents Wright's own life, it is . . . (I do not wish to use the word "lie" so let's say simply that Wright availed himself of a literary convention). Anyone wishing to view the distance between the benighted Bigger Thomas and the enlightened Richard Wright with more accurate measurement should compare, for example, Wright's attitude towards white women in his fiction and his attitude towards them in his biography and his autobiographical works. By insisting on the disparity between Wright's life and the social reality he created, I am not saying that Wright was dishonest and that he betrayed (however unwittingly) the values of the black community; rather, to emphasize the extent to which literature is dependent, for its impetus and impact, on literary fashions and conventions. One should avoid the implication of Wright's social reality, that South Chicago was worse in the 40s than it is now. Wright wrote about Chicago in the manner that he did because that was what white America was ready to accept (in terms of literary fashion and social imagery), or more accurately, *needed* to accept.

White America branded Wright the Official Negro Protester, the genuine article; to reject him was to reject official, genuine Negro protest, no matter what your own experience as a Negro might have been. In terms of popularity, Wright was the Great American Writer, and in Europe even more so—and probably for the same reason that *Patch of Blue* was so popular in Denmark. I remember walking out of that movie in Copenhagen trying to explain to sympathetic Danish friends ("It's not *that* simple; I mean it's more *complex*") why I rejected the movie's reality.

To reject Wright's art is not to reject protest; it is to reject negative protest, to reject the white man's concept of protest, which is that of a raging, ferocious, uncool, demoralized black boy banging on the immaculate door of White Society, begging, not so much for political justice as for his own identity, and in the process, consuming himself, so that in the final analysis, his destiny is at the mercy of the White Man. No, to reject Wright is not to reject protest, it is to reject negative protest. Every black person who realizes how sick American white society is, by the logic of this awareness, makes a protest, a positive protest. This is a delicate point which the oversimplification of Wright's social reality has obscured.

Positive protest that creates as it eliminates: it deals with the opposition's ugliness by concentrating on its own beauty. LeRoi Jones's prose is positive protest, because it is witty and beautiful to black people—which means simply white people cannot understand it; black children in the doorways of the ghetto doing the James Brown or the Uptight are positive protest directed against white people, because white people can't dance; *Negro Digest* is positive protest against the *Reader's Digest*;

every ghetto—I do not mean slum—is positive protest against white insipid suburbs; black people together, involved with their lives, carrying on with their black and bluesy culture, is positive protest against the simpleness and the uninterestedness that haunt the abstracted lives of middle-class whites.

II

The argument that the value in Richard Wright's work lies in how well it describes the "specific social climate" that produced it is nothing more than a rationalization for the man's success, and an erroneous one at that; for it misses the point that it was Wright's attitude towards the Negro writer and Negro literature that led him to believe there was a gold mine in explaining to White America the lives of Black People; it was his definition of "Negro Writer" that led him to select from his own vast and rich experiences those horrifying scraps from which emerged a dozen or so unbelievably dumb Negroes. Just as the monster was created not by Frankenstein but by Mary Shelley, so Wright's creation cannot be foisted off on society; if we want to get to the key to Wright's work, we would do best by examining the theories of fiction Wright accepted during his day. A crucial question in Wright's definition of the Negro writer had to do with subject-matter, which stated simply that a Negro writer was someone who wrote about Negro life (Jesus, this would make Jessie Hill Ford, Nat Hentoff, Robert Penn Warren and William Faulkner Negro writers!) and, as though this was not enough, there was definite itemized catalog (*i.e.* set-pieces) of what constituted "Negro life"—this, of course, was a much easier way out than saying "Negro life" is anything that a Negro does, because this leaves a definition of "Negro" too opened and, baby, white people weren't having that just yet! An intellectual life, literary success, marriage to a white woman, for example, did not constitute "Negro life" (at least not for the white reading public), which explains why Wright published not one scratch about *this* aspect of his life. (In order to see how Black Writing handles this, compare, for example, the manner in which LeRoi Jones handles these aspects of his life in plays *Dutchman* and *The Slave.*)

Wright believed, as far too many people still do, that there are certain categories which constitute black experience and others white experience, that these white and black categories are (and this is a shame) ascribed, with you when you are born, and cannot be shaken by individual will. For Wright, it was his damnation to be born black, and his will to achieve whiteness—*i.e.* to pull himself up to the literary standards of white America.

The tenets of Black Writing today are the reverse of what Wright believed. For Black Writing, a black writer is first of all black, which means simply that he accepts the standards of black people *over* those of White America. Every Negro baby in America is born white, born, that is, into a world of white values, and if he is to survive that world, he has to *achieve* blackness; somewhere in the marrow of his youth must be that experience, that awakening, that *rebirth* Jesus talked so much about, which must carry him over to accept the reality of blackness. This journey is ultimately an achievement of both grace and one's own will. One must, as Ellison so strongly insists upon, *will* to be a Negro: ". . . . . being a Negro American involves a *willed* (who wills to be a Negro? *I* do!) affirmation of self against all outside pressures." But the Irving Howe types ("Freedom can be fought for, but it cannot always be willed or asserted into existence") wishes this weren't so.

So then, a Black Writer is not just some colored person trying to prove to White Society that he is not a "nigger," or/and that if he is, White Society is to blame. No, when we meet the black writer in the pages of his work, we encounter someone who has *achieved* and *willed* an identity of blackness, someone who has accepted Negro life not as a burden, as Ellison puts it, but as a discipline.

Subject-matter, then, is not part of the criteria in determining a black writer, but quality of life, will, discipline and moral courage are. A black writer can write about anything, I mean this literally, and what he has to say will still be said by a black man. As LeRoi Jones puts it: "If I say, 'I am a black man. All my writing is done by a black man,' whether I label each thing I write, 'Written by a black' it's still written by a black man, so that if I point out a bird, a black man has pointed out that bird, and it is the weight of that experience in me and the way I get it from where it is to you that says whether or not I am a writer." (*Anger, and Beyond*, p. 56.)

The tragedy of Richard Wright's life is that he subscribed to a definition of the Negro writer that was perniciously paradoxical: on the one hand the role of the Negro writer, as Wright saw it, allowed him the potent power of the raging satirist, while at the very same time rendered him, in the last years of his life, impotent and exiled. It was near impossible for Wright to change his ideas about the function of the writer, because such ideas were, as always, intricately woven into the writer's definition of his *self*. "To me Wright as *writer* was less interesting than the enigma he personified," Ellison can say, "that he could so dissociate himself from the complexity of his background while trying so hard to improve the condition of black men everywhere; that he could be so wonderful an example of human possibility but could not for ideological reasons depict a Negro as intelligent, as creative or as dedicated as himself" (*Anger and Beyond*, p. 26). Wright's idea of a Negro Writer was extremely middle-class, which means that he believed that what white society thought to be Negro reality was more important than what Negroes knew to be their reality.

Wright was exiled because his definition of "Negro life" was too narrow, too confining, too puny, and too dependent on White Society. Wright was afraid to define "Negro life" too broadly for fear it would cease to be Negro. A weird kind of insecurity.

III

It was Wright's conception of what he thought his function as a Negro writer should be that is primarily responsible for his style (*i.e.* his attitude towards his reader and his characters.)

The Negro world that Wright wrote about was so strange, so far from the lives of his white audience, that Wright indulged, too often, in the explanatory. The Negro Characters that he created are usually so sub-human, so dumb that, for the most part, Wright was forced to stand in the pages of his fiction as a kind of "Negro

Spokesman." In order for a work of fiction to mean anything, it must first of all involve the reader. For a black reader, it is difficult to become involved—I mean really involved—with Wright's characters because he is always there intruding with his commentary, explaining, as it were, what to a black reader needs no apologetic explanation. This explanatory mood of Wright's resulted, finally, in a dull, desiccated, prosaic sentence structure that leaves nothing to the reader's imagination.

It is not, as some critics have stated, that Wright doesn't have a sense of humor, in his fiction; it is simply that his prose style strangles his humor, which, like most elements of black culture, has nuances that are difficult to grasp with discursive prose. It is only after we have laid the story aside for some time and have allowed our minds to re-arrange the images, the setting, the tone, of Wright's stories, only after that methodical and plodding rhythm of his prose has ceased to reverberate in our minds, that we appreciate his humour.

One of the reasons, incidentally, that LeRoi Jones is such a funny writer ("The Alternative" has to be one of the funniest stories ever written in America) is that his style is essentially poetic; and this is why, too, in *Tales* he can convey so much of Negro life. Poetry, rather than prose, seems to be the tool that is best for conveying the subtleties, the nuances, the complexity of Negro culture. Wright's style is about as close to poetry as, say, Booker T. Washington's or Richard Nixon's.

With the exception of two stories, "Man of All Work," and "Man, God Ain't like That . . . ," both of which were written in dialogue, which was Wright's forte, the book, *Eight Men*, is the dullest I have ever read. Everywhere the reader turns in the book there is the dumb, sub-human, animal-like nigger, and his eloquent interpreter who, possessing some smattering of sociological theories, usually has the responsibility of forging the animal's actions into some acceptable "universal" or "literary" theme.

Take, for instance, the first few lines of the very first story, "The Man Who Was Almost a Man":

> Dave struck out across the fields, looking homeward through paling light. Whut's the use talkin wid em niggers in the field? Anyhow, his mother was putting supper on the table. Them niggers can't understan' nothing. One of these days he was going to get a gun and practice shooting, then they couldn't talk to him as though he were a little boy (p. 11).

The first sentence is by the intelligent, objective, omniscient narrator whom we may presume is also the author; the second that of some Negro who seems to be thinking to himself, and I say *seems* because Wright's Negroes *never* think (although, Wright will *tell* you they do), this is left up to Wright—as Ellison said, "Wright could imagine Bigger, but Bigger could not possibly imagine Richard Wright. Wright saw to that"; the third is by the narrator (*i.e.* Wright), but it is— and this is important—only an interpretation of what presumably the character is thinking; the fourth, which is Dave speaking again, is fused with the narrator's interpretation; and finally, the fifth sentence, although written in the language of the narrator, is the thoughts of the boy—or, is it the narrator putting words into the boy's mouth? The problem is this: we believe we know something about the boy's mind, but we can't be sure, for after all, it was *reported* to us by the narrator.

We can never really know the boy, the narrator stands between us, such that, at the end of the story our feeling towards the boy are ambivalent and anxious. This anxiety builds up to disastrous proportions if in the course of the story, the protagonist is the victim of violence, because one is forced to feel great sympathy for someone one does not know, and does not know why. Maybe this is why upon finishing each of these stories, I felt a bit frustrated and unsatisfied.

The long, short story, "The Man Who Lived Underground," collected in *Eight Men*, suffers greatly from Wright's dumb Negro–eloquent spokesman device. The story cites the adventures of a Negro murderer, Fred, who lives in a manhole, making Robinson Crusoe–type discoveries; Fred is quite childish, and when he finds a stack of money, unlike Crusoe with his mature sense of what money can do in English society. Fred is only "intrigued with the form and color of [it]." He steals a typewriter and radio upon which he literally spends hours, tinkering like a 10-year-old; but it is not of a child Wright wants us to think; his is imagining Fred as a sub-human, as some human who has become less human because he has been shut out of White Society, and this is what is behind Wright's statement about Fred": . . . never in [Fred's] life had he used [a typewriter]. It was a queer instrument of business *something beyond the rim of his life*" (Italics added)—as though using a typewriter is going to add something to the quality of one's life! (One is reminded, of course, of the demoralized Bigger Thomas who wants "to do things," "to fly airplanes" like white boys. A cryin shame.)

Yet this sub-human who has no humanity to speak of or at least one is not convinced of it, is transformed into an intellectual before the story ends—because Wright has to give the thing a universal theme. He selects the theme of Orestes and the furies. Fred, then, marches out of his man-hole into the police station and confesses he is "guilty." The police try to convince him that they had already caught the murderer of the woman whom Fred claims he killed.

The story ends when Fred finally persuades two policemen to go down into the underground to witness what he had experienced, so that "At last he would be free of his burden"; when they are deep in the tunnel, one of the police shoots him, with the explanation, "You've got to shoot his kind. They'd wreck things." Wright not only ended up with the "universal theme" but he even achieved a bit of tear-jerker. What Black Writing has come to realize is that meaning (*i.e.*, theme) is always implied in the image. One has only to paint the metaphor of blackness— the whole community, despite its pretense to the contrary, knows that the meaning is. And again, the history of black people in this country is within itself a universal theme—the most universal of themes. (What "Universal Theme" means, that is in Wright, is to write so white people can understand—*i.e.* without really understanding.)

In the few stories in which Wright left off the discursive prose, and let his character do their own explaining, he created masterpieces. In *Lawd Today*, for example, the dialogue gets as close to poetry as Wright ever got. In this novel the dialogue is fascinating, because it is used to provoke the atmosphere, the mood of black people that the most skilled prose writer would have difficulty in capturing. The last fourth of the book is the best piece of writing Wright accomplished, the proof of this being in the fact that one can return to it and re-read it again and again. The novel depicts one day in the life of a postal clerk, and in order to give the events his inevitable commentary, Wright has that day happen on February 12, Abraham Lincoln's birthday. Throughout the novel, there are brief reminders of the Civil War, reminders that are so planted in the novel as to remind the reader that these Negroes, although wrapped in their own black culture, are not free yet. If this novel, in its celebration of Negro life, could shake itself free of Wright's commentary device it would rival *Native Son* as being Wright's most valuable book.

IV

I have been talking about technique and style and how they were influenced by Wright's definition of the Negro writer. Let me now deal with the treatment of theme, which in Wright's work was as subject to being dictated by white Society as well as style. Let us take for example the theme of the white woman and her relationship with the black man. There is only one kind of interaction between these two, and that is one of unadulterated violence inflicted by the black male, who is imaged as an animal. This relationship is as rigid and codified as any element of medieval symbolism. The idea that a white woman is only a human being and one to whom it is possible to feel something other than hate is an idea that Wright's blacks are incapable of; this, despite the fact that Wright's own experience taught him otherwise.

When Max is questioning Bigger Thomas about his alleged rape and murder of the white girl, Mary Dalton, he suggests that Bigger might have liked Mary. Bigger's reaction is depicted as that of an animal's:

"Did you like her," Max asked?

"*Like* her?"

"Bigger's voice *boomed so suddenly from his throat* that Max started. Bigger *leaped to his feet*; his *eyes widened* and his hands *lifted* midway to face, *trembling*. (Italics added.)

"No! No! Bigger . . ." Max said (p. 323).

Thus, Bigger, the prototype nigger, in his attitude towards the White woman, is more of a creation of white society (which is why white men like Irving Howe can so eagerly lay claim to him) than he is of any black man's: and so are those other black males in the pages of Wright's fiction whose only response to white women is to chop off their heads.

Concerning this, Baldwin has written: "In most of the novels by Negroes until today . . . there is a great space where sex ought to be; and what usually fills this space is violence. This violence, as in so much of Wright's work, is gratuitous and compulsive. It is one of the severest criticisms that can be leveled against his work. The violence is never examined."

I do not believe that Wright did not examine that violence, if it existed, in his personal life; what seems to be the case is that Wright subscribed to a literary convention that had as much to do with life as, say, menthol cigarettes, a convention responsible only to White Society. One could look, for example, at the treatment of the theme of the white woman in an autobiographical story called "The Man Who Went to Chicago," in which, the hero is an intelligent young man whom we must recognize as none other than the author; and his attitude towards white women is, simply, normal. It is only when Wright had to create fictional characters that he insisted on gratuitous violence.

V. NATIVE SON

Bigger Thomas, like Othello, another victim of white society, is dumb, but whereas Othello's error lies in Othello, in his perception, Bigger's lies in bad style, in Richard Wright. Bigger's dumbness is only a thematic device. Wright is not so much interested in the character of Bigger as he is in using whatever literary conventions to make an ideological point. Thus, at the beginning of the novel, it is convenient to have Bigger extremely stupid, for purposes of motivation; and after the murder, again it is convenient to give Bigger some awareness of his crime, thus adding to the significance of the crime as a theme. So that on page 35, Bigger is so stupid that he doesn't know what a communist is (when his friend helps him with "a communist is a red" he dumbly asks, "What's a red?"); yet, on page 109, he is suddenly ruminating on world issues: "Of late he had liked to hear tell of men who could rule others, for in actions such as these he felt that here was an escape from his tight morass of fear and shame that sapped at the base of his life. He liked to hear of how Japan was conquering China; of how Hitler was running the Jews to the ground; of how Mussolini was invading Spain." One ceases to believe in Bigger as a character, and there are moments when the reader grasps at Bigger's action and the ideas behind them with the same awe and lack of understanding that his own family did. And this happens because one feels he does not know Bigger, which is because he doesn't exist as a human being.

A rebel without a brain, Bigger's tragedy is a personal one, and it exists in the fact that he simply refuses to (cannot) see; Wright's tragedy is that he fails to condemn this blindness. Though, it may be that Bigger's demoralization is Wright's, *i.e.* Wright as artist. Bigger, for instance, prides himself on the knowledge that no one would ever think that a black timid Negro like himself was responsible (Or is this Wright putting words in his mouth?): ". . . for he felt that they [white people] ruled him, even when they were far away and not thinking of him, ruled him by conditioning him in his relations to his own people" (p. 110). Bigger is only embodying a fantasy White Society created for him long ago, and this is why he feels that the murder is an act of creation; he talks about the murder bringing out the "hidden meaning of his life." This has to be taken ironically, because what is really meant is that Bigger, a kind of racial correlative objective, was created to serve White Society.

Bigger wanted to be white, but he wasn't smart enough to see that what can be had in whiteness can most certainly be had in blackness. Why couldn't Wright see this?

VI. CRITICS—BLACK AND WHITE

The distance between Bigger Thomas and Richard Wright, even after the publication of *Black Boy*, was so notoriously great that Ellison, in his famous essay, "Richard Wright's Blues," set out to explain it: "By discussing some of its cultural sources I hope to answer those critics who would make of the book a miracle and of its author a mystery." One of those "cultural sources" Ellison took to be the blues, and so began his essay a much quoted paragraph on the function of the blues; after this insightful opening, Ellison dwindles into some well-stated sociology about the southern rural family, and has nothing else to say about the blues, except in the last paragraph.

Despite its title and general intent, Ellison's essay, in retrospect, sheds much doubt on whether Wright ever really understood the blues. In another essay, "A Rejoinder," published 19 years later, Ellison disparages Wright's knowledge of blues, and says "Hemingway was more important to me than Wright. Not because he was white, or more 'accepted' but because he appreciated the things of this earth which I love and which Wright was too driven or deprived or inexperienced to know." Hemingway's love for life, Ellison says in counterdistinction, "was very close to the feeling of the Blues." In terms of "explaining" Wright, I think Ellison was much closer when he said recently that Wright "was as much a product of his reading as of his painful experiences, and he made himself a writer by subjecting himself to the writer's discipline—as he understood it."

This changing critical attitude of Ellison's toward Wright I cite as an example of how critical theory has changed in the last 20 years. It is interesting, too, that during the writing of his essay, Ellison's criticism was about as equally imbued with sociological theories as was Wright's writing. Baldwin's criticism of the protest novel ("Everybody's Protest Novel") in general, and his essay, "Alas, Poor Richard," in particular, is very good critically on Wright, and precisely because Baldwin stayed clear of theories—well, at least sociological ones.

Irving Howe is typical of the white critics who harbor a vested interest in Richard Wright's Negroes. In his now famous essay, "Black Boys and Native Sons," Howe claims his disagreement with Ellison and Baldwin has something to do with protest, but Howe's real objection is that these writers, unlike Wright, refuse to create demoralized, unintelligible, sub-humans whose sole life-time concern is consumed in hating the invincible force (as Howe likes to imagine it) of the White World; rather, these writers have given us humane, courageous, profound, aware, conscious heroes, who are really more concerned with themselves and their own realities than with those of white Jewish intellectuals like Howe, whom Wright, apparently, was so respectful of; Howe accuses Baldwin and Ellison of not protesting, but what he refuses to acknowledge is that Baldwin and Ellison, for all their faults, by virtue of their existence as excellent, moral craftsmen, are protesting; their protest is positive protest because, in addition to blasting the white world (*i.e.* not letting White people get to them), they erect black positive images.

Richard Wright begged; Baldwin, Ellison, LeRoi Jones, Eldridge Cleaver are not begging, and this upsets the Howe-types, because they need to hear the rasping, rage of groveling, demoralized Bigger Thomases at the door of White Society in order to be assured themselves that White Society still exists as the only possible alternative for the Negro personality.

Howe writes, for example, that in *Native Son*, Wright struggles to "transcend" violence. "That he did not fully succeed seems obvious; one may doubt that any

Negro writer could." Now this cracker must be kidding, because almost every black writer I know of has "transcended" violence, at least that violence of Bigger's. Howe, like Wright, believes that "violence" is the Negro writer's lot; not to write about violence is to avoid writing about Negro life. This is why he finds *Giovanni's Room* "a flat failure," because, "it abandons Negro Life entirely."

Finally, Howe assigns Wright as spiritual father to both Ellison and Baldwin— Ellison, because he didn't come around to protest, is suffering as a result; but Baldwin has come around: "Baldwin's most recent novel, *Another Country*, is a protest novel quite as much as *Native Son* . . . No longer is Baldwin's prose so elegant or suave as it once was; in this book it is *harsh, clumsy, heavy-breathing* with the pant of *suppressed bitterness.*" Obviously, this white man is speaking of negative protest, demoralized protest, and not the protest of James Brown or LeRoi Jones. In other words, positive protest that asserts its own beauty, if you will, *its own elegance* as it protests is not viable? Well, Howe and his buddies had better wake up. Or not wake up, as they wish.

SONGS OF
A RACIAL SELF

On Sterling A. Brown

HENRY LOUIS GATES, JR. is a MacArthur
Fellow, former professor at Yale, Cornell, and Duke Universities, editor
of numerous books and author of many articles in both popular and
academic publications. He is currently the chair of African-American
Studies at Harvard University. "Songs of a Racial Self: On Sterling A.
Brown" first appeared as a *New York Times* book review on January 11,
1981. It was reprinted in Gates's collection of essays, *Figures in Black:
Words, Signs, and the "Racial" Self* (1987).

"Nigger, your breed ain't metaphysical."
—ROBERT PENN WARREN, "Pondy Woods," 1928

"Cracker, your breed ain't exegetical."
—STERLING BROWN, interview, 1973

B y 1932, when Sterling Brown published *Southern Road*, his first book of
poems, the use of black vernacular structures in Afro-American poetry
was controversial indeed. Of all the arts, it was only through music that
blacks had invented and fully defined a tradition both widely regarded and acknowl-
edged to be uniquely their own. Black folktales, while roundly popular, were
commonly thought to be the amusing fantasies of a childlike people, whose sagas
and anecdotes about rabbits and bears held nothing deeper than the attention span
of a child, à la Uncle Remus or even *Green Pastures*. And what was generally called
dialect, the unique form of English that Afro-Americans spoke, was thought by
whites to reinforce received assumptions about the Negro's mental inferiority.

Dorothy Van Doren simply said out loud what so many other white critics
thought privately. "It may be that [the Negro] can express himself only by music
and rhythm," she wrote in 1931, "and not by words."

Middle-class blacks, despite the notoriety his dialect verse had garnered for

Paul Laurence Dunbar and the Negro, thought that dialect was an embarrassment, the linguistic remnant of an enslavement they all longed to forget. The example of Dunbar's popular and widely reviewed "jingles in a broken tongue," coinciding with the conservatism of Booker T. Washington, was an episode best not repeated. Blacks stood in line to attack dialect poetry. William Stanley Braithwaite, Countee Cullen, and especially James Weldon Johnson argued fervently that dialect stood in the shadow of the plantation tradition of Joel Chandler Harris, James Whitcomb Riley, and Thomas Nelson Page. Dialect poetry, Johnson continued, possessed "but two full stops, humor and pathos." By 1931, Johnson, whose own "Jingles and Croons" (1917) embodied the worst in this tradition, could assert assuredly that "the passing of traditional dialect as a medium for Negro poets is complete."

As if these matters of sensibility were not barrier enough, Johnson believed, somehow that until a black person ("full-blooded" at that) created a written master-piece of art, black Americans would remain substandard citizens.

Johnson here echoed William Dean Howells's sentiments. Howells wrote that Paul Laurence Dunbar's dialect verse "makes a stronger claim for the negro than the negro yet has done. Here in the artistic effect at least is white thinking and white feeling in a black man. . . . Perhaps the proof [of human unity] is to appear in the arts, and our hostilities and prejudices are to vanish in them." Even as late as 1925, Heywood Broun could reiterate this curious idea: "A supremely great negro artist who could catch the imagination of the world, would do more than any other agency to remove the disabilities against which the negro now labors." Broun concluded that this black redeemer with a pen could come at any time, and asked his audience to remain silent for ten seconds to imagine such a miracle! In short, the Black Christ would be a poet. If no one quite knew the precise form this Black Christ would assume, at least they all agreed on three things he could not possibly be: he would not be a woman like feminist Zora Neale Hurston; he would not be gay like Countee Cullen or Alain Locke; and he would most definitely not write dialect poetry. Given all this, it is ironic that Brown used dialect at all. For a "New Negro" generation too conscious of character and class as color (and vice versa), Brown had all the signs of the good life: he was a mulatto with "good hair" whose father was a well-known author, professor at Howard, pastor of the Lincoln Temple Congregational Church, and member of the D.C. Board of Education who had numbered among his closest friends both Frederick Douglass and Paul Laurence Dunbar. Brown, moreover, had received a classically liberated education at Dunbar High School, Williams College, and Harvard, where he took an M.A. in English in 1923. Indeed, perhaps it was just this remarkably secure black aristocratic heritage that motivated Brown to turn to the folk.

Just one year after he had performed the postmortem on dialect poetry, James Weldon Johnson, in the preface to Brown's *Southern Road*, reluctantly admitted that he had been wrong about dialect. Brown's book of poetry, even more profoundly than the market crash of 1929, truly ended the Harlem Renaissance, primarily because it contained a new and distinctly black poetic diction and not merely the vapid and pathetic claim for one.

To the surprise of the Harlem Renaissance's "New Negroes," the reviews were of the sort one imagines Heywood Broun's redeemer–poet was to have gotten. The *New York Times Book Review* said that *Southern Road* is a book whose importance is considerable: "It not only indicates how far the Negro artist has progressed since the years when he began to find his voice, but it proves that the Negro artist is abundantly capable of making an original and genuine contribution to American literature." Brown's work was marked by a "dignity that respects itself. . . . There is everywhere art." Louis Untermeyer agreed: "He does not paint himself blacker than he is." Even Alain Locke, two years later, called it "a new era in Negro poetry." *Southern Road's* artistic achievement ended the Harlem Renaissance, for that slim book undermined all of the New Negro's assumptions about the nature of the black tradition and its relation to individual talent. Not only were most of Brown's poems composed in dialect, but they also had as their subjects distinctively black archetypal mythic characters, as well as the black common man whose roots were rural and Southern. Brown called his poetry "portraitures," close and vivid detailings of an action of a carefully delineated subject to suggest a sense of place, in much the same way as Toulouse-Lautrec's works continue to do. These portraitures, drawn "in a manner constant with them," Brown renders in a style that emerged from several forms of folk discourse, a black vernacular matrix that includes the blues and ballads, the spirituals and worksongs. Indeed, Brown's ultimate referents are black music and mythology. His language, densely symbolic, ironical, and naturally indirect, draws upon the idioms, figures, and tones of both the sacred and the profane vernacular traditions, mediating between these in a manner unmatched before or since. Although Langston Hughes had attempted to do roughly the same, Hughes seemed content to transcribe the popular structures he received, rather than to transcend or elaborate upon them, as in "To Midnight Man at LeRoy's": "Hear dat music . . . / Jungle music / Hear dat music . . . / And the moon was white."

But it is not merely the translation of the vernacular that makes Brown's work major, informed by these forms as his best work is; it is rather the deft manner in which he created his own poetic diction by fusing several black traditions with various models provided by Anglo-American poets to form a unified and complex structure of feeling, a sort of song of a racial self. Above all else, Brown is a regionalist whose poems embody William Carlos Williams's notion that the classic is the local, fully realized. Yet Brown's region is not so much the South or Spoon River, Tilbury or Yoknapatawpha as it is "the private Negro mind," as Alain Locke put it, "this private thought and speech," or, as Zora Neale Hurston put it, "how it feels to be colored me," the very textual milieu of blackness itself. Boldly, Brown merged the Afro-American vernacular traditions of dialect and myth with the Anglo-American poetic tradition and, drawing upon the example of Jean Toomer, introduced the Afro-American modernist lyrical mode into black literature. Indeed, Brown, Toomer, and Hurston comprise three cardinal points on a triangle of influence out of which emerged, among others, Ralph Ellison, Toni Morrison, Alice Walker, and Leon Forrest.

Brown's poetic influences are various. From Walt Whitman, Brown took the oracular, demotic voice of the "I" and the racial "eye," as well as his notion that "new words, new potentialities of speech" were to be had in the use of popular forms such as the ballad. From Edward Arlington Robinson, Brown took the use of the dramatic situation and the ballad, as well as what Brown calls the subject of "the undistinguished, the extraordinary in the ordinary." Certainly Brown's poems "Maumee Ruth," "Southern Cop," "Georgie Grimes," and "Sam Smiley" suggest the same art that created Miniver Cheevy and Richard Cory. From A. E. Housman, Brown borrowed the dramatic voice and tone, as well as key figures: Housman's blackbird in "When Smoke Stood Up from Ludlow" Brown refigures as a buzzard in "Old Man Buzzard." Both Housman's "When I Was One and Twenty" and Brown's "Telling Fortunes" use the figure of "women with dark eyes," just as Brown's "Mill Mountain" echoes Housman's "Terence, This Is Stupid Stuff." Housman, Heinrich Heine, and Thomas Hardy seem to be Brown's central influence of tone. Robert Burns's Scottish dialect and John Millington Synge's mythical dialect of the Aran Islander in part inform Brown's use of black dialect, just as Robert Frost's realism, stoicism, and sparseness, as in "Out, Out—," "Death of the Hired Man," "Birches," "Mending Wall," and "In Dives' Dive" inform "Southern Road," "Memphis Blues," and "Strange Legacies." Brown's choice of subject matter and everyday speech are fundamentally related to the New Poetry and the work of Amy Lowell, Vachel Lindsay, Edgar Lee Masters, and Carl Sandburg, as well as to the common language emphasis of the Imagists. In lines such as "bits of cloud-filled sky . . . framed in bracken pools" and "vagrant flowers that fleck unkempt meadows," William Wordsworth's *Lyrical Ballads* resound. Brown rejected the "puzzle poetry" of Ezra Pound and T. S. Eliot and severely reviewed the Southern Agrarians' "I'll Take My Stand" as politically dishonest, saccharine nostalgia for a medieval never-neverland that never was. Brown never merely borrows from any of these poets; he transforms their influence by grafting them onto black poetic roots. These transplants are splendid creations indeed.

Michael Harper has collected nearly the whole of Brown's body of poetry, including *Southern Road*, *The Last Ride of Wild Bill* (1975), and the previously unpublished *No Hiding Place*, Brown's second book of poems which was rejected for publication in the late thirties because of its political subjects and which seems to have discouraged Brown from attempting another volume until 1975. Inexplicably, two poems of the five-part "Slim Greer" cycle, "Slim in Hell" and "Slim Hears 'The Call,' " are missing, as is the major part of "Cloteel" and the final stanza of "Bitter Fruit of the Tree," oversights that a second edition should correct. Nevertheless, this splendid collection at last makes it possible to review the whole of Brown's works after years when his work remained out of print or difficult to get. Forty-two years separated the first and second editions of *Southern Road*.

Rereading Brown, I was struck by how consistently he shapes the tone of his poems by the meticulous selection of the right word to suggest succinctly complex images and feelings "stripped to form," in Frost's phrase. Unlike so many of his contemporaries, Brown never lapses into pathos or sentimentality. Brown renders the oppressive relation of self to natural and (black and white) man-made environment in the broadest terms, as does the blues. Yet Brown's characters confront catastrophe with all of the irony and stoicism of the blues and black folklore. Brown's protagonists laugh and cry, fall in and out of love, and muse about death in ways not often explored in black literature. Finally, his great theme seems to be the relation of being to the individual will, rendered always in a sensuous diction, echoing what critic Joanne Gabbin calls "touchstones" of the blues lyric, such as "Don't your bed look lonesome / When your babe packs up to leave," "I'm gonna leave heah dis mawnin' ef I have to ride de blind," "Did you ever wake up in de mo'nin', yo' mind rollin' two different ways—/ One mind to leave your baby, and one mind to stay?" or "De quagmire don't hang out no signs." What's more, he is able to realize such splendid results in a variety of forms, including the classic and standard blues, the ballad, a new form that Stephen Henderson calls the blues-ballad, the sonnet, and free verse. For the first time, we can appreciate Brown's full range, his mastery of so many traditions.

In the five-poem ballad cycle "Slim Greer," Brown has created the most memorable character in black literature, the trickster. In "Slim in Atlanta," segregation is so bad that blacks are allowed to laugh only in a phone booth:

> Hope to Gawd I may die
> If I ain't speakin' truth
> Make de niggers do their laughin'
> In a telefoam booth.

In "Slim Greer," the wily Greer in "Arkansaw" "Passed for white, / An' he no lighter / Than a dark midnight / Found a nice white woman / At a dance, / Thought he was from Spain / Or else from France." Finally, it is Slim's uncontainable rhythm that betrays:

> An' he started a-tinklin'
> Some mo'nful blues,
> An' a-pattin' the time
> With No. Fourteen shoes.
>
> The cracker listened
> An' then he spat
> An' said, "No white man
> Could play like that. . . ."
>
> Heard Slim's music
> An' then, hot damn!
> Shouted sharp—"Nigger!"
> An' Slim said, "Ma'am?"

Brown balances this sort of humor against a sort of "literate" blues, such as "Tornado Blues," not meant to be sung:

> Destruction was a-drivin' it and close behind was Fear,
> Destruction was a-drivin' it hand in hand with Fear,
> Grinnin' Death and skinny Sorrow was a-bringin' up de Rear.
>
> Dey got some ofays, but dey mostly got de Jews an' us,

Got some ofays, but mostly got de Jews an' us,
Many po' boys castle done settled to a heap o'dus'.

Contrast with this stanza the meter of "Long Track Blues," a poem Brown recorded with piano accompaniment:

Heard a train callin'
Blowin' long ways down the track;
Ain't no train due here,
Baby, what can bring you back?

Dog in the freight room
Howlin' like he los' his mind;
Might howl myself,
If I was the howlin' kind.

In "Southern Road," Brown uses the structure of the worksong, modified by the call-and-response pattern of a traditional blues stanza:

Doubleshackled—hunh—
Guard behin';
Doubleshackled—hunh—
Guard behin';
Ball an' chain, bebby,
On my min'.

White man tells me—hunh—
Damn yo' soul;
White man tells me—hunh—
Damn yo' soul;
Get no need, bebby,
To be tole.

Brown is a versatile craftsman, capable of representing even destruction and death in impressively various ways. In "Sam Smiley," for example, he describes a lynching in the most detached manner: "The mob was in fine fettle, yet / The dogs were stupid-nosed; and day / Was far spent when the men drew round / The scrawny wood where Smiley lay. / The oaken leaves drowsed prettily, / The moon shone benignly there; / And big Sam Smiley, King Buckdancer, / Buckdanced on the midnight air." On the other hand, there is a certain irony in "Children of the Mississippi": "De Lord tole Norah / Dat de flood was due / Norah listened to de Lord / An' got his stock on board, / Wish dat de Lord / Had tole us too."

Brown also uses the folk-rhyme form, the sort of chant to which children skip rope: "Women as purty / As Kingdom Come / Ain't got no woman / Cause I'm black and dumb." He also combines sources as unlike as Scott's "Lady of the Lake" and the black folk ballad "Wild Negro Bill" in his most extended ballad, "The Last Ride of Wild Bill." Often, he takes lines directly from the classic blues, as in "Ma Rainey," where three lines of Bessie Smith's "Backwater Blues" appear. Perhaps

Brown is at his best when he writes of death, a subject he treats with a haunting lyricism, as in "Odyssey of Big Boy":

> Lemme be wid Casey Jones,
>   Lemme be wid Stagolee,
> Lemme be wid such like men
>   When Death takes hol' on me,
>   When Death takes hol' on me. . . .
>
> Done took my livin' as it came,
>   Done grabbed my joy, done risked my life;
> Train done caught me on de trestle,
>   Man done caught me wid his wife,
>   His doggone purty wife.

He achieves a similar effect in "After Winter," with lines such as "He snuggles his fingers / In the blacker loam" and "Ten acres unplanted / To raise dreams on / Butterbeans fo' Clara / Sugar corn fo' Grace / An' fo' de little feller / Runnin' space." When I asked why he chose the black folk as his subject, Brown replied:

> Where Sandburg said, "The people, yes," and Frost, "The people, yes, maybe," I said, "The people, maybe, I hope!" I didn't want to attack a stereotype by idealizing. I wanted to deepen it. I wanted to understand my people. I wanted to understand what it meant to be a Negro, what the qualities of life were. With their imagination, they combine two great loves: the love of words and the love of life. Poetry results.

Just as Brown's importance as a teacher can be measured through his students (such as LeRoi Jones, Kenneth Clarke, Ossie Davis, and many more), so too can his place as a poet be measured by his influence on other poets, such as Leopold Senghor, Aimé Césaire, Nicolas Guillen, and Michael Harper, to list only a few. Out of Brown's realism, further, came Richard Wright's naturalism; out of his lyricism came Hurston's *Their Eyes Were Watching God*; his implicit notion that "De eye dat sees / Is de I dat be's" forms the underlying structure of *Invisible Man*. In his poetry, several somehow black structures of meaning have converged to form a unified and complex structure of feeling, a poetry as black as it is Brown's. This volume of poems, some of which are recorded on two Folkways albums, along with his collected prose (three major books of criticism, dozens of essays, reviews, and a still unsurpassed anthology of black literature) being edited by Robert O'Meally and a splendid literary biography by Joanne Gabbin, all guarantee Brown's place in literary history. Brown's prolific output coupled with a life that spans the Age of Booker T. Washington through the era of Black Power, makes him not only the bridge between nineteenth- and twentieth-century black literature but also the last of the great "race men," the Afro-American men of letters, a tradition best epitomized by W. E. B. Du Bois. Indeed, such a life demands an autobiography. A self-styled "Old Negro," Sterling Brown is not only the Afro-American poet laureate; he is a great poet.

TRICKSTER TALES

DARRYL PINCKNEY grew up in Indiana and is a regular reviewer for *The New York Review of Books*. He won the prestigious Whiting Writer's prize of $25,000 in 1986. This review-essay on Ishmael Reed appeared in *The New York Review of Books*, October 12, 1989. His first novel, *High Cotton*, was published in 1992.

The slave narratives tell of spirits riding people at night, of elixirs dearly bought from conjure men, chicken bones rubbed on those from whom love was wanted, and of dreams taken as omens. Harriet Tubman heeded visions which she described in the wildest poetry. VooDoo, magic, spirit worship as the concealed religious heritage of the black masses, and literacy, control of the word as a powerful talisman, are among the folk sources of what Ishmael Reed calls the "Neo-HooDoo aesthetic" of his polemical essays, contentious poems and pugnacious elliptical fictions.

Reed's "Neo-HooDooism" is so esoteric that it is difficult to say what he intends by it, whether it is meant to be taken as a system of belief, a revival of HooDoo, the Afro-American form of Haitian VooDoo, or, as he has also suggested as a device, a method of composition. Mostly Neo-HooDooism seems to be a literary version of black cultural nationalism determined to find its origins in history, just as black militants of the 1960s invoked Marcus Garvey or the slave rebellions. Neo-HooDooism, then is a school of revisionism in which Reed passes control to the otherwise powerless, and black history becomes one big saga of revenge.

Black writers, Leslie Fiedler once pointed out, have been attempting to "remythologize" themselves and black people since the time of Jean Toomer, but in Neo-HooDooism, writing itself becomes an act of retribution. Reed puts a hex or a curse on white society, or on any group in black life that he doesn't like simply by exposing them to ridicule: the whammy hits Rutherford B. Hayes, Millard Fillmore, Lincoln,

Woodrow Wilson, black nationalists, black Maoists reading "Chinese Ping-Pong manuals," black feminists, white feminists, white radicals, television, what he conceives of as secret societies of Anglos, the master caste, and those who control the canon, the dreaded C word, and ignore Asian-American, Native American, and Hispanic literature, and get Afro-American literature all wrong. There is also much beating up of Christianity and the Catholic Church.

Fantastic in plot, satirical in tone, colloquial in style, and always revolving around what Zora Neale Hurston identified as the "wish-fulfillment hero of the race" in folklore, Reed's novels, with one smooth black after another blowing the whistle on covert forces that rule the world, are latter-day trickster tales with enough historical foundation to tease.

Reed came of age in the 1960s, "the decade that screamed." His family roots are in Chattanooga, Tennessee. He was born in 1938, grew up in Buffalo, New York, dropped out of the university there in 1960, worked for a local militant newspaper where he defended black prostitutes against the brutality of the police, wrote a play, and in 1962 took his belongings in a plastic bag to downtown Manhattan. The black movement was beginning to heat up; avant-grade black magazines appeared on the scene. Leroi Jones, Reed's contemporary, had been to Cuba and had ceased to be a Beat poet. Reed joined the Umbra Workshop, a forerunner of Jones's Black Arts Repertory School. In 1965, the year Jones established his school in Harlem and turned away from interracial politics, Reed headed a black newspaper in Newark. (He was later to be associated with the magazine *Yardbird* and to run his own small press.) In 1968, he moved to Berkeley where he has been teaching ever since, and in 1979 settled into the kind of neighborhood in Oakland that he says, his stepfather and mother "spent about a third of their lives trying to escape."

Many black intellectuals in the 1960s sought to rehabilitate their identity through Islam, Black Power, or the principles of Ron Karenga, who held that black art must show up the enemy, praise the people, and support the revolution. Words were seen as weapons and whites were accused of "the intellectual rape of a race of people," but Reed was too quirky to become merely a black separatist. At his most rhetorical he claims to have a multinational, multi-ethnic view of the United States. He concocted his personal brand of chauvinism, one designed to dispense with the black writer's burden of interpreting the black experience.

The ground under the naturalistic problem novel of the 1940s, which depended on oppression for its themes, was eroded by the possibilities of the integration movement, and it led black writers in the 1950s to turn inward. But the black revolt of the 1960s brought a resurgence of protest literature. Though Reed shared its anti-assimilationist urges, maybe he didn't want to sound like everyone else who was hurling invective against the injustices in American society. Reed's work aims to dissolve or transcend the dilemma of the double consciousness of the black writer as an American and as a black that has characterized black writing since the slave narratives. Chester Himes, half of whose ten novels are hard-boiled detective stories from which Reed got a good deal, complained in his autobiography, *The Quality of Hurt* (1973), that white readers only wanted books in which black characters suffer. "Fuck pain," Reed said. "The crying towel doesn't show up in my writing."

To disarm racism and make room for his comic sense of the irrational, to free himself from the tradition of the black writer's double consciousness, Reed got rid of the confessional voice, the autobiographical atmosphere of Afro-American literature, those "suffering books" about the old neighborhood in which "every gum drop machine is in place." His first novel, *The Free-Lance Pallbearers* (1967), is a fitful, irreverent parody of the literature of self-discovery. The narrator, Bukka Doopeyduk, a luckless believer in "the Nazarene Creed," lives in a place called HARRY SAM, which is ruled by SAM, who is rumored to eat children, has been enthroned on a commode in a motel for thirty years, and rants about "all the rest what ain't like us."

The novel is madly scatological, waste overruns everything. Doopeyduk, "a brainwashed Negro" of the projects who listens to Mahler, becomes by accident, a media star until he witnesses the "sheer evil" of SAM—performing backroom anal sex. He then tries to grab power, fails, and is crucified on meat hooks.

Along the way to doom Doopeyduk meets opportunistic black leaders, voyeuristic white radicals, academics, slumlords, television talk show hosts, all of whom Reed lampoons. Given the climate of the late 1960s, with antipoverty programs like HARYOU and best sellers about the inner city in which self-exploration often had an element of self-exploitation, Reed's baiting of almost everyone has the calculated exhibitionism of funky stand-up comedy. For outrageousness, Reed's only peer is Richard Pryor.

There isn't much in this novel that Reed won't try to take the piss out of, including the legacy of *Black Boy* and *Invisible Man*; reports about the Vietnam War; the Book of Revelations; and militant rhetoric, which comes off as sell-out entertainment for masochistic white audiences.

HEAH THAT. WHITEY, ON THE NEXT
SUNNY DAY YOU WILL MEET YOUR
DEMISE. YOU BEASTS CREATURES OF
THE DEEP. 'CAUSE YOU CANT HOLD UP
A CANDLE TO US VIRILE BLACK PEOPLE.
LOOK AT THAT MUSCLE. COME ON UP
HERE CHARLIE AND FEEL THAT MUSCLE.

Reed makes fun of HooDoo in *The Free Lance Pallbearers*. Doopeyduk's wife's grandmother takes conjure lessons through the mail under the "Mojo Retraining Act," and while studying for her "sorcery exams" tries to shove her granddaughter in the oven to practice an exercise from the "witchcraft syllabus." VooDoo is part of the pervasive corruption in HARRY SAM, one more ridiculous thing about life.

But in his second novel, *Yellow Back Radio Broke-Down* (1969), Reed is serious about possession and spells, at least as a pose, though he is capable of saying anything to be sensational. Here in order to get away from white fiction as a model, and to return to a "dark heathenism," Reed puts Neo-HooDooism to the forefront in place of the crying towel of his experience as a black man in America. Anything that Reed approves of historically he says comes from HooDoo. "HooDoo is the strange and beautiful 'fits' the Black slave Tituba gave the children of Salem."

Ragtime and jazz were manifestations of HooDoo, messages from the underground, and in his own day Neo-HooDoo signs are everywhere, like charges in an electric field.

Reed's Neo-HooDooism shares the syncretism of its model. Just as VooDoo absorbs Catholic saints to represent its spirits, Neo-HooDooism is comfortable enough with a California out-of-it-ness to become "a beautiful art form of tapestry, desire, song, good food, healthful herbs." Tall tales of how the weak overcome the strong through wit, toasts of the urban tradition, "positive" humor, and other "neo-African" literary forms—the entire folk tradition is, to Reed, a vast reservoir of HooDoo ideas to which he, its conservator, hopes in Neo-HooDooism to add "fresh interpretations" by "modernizing its styles."

Yellow Back Radio Broke-Down is a full-blown "horse opera" (spirits ride human hosts), a surrealistic spoof of the Western with Indian chiefs aboard helicopters, stagecoaches and closed-circuit TVs, cavalry charges of taxis. The wish-fulfillment hero in this novel is the Loop Garoo Kid, a HooDoo cowboy, not only "a desperado so ornery he made the Pope cry and the most powerful of cattlemen shed his head to the Executioner's swine," but also a trickster Satan. Loop Garoo conducts "micro HooDoo masses" to end "2000 years of bad news." He fights ranchers, the U.S. government, and then Pope Innocent on behalf of the youth of Yellow Back Radio, an intersection of historical and psychic worlds, a beleaguered town where the rule of the elders has been temporarily overthrown by an anarchist revolt that resembles the counterculture of the late Sixties. The Pope wants Loop to "come home," to make peace with the Big Guy.

Like Reed's subsequent novels, *Yellow Back Radio Broke-Down* is about many things and all at once. Pages flash with allusions to great issues of the moment, the novel seems to unravel, to carelessly shed its best layers, in order to get to an impatient message: the hero must not suffer, must win out over the whites in power, or at least dazzle them to a draw. Black magic, and black culture, must be recognized as a force as powerful as any other. Pope Innocent concedes that the Catholic Church failed to change the pantheon of the African slaves because its own "insipid and uninspiring saints were no match" against the slaves' juju, that "German Aryan scholars faked the history of the Egyptians by claiming them to be white"—all these assertions of black culture's strengths, of theories that have as much to do with race pride as with scholarship, were heard on every corner of the 1960s.

But curiously, while Reed approaches historical black culture with the enthusiasm of one who has just come across an offbeat work that supports his anti-establishment convictions on current matters, like whether the police have a hard job or whether black militants are anti-achievement in their vilification of the black middle class, he does not hesitate to go against received black opinion, to deplore the lack of skepticism among his black critics, as if each side of his mouth were aimed at a different audience and his purpose were to discomfort both.

He can find the good fight anywhere, often with other black writers. "Even the malice and vengeance side of HooDoo finds a place in contemporary Afro-American fiction," Reed says, a fish in its own water. Already in his second novel Reed is defending himself against the Black Aesthetic critics, the followers of the

Black Arts movement, the "field niggers" who got "all the play" in the 1960s, denounced individualism, and endorsed the line that there was a uniform black experience, that blacks have only one language, that of their liberation. Reed has this Loop Garoo Kid meet up with Bo Shmo, a "neo-socialist" who tells Loop that he's too abstract, "a crazy dada nigger" whose work is just "a blur and a doodle." Loop says:

> What's your beef with me, Bo Shmo, what if I write circuses? No one says a novel has to be one thing. It can be anything it wants to be, a vaudeville show, the six o'clock news, the mumblings of a wild man saddled by demons.

Bo Shmo says:

> All art must be for the end of liberating the masses. A landscape is only good when it shows the oppressor hanging from a tree.

Reed says he uses "the techniques and forms painters, dancers, film makers, musicians in the West have taken for granted for at least fifty years, and artists of many other cultures for thousands of years," but this seems a device to protect the structural weaknesses of his madcap novels. Reed does not create characters, he employs types to represent categories, points of view. Plot, however, he has in overabundance, ever since his most ambitious novel, *Mumbo Jumbo* (1972), in which he began to use the detective story as the vehicle for his history of the Western world according to Neo-HooDooism.

What Reed probably finds most congenial about the suspense genre, in addition to its law of cause and effect, is the recognition scene in the library where the hero makes arrests and explains how he solved the case, which in *Mumbo Jumbo* means a lengthy deposition on the mysteries of black culture. The exposition comes as a relief because of the complexity of the narrative, the noisy feeling of several voices going on at the same time. *Mumbo Jumbo* is dense with subplots, digressions, hidden meanings, lectures ("The Book of Mormon is a fraud. If we Blacks came up with something as corny as the Angel of Moroni . . ."). It is packed with epigrams, quotations, newsclips. The written text is interpolated with reproductions of drawings and photographs, illustrations that function as a kind of speech. Reed even appends a long bibliography about VooDoo, dance, Freud, art, music, ancient history, presidents, as if to say, "If you don't believe me look it up."

Mumbo Jumbo is set in the 1920s because of the parallels between the "negromania" that swept America during the Jazz Age and that of the late 1960s. A HooDoo detective, PaPa LaBas, tries to track down the source of the phenomenon Jes Grew, as the nationwide outbreak of dancing and bizarre behavior—"stupid sensual things," "lusting after relevance," and "uncontrollable frenzy"—is called. Jes Grew knows "no class no race no consciousness," and causes people to speak in tongues, hear shank bones, bagpipes, kazoos. It is "an anti-plague" that enlivens the host, fills the air with the aroma of roses. This creeping thing like Topsy, "jes grew," as James Weldon Johnson said of ragtime, and in *Mumbo Jumbo* it could mean many things in black culture. "Slang is Jes Grew."

In trying to give black feeling an ancient history, Reed reaches back to unexpected allies like Julian the Apostate who foresaw the "Bad News" of a Christian Europe, and eventually into Egyptian myth, to Set's murderous jealousy of his brother, Osiris. Reed believes that the past can be used to prophesy about the future, "a process our ancestors called necromancy," and in *Mumbo Jumbo* the earthiness of black culture and the repressiveness of white societies are a legacy of Set's uptightness.

The message of *Mumbo Jumbo* is difficult to grasp because of an abstraction on which the action of the novel hinges. "Jes Grew is seeking its text. Its words. For what good is a liturgy without a text?" An elite military group that defends the "cherished traditions of the West" successfully conspires to contain Jes Grew, to keep it from uniting with its text, its key of truth, which Reed calls the Book of Thoth, "the 1st anthology by the 1st choreographer." Jes Grew withers away without this text, but LaBas goes on with his obeah stick into the 1960s to tell college audiences about the good times that almost were and might be.

That the nature of the lost text is left for us to conjecture makes it hard to guess what Reed has in mind here as the written tradition for what he sees as the Neo-HooDoo aesthetic. The novel is anticlimactic, though Reed may mean that the mysteries of black culture can't be written down, that Jes Grew must remain in the air, always possible, but beyond the page. In fact, the suggestiveness of *Mumbo Jumbo* has made it a rich mine among poststructuralists who see it as a handbook of signs, a textbook of signifiers on prejudices about the quality of blackness since Plato, and an example of black literary autonomy. It has also been read "as a critique of the Harlem Renaissance for its failure to come up with a distinct Afro-American voice."[1]

Reed's novels after *Mumbo Jumbo* are variations on the theme of a total license that is not as liberating as it would seem. In them the hold of neo-HooDooism begins to fade, or sinks into their soil. The later novels resort more to riddles, and reduce the detective novel to a hasty cycle of situation and exposition. The targets narrow. *The Last Days of Louisiana Red* (1974) puts PaPa LaBas in Berkeley. He rescues a HooDoo business, the Solid Gumbo Works, which performs good deeds, offers its clients a cure for cancer, and almost finds a cure for heroin addiction. This time HooDoo doesn't do battle with white theocrats, but with bad HooDoo, Louisiana Red, as practiced by the Moochers.

This is a satire on the hustlers of Black Power politics, with rallies and veiled references to Huey Newton in his chair.

> You can't keep the Street Gang going forever. . . . All you knew how to do was destroy. Maybe destruction was good then, it showed our enemies we meant business. But we can't continue to be kids, burning matches while the old folks are away.

The plot involves opportunists in North African exile, a preacher who because he can't preach uses $100,000 of audio-visual equipment, and Minnie the Moocher, a heroine oppressed by the exaltation of her followers. Included in the "Moocher high command" is a "Lit. teacher from New York," a white man so caught up in his study of *Native Son* that he dreams he is Mary Dalton and longs to be molested by Bigger, who just wants to take his employer's Buick for a joy ride.

Reed also draws on *Antigone* for this novel, offering a timid sister, brothers, who slay each other, and a chorus, or Chorus, an "uncharacterized character," a vaudevillian in white tails, like Cab Calloway, who complains about his role declined because Antigone talked too much. Instead of being one who would not yield to earthly authority, a woman who did not believe that a man's death belonged to the state, Antigone, to Reed, is a selfish girl who wanted to have things her way. "You wrong girl," Reed says in a poem, "Antigone, This Is It," "you would gut a nursery to make the papers," which makes her sound more like Medea. Nevertheless, she represents to Reed implacable hostility toward men and misuse of a woman's powers. Minnie the Moocher, Antigone's comic reincarnation, and her followers, dupes of the handed-down, hammered-in philosophy of the inferiority of slaves, are accused of not being able to "stand negro men attempting to build something: if we were on the corner sipping Ripple, then you would love us." LaBas goes on to lose his cool completely:

> Have you ever heard the term "pussy-whipped" or "pussy-chained"? These expressions may be crude, but they smack of the truth. A woman uses her cunt power to threaten and intimidate, even to blackmail. . . . Women use our children as hostages against us. We walk the street in need of women and make fools of ourselves over women; fight each other, put Louisiana Red on each other, about maim each other. The original blood-sucking vampire was a woman. . . . Your cunt is the most powerful weapon of any creature on this earth. . . . I can't understand why you want to be liberated. You already free. . . . We're the ones who are slaves; two-thirds of the men on skid row were driven there by their mothers, wives, daughters, their mistresses and their sisters. I've never known a woman who needed it as much as a man. Women rarely cruise or rape.

In *Flight to Canada* (1976), Reed's takeoff on the antebellum South, black women are also prominent among the boogey persons who get theirs. A black mammy in velvet, loyal to the incestuous, necrophiliac master, claims that Jesus got tired of Harriet Beecher Stowe, who ripped off *Uncle Tom's Cabin* from the narrative of Josiah Henson, and therefore caused one of her sons to be wounded in the war and the other to get "drowned." The light-skinned overseer tells the master, "I armed the women slaves. They'll keep order. They'll dismember them niggers with horrifying detail." The fugitive hero, Raven Quickskill, has a beautiful Indian lover and when they enter a tavern two of the female slaves help begin to "let out their slave cackle, giving them signifying looks." No black matriarchy for Reed.

In a "Self-interview" in *Shrovetide in Old New Orleans* (1978) Reed asks himself, "Why you so mean and hard?"

> A. Because I am an Afro American male, the most exploited and feared class in this country. All of the gentlemen, all of the ones who tried to be nice, are in the cemetery or sitting on a stoop humiliated and degraded and waiting for someone to hand them a bar of soap or waiting for the law some woman has called on them.

This is as much a flashback to the Sixties when the black male was an envied species as it is a reminder of current statistics about the low life-expectancy of black men.

Reed can't resist excess, overstating his case, even when he has a valid one, as in *Reckless Eyeballing* (1986), another whodunit busy with plot, about the historical distortions of feminism. Whereas his quarrel in the books of the Seventies was with the Stalinesque rigidity of black aesthetic writers, he now takes on black women writers who have received attention, as if Alice Walker's finding the goddess within her were a distraction from his story of black men versus white men. The title of his latest collection of essays, *Writin' Is Fightin'*, comes from Muhammad Ali, and Reed compares his own style of not mincing words to that of Larry Holmes in the ring. "A black boxer's career is the perfect metaphor for the career of the black male." Daily life is "sparring with impersonal opponents as one faces the rudeness and hostility that a black male must confront in the United States, where he is the object of both fear and fascination."

The Terrible Twos (1982) and its sequel, his most recent novel, *The Terrible Threes*, are set in the not-so-distant future mostly to address the Reagan years. The detective in both books, Nance Saturday, who gets lost in the thick plots, remains aloof from the madness of trying to make it in the new white world, and becomes celibate out of a fear of infection. Neo-HooDooism itself has been pushed offstage entirely by a sort of Gnostic sect of questionable sincerity.

Reed is aware of the shift in the country's attention during the Eighties. *The Terrible Twos* opens with the "Scrooge Christmas of 1980," when it feels good to be a white man again and whites aren't afraid to tell blacks they aren't interesting anymore. There are more pressing problems. Reed's campaign to mention everything that has gone wrong in America results in a narrative that is all over the place, as if he were trying to work in everything from crime against the environment to offenses against the homeless. Instead of suspense or satire one is confronted with an extended editorial rebuttal.

The Terrible Twos is a souped-up version of *A Christmas Carol*. The northern hemisphere isn't "as much fun as it used to be." Hitler's birthday has become a national holiday, but the White House is alarmed by the number of "surplus people," worries that the world will turn "brown and muddy and resound with bongo drums" and the "vital people" will be squeezed out. A conspiracy unfolds to nuke New York and Miami and blame the destruction on Nigeria. Meanwhile, oil companies control Christmas, the Supreme Court grants one store exclusive rights to Santa Claus, and the economy depends on every day being Christmas for the "vitals." The conspiracy is threatened by the followers of Saint Nicholas and his servant or rival in legend, Black Peter. Saint Nicholas converts the President, a former model, by taking him to hell where Truman is the most tormented. The President is declared incapacitated when he reveals the conspiracy.

America has worsened in the new novel, *The Terrible Threes*. The temperature has dropped, larceny fills every heart, mobs roam the cities in search of food, evangelists who believe Jews and blacks are the children of the devil control the government and hope to establish a Christian fundamentalist state. "Who needs the yellows, the browns, the reds, the blacks?" These people are "the wastes of history." Saint Nicholas and Black Peter, a figure similar to Reed's earlier renegade heroes, compete to enlighten and to help people, and nearly bring back an age of liberalism until Lucifer himself interferes. To top it off, extraterrestrials, contemptuous of human beings, have their own plans for earth.

In this latest novel Reed writes of a country that has lost its soul, but he, too, seems uncertain of direction. His picture of "Scroogelike" America, "kissing cousin of South Africa, of yuppies for whom the buck is the bottom line; of black people marooned in drug neighborhoods, is extremely bleak. Even Black Peter is chastised, ambivalent, exhausted. The extraterrestrials come like an afterthought, as if Reed were making a last-ditch effort to deny power over the future to Neo-HooDoo's opponents. His work has always had a certain bitterness, but that was part of its fuel. Compared to his reconstruction of recent American history as a sequence of Terribles (the first one, Reed says, began on November 22, 1963), of genocidal policies and coverups, his previous novels seem almost utopian.

But the problem with his parodies of the obvious and the obscure, his allegorical burlesques, pastiches of the fantastic—the problem with this gumbo (his analogy) is that he can't move beyond their negations. Neo-HooDooism needs what Reed would call Anglo un-freedom the way Christianity needs Judas's lips or, as the movie says, the way the ax needs the turkey. Similarly, Reed may have declined to take on the old-fashioned subject of the Afro-American's double consciousness, but his fictions are as dualistic in their representations of the egalitarian versus the hierarchical, HooDoo versus the Cop Religion. They buzz with conspiracy theories that pretend to explain the world, with the determination to set the world straight about the hypocrisy of "patriotic history." "Jefferson Davis died with a smile on his face." Paranoia, Burroughs said, is just having the facts, but a few facts are not as dangerous as Reed would have us think.

Reed's subjects involve large cultural questions, but often the transplant from the headlines is the quickest of operations. His novels are entirely of their day, nostalgic in their defiance of "the Judeo-Christian domination of our affairs," and vividly recall the era when the lightness of blackness was a revelation, when blacks were the catalysts of social change. Neo-HooDooism gave Reed a way to work with this, to reimagine it. Back then, in the "Neo-HooDoo Manisfesto," Reed could describe it as the "Now Locomotive swinging up the Tracks of the American Soul."

The shift in the cultural climate, the loss of that moment, may help to explain why in the Terribles, Reed's remarkable fluency has dried up. The supporting atmosphere is missing, without which his books are suddenly vulnerable. This fluency, this back talk, is what animates Reed's work, for Neo-HooDooism is not the sort of mysticism or system that provides a language of symbols or infuses imagery, it has no widening gyres, no junkie codes. It is Reed's language that carries his mission of exasperation—the old black faith in the power of the word. The police commissioner fronting as the Curator of the Center of Art Detention in *Mumbo Jumbo* is made to pay the supreme compliment:

Son, these niggers writing. Profaning our sacred words. Taking them from us and beating them on the anvil of BoogieWoogie, putting their black hands on them so that they shine like burnished amulets. Taking our words, son, these filthy niggers and using them like . . . god-given pussy.

Whether Reed's fictions are argument for the reenchantment of Afro-American literature, are unmaskings of Western culture by written formulation, or are self-congratulatory texts about HooDoo as an untainted supply of material does not change the fact that his literary separatism is doomed to obsolescence because Afro-American writing only comes to life as a junction of traditions. Reed questions not only the social reality presented in Afro-American literature, but also the narrative tradition itself. To do so, he takes shelter in the black oral tradition without realizing that it makes him no more free than contemporary white novelists. Reed often speaks of his hero as "scatting," or uses Charlie Parker as an example of the Neo-HooDoo artists, free of the rules, blowing, improvising, and this wish-fulfillment hero becomes a stand-in for Reed himself, the black writer floating far above an alien tradition in which he doesn't feel at home. But perhaps there's no way back, for black writers, to an innocent folk state. The writers of the Harlem Renaissance inadvertently discovered that there is no literary equivalent to dance or music, and no reconciliation either.

Once it's written down, the oral tradition becomes literature, as Neil Schmitz pointed out, and the experience of the black man in the library intervenes with the experience of the black man in the street, in Reed as much as it does in any other black writers. Reed's Neo-HooDoo tales are not as tall as the ones blacks used to tell. Still there's much to say for his own tales: after all, not to make fun of racist absurdities is to be still afraid of them.

NOTES

1. See *The Signifying Monkey: A Theory of Afro-American Literary Criticism* by Henry Louis Gates, Jr. (Oxford University Press, 1988); *Ishmael Reed and the New Black Aesthetic Critics* by Reginald Martin (St. Martin's Press, 1988); *Conscientious Sorcerers* by Robert Elliot Fox (Greenwood Press, 1987); and "Neo-HooDoo: The Experimental Fiction of Ishmael Reed," by Neil Schmitz (*Twentieth Century Literature*, Vol. XX, April 1974).

NOVELIST ALICE WALKER

Telling the Black
Woman's Story

DAVID BRADLEY attended the University of
Pennsylvania and is currently a creative writing teacher at Temple
University. His second novel, *The Chaneysville Incident* (1981), was
highly acclaimed and earned Bradley the renowned PEN-FAULKNER
Prize. He has written numerous articles for various magazines. This piece
on Alice Walker appeared in the *New York Times Magazine* on January
8, 1984.

first met Alice Walker the way people used to: Someone I liked and respected
pressed a dogeared copy of one of her books into my hands and said, "You've
got to read this." The book was "In Love & Trouble," a collection of stories
written between 1967 and 1973. Some of them had been published previously in
periodicals directed at a primarily black readership, in the feminist standard, *Ms.*,
and in mainstream magazines like *Harper's*, a spectrum that hinted at the range of
Alice Walker's appeal, just as the book's eventual winning of the American Academy
and Institute of Arts and Letters' Rosenthal Award was a harbinger of honors to
come, including the Pulitzer Prize for fiction.

My reaction to the book was complicated. Some of the stories I judged profes-
sionally. "The Revenge of Hannah Kemhuff," the story of an old black woman
who comes to a conjurer seeking revenge against a white woman who had humiliated
her long ago, does not really work; the use of an educated apprentice to tell the tale
seems intrusive and false. On the same professional basis, I liked "Roselily," a stark
tableau of a wedding between a Northern Muslim and a black Southern woman.

But my reaction to other stories forced me out of the shelter of professional
detachment. I was moved deeply by "The Welcome Table," in which an old, dying
black woman is expelled bodily from a white church, but meets up with Jesus on the
highway. I was horrified yet mesmerized by "The Child Who Favored Daughter," in

which a bitter, sullen, Bible-thumping sharecropper, full of confusion and guilt over the wanton life and eventual suicide of his sister, imprisons, tortures and eventually kills (by hacking off her breasts) his own daughter, who has shown an interest in boys.

My response, in the end, was overwhelming admiration. For I was, at the time, trying to figure out how a writer should balance the demands of technique with the demands of emotion, of honest plotting and storytelling with larger political concerns. Alice Walker seemed to have found some kind of answer. Her technique was flawless—her plots inexorable, her images perfect, her control, even of the roiling Freudian undercurrents in "The Child Who Favored Daughter," unwavering. Yet there was in every story, even the ones that did not seem to work, a sense of someone writing not simply to be writing, but because she wanted to make people see things.

I did not resolve to imitate her—I had enough sense to know that her way was not precisely mine—but I did decide to emulate her. I also decided to read everything she ever wrote (which now includes 10 books, the latest being "In Search of Our Mothers' Gardens: Womanist Prose").

I first met Alice Walker in person in the summer of 1975, when she accepted my invitation to lunch. Alice Walker, who is now 39, was then 31; I was only 24. By that time, I had gone a long way toward reading everything she had ever published. I had only skimmed her first book of poems, *Once*, which was published in 1968 when she was 24, but completed by the time she was 21. But I had studied her second volume of poems, *Revolutionary Petunias & Other Poems*, which came out in 1973.

I was no lover of contemporary poetry, particularly the "radical" poetry of the 1960s and early 1970s. Some of it had moral force and authenticity, and some of the poets had a sense of craft. But the sentiments of nonjudgmental liberalism that characterized the movements of the period had made it possible for every idiot with a Bic pen and a Big Chief pencil tablet to claim to be a poet, so long as he or she was a member of some oppressed group, imitated Orwell's use of pigs as the symbol of the oppressor and occasionally stapled together a rudimentary chapbook of poems that seemed unified only because they were repetitious.

But Alice Walker's *Revolutionary Petunias* was about as far from that airheaded tradition as Leonardo da Vinci is from Andy Warhol. Her sense of line was precise, her images clear, simple, bitingly ironic, the book unified by the symbol of flowers. "These poems," Alice Walker writes, "are about . . . (and for) those few embattled souls who remain painfully committed to beauty and to love even while facing the firing squad."

Those "embattled souls" included members of her own large (eight children) family: a sister who escaped, through education, the narrow and impoverished world of Alice Walker's native Eatonton, Georgia ("*Who saw me grow through letters/ The words misspelled But not/ The longing*"); her uncles visiting from the North ("*They were uncles. . . ./ Who noticed how/ Much/ They drank/ And acted womanish/ With they do-rags*"); her grandfather, seen at the funeral of her grandmother, Rachel Walker:

My grandfather turns his creaking head
away from the lavender box.
He does not cry. But looks afraid.
For years he called her "Woman";
shortened over the decades to
" 'Oman."
On the cut stone for " 'Oman's" grave
he did not notice
they had misspelled her name.

They also included the women and the old men of Eatonton, and they also included figures from the larger world of political struggle. She mourned:

The quietly pacifist peaceful
always die
to make room for men
Who shout. Who tell lies to
children, and crush the corners
off of old men's dreams.

And she attacked on their behalf the con men of the revolution who: ". . . *said come/ Let me exploit you;/ Somebody must do it/ And wouldn't you/ Prefer a brother?"*

Those embattled souls included Alice Walker herself. She writes with sadness and defiance of the price she had paid for loving and marrying a white man, a civil-rights lawyer named Mel Leventhal. In "While Love Is Unfashionable," she writes:

While love is dangerous
let us walk bareheaded
beside the Great River.
Let us gather blossoms
under fire.

She made clear her love of peacefulness, but left no doubt as to her determination to ignore the standards of society and appeal to higher judges: *"Be nobody's darling;/ Be an outcast./ Qualified to live/ Among your dead."*

It took no unique perception to be enthralled by *Revolutionary Petunias*, which had already been enthusiastically reviewed, nominated for the National Book Award and given the Lillian Smith Award. However, unlike a number of reviewers, I was even more taken with Alice Walker's first novel. *The Third Life of Grange Copeland.* published in 1970, in which a black sharecropper, enslaved by circumstances and eternal debt, breaks free of the destructive cycle at the point where he would have slain his wife, who has betrayed him with the white landowner. Instead, he abandons her and his son, Brownfield, and heads north. Consumed with hatred for Grange, Brownfield nevertheless echoes his father's sins in more sinister harmonic; he destroys his wife's intellect, batters her and their three daughters and eventually kills her. The youngest daughter, Ruth, is taken in by Grange, now returned and transformed by time and experience into a wise and saintly old man. He nurtures and protects Ruth, in the end to the point of killing his own son and sacrificing his own life.

There is, to be fair to its critics, a lot not to like about the novel. Its structure is weak; despite the basic three-part plot implied by the title, the book is chopped up into 11 "parts" and 48 short chapters. The plot itself is both episodic and elliptical; the crucial "second life," which would have shown Grange Copeland's transformation, is largely missing.

But there is much to admire, especially in the "third life," in which Grange Copeland emerges as one of the richest, wisest and most moving old men in fiction. His speeches, never preachy, always set perfectly in context, ring with complex truth. Speaking of the difference between himself and his son:

> "But when he become a man himself, with his own opportunity to righten the wrong I done him by being good to his own children, he had a chance to become a real man, a daddy in his own right. That was the time he should have just forgot about what I done to him—and to his ma. But he messed up with his children, his wife and his home, and never yet blamed hisself. And never blaming hisself done made him weak . . . By George, I *know* the danger of putting all the blame on somebody else . . . And I'm bound to believe that that's the way the white folks can corrupt you even when you done held up before. 'Cause when they got you thinking that they're to blame for *every*thing they have you thinking they's some kind of gods!"

Much of Grange's humanity comes out in his interactions with Ruth, a sweet, sassy, feisty, precocious child ("I never in my life seen a more womanish gal," says Grange). Their dialogues are dramatic expressions of an unabashedly universalist philosophy.

But much as I admired *Revolutionary Petunias* and *The Third Life of Grange Copeland*, it was one of Alice Walker's essays, "The Unglamorous but Worthwhile Duties of the Black Revolutionary Artist," that compelled me to meet her. At the time, I was awaiting the publication of my first novel and trying to figure out how I would deal with the political nonsense that seems to always attend the appearance of even the most nonpolitical book by a black.

Alice Walker "told" me: "The truest and most enduring impulse I have is simply to write. It seems necessary for me to forget all the titles, all the labels and all the hours of talk, and to concentrate on the mountain of work I find before me. My major advice to young black artists would be that they shut themselves up somewhere away from all the debates about who they are and what color they are and just turn out paintings and poems and short stories and novels."

I wanted to meet Alice Walker, I realized, because there were things I needed to learn from her.

We ate in a deli on Lexington Avenue in Manhattan and talked of many things— of the 1930s anthropologist and novelist Zora Neale Hurston, whose work Alice

Walker had discovered while doing research "in order to write a story that used *authentic* black witchcraft." The results had been "The Revenge of Hannah Kemhuff," and something less purely professional. Alice Walker fell in love with Hurston. "What I had discovered," she had told the Modern Language Association a few months before our lunch, "was a model. A model who, as it happened, had provided . . . as if she knew someday I would come along wandering in the wilderness, a nearly complete record of her life."

We talked of my own model, Jean Toomer, one of Hurston's forerunners of whose major work, "Cane," Alice Walker had written, "*I love it passionately*; could not possibly exist without it."

She spoke of her years in the South, her impoverished childhood in Eatonton, the two years she had spent at Atlanta's elite black women's college, Spelman, before she found a way to escape from what she felt to be its puritanical atmosphere to an elite white women's college, Sarah Lawrence; her years in Mississippi as a civil-rights worker and teacher, a vulnerable position made more so because of her marriage to Leventhal. She spoke, too, of her turning away from formal religion. "I just need a wider recognition of the universe," she would explain years later.

She had little to say about publishing. Breaking into the business had not required the usual years of frustration. She had written most of the poems in "Once" during a short, frenzied week following a traumatic abortion while at Sarah Lawrence. One of her teachers, the poet Muriel Rukeyser, gave them to her own agent, who showed them to Hiram Haydn, then an editor at Harcourt Brace Jovanovich, who almost immediately accepted them.

Alice Walker in person was as many faceted as Alice Walker in print. She was a scholar of impressive range, from African literature to Oscar Lewis, the noted anthropologist. She was an earthy Southern "gal"—as opposed to lady. Her speech was salted with down-home expressions, but peppered with rarified literary allusions. She was an uncompromising feminist, capable of hard-nosed, clear-eyed analysis; she was also given to artless touching and innocent flirtation. She had a sneaky laugh that started as a chuckle and exploded like a bomb. Her eyes sparkled—I did not know then, and surely could not tell, that one of them had been blinded in a childhood accident.

I left Alice Walker in the lobby of the building that housed *Ms.* magazine, of which she was then a contributing editor, feeling both elated and uneasy—elated because I had liked her every bit as much as I had liked her books, and uneasy because I thought, as I had watched her walk toward the elevators, that the world into which she was moving was a steamdriven meat grinder, and she the tenderest of meat. The black movement, with which she still identified, was split on questions of anti-Semitism, integration, class, region, religion and, increasingly, sex. The women's movement, of which she was perhaps the most artistic and evocative contemporary spokesperson, was increasingly being accused of racism, and had factions of its own.

Alice Walker was black, a pacifist but a rejector of the organized religions to which that tradition belonged. She was married to a white, indeed, a Jew. She was a rejector of black middle-class education and pretensions, and an acceptor of white upper-class education—but not pretensions. She was a Southerner in the "liberal" North, a feminist who was also a wife and a mother. She was also sensitive enough to be hurt by criticism.

I worried for her. I watched her go. I wished her well.

I saw Alice Walker only twice in the next seven years: once, in 1976 at a party celebrating the publication of her second novel, *Meridian*; again, in 1983, at the ceremony where she accepted the American Book Award for her third novel, *The Color Purple*, which would, a few days later, be announced as the winner of the Pulitzer Prize. Between those occasions, I had no real conversations with her; I had even allowed our real acquaintance, based on her work, to lapse.

That was, in part, because I had become busy with my own writing and teaching. But I had also been terribly disappointed by *Meridian* and the collection of short stories that followed in 1981, *You Can't Keep a Good Woman Down*.

In this I was, to all appearances, alone. *Meridian* had been touted by *Newsweek* as "ruthless and tender," by *Ms.* as "a classic novel of both feminism and the civil rights movement," and by *The New York Times Book Review* as "a fine, taut novel that . . . goes down like clear water." But to me it seemed far more elliptical and episodic (three parts, 34 chapters) than her first novel, without having that novel's warmth and simplicity. The title character, an itinerant civil-rights worker, seems less pacifist than passive. She suffers from an intermittent paralysis of vague origins that, by the end of the book, she has managed to pass off to a weak skunk of a man named Truman Held, a former lover who repeatedly betrayed her in order to be with white women. He seems to redeem himself years later by mothering her, accepting her illness and ignoring her sexuality.

The dialogue between Meridian and Truman Held, especially when compared to the easy conversation of Grange Copeland and Ruth, is just plain awful. ("Hah," he said bitterly, "why don't you admit you learned to hate me, to disrespect me, to wish I were dead. It was your contempt for me that made it impossible for me to forget.") The symbolic unity, so powerful in *Revolutionary Petunias*, is missing.

Many of the stories in *You Can't Keep a Good Woman Down* show the complexity and artistry of "In Love & Trouble." There is "A Sudden Trip Home in the Spring," in which a young, Southern black girl, a student at a Northern women's college, returns home for the funeral of her father, whom she has never understood, and discovers new sources of strength in her older brother and her grandfather. And there is "Fame," a day in the life of Andrea Clement White, an aging and proper black woman of letters, who goes to a literary-awards luncheon uttering acerbic comments: ". . . white liberals told you they considered what you said or wrote to be new in the world (and one was expected to fall for this flattery); one never expected them to know one's history well enough to recognize an evolution, a variation, when they saw it; they meant *new* to *them*."

But many of the stories are flawed by unassimilated rhetoric, simplistic politics and a total lack of plot and characterization. Some are hardly stories. One unsatisfying piece, "Coming Apart," through its complex publication history, hinted at what was going wrong. Commissioned as an introduction to a chapter on third-world women in a feminist collection of essays on pornography, the "story" had been published in *Ms.*, entitled "A Fable," then republished in *You Can't Keep a Good Woman Down*, retitled and with a polemical, confusing and somewhat inaccurate introduction: ". . . the more ancient roots of modern pornography are to be found in the almost always pornographic treatment of black women who, from the moment they entered slavery, even in their own homelands, were subjected to rape as the 'logical' convergence of sex and violence."

Meridian and *You Can't Keep a Good Woman Down* upset me. Alice Walker seemed to have lost the balance of form and content that had made her earlier work so forceful. She had ignored the human power of situations in favor of polemical symbolism. Worse, she appeared to have got caught up in the business she had advised young writers to avoid—advice I had taken to the heart of my own existence. I was furious at Alice Walker. I felt . . . misled.

By the time I watched her receive the American Book Award, my anger had faded. By then, I had had some taste of what it is like to scribble in obscurity and then suddenly have people ripping manuscripts out of your hands before you have satisfied yourself and publishing them for reasons and standards far removed from yours. I no longer felt that Alice Walker had misled me; I believed she had been misled, and pressured in ways she could not possibly ignore. When Gloria Naylor, the black woman who won the American Book Award for first novels in 1983, acknowledged the debt that she and other black female writers owed Alice Walker, I could only think, what a heavy burden that tribute must be.

When Alice Walker rose to make her own acceptance speech, I could not help thinking of Andrea Clement White, who tells an interviewer, "In order to *see* anything, and therefore to create . . . one must not be famous" and could only summon up the energy to accept her "one hundred and eleventh major award" after hearing a small, dark-skinned girl sing an old slave song. I wondered who, if anybody, was singing for Alice Walker. I had not then, you see, read *The Color Purple*.

I rediscovered Alice Walker through reading *The Color Purple*. In my case, though, the rediscovery almost did not happen. I had read enough about the book to want to avoid it like the plague.

I had read that it was an epistolary novel, with most of the letters written by Celie, a black Southern woman, the victim of every virulent form of male oppression short of actual femicide, who eventually finds true love and orgasm in the arms of another woman. The description made me fear the book would be as disjointed as *Meridian* and as polemical as most of *You Can't Keep a Good Woman Down*.

I also sensed that *The Color Purple* was going to be ground zero at a Hiroshima of controversy. In June 1982, Gloria Steinem, in a profile of Alice Walker published in *Ms.*, had written about an "angry young novelist," male and implicitly black, who had been miraculously tamed by Alice Walker's writing. This, Miss Steinem said, was "a frequent reaction of her readers who are black men." But she then went on to question the thoroughness, integrity and motivation of all Alice Walker's reviewers, especially those black and male. "It's true," she wrote, "that a disproportionate number of her hurtful, negative reviews have been by black men. But those few seem to be reviewing their own conviction that black men should have everything white men have had, including dominance over women. . . ." That position would make expressing any reservations about *The Color Purple* risky business for a black man, and indeed, I had heard rumblings about the review Mel Watkins, a black man, had written in *The New York Times*, because he had criticized the male portraits as "pallid" and the letters not written by Celie as "lackluster and intrusive" even though he termed the book "striking and consummately well written."

At the same time, I had heard some people—not all of them white and/or male—expressing some misgivings about the book. One black poet, Sonia Sanchez, criticized Alice Walker's theme of black male brutality as an overemphasis. Another black woman told me *The Color Purple* was "a begging kind of piece" and she was "getting tired of being beat over the head with this women's lib stuff, and this whole black woman/black man, 'Lord have mercy on us po' sisters,' kind of thing" in Alice Walker's work.

On the other hand, one white woman told me that once she had gotten through the first few depressing letters, "The rest was so uplifting and *true*, it made me cry."

All this considered, *The Color Purple* seemed a good book to stay away from. But then someone I liked and respected pressed a dogeared copy of *The Color Purple* into my hands and said, "You've got to read this."

I did and discovered a novel that seems a perfect expression of what, in my mind, makes Alice Walker Alice Walker. The epistolary form is perfectly suited to her experience and expertise with short forms—what in another book would have been choppiness is short and sweet. There is plenty of political consciousness, but it emerges naturally from the characters, instead of being thrust upon them. That Celie—after being repeatedly raped and beaten by a man she thinks of as her father, having him take the children she bears him away, and then, knowing that his brutality has rendered her sterile, hearing him tell her future husband, "And God done fixed her. You can do everything just like you want to and she ain't gonna make you feed it or clothe it"—should find herself uninspired by the thought of sex with men, and be drawn to a woman who shows her love and introduces her to ecstasy seems less a "message" of radical feminist politics and more an examination of human motivation. That the other woman, Shug Avery, should fall in love with a man gives any such message a counterpoint.

No matter what polemical byways Alice Walker might have strayed into, she had, in the process of creating *The Color Purple*, become a writer far more powerful than she had been. Before she had touched me and inspired me. This time, along about page 75, she made me cry.

On an airplane at 35,000 feet, I was suddenly scared to death. I was on my way to talk to Alice Walker, preparatory to writing about her, and I was reading my homework; galley proofs of Alice Walker's newest book, *In Search of Our Mothers' Gardens: Womanist Prose*, essays, speeches and reviews written over 17 years— nearly her entire adult life.

The book made me see an error in my thinking about Alice Walker. I had allowed myself to become so mesmerized by *The Color Purple* and the fond recollections it inspired of *Revolutionary Petunias* and *The Third Life of Grange Copeland* that I had forgotten the works that came between. I had, therefore, set out to write about Alice Walker confident I would not be doing anything "hurtful," but rather testifying that she has a miraculous ability to transubstantiate the crackers and grape juice of political cant into the body and blood of human experience.

Yet Alice Walker, in her time, has produced some crackers and some grape juice, and that surely must show up in a collection such as *In Search of Our Mothers' Gardens*. Reading it, I realized I had more or less refused to really *see* Alice Walker. I had picked and chosen aspects of her, deciding which I would respond to, which I would not.

In Search of Our Mothers' Gardens forced me to look at all of her. As it turned out, much in the book is not only pleasing, but impressive and moving. Alice Walker, the award-winning poet, novelist and short-story writer, proves herself the master of yet another form. Her descriptions are elegant. Her sarcasm is biting, her humor pointed.

Nor is her artistry merely a matter of rhetorical form. The content of much of her statements places so many troublesome controversies in proportion and perspective. Her 1976 speech, "Saving the Life That Is Your Own," deposits the question of differences between literature written by blacks and whites into the appropriate circular file.

But there is also much that dismays me. Some of those things can be written off to polemical excess, such as her discounting of the ability of literature to reach across racial lines or her proclamation that she had once attempted to "suppress" statements made by another black female writer.

But other excesses are more troubling because they form, it seems, a pattern indicating Alice Walker has a high level of enmity toward black men. Her early praise of individual male writers seems to have been transformed over time to dismissal and disdain: Richard Wright's exile from Mississippi she no longer finds "offensive" but proof of his place of favor; Toomer is no longer a genius not to be thrown away but a disposable commodity ("*Cane* . . . is a parting gift . . . I think Jean Toomer would want us to keep its beauty but let him go"). Black male writers, in general, are possibly less insightful than their white male counterparts who, "It is possible . . . are more conscious of their own evil," and are guilty of "usually presenting black females as witches and warlocks."

Her acidity flows beyond black male writers. It pours over men who are attracted to light-skinned women—including, apparently, the Rev. Dr. Martin Luther King Jr. ("Only Malcolm X, among our recent male leaders, chose to affirm, by publicly loving and marrying her, a black woman.") It spatters, in general, men she considers fundamentally illiterate: "And look at the ignorance of black men about black women. Though black women have religiously read every black male writer who came down the pike . . . few black men have thought it of any interest at all to read black women."

The pattern makes me see that some of the "hurtful" criticism is demonstrably true: Black men in Alice Walker's fiction and poetry seem capable of goodness only when they become old like Grange Copeland, or paralyzed and feminized, like Truman Held. If they are not thus rendered symbolically impotent, they are figures of malevolence, like Ruth's murderous father, Brownfield, or the black "brothers" in *Revolutionary Petunias* ("*and the word/ 'sister'/ hissed by snakes/ belly-low,/ poisonous,/ in the grass./ Waiting with sex/ or tongue/ to strike./ Behold the brothers!*").

Yet *In Search of Our Mothers' Gardens* has a wealth of honest self-revelation, enough to help me understand where some of that pattern—as well as some of Alice Walker's brilliance—came from. She writes of the aftermath of an accident that befell her at age 8, when her brother accidentally shot her with a BB gun, blinding an eye and filling her with a dread of total blindness as well as leaving her with a disfiguring scar.

After that accident, she felt her family had failed her, especially her father. She felt he had ceased to favor her, and, as a child, blamed him for the poverty that kept her from receiving adequate medical care. He also, she implies, whipped and imprisoned her sister, who had shown too much of an interest in boys, as had the farmer in "The Child Who Favored Daughter." In company with her brothers, her father had failed to "give me male models I could respect."

The picture that emerged is of a very unhappy existence, but, ironically, the loss of her sight enabled her to see those truths that imbue her writing: "For a long time, I thought I was ugly and disfigured. This made me shy and timid, and I often reacted to insults that were not intended . . . I believe, though, that it was from this period . . . that I really began to see people and things. . . ."

Five years ago, Alice Walker sold her small house in Brooklyn and flew to San Francisco in search of a place she had dreamed of without ever seeing, "a place that had mountains and the ocean." In time, she and her companion, Robert Allen, a writer and editor of the journal *Black Scholar* (she is divorced from Leventhal), found a small, affordable house in Mendocino County, north of the city, in a locale that looked, to Alice Walker, like Georgia. She planted a hundred fruit trees around the house, just as her mother had "routinely adorned with flowers whatever shabby house we were forced to live in."

In San Francisco itself, Alice Walker also found an apartment, which she decorated to her taste—wood, clay, earth tones and, of course, several shades of purple. The apartment, a four-room, third-floor walkup, is in close proximity to Divisadero Street, the main thoroughfare in the black ghetto many San Franciscans maintain does not exist. Alice Walker has traveled far, but has not removed herself from anything. As I settle down in her apartment to talk to her for the first time in the better part of a decade, I wish she had; fatigue is obvious in her features and the tone of her voice. Once she had reminded me of Ruth; now, she reminds me of Meridian.

But unlike Meridian, Alice Walker is not paralyzed. She sits in a comfortable wooden rocker, in constant, rhythmic motion, and talks of the fight she has put up to keep the term "womanist" in the subtitle of *In Search of Our Mothers' Gardens*.

"I just like to have words," she explains, "that describe things *correctly*. Now to me, 'black feminist' does not do that. I need a word that is organic, that really comes out of the culture, that really expresses the spirit that we see in black women. And it's just . . . *womanish.*" Her voice slips into a down-home accent. "You know, the posture with the hand on the hip, 'Honey, don't you get in my way.' " She laughs. It is almost the same laugh that she used in the Lexington Avenue deli, but now it is deeper, fuller, more certain.

She goes on, expounding on a theme that had grown through *You Can't Keep a Good Woman Down* and her later essays: her dissatisfaction with white feminists.

"You see," she says, "one of the problems with white feminism is that it is not a tradition that teaches white women that they are capable. Whereas my tradition *assumes* I'm capable. I have a tradition of people not letting me get the skills, but I have cleared fields, I have lifted whatever, I have *done* it. It ain't not a tradition of wondering whether or not I could do it because I'm a woman."

But womanism, in Alice Walker's definition, is not just different from feminism; it is better. "Part of our tradition as black women is that we are universalists. Black children, yellow children, red children, brown children, that is the black woman's normal, day-to-day relationship. In my family alone, we are about four different colors. When a black woman looks at the world, it is so different . . . when I look at the people in Iran they look like kinfolk. When I look at the people in Cuba, they look like my uncles and nieces."

One of them looked like her father. The resemblance was part of the inspiration for one of her most moving essays, "My Father's Country Is the Poor."

I ask her about her father.

"He died in '73," she says sadly. "He was racked with every poor man's disease—diabetes, heart trouble. You know, his death was harder than I had thought at the time. We were so estranged that when I heard—I was in an airport somewhere—I didn't think I felt anything. It was years later that I really felt it. We had a wonderful reconciliation after he died."

I laugh, thinking that she is alluding to something she had written in the essay, that it is "much easier . . . to approve of dead people than of live ones." But she is serious: "I didn't cry when he died, but that summer I was in terrible shape. And I went to Georgia and I went to the cemetery and I laid down on top of his grave. I wanted to see what he could see, if he could look up. And I started to cry. And all of the knottedness that had been in our relationship dissolved. And we're fine now."

That year was the epicenter of some general upheaval in her life. In 1973, she wrote the answers to questions published in a collection called *Interviews with Black Writers,* and later in *In Search of Our Mothers' Gardens.* "Writing poems," she writes, "is my way of celebrating with the world that I have not committed suicide the evening before."

"I don't even remember," she says at first, when I ask if 1973 had been a particularly difficult year, but then she goes on to recall that it marked, besides the death of her father, her escape from Mississippi, which had "just about driven me around the bend," a period of physical separation from her husband, who had stayed behind to work, while she and her daughter, Rebecca, went to Cambridge,

Massachusetts. There she had discovered that "when I am ill and feel pain, things take on a certain extra clarity . . . something opens up and you begin to see things that you just wouldn't if you were surrounded by happy-go-lucky folk."

I remind her of another time of trauma she had written in that interview, when she, young, alone, pregnant and suicidal, "allowed myself exactly two self-pitying tears. . . . But I hated myself for crying, so I stopped."

Alice Walker laughs about that now. "Well, you know, I cry so much less than I used to. I used to be one of the most teary people. But I've been really happy here."

But writing is also a part of the reason she cries less. "I think," she says, "writing really helps you heal yourself. I think if you write long enough, you will be a healthy person. That is, if you write what you need to write, as opposed to what will make money, or what will make fame."

As when we talked before, and as when I have read Alice Walker at her best, I find myself being enchanted by her vision of things. She sees the writing process as a kind of visitation of spirits. She eschews the outline and other organizing techniques, and believes that big books are somehow antithetical to the female consciousness ("the books women write can be more like us—much thinner, much leaner, much cleaner"). Later, I will realize that her methods would make it well nigh impossible for her to write a long, sustained narrative and suspect the belief is something of a rationalization—and the kind of sexist comment a male critic would be pilloried for making. Yet when she says it, it seems a wonderful, magical way to write a book. But there is nothing mystical about what she sees as her role in life.

"I was brought up to try to see what was wrong and right it. Since I am a writer, writing is how I right it. I was brought up to look at things that are out of joint, out of balance, and to try to bring them into balance. And as a writer that's what I do. I just always expected people to understand. Black men, because of their oppression, I always thought, would understand. So the criticism that I have had from black men, especially, who don't want me to write about these things, I'm just amazed."

"You come down very heavy on the men," I say. "How about the black women?"

"Oh, I get to them. But I am really aware that they are under two layers of oppression and that even though everybody, the men and the women, get twisted terribly, the women have less choice than the men. And the things that they do, the bad choices that they make, are not done out of meanness, out of a need to take stuff out on people. . . ."

Her statement seems contradictory.

"In your writing," I suggest, "it's clear that you love old men. But they don't make out too well when they're young. None of them do."

"Well," she says, "one theory is that men don't start to mature until they're 40." She laughs, and I start to laugh, too. But then I realize her voice has taken on a certain rhetorical tone, and it makes me angry—because she herself is not yet 40. Then she slips out of the rhetorical tone, begins to explain, as she often does, how her perception of the general comes from intense feelings about the personal: "I knew both my grandfathers, and they were just doting, indulgent, sweet old men. I just loved them both and they were crazy about me. However, as young men, middle-aged men, they were . . . brutal. One grandfather knocked my grandmother out of a window. He beat one of his children so severely that the child had epilepsy. Just a horrible, horrible man. But when I knew him, he was a sensitive, wonderful man."

"Do you think your father would have eventually gotten to be like your grandfather?" I asked her.

"Oh," she says wistfully, "he had it in him to be."

I ask her how her political involvements have affected her writing; if she has ever become aware of how the "brotherhood" or the "sisterhood" might see a particular piece, and thought about changing it.

"I often think about how they will see it, some of them," she says. "I always know that there will be many who will see it negatively, but I always know there will be one or two who will really understand. I've been so out of favor with black people, I figure if I can take that, I can be out of favor with anybody. In some ways. I'm just now becoming a writer who is directed toward 'my' people. My audience is really more my spirit helpers." She explains what a spirit helper does by describing a dream she had recently about one of them, Langston Hughes: "It was as if we were lovers, but we were not sexual lovers, we were just . . . loving lovers. Knowing it was a dream made me so unhappy. But then Langston, in his role of spirit helper, sort of said, 'But you know, the dream is real. And that is where we will always have a place.' I feel like that with all of them. They're as real to me as most people. More real."

Later, alone in my hotel room, I try to make sense of Alice Walker or, more correctly, of my feelings about her. I am not sure that I like her as much as I once did, that she sees as deeply and as clearly as I thought. Yet I am sure that there is no one I like more as a writer, or who is possessed of more wisdom—that there is no writer in this country more worthy of the term seer. I would like to forget about 30 percent of what she has written and said. And yet the remaining 70 percent is so powerful that, even in this quandary, I am listening to the tapes of our conversation, and thumbing through her books, looking for an answer.

And it is there. On the tape, I hear her talking of her own reaction to her beloved Zora Neale Hurston: "I can't remember all the times that I would be apalled by some of the views that she held. But it wasn't her fault that she had to report things a certain way. That was what *she* found." And in the final essay in *In Search of Our Mothers' Gardens*, Alice Walker writes of how her daughter had finally liberated her from her sense that she is disfigured, and her fear that her own child will be alienated by her artificial eye. "Mommy," Rebecca tells her, "there's a *world* in your eye."

Yes indeed, I think, there *is* a world in Alice Walker's eye. It is etched there by pain and sacrifice, and it is probably too much to expect that anything so violently created would be free of some distortion. But it is nevertheless a real world, full of imaginary people capable of teaching real lessons, of imparting real wisdom capable of teaching real lessons.

IX

PORTRAITS,
VOLUME 4

A. PHILIP RANDOLPH

BAYARD RUSTIN (1910?–1987) was a passionate believer in pacifism and nonviolent social change. A Quaker by religious faith, he spent 28 months in prison for refusing military service during World War II. He spent weeks on a North Carolina chain gang for violating bus seating laws in 1947. He was the organizing force behind the historic 1963 March on Washington. His strong support of Israel and black–Jewish ties made him suspect with many blacks, and his homosexuality estranged him from others. But Rustin was an extraordinary man and was an instrumental player in the civil rights crusade. Rustin's lovely essay on his good friend and mentor, A. Philip Randolph (1889–1979), the great black labor leader, was originally published in the *Yale Review*, Spring 1987.

In my fifty years as a social and human rights activist, I have met and worked with some of the leading figures in the struggle for justice—Gandhi, Norman Thomas, Martin Luther King, Jr., Lech Walesa. But the man who most closely touched my life, whose ideas, character, and work helped shape my destiny, was Asa Philip Randolph, this country's premier black labor and civil rights leader. I have chosen to write about Mr. Randolph for two reasons. First, our association was a long and fruitful one. I had the privilege and good fortune of working with Mr. Randolph from about 1939 until his death in 1979 at the age of ninety. Second, though much heralded in his time, Mr. Randolph and his ground-breaking achievements in the struggle for racial and economic equality have been obscured by the passage of time. This was a man whom every major civil rights leader, from Roy Wilkins to Martin Luther King, affectionately and respectfully called "the Chief."

Mr. Randolph was, in the truest sense of the word, a pathfinder. Tall, aristocratic, with just a touch of vanity about his appearance, he was an intellectual imbued with unflappable dignity and courage, who used his outward reserve and quiet demeanor as a potent weapon in the formative years of the civil rights struggle. As a member of the Socialist Party, he ran for New York Secretary of State in 1922 and received an impressive two hundred thousand votes. Three years later, he organized the Brotherhood of Sleeping Car Porters. In subsequent years, he tangled with corporate executives, presidents, and this country's most powerful labor leaders, and more often than not, his dignity and steadfastness won concessions that paved the way for black social, economic, and political advancement.

Confronted with the humiliations of racism, insults, and resistance, he never lost his poise, and he never lost his nerve. He was imperturbable and implacable in his single-minded commitment to his ideals and principles. He was a self-made gentleman and a prudent tactician with the grit and toughness of a boxer. Mr. Randolph was a man of quiet courage, of resoluteness without flashiness, of perseverance without pretension.

Many of these attributes were evident to me at our first meeting, which occurred in 1938 when I was a student at the City College of New York. I had shown a friend of mine a paper I had written in which I concluded that the Communists were the only party sensitive to the needs of blacks. Now this was the time of the Scottsboro trials, in which the Communists were actively involved. Well, my friend disagreed with my analysis, and asked me if I had ever met A. Philip Randolph, a socialist who was firmly anticommunist. Of course I had heard of Mr. Randolph, but never met him. After some discussion, my friend suggested that we arrange to visit Mr. Randolph at the Brotherhood of Sleeping Car Porters headquarters up on 125th Street in Harlem. I was sure that a man of Randolph's stature would not bother with two young and unknown college kids.

Much to my surprise, we got a call from Mr. Randolph's secretary, who told us that he would see us. At that initial meeting, Randolph did three simple things that I saw him do countless times during our long association, and which illustrate the decorum and gentility that characterized his dealings with people and which, I feel, were a small but integral part of his successes.

When we arrived at Randolph's modest offices for our appointment, it was clear that he was busy and running late. But rather than just keep us waiting, we heard him come over to the door and tell his secretary, loud enough for us to hear, "Tell the two gentlemen from City College that I will be a little late." For years and years, when Mr. Randolph had to keep someone waiting, he would either send his secretary or come out in person and explain the delay. The courteousness and thoughtfulness made quite an impression on me.

The second thing that really impressed me happened as we were ushered into Mr. Randolph's office. This important man, instead of sitting smugly behind his desk waiting to receive us, got out of his chair, walked toward us, and shook our hands. He then did something which seemed most unusual. As he showed us to two seats near his desk, he gestured with his hand for us to sit down, but not like most people do by merely pointing to the chair. He made a gesture as if he were brushing or dusting the seat before we sat down, something I also saw him do for years and years.

Although these displays of civility may seem like insignificant and even overly obsequious acts, they were not. I later realized that it was Randolph's courtliness, his staid manners and reserve, that made it so extraordinarily difficult for opponents to dismiss him. In fact, his restrained manner was often totally disarming; it was a type of moral judo that threw opponents, including presidents and other officials, off balance. Although these qualities were an innate part of his personality, they were also an effective tactic.

At that initial meeting, Randolph discussed his socialist beliefs, outlining his positions on child labor, the six-day work week, trade union rights, black economic progress, and other matters. I was awed by his eloquence, his equanimity, his bearing, and his grasp of the issues.

I was so taken with Mr. Randolph after that first meeting that a year later I went to work for him in his major campaign to organize a march on Washington to press for an executive order banning segregation in defense plants. During the planning stages of the effort I got to know Randolph better. And he told me a remarkable story of a negotiating meeting between the Brotherhood of Sleeping Car Porters and the Pullman Company which further underscored his style and shrewdness.

Although always mindful of his dignity and decorum, sometimes Randolph let other, more indelicate spokesmen take the floor when things got nasty or when blunt or indecorous language had to be used to make a point. In 1937, representatives of the Pullman Company sat down with leaders of the Brotherhood of Sleeping Car Porters, some twelve years after the union was formed. Well, the company representatives were condescending and coarse. They freely used the terms *nigger* and *darkie* when referring to the porters. After several minutes of these insults, Mr. Randolph, never losing his composure and never mentioning their ill manners, responded with some brief comments and then turned to Milton Webster, the head of the Midwest region of the union, and said: "Mr. Webster, have you anything to say?" Now, Milton Webster was a huge, imposing man, who must have been about six feet five inches tall and weighed 260 pounds. He was a tough, no-nonsense man, known for his outspokenness and his temper. Webster lit into the Pullman executives, calling them every vile name under the sun, questioning their ancestry, and thundering that the porters didn't have to put up with any crap from high-handed white bastards. Just as Webster was hitting his stride, Randolph quietly interrupted, and in his measured and aristocratic tone said, "Mr. Webster, if I may interrupt, I think we ought to proceed with the business at hand." Randolph would never have personally cursed out the Pullman representatives, but by calling on Webster, he knew the company men would get the message, in no uncertain terms, that the porters were not to be patronized. The point made, the meeting proceeded without any more insults from the Pullman representatives. After a series of meetings, the Pullman Company signed a contract with the union, the first time a black union had won an agreement with a white company. Throughout the negotiations, Randolph maintained that air of measured restraint and ultimately won the day.

Randolph also used "deliberate" dignity—that is, dignity for a powerful purpose—in his campaign to end discrimination in the defense industry. Before Pearl Harbor, Randolph had been pressing Franklin Roosevelt to issue an executive order ending segregation in defense plants. When the president hedged, Randolph planned a march on Washington in 1941 to push his demands. At a meeting with Randolph, an exasperated FDR—who was not too eager to desegregate—complained that if a hundred thousand blacks came into Washington, which was a segregated city, there would be no place for them to eat, to sleep, to go to the toilet. After a brief pause, Randolph told the president that if people wanted to come to Washington he was in no position to stop them. Then, in a quiet, even voice, he told the president that if he was really so concerned about where the marchers would eat, sleep, or go to the toilet, he could, by merely picking up a pen, issue an executive order desegregating public accommodations in the entire city. Randolph spoke so quietly and matter-of-factly that it took a moment for the implications of his words to sink in, but when they did, Roosevelt's cigarette-holder nearly fell from his mouth. Randolph had come to talk about desegregating defense plants, and here he was escalating his demands and talking about desegregating public facilities in the whole city. Six months before Pearl Harbor, Roosevelt signed a fair employment practices order which called for an end to discrimination in defense plant jobs. As a result, Randolph called off the march.

But he did not halt his efforts to end discrimination in the armed services, and this led to several clashes with President Truman and other politicians, notably Senator Wayne Morse of Oregon. And it also led to a serious clash between me and Mr. Randolph, the only one in the four decades of our collaboration.

In 1948, Mr. Randolph appointed me executive secretary of the League for Nonviolent Civil Disobedience Against Military Segregation. I had served a three-year sentence in Lewisburg Penitentiary as a conscientious objector during World War II. On 22 March 1948, Randolph and a group of black leaders met with Truman, telling him that unless an executive order were issued barring segregation in the military, blacks would refuse to bear arms in defense of the country and would engage in other acts of civil disobedience. Truman, ever blunt, said he didn't care to hear such talk, and simply adjourned the meeting. By this time, we had some fifty blacks in jail for evading the draft. Undeterred by Truman's rebuff, Randolph went before the Senate Armed Services Committee, testifying that he would personally continue to advise blacks "to refuse to fight as slaves for a democracy they cannot possess and cannot enjoy." This open defiance was too much even for Senator Morse, a liberal and one of Randolph's admirers on the committee. He asked Randolph if he would continue to counsel disobedience and draft evasion even in the event of war. When Randolph said he would because such action was "in the interest of the soul of the country," Morse shot back that such action would be construed by the government as treason. Unflustered, Randolph replied: "We would be willing to absorb the violence, absorb the terrorism, to face the music and to take whatever comes, and we, as a matter of fact, consider that we are more loyal to our country than the people who perpetrate segregation and discrimination upon Negroes because of color or race."

Later that day, Randolph was more emphatic. Speaking to a group of young people at the March on Washington headquarters, he said: "I am prepared to oppose a Jim Crow army until I rot in jail." What made Randolph's position even more courageous was that there were large segments of the black leadership and media that opposed his stand. The influential *Amsterdam News*, the widely read New York paper considered the voice of the black community in America, was against him. Several prominent blacks wrote President Truman assuring him that Randolph spoke only for a small, militant minority of blacks. Even the Urban League had doubts about the wisdom of Randolph's radical stand.

But as was usually the case, Randolph had accurately read the mood of the black people. A poll of young black men in Harlem showed that seventy-one percent favored a civil disobedience campaign against the draft. In July 1948, Randolph led a group of picketers at the Democratic National Convention in Philadelphia. Later that month, President Truman issued Executive Order 9981, calling for an end to military discrimination "as rapidly as possible." After receiving confirmation from presidential advisors that the order did indeed ban segregation, Randolph called off the civil disobedience campaign and moved to disband the League for Nonviolent Civil Disobedience.

Being young and impetuous at the time, I argued that dissolving the League would be unfair to those blacks who were still in jail for refusing to serve in the armed forces. Randolph, always a man of great honor, would not be swayed, noting that he had given his solemn word to the president of the United States. He had demanded an executive order, and that demand had been met. Unsatisfied with that answer, a number of "Young Turks" and I decided to outflank Mr. Randolph. He had asked me to call a press conference for four o'clock on 17 August 1948 in order to announce the dissolution of the League. Well, we called a press conference of our own for ten o'clock that morning, during which we denounced Randolph as an Uncle Tom, a sellout, a reactionary, and an old fogey out of touch with the times. Of course, we got all the headlines. For months we continued to operate the League, sending out correspondence and continuing to embarrass Mr. Randolph. Finally, Randolph was forced to issue a statement. Always a man of great tact and patience, he did not blast us for our impertinence. He merely said that the League had been co-opted by a pacifist element that, while useful to keep the movement nonviolent, now had its own agenda.

Such was Randolph's stature that the League lost all influence and resources quickly dried up. It finally collapsed in November 1948. Guilt-ridden and ashamed, and sure that Randolph would never forgive me for my treachery, I avoided him for two whole years. I was convinced that even a man of such understanding, dignity, and forbearance would never forget being stabbed in the back by trusted confidants and friends. When I finally mustered the courage to go see him, I went to his modest union office on 125th Street, the very place I had first met him some ten years earlier, expecting to be chastised for my recklessness. As I was ushered in, there he was, distinguished and dapper as ever, with arms outstretched, waiting to greet me, the way he had done a decade ago. Motioning me to sit down with that same sweep of his arm, he looked at me, and in a calm, even voice said: "Bayard, where have you been? You know that I have needed you." I was moved and overwhelmed. For the rest of our long friendship, he never, ever mentioned what I had done to him.

Mr. Randolph's crowning achievement, the 1963 March on Washington, which led to a confrontation with President Kennedy, also included a dramatic and trying episode that threatened my personal reputation and the march itself. Again, Randolph's dignity and nerve saved my career and what was to become a watershed event of the civil rights movement.

When Randolph asked me to organize the march, he envisioned it as a march for jobs and freedom. By now a member of the AFL–CIO Executive Council (the first black to hold this position), Randolph understood that the upcoming phase of the civil rights movement would involve economic justice. In planning the march, Randolph did not consult with the other black leaders until all the mechanisms were in place, presenting them with a fait accompli they would find hard to refuse. When final preparations were being made, a nervous President Kennedy, who had been working to get civil rights legislation passed in Congress, called a meeting of a number of top black leaders on 22 June 1963. The president voiced his concern about possible violence and the fact that some congressmen might not vote for the legislation if they felt pressured by a mass demonstration in the nation's capital. His position was that one simply could not bully Congress. After comments from other black leaders, Randolph took the floor, speaking with, as Arthur Schlesinger would later recall, "the quiet dignity which touched Kennedy as it had touched Roosevelt before him." Noting the inevitability of the march, Randolph said: "Mr. President, the Negroes are already in the streets. It is very likely impossible to get them off. If they are bound to be in the streets in any case, is it not better that they be led by organizations dedicated to civil rights and disciplined by struggle rather than to leave them to other leaders who care neither about civil rights nor nonviolence?"

With those words, Randolph not only convinced Kennedy that the march was unstoppable, but got him to endorse it as well.

But just as plans were being made final, a serious crisis arose that would test Randolph's trust in me and all his skills as a leader. Six weeks before the march, Senator Strom Thurmond stood before the Senate and for over three-quarters of an hour attacked me as the organizer of the march in an effort to disrupt and divide the black leadership. He accused me of being a draft-dodger, a Communist, and a homosexual. The papers jumped all over the story. It made the front page of the *New York Times*, and it was plastered in papers around the country. By this time, the march had gained international attention. As expected, Senator Thurmond's accusations caused pandemonium among the black leadership. Roy Wilkins had predicted that if I were made chief organizer of the march these charges would be made.

Randolph quickly called the black leaders together, and there was a fierce debate over my future role. He said that the purpose of Thurmond's remarks was to destroy the march, and that the purpose of the meeting was to make certain that he did not succeed. He then said he had already prepared a statement which he wanted all the leaders of the march to sign, adding that he had called a press conference for the next day at which he would read the statement and tell the media that all the leaders had agreed to it. The statement read: "We have absolute confidence in Bayard Rustin's ability and character, and he will continue to organize the march, which we know will be a great success." Many of the leaders expressed concern that the press would hound them for further comments, to which Mr. Randolph said that the only way to put an end to the controversy was for all of them to repeat the simple statement he had just read.

The next morning, Mr. Randolph met the press alone. It was the biggest press conference to date dealing with the march. There must have been fifty people there from newspapers and radio and television stations around the country. For ten minutes after he read the statement, the press tried to goad Mr. Randolph to say more. They badgered him with questions. With his customary self-control and calm, Randolph simply repeated the one-line statement. He said it so quietly that the press corps had to lean in to hear him. And the reporters, who had been incessantly pumping Randolph for more information, recognized the inner strength of this dignified man and burst into spontaneous applause. It was an unbelievable moment. And six weeks later, on 28 August, over 250,000 people gathered in Washington for the largest demonstration ever held in the capital. Only a person of Mr. Randolph's impeccable character and integrity could have pulled the whole thing out of the fire.

The way Mr. Randolph decisively handled the crisis that arose before the march taught me lessons that would later help me act quickly to protect his dignity. After the March on Selma in 1965, during which he walked several grueling miles in the blazing sun, Mr. Randolph, who was already over seventy and suffered from a serious heart condition, passed out at the train station. Almost immediately, press photographers rushed over, trying to get a picture of the stricken warrior lying on the ground. I quickly got together a group of tough, brawny associates, and we formed a human wall to keep the photographers away. At one point, in the heat of the moment, I unfortunately snatched a camera from someone who had taken a picture and ripped the film out. To this day I regret losing my temper. My associates and I surrounded the Chief until I managed to get Dick Gregory's plane to fly Mr. Randolph to New York and get him to a hospital. Later, a reporter came up to me and complained that the press had to make a living, and the fact that Mr. Randolph had collapsed after the march was news. I recall saying to the man: "It will be over my dead body that anyone ever sees a man of Mr. Randolph's dignity lying helpless on the ground." For over four decades Phil Randolph, with moral fortitude and nobility, had won victories that were the key stepping-stones to racial and economic equality for blacks. He had become a symbol of strength and progress. At that moment in Selma, a critical juncture for the civil rights movement he helped launch, I knew I could not allow any impression, any suggestion to emerge, even for a moment, that our gentle warrior was vanquished.

CICELY TYSON

Reflections on a
Lone Black Rose

MAYA ANGELOU was born in 1928 and has been an actress, cook, dancer, unwed mother, street car driver, streetwalker, writer, professor, and lecturer. Her series of autobiographies, starting with *I Know Why the Caged Bird Sings* (1970), have been best-sellers. Her poetry is used frequently for dramatic readings. This essay on her friend, actress Cicely Tyson, was published in *Ladies' Home Journal* in February 1977.

Would I write an article on Cicely Tyson? When *Ladies' Home Journal* asked me, I jumped at the chance. I had known Cicely for 15 years or more, admired her talents and loved her sense of humor. But my heart halted in mid-jump. How could she take two days of her time to sit and talk to me? And what about my full schedule? The last time I had seen her, for three spring days in 1976, we had worked together in Savannah, Georgia, performing in the television adaptation of Alex Haley's powerful saga, *Roots*. She had played the mother of the young hero, and I had acted the role of the grandmother. Now she was in Hollywood filming *A Hero Ain't Nothing but a Sandwich*, and I was about to begin a promotion tour for my new book. She was a serious, busy working woman—and so was I.

I telephoned Cicely.

"Hey, Beauty."

"Hey, Lady."

Giggle, giggle.

"I want to do an article on you."

"Fabulous. Really? When?"

"I need some time to talk. I could come to Hollywood, but I think we'd be disturbed there. Can you come to Sonoma County? We can sit under oak trees and walk through the grass down to the horse corral."

She hesitated. "Well . . ."

"I grow all my own vegetables and you can eat corn, green peppers and tomatoes straight out of the garden."

"I'll come. Okay. You've got me convinced. I'll come."

Cicely arrived carrying her little white dog; she was thinner than she had been some months before in Savannah. Now, here in the country, she seemed smaller. As beautiful but more frail. Her eyes are black and slanted and almost too large for such a small face; they glint with excitement. She turns her head and nods in quick, smooth movements and her thin, pointed fingers wave as if they play on an invisible reed instrument. Her photographs do not prepare one for her ruggedness; and, hearing her mellifluous voice, one is not ready for her wiry, hard surface.

Ms. Tyson presents a series of complications and contradictions that astound. She has won fame as a film and stage actress, yet she is a pianist of concert standard. She has given recitals at many of New York's concert halls, but now not only refuses to play but is reluctant to speak of her concertizing days. Her mother had been fierce in dictating Cicely's piano rehearsal schedule and piano performing schedule. "I decided when I could dictate my own life, I would never touch another piano. I realize that was youthful rebellion. I did pretty much the same thing with marriage. When I was eighteen, I married nearly the first person who proposed. As soon as the ceremony was over and I was out of my mother's house, the marriage was over and I was out of my husband's house. I decided I had done marriage. So I never had to marry again. That, too, represents youthful rebellion. Now I am moving closer to maturity. I might play the piano again, I might, maybe. But as for marriage," she laughs, "don't ask."

She is a young, passionate woman who says she is able to control her romantic energy and totally enjoy being alone. "I sublimate," she explains. "I take all my passion and jam it into the passion of the character I'm playing. It always works." She appreciates an occasional gourmet dinner, but could exist happily on a diet of fresh fruits, nuts and vegetables.

She sits curled up, barefoot, in the corner of my large and comfortable sofa, seeming to relish the luxury as much as a cat loves a soft place before a fire. Yet she has come to the sofa only after having run three miles along unfamiliar country roads in Northern California's Sonoma County.

She is small (5 feet 3 inches and 100 pounds), yet when she shakes hands her thrust is thorough, completely encountering the invited hand, and her grasp is strong and powerful.

Cicely Tyson, one-time model, one-time concert pianist, heralded now as one of America's most talented actresses. Who is she?

"I am a puzzlement. I am a puzzle to myself. Sometimes I know that I am involved in a lifelong search and I even know what I am searching for."

She hesitates, living in a quiet moment, then her hands begin to fly around in the air like two dark birds frightened out of their nest.

"And at other times, I not only don't know what I'm searching for, but I even have difficulty understanding the search at all."

She laughs. Reddened lips stretch across her large white teeth, which protrude just enough to make her smile distinctive. Cicely Tyson is considered one of the great American beauties. Her picture looks out of the nation's slick magazines, surrounded by the photographs of Faye Dunaway and Ali MacGraw and other current beauties; yet if her teeth thrust out one more millimeter, she would lose her place in a beauty contest because of an overbite.

I first met Cicely Tyson at New York City's St. Mark Playhouse in 1961. I had auditioned for a role in Jean Genet's *The Blacks*, which was to open three weeks later. When I was told that I had been chosen to play the role of the White Queen, I responded with trembling dread. It was not stage fright that caused me such discomfort, but rather the insecurity a country person feels in the company of city-bred people. Although I had once studied in New York City and had sung from time to time in Manhattan night clubs, I always felt I still had one foot on the dirt roads of the Arkansas small town where I grew up.

When I arrived, the theater was dark and the only light on the stage dim and eerie. A few people sat in the front rows, while a lone man sat on a chair mid-stage. He had been talking when I entered. I walked down the aisle toward the stage, and the man looked up and abruptly shouted, "Who are you? Who are you? What do you want?" I told him my name, and if he relented his severity, I couldn't tell. "Well, come on down and meet the rest of the cast." In the front row I was introduced to a group of sophisticates who seemed to be as at ease in a theater as Alfred Lunt and Lynn Fontanne would be. Except for Abby Lincoln, who was my closest friend, and Godfrey Cambridge, with whom I had worked, the rest—among them Cicely Tyson—were strangers.

We immediately began a course of work that was to strain nearly everyone to the breaking point. After a week of ten-hour daily rehearsals, the social graces began to disappear as if they had melted in the perspiration of hard work. Only Cicely seemed immune to the erosive power of repetitive rehearsal. She was the smallest member of the cast, as finely made as Venetian blown glass and more beautiful. Her composure never wavered; in fact, she became increasingly kinder, more tolerant, more gracious. Admittedly, there was a coolness about her, a distance that was neither hostile nor benevolent.

"I need the time. I need the moment. I must withdraw. I must discover what my soul has to tell me. What I must say to my soul. As long as I can remember, I have always needed to withdraw myself from company. I like people, but I also like being alone. Solitude is friendly to me. I need time to turn myself around. That's what I call it."

When I first read *The Blacks*, and even after hearing the dialogue in rehearsal, I believed that of all the characters Virtue (Cicely's role) was the most frivolous, the easiest to comprehend. Her lines did not puzzle me and I thought her motivation obvious. Gradually, however, the role began to change and grow. Gradually, Virtue became a clearly dominant character in a cast loaded with dominant characters. Cicely changed the woman from a flirtatious madcap into a determined vamp.

She could slither across the stage, as sinuous as Eden's serpent and with no less deadlines than Cleopatra's asp. By opening night, Virtue was not just sexy—

she had become sex itself. Cicely won the prestigious Obie (Off-Broadway award) for her performance. I wondered how a little woman like that could project such sensuality.

DADDY'S FAVORITE

Cicely leaned back into the sofa, bouncing a California orange in her dark hand. "My mother was strict. I mean, my sister, who is two years older, could have company. She could always, really, do anything she wanted to do. But not I. Mother watched me like a hawk. Mother had left my father, who had a produce stall in Harlem, and she always said that I was Daddy's baby. She seemed to resent that and that I favored him so much and that I had been his favorite. So she made me pay for that for years. I was always the one who got the beatings, and I suppose I understand why. She knew if anything happened to me, I mean, if I 'went wrong,' my father would never forgive her and there would be hell to pay. So my mother watched me like a hawk."

"When I grew up in Harlem, every girl I knew had at least one boyfriend. Of course, I didn't expect boys would be very interested in me anyway. I was tall. Well, I was! I was taller than anyone else. And I was skinny. They called me string bean. I wasn't pretty, either. I sucked my thumb until I was twelve years old. That's why my teeth are like what they are today. Nothing my mother did could break me of that habit. And she tried everything. Taping it up, wrapping it, putting red pepper on it. I would just scrape whatever she had put on off and pop my thumb back in my mouth.

"Then one morning I woke up, put my thumb in my mouth and it didn't feel right. I took it out and looked at it. I turned my hand around as far as it would go, back around again, examining my thumb. It seemed the same, so I stuck it back in. It still didn't taste right, so I took it out and never, never sucked my thumb again. But years of the habit caused my teeth to protrude, so boys didn't notice me much. Then my breasts began to develop and develop and develop even more, until just naturally I hunched my shoulders to try to hide my bust. I was sixteen before I ever kissed a boy. Can you believe it? I can still remember his name. And the kiss. He was Joe and the kiss was delicious. That was my introduction to sex. A single kiss from Joe in a doorway on a summer afternoon."

After a few months, I left Cicely and the rest of the cast of *The Blacks* and joined my husband in Egypt. I went to work as a journalist and my life became concerned with political issues, news bulletins, keeping a marriage in balance and raising a son. After two years my son and I moved to Ghana, and I began to work as the University of Ghana as administrative assistant. The theater and its artists had receded from my consciousness as if they had never been. I had taken on the sober attitudes of a civil servant and the stiffness of a bureaucrat. Then one morning I received a telegram from New York.

Maya Angelou: The original company of *The Blacks* has been invited to perform at Berlin's Folk Opera and at the Venice Bienale. Stop. Are you interested? Stop. Signed: Sidney Bernstein, Producer.

Interested? Were the pyramids stone?

ALL CHANGED EXCEPT CICELY

In Berlin I found the cast older, even more sophisticated, more assured. When we met in the rehearsal hall, I noticed a few lines creasing the familiar faces. Voices seemed deeper, a little tired, a little blasé. Everyone seemed changed—except Cicely. She still had the little girl look, the pealing laughter as high and clear as chimes. We found adjoining rooms and talked late into the German nights. I told her about my life in Africa and asked how she could retain such youthful simplicity while playing a relentless siren for four years and being heralded as an extraordinarily talented actress. Years later, Tyson would astonish viewers of *The Autobiography of Miss Jane Pittman* by playing a 20-year-old woman, the same woman at 40 and the same character 64 years later.

"Age is a concept. People think if you look sixteen you should play sixteen. If you look sixty, you should play sixty. I don't agree. I have never agreed with that. I believe you can be two years old if you want to. You can be it by being it. Being. Being two. I could play Dorothy in *The Wizard of Oz*, if I chose. Because I believe age is a concept I agreed to play Jane Pittman. I visited old people. I sat and listened to them talk. I watched them walk. I studied their bodies, their hands, their eyes and when I got ready to play one hundred years old, I became one hundred years old. Many people wonder how old I actually am. Some even have the nerve to ask me. I never tell them because they are asking me not for myself, for who or what I am, but for the numbers I can tell them. Age is not numbers. Age is a concept of Being."

After my second stint with *The Blacks*, I returned to the U.S. The years passed. Cicely and I met in theater lobbies, at little intimate parties and sometimes in the street. She played in a television series with George C. Scott, becoming the first black woman on national television to sport an Afro. Then suddenly she dropped from the theatrical scene. One second, she was there, heralded as one of America's most promising actresses, and the next she seemed nowhere. Cicely had fallen in love. Miles Davis, the famous trumpet player, had taken her heart and for three years, from 1965 to 1968, she gave to him all the energy that she had formerly put into her profession. She appeared so ambitious before, so certain of where she was going and how she would arrive at her desired destination, that it seemed improbable that she would completely surrender her art, her intent, her profession. And yet, as she explains it, it all fits.

"I can only do one thing at a time. I loved Miles and he loved me. I wanted to be all things to him. His love, his woman, his friend, his buddy. I could not do otherwise. I was never really interested in formal marriage. I gave him all I had to give and that satisfied me. I took all he had to give and thought myself a very lucky woman. When we had no more to give each other, our relationship was over. I could no more act while I was with him than I could fly while swimming. I am glad I did it. I would do it again. I am richer for the experience. Now I am acting. Theater is my world. I don't mean I don't have friends, some companionship, some intimacy. But the great love? That all-in romance. Not now. When I finish filming this picture, I shall withdraw again. I shall go alone somewhere to be close to myself. I shall find out what my soul is saying. I shall get recharged. I shall turn myself around again. Solitude is friendly to me."

Now she lives alone in a beach house in Southern California. "I need the sound of the sea, the waves, the breakers. Funny, huh? I was born in New York City in the heart of Harlem, but when I heard the roar of the Pacific Ocean, I decided I had found my way home."

As she speaks her face relaxes, her hands become still. She has already withdrawn from the interview.

I turn to you . . .
I see the flowering night
Cameo condensed
into the lone black rose
of your face.
—*Flowers of Darkness* by Frank M. Davis

GLAMOUR BOY

ROI OTTLEY was born on August 2, 1906. A New Yorker by birth and habit, he spent his career as a social worker and newspaper man, writing for such black newspapers as the *New York Amsterdam News*. He ended his career writing for the *Chicago Tribune*. Ottley knew the streets of the big city and understood the city black and his haunts better than most. "Glamour Boy," on the famous Harlem minister and politician Adam Clayton Powell, Jr. (Powell was not a congressman at the time the piece was written) appeared in *New World A-Coming* (1943).

Young man, young man,
Your arm's too short to box with God.

—James Weldon Johnson

Big, booming Adam Clayton Powell, Jr., preacher, editor, and legislator, is one of the handsomest men in Black America. Women sometimes call him "Mr. Jesus." Therein lies the source of his extraordinary popularity. He is six feet three inches in height, and weighs two hundred and ten pounds. Sloppy tweeds hang on his powerful frame with *Esquire* distinction. He is a white man to all appearances, having blue eyes, an aquiline nose, and light, almost blond hair. At thirty-four years of age, he is going places in a rush. Impatiently ambitious, he seeks to lead the working-class whites as well as Negroes in a "People's Movement," and is one of the first Negroes to aspire to the leadership of both people. Such a leadership, should he realize his ambition, would be noisy, militant, and opportunistic. "Do it, Brother Powell!"

Somewhat the careerist—aggressive, articulate, unpredictable—no more contradictory character exists in Negro life. He is an incredible combination of showman, black parson, and Tammany Hall. He is at once a salvationist and a politician, an economic messiah and a super-opportunist, an important mass leader and a light-hearted playboy. This young man on horseback—with a love for pleasure, quest for power, and unusual capacity for work—combines qualities which defy clear pigeonholing. To some he is a demagogue; to others the anointed leader. To all, though, he is a thoroughly engaging personality, whose weaknesses as a man are his virtues as a public figure.

If personal qualities alone are not sufficient to snatch the national Negro leadership, he possesses the instruments for pushing himself forward. As pastor of the largest Negro church in America, the Abyssinian Baptist, with a membership of fourteen thousand, he has a platform and to all practical purposes a powerful, cohesive political bloc. As the only Negro member of the City Council, he has prestige and a public sounding-board with echoes in the metropolitan press. As editor and co-publisher of a newspaper, the *People's Voice*, he can reach those thousands of Negroes who never darken the doorways of churches or political clubs. And as the leader of the Greater New York Coordinating Committee for the Employment of Negroes, a mass organization which has obtained hundreds of jobs for Negroes, he is provided with a mobile pressure group.

In short, he is the new and different kind of leader that the Negro church has produced—as modern as jive talk!

There are approximately four million Negro Baptists and about one and a half million Negro Methodists in the United States. The Baptist Church attracts the great masses. The Methodist with its hierarchy and formal ritualism does not have quite so strong an appeal. The other religious denominations trail in Negro attendance, tho igh in recent years the missionary work of the Roman Catholic Church has made pron(unced headway. However, those denominations which are controlled by a white hierarchy are at a disadvantage in attracting Negroes, for the Negro church, developed by the Negro in slavery, is his very own to an extent equaled by few other institutions. Not alone is the church the center of the Negro's independent existence, but it is one of the most important tools the Negro has in his struggle for status.

By fostering race-consciousness the Negro church helps to solidify the race, a function the white church can hardly perform. There was talk some years ago by Negroes, when Saint Benedict, the Moor Roman Catholic Church, was being redecorated, to have the pink cherubs pictured on the ceiling painted *black*! The church being led by a white priest, this business never came to pass.

In recent years the Negro church has been sharply criticized for assuming a passive, sometimes indifferent rôle toward the Negro's social and economic problems, even indeed advocating submission to white domination. Some Negroes declare that the church exploits its members. H. L. Mencken, none too generously, called the Negro clergymen "barnyard theologians" and the church a "hogwaller of Christianity." While the Negro church of today does not approximate the vigorous instrument it was in the antislavery period, individual ministers nonetheless have spoken out clearly and have frequently mobilized forces for aggressive action in the Negro's cause. By writing letters, holding mass meetings, and threatening economic boycotts, certain ministers have helped to break down economic discriminations against the race. A survey conducted recently by Jerome H. Holland, a Negro professor at Lincoln University, to determine the attitude of the Negro clergy toward social injustice, showed that only 23 were opposed to any action being taken by the Negro ministers out of a possible 776 answers. Asked whether they thought immediate action was imperative, 597 replied in the affirmative.

For a number of years following the first World War, the press rivaled the church as a medium of racial self-expression, concerned as the church was with purely religious functions. Today, the Negro church is attempting to recapture its former place in the secular life of the black man. New types of leaders are taking over—men who are trained, socially conscious, and forward-looking, with their fingers on the pulse of the Negro. First-rate seminaries are turning out men prepared not only in the Scriptures but in the importance of health, employment, and housing, from such institutions as Gammon Theological Seminary, a Methodist school in Atlanta, and Howard University in Washington.

It was, for instance, J. C. Austin, pastor of Pilgrim Baptist Church, who first led the Jobs-for-Negroes campaign in Chicago; and in New York it was John H. Johnson, pastor of Saint Martin's Protestant Episcopal Church, who took the helm in Harlem's jobs campaign. Stanley High, a white journalist, visited the Chicago church and there saw a huge sign hanging beside the entrance which, in the distance, he took to be an announcement of revival meetings. The first sentence read, "What Must We Do to Be Saved?" The answer surprised him. It was this: "Beset by Rent Hogs, Overcrowded in Hovels. Come to the Housing Mass Meeting on Thursday Noon. The United Front."

For a number of years, the only Negro member of the Pennsylvania state legislature was Marshall L. Shepard, pastor of Mount Olivet Tabernacle in Philadelphia. He attracted national attention in 1936 when he rose to deliver the opening prayer at the Democratic National Convention in Philadelphia and Senator Ellison D. ("Cotton Ed") Smith of South Carolina marched out in protest—"racial pandering," the Southern politician called it. Two years later Shepard was awarded a medal for meritorious service to his state.

Twenty years ago it is doubtful if any Negro church anywhere would have opened it doors, much less given the freedom of its pulpit, to a Socialist. Today, there is indeed a Socialist minister—the Reverend Ethelred Brown of Harlem. Moreover, James W. Ford, the Negro Communist candidate for Vice President, has spoken in Negro churches all over the country. He attracted two thousand in 1934 at the Ebenezer Baptist Church in Pittsburgh, and similar numbers at the Abyssinian Baptist Church. The Scottsboro boys, who, after their release, made a triumphal tour through Negro communities under the wing of the Communist Party, had church pulpits offered them wherever they went.

"We've had enough," one young preacher was heard to say, "of the gospel of 'dem golden slippers.' What we want is the gospel of thick-soled shoes."

What is happening to the church is a reflection of what is happening to Negroes. Though the Negro church appeared to be slipping some years ago, it will never completely lose its place in the Negro's life so long as the race is discriminated against. For, within its portals, Negroes find entertainment, culture, and self-expression as well as political guidance and spiritual nourishment. The fact that the ministers have again stepped to the front has reinforced the church's hold on the Negro. Yet, curiously enough, not one clergyman can be called a national leader.

To corral the Negro vote, though, the Democratic Party crowds its stationery with the names of outstanding Negro clergymen. Topping the list is Doctor R. R. Wright, bishop of the African Methodist Episcopal Church. During the 1936 campaign, Bishop Wright was given permission to delay his sailing to his African mission in order to labor in the political field. Another bishop, Doctor Reverdy C. Ransom, is a very large figure among Negroes in the Midwest—both as a clergyman and as a politician. Elder Solomon Lightfoot Michaux, famed radio preacher of Washington's Church of God, is something of a pet among Democratic politicians, and is frequently called out to beat the drum in campaigns.

Adam Clayton Powell, Harlem's crusading preacher, was born with a silver spoon in his mouth which he is using as a lever to lift himself up in the world. His father, Doctor A. Clayton Powell, Sr., born of Virginia slaves and today a man of considerable means, was pastor for some thirty years of that great Gothic structure of New York bluestone which is the Abyssinian Baptist Church. Before he moved the church to Harlem, it occupied a building on West Fortieth Street, opposite the site of the present *Herald Tribune*. In 1921 the church sold the site for $190,000 and erected the present edifice at a cost of $350,000. It has an amphitheater auditorium seating two thousand, a pulpit constructed out of Italian marble, and a community house with offices, lecture rooms, gymnasium, showerbaths, reading-rooms, and a roof garden. The mortgage was publicly burned in 1928, after the church's membership had observed a rigorous tithing system. Today, the cost of maintenance and manifold activities is estimated at seventy-five thousand dollars annually.

The Abyssinian Baptist Church, organized by eighteen Negroes in a building on Anthony Street, was one of those religious bodies which separated from the white churches at the turn of the last century. With the migration of Negroes to Harlem the downtown churches were forced to pursue their flocks, and an era set in of large-scale buying and building. Today, scattered throughout New York are more than two hundred and fifty established Negro churches. The most significant commentary on this phase of Negro life is the fact that ten million dollars is invested in Harlem temples of worship, and some seventy thousand Negroes—most of them women—are members.

Before the government launched the public-relief program, during the Depression, the elder Powell established a relief bureau in the Abyssinian Church and appointed his son as director. This brought young Powell to the front for the first time. Suffering thousands were given clothes, coal, kerosene, and medical care, and two thousand persons were fed daily in a free food kitchen conducted in the gymnasium of the community house. The newspapers reported that Powell *père* had contributed one thousand dollars to start operations. When he publicly called upon the Negro ministers throughout the country to do likewise, if they could afford it, a bitter and acrimonious battle began to rage within the Negro church. One clergyman, manifestly resentful of the publicity that Doctor Powell had received, said that "It is a mooted question whether the church should actively engage in making medicine, serving soups, and juggling jobs." To which another preacher replied, "If the newspapers don't publish what you do, remember that 'Thy Father which seeth in secret, Himself shall reward you openly.' "

"My father," young Powell once told an audience, "said he built the church and I would interpret it." The Abyssinian Baptist Church is indeed a Powell institution, unaffiliated as it is with any denomination. This fact, perhaps, is the secret of its challenging policies. At any rate, the elder Powell forged the instrument, and young Powell has streamlined it. The church's letterhead speaks of it as "The Church of the Masses." One Sunday morning he said to his flock: "At times it seemed as if we were going to become a society church with a so-called mythical Negro upper class. At other times we drifted into what seemed to be an intellectual church, then again a church for radicals, but today we have come of age, we are *The People's Church*. All classes, all races, all schools of thought—that is our parish."

That boast is supported by a vast institutional program, which attracts all sections of the population. The church has become a complex organization of men's clubs, women's societies, and young people's groups sponsoring a host of activities for children. The church's bulletin boards are fair indexes of the activities. They are loaded down with announcements of labor and political meetings, notices to those on relief, calls for jobs, and a variety of social gatherings. The church provides a clearing house for the multitude of community interests. Powell, alert to social trends, sponsors forums with speakers whose views range from those of James W. Ford, the Negro Communist, and Margaret Sanger, the birth-control advocate, to those of Evangeline Booth, the Salvation Army leader, and Rabbi Stephen S. Wise, pastor of the Free Synagogue.

Before assuming the assistant pastorship in 1930, young Powell was graduated from Colgate University and then spent a year traveling in Europe and Africa. He attributes his present progressive views to the oppression of colonial peoples which he witnessed while in Africa. Perhaps the accident of his having worked as a bellhop in the Equinox House, a summer resort in Manchester, Vermont, where he met Robert Lincoln, son of the Emancipator, had a more profound influence upon him. Lincoln, it seems, manifestly disliked Negroes. He even forbade any of the Negro help to touch his personal possessions—luggage, clothes, even his automobile. If one did, with his cane he soundly rapped the offender on the knuckles. Powell, whom Lincoln mistook for a white man, was the only Negro member of the help whom he would allow to wait on him. The other Negro bellhops thought the incident humorous, but the future Negro leader never forgot it.

Even more important in his development was the fight he waged against his parents and the deacons of the church some years after becoming the assistant pastor, to marry Isabel Washington, a lovely and talented actress, who was then starring on Broadway in Vinton Freedley's *Singin' the Blues*. He told Richard O. Boyer, in an interview, that the affair revealed to him the unreasonable formalism of the Baptist Church, and from that day he learned to stand alone. Actually, he didn't stand alone. She immediately gave up a bright and profitable career in the theater. The affair assumed the proportions of a public issue, with people taking vocal sides. There were perhaps more people standing with him, supporting his right to marry the woman he loved, than those who opposed. He finally married her, with the applause of Harlem ringing in his ears. The deacons relented and in

1937 formally called him to the pastorate, to succeed his father, who today is pastor emeritus. In winning out, young Powell gained considerable confidence in his ability to meet a tight situation. But more important is the fact that he won his first important following beyond the corridors of his church.

From that day he really spread his wings. He joined the Jobs-for-Negroes Movement, which was then languishing in the hands of anti-Semites, and returned it to lusty life. In association with the Reverend William Lloyd Imes, then pastor of Saint James's Presbyterian Church, and A. Philip Randolph, president of the Brotherhood of Sleeping Car Porters, he formed the Greater New York Coordinating Committee for the Employment of Negroes. Before long, it had become a Powell organization. In the spring of 1938 he led the committee in a "Black-Out Boycott" of the Consolidated Edison Company to force it to hire Negroes in capacities other than menials. Every Tuesday night, in waging this unique economic battle, in many Harlem homes electric lights gave way to two-cent candles.

When the boycott tactic produced few gains, Powell geared his organization for sharper action. At a mass meeting he sounded the keynote of the new drive: "Harlem is sick and tired of promises. The hour has struck to march!" A billpayers' parade was staged in which hundreds converged on the company's Harlem offices daily and paid their bills in nickels and pennies—obviously a stratagem to disrupt service. Simultaneously, action against other public utilities was taken. Picket lines were thrown before their offices, led by Powell immaculately dressed in a white linen suit. Attention also was again focused on the 125th Street merchants, with chanting picketeers loudly telling the world of their economic woes.

After months of intensified agitation from soapbox, newspaper, and pulpit— with, incidentally, the black nationalists rallying to his banner—the Harlem Chamber of Commerce, representing the white merchants, negotiated a contract with the Coordinating Committee which guaranteed jobs to Negroes on a basis of their numbers in the population. The *Times* commented favorably on the impressive gains. One thousand persons were employed over a period of one year. The Consolidated Edison Company capitulated and placed a number of Negroes in white-collar positions, ending the policy of hiring Negroes for menial tasks exclusively. The New York Telephone Company followed suit in handsome fashion. It staffed its entire Harlem office with a Negro personnel, and appointed a Negro as manager. The gleaming feather in Powell's cap, however, was the contract signed with the Fifth Avenue Coach Company and the New York City Omnibus Corporation which, for the first time in the history of the city, hired Negro drivers and mechanics. This was an achievement of no small proportion in the eyes of Negroes, and they loudly applauded. Every time they board a bus today and see Negroes at the wheel, they swell with pride.

The Jobs-for-Negroes movement is profoundly serious business to Negroes, but Powell always has an immense time. He enjoys himself so thoroughly that some are inclined to doubt his sincerity. Perhaps his vast sense of humor is discomforting. At any rate, he is too vibrant and happy to be a solemn reformer. Some people turn to gambling for excitement. Powell gets his in the daily rough-and-tumble of industrial strife. Once a movement bogs down, he soon wearies and turns to

something else. If nothing is cooking, Powell discovers something that needs imme-
diate action. For instance, take the letter he addressed to the thousands on his
mailing list, calling them out for a mass demonstration:

My dear friend:
A crisis has arisen in Harlem.
A Negro—Wallace Armstrong, 168 W. 128th St.—was brutally beaten and
    then killed by over 15 policemen.
He was shot down like a dog.
This marks the third inexcusable killing this year in New York City of Negro
    people.
NOT ONE KILLER HAS BEEN ARRESTED.
IT IS OUR FAULT.
YOU MUST BE PRESENT, May 14, at 9:30 sharp at the Abyssinian Community
    House to stage a MONSTER CITIZENS' PROTEST MEETING for This Sunday,
    May 17, at 5 p.m., at the Golden Gate (Ballroom) and to PLAN A MARCH-
    ON-CITY HALL.
DO NOT FAIL THE PEOPLE. LAY ASIDE EVERYTHING.

Yours for People's Victory,
(Signed) A. CLAYTON POWELL, JR.

What first comes to mind about Powell is his overwhelming charm, to which
men and women alike succumb. He is boyish, affectionate, and playful. Once an
athlete, he has never lost his love of sports. In the well-cushioned study of his Sugar
Hill private home, he is relaxed, even reflective. He has a sharp, brittle mind,
which is allergic to old ideas. In relating some new idea, he wags his head happily,
chortles through his teeth, while gripping a pipestem tightly. In the midst of a
conversation he will bounce out of his chair and say, 'How about a game of ping-
pong?' Between strokes, the conversation continues as if never interrupted. He is
never complex or ponderous. Hundreds of admirers flock in and out of his home,
some hoping to bask in reflected glory.

He prides himself on being the perfectionist as an executive. His half a dozen
jobs keep him going at high speed, and overwork two secretaries. His office is almost
a confessional—he is a political boss, economic consultant, and seven-days-a-week
pastor. Beside his desk is a dictaphone into which he delivers his mail, and when
he travels he takes the machine along, preparing speeches, notes, and directives for
his office staff. His study, too, is equipped with a dictaphone.

He works with his bare hands in the political pastures. He is a man without a
political party behind him—though lately he has been close to the Communist
Party. The Socialist Party is openly suspicious of him. A lot of Democrats and
Republicans hate him because he is too far ahead of their parties, yet he has friends
in both parties. He moves independently under the force of his own personality,
his courage, and a whole lot of insight into what is going on about him. He preaches
no Valley-and-Dry Bones sermons, but salts down his speeches with nicely chosen
Negro idioms about everyday issues. But it is not so much what he says as the way

he says it—loud, dramatic, and often. He is perhaps the outstanding orator in the race, and a spellbinder of no small proportions. Sometimes he becomes entranced with his own words, and, on at least one occasion, has been so moved as to weep publicly. Negroes like their leaders emotional. Powell drips with emotion. Yet thousands follow him because he has vigor, brains, and understanding, and has identified himself with the aspirations of the black rank-and-file.

But there are Negroes who complain that he is "a stranger in our midst." Perhaps his light complexion is the source of this feeling. For Negroes are very conscious, maybe envious, of the fact that he can visit hotels, restaurants, and cafés run by whites and not suffer any racial indignities. But to other sections of the black population, he is the idolized "White Hope!" Dan Burley, witty editor of Harlem's *Amsterdam-Star News*, is not the least bit worried about Powell's color. He once remarked that Negroes need have no fear of him as a leader because "being *white* he constantly has to prove he's a *Negro* to Negroes." If Powell is aware of this banter about his complexion, no one would know it. His racial patriotism is unquestioned. The unkind cuts at the race reach him as deeply as they do black men.

His every act is done with flamboyant suddenness. A Sunday morning late in the summer of 1941, for example, Pastor Powell mounted the marble rostrum of his church in an unusually serious mood. "Brother pastor must be sick," said one old woman. When he closed his sermon, appropriately chosen for the occasion, he walked down to the edge of the rostrum and rather intimately announced that he was running for a place in the City Council. For a few moments the packed auditorium was motionless. "Then," according to one newspaper report, "as if blitzkrieged with religious fervor, the congregation suddenly turned the sacred meeting into a bedlam of hallelujahs and vociferous hand clappings, lasting twenty minutes, leaving no doubt that the pastor would have the full backing of his membership."

When he flung his hat into the political pot, three other Negroes were already in the field—Doctor Channing H. Tobias, candidate of the Fusion Party; Doctor Max Yergan, president of the National Negro Congress and American Labor Party standard-bearer; and a lawyer, Herman C. Stoute, the Tammany Hall choice. Powell lost no time in persuading Doctor Yergan and Doctor Tobias to withdraw in his favor, and without the backing of any political party he launched a campaign which startled even old heads at the game. He first formed the People's Committee, with his Coordinating Committee as a nucleus, and selected an imposing list of white and Negro sponsors. He announced a platform which pledged a fight for "Jobs! Jobs! Jobs!" He established headquarters, staffed by almost a thousand volunteers who worked with religious zeal. When he began to show strength, the American Labor, Republican, and Fusion Parties endorsed him—not, however, without some behind-the-barn dickering. At a formal session of the New York State Colored Baptist Convention, Mayor La Guardia finally threw his support to the Negro minister.

Powell spoke every day and night to any group that would listen. Always carefully groomed for these occasions, he wore tweeds when he addressed white people and pallbearer blues before Negro audiences. All during the campaign it was impossible to keep placards with his picture in their appointed places—women cut them out as souvenirs! He waged an unorthodox political fight, even to turning out a parody on a song popular in Harlem, "Why Don't You Do Right?" The heat churned up in this campaign was reminiscent of his stormy job crusades. And he was elected—receiving the third highest number of votes in the city. He received a tremendously large white liberal vote. This opened his eyes to the possibilities of becoming the leader of a people's movement! His election cost twenty-five hundred dollars, whereas one losing candidate had spent twenty thousand dollars. The job pays five thousand dollars annually!

Councilman Powell, measured by ordinary standards, has been no flaming success as a legislator. Standing pretty much alone, he is without organized support for any legislation he would like to see enacted. But he does manage to make his presence felt—however flamboyantly. His initial act as a councilman was to charge the New York colleges with racial discrimination, because of the absence of Negro professors on the teaching staffs. The old-line Tammany politicians who dominate the council, pinned back his ears on this one. Instead of tabling his motion as was no doubt expected, they promptly supported his plea for an investigation. Nice boys!

A public hearing was held at which the college presidents testified that Negroes had never made application for teaching appointments! This closed the matter, and the Negro and white press criticized Powell's impetuousness and baseless charges. Actually, he was absolutely right. Of the 2232 faculty members of the city's four colleges, none are Negroes, but he presented few cases to prove racial discrimination—not because they did not exist, but because he had failed to take the trouble to consult with those responsible agencies concerned with this specific problem. He was vindicated in a measure when some months later City College made a gesture by appointing Doctor Abram L. Harris, Howard University professor of economics, for the summer session.

Possessed of amazing buoyancy, Powell was little dismayed by this setback. Unable to offer but few tangible accomplishments as a legislator, he insists that his *presence* there is sufficient. For, to the young leader, a public office is a platform and he sounds off regularly in behalf of the Negro. To further his political career, he entered into partnership with Charles Buchanan, manager of the Savoy Ballroom, to publish the *People's Voice*. It has become another platform from which he dins his name into the consciousness of the public. His editorials, captioned "The Soapbox," are the wordy diatribes of a speech-maker, but they also are forceful denunciations of the evils of our times and attract followers. Here is a sample:

> We are fighting FOR equality of races, blackout of discrimination, just economic opportunity, and decent housing anywhere, on either side of the tracks. . . .
> We are all men together. We are demanding a share in carrying this cross of world conflict, and just as strongly as we demand that, we demand a share of the crown of victory. . . .

Powell's immediate political aspiration is Congress. Once provided with this national platform, he will attempt to seize national leadership of the Negro people. He frankly says he has no program—beyond seeking the total integration of Negroes in the political and economic scheme of America. But already he has formidable enemies arrayed against him among the intellectuals and mass-organization leaders. While loudly applauding his achievements, Negroes frankly distrust him. They resent, too, his playing both ends against the middle. His frequently changing political alignments do not inspire confidence. Moreover, no one seems to know exactly what is his ultimate goal—beyond having power. He stirs the emotions, and drives people to action. But it is left to others to formulate concrete programs. Actually, Negroes are more dazzled than lifted by him—which indeed makes him a tough man to beat.

ACKNOWLEDGMENTS

Every effort has been made to contact copyright holders; in the event of an inadvertent omission or error, the editor should be notified.

"Black Heavies" by Jervis Anderson is reprinted from *The American Scholar*, Volume 47, Number 3, Summer 1978. Copyright © 1978 by Jervis Anderson. By permission of *The American Scholar*.

"Cicely Tyson: Reflections on a Lone Black Rose" by Maya Angelou. Copyright © 1977 by the Meredith Corporation. All rights reserved. Reprinted from *Ladies' Home Journal* magazine with permission of the author.

"The Harlem Ghetto" is from *Notes of a Native Son* by James Baldwin. Copyright © 1955, 1983 by Beacon Press. Reprinted by permission of Beacon Press.

"Novelist Alice Walker: Telling the Black Woman's Story" by David Bradley is reprinted by permission of The Wendy Weil Agency, Inc. Copyright © 1984 by David Bradley.

"Richard Wright's Complexes and Black Writing Today" by Cecil Brown is from *Negro Digest*, December 1968. Reprinted by permission of the author.

"Why I Am a Communist" by Benjamin J. Davis is reprinted by permission of *Phylon*.

"On Being Black" by W. E. B. Du Bois originally appeared in the *New Republic*.

"The Black Intellectual and the Sport of Prizefighting" by Gerald Early first appeared in *The Kenyon Review*. Reprinted by permission of the author.

"The Charlie Christian Story" from *Shadow and Act* by Ralph Ellison. Copyright © 1953, 1964 by Ralph Ellison. Reprinted by permission of Random House, Inc.

"Henry Ossawa Tanner" by Jessie Redmon Fauset is reprinted from *The Crisis*, April 1924, by permission of the publisher.

"Songs of a Racial Self: On Sterling A. Brown" is from *Figures in Black: Words, Signs, and the "Racial" Self* by Henry Louis Gates, Jr. Copyright © 1987 by Henry Louis Gates, Jr. Reprinted by permission of Oxford University Press, Inc.

"Black Pride" by Kimbal (Stroud) Goffman is reprinted from *Atlantic Monthly*. Used by permission.

"A Study of the Black Fighter" by Nathan Hare is from *The Black Scholar*, November 1971. Reprinted with permission from *The Black Scholar*.

"Down Under in Harlem" by Langston Hughes is reprinted by permission of the *New Republic*.

"My Adventures as a Social Poet" by Langston Hughes is reprinted by permission of *Phylon*.

"Restoring the Perspective: Robert Hayden's 'The Dream' " by Gayl Jones first appeared in *Obsidian*, Spring 1981. Reprinted by permission.

"The Poor Pay More, Even for Their Dreams" is from *Black Voices from Prison* by Etheridge Knight, Pathfinder Press, 1970. By permission of the author.

"On Being Black: The Burden of Race and Class" originally appeared in *Blackwater: Historical Studies in Race, Class, Consciousness and Revolution* by Manning Marable (Dayton: Black Praxis Press, 1981), pp. 69–77.

"The Numbers Writer: A Portrait" by Julian Mayfield is reprinted from *The Nation*, 14 May 1960, courtesy of *The Nation* magazine / The Nation Company, Inc. Reprinted by arrangement with the Estate of Julian Mayfield.